WHITTIER

INDEPENDENT COLLEGE IN CALIFORNIA

WHITTIER

INDEPENDENT COLLEGE
IN CALIFORNIA

Founded by Quakers, 1887

By CHARLES W. COOPER
with a preface by
JESSAMYN WEST

THE WARD RITCHIE PRESS
Los Angeles, California

1967

CONTENTS

ILLUSTRATIONS

PREFACE

NUMEROUS NOVELS have taken life on the campus as their subject matter. None, insofar as I know, has used the *establishment* of a college as the focus of its narrative. After reading Charles Cooper's account of Whittier College one wonders why. All the elements of a stirring fiction are present: a cast as large and issues as fundamental as those of *War and Peace*; though the subject matter is of course particularly American.

The founding of small denominational colleges has been as American as baseball; and though financially a more shaky operation, it has required almost as much skill and aggressiveness; and on occasion has had about as little to do with any activity that could be called intellectual.

The history of America is written in small in the histories of these colleges. In their development is reflected the unprecedented American belief in the value of education; though in the beginning the belief of the founders of small denominational colleges that sound education involved the indoctrination of students with their own religious tenets, involved wearisome and educationally nullifying struggles; there was often little agreement among the founders themselves about their own religious tenets. Considerable progress had been made before William Matlock, a Whittier professor, could say, "You are to be made intellectual men that you may be fit moral agents." In the early days of Whittier, that statement would have concluded, "fit members of the orthodox, pastoral and evangelistic branch of the Society of Friends, West."

Can the history of all denominational colleges provide reading as fascinating as Charles Cooper's account of the Quaker College in California? I think it unlikely for two reasons. The first has to do with Cooper's ability as a narrator; his skill in melding the confusing and often confused happenings of eighty years into a coherent, and frequently eloquent and moving, story.

The second reason has to do not with the skill of the historian, but with the nature of the history. Quakers have always been considered quirky; and names similar, though less affectionate, have been used to describe Southern Californians. The collision or collusion, depending upon your viewpoint, between the Quaker temperament and the Southern California mystique produced a series of events which could scarcely have been equalled by college-founding Quakers in Oskaloosa, Iowa or Wichita, Kansas.

It is unlikely that any other college of any denomination had its beginnings in a town with the makeup of Whittier in 1887. This "magic little city" Cooper quotes but does not give the source of this catchy phrase; though its source is surely Chamber of Commerce, rather than Quarterly Meeting—had 800 citizens served by the following places of business: "two general stores, a butcher and a milk dealer, a drug store and postoffice, three restaurants, three hotels, three livery stables—and twelve real estate offices"! (Exclamation mark mine.)

Aquilla Pickering, founding father of the "magic little city," had two interests in Whittier: real estate *and* reform. As a "special colonization agent" for both the Union and Southern Pacific he was dealing in real estate. As a Quaker he hoped that by establishing a Quaker colony in Whittier the Quakers would "assist in bringing about much needed reforms" amongst those already in residence. He was successful in both attempts. A colony was established and it did assist in bringing about reforms.

The first recorded sit-in in history was staged in Whittier by ladies intent, not on being served themselves, but in seeing that others were not served. They sat, knitting and crocheting in Whittier's only saloon, making it impossible for men of 1888 to subject females to the coarse sight of men pouring alcoholic drinks down their gullets. Some of the coarser men persisted in doing so. Quakers, foregoing for the time (as Whittier Quakers have continued to do during two world wars) their early belief in non-violence, joined with fellow reformers in pulling down the first saloon that set up business in Whittier.

It would clearly be impossible, and Charles Cooper does not make the attempt, to determine the exact motivations of the founders of the "magic little city" in attempting to establish in 1887-88 a "Friends' College." True, the Quakers had from the beginning placed much emphasis on education, and on educational institutions which taught Quaker "truths."

This last, Daniel J. Boorstin, who devotes a considerable section of his book, *The Americans*, to a study of early American Quakerism, considers a mistake. "In the late 17th century," says Boorstin, "Quakerism had many qualities which would have suited it to become the dominant American religion. . . . The Quakers possessed a set of attitudes which fit later textbook definitions of American democracy. . . ." Quakerism did not become the dominant American religion because, says Boorstin, "Quakers had a preoccupation with the purity of their own souls." This purity they fostered by the establishment of their own denominational schools.

Quite possibly most Quakers had no desire to have their beliefs become "the dominant American belief." This does not interest Boorstin. The question that interests him, and that should possibly have interested Quakers, was: Would an America with the beliefs of 17th century Quakers be a better America?

This question ignores also the fact that in 1887 the Orthodox pastoral Quakers of Whittier were no longer themselves "17th century Quakers." And it leaves still another question unanswered. Was "Friends' College" founded (or the attempt made to found it, since it never actually came into being) because of a preoccupation of Quakers with "the purity of their souls?"

There were certainly times when this motivation appears minimal; when what Frederick Tolles has characterized as "the shift from Meeting House to Counting House" appears to have taken place in the thinking of many concerned with the development of a college. In a town so small, with a preparatory school just starting, and with colleges already being established in nearby towns, the real purpose of a college often appears to have been to provide a come-on for advertising lots for sale in "a college town."

Not that this was in itself inherently wrong. John Greenleaf Whittier himself, for whom the town was named, had urged Whittier's founders to make their Quakerism "of the old practical kind, diligent in business *and* serving the Lord." (Italics mine.)

Diligent, and Lord serving (according to their lights), the founding fathers undoubtedly were. Practical they were not. And the college, real-estate linked, became, literally a hole in the ground when the real estate boom of '87 was followed by the bust of '88. What had been intended as a basement for Friends' College became, when the building which was to rest above it did not materialize, the town reservoir.

I find it personally ironic that the scene of that early institutional demise became later the intended locale for my own demise. At seventeen, shamed forever, I thought, when a paper of mine entitled "Live Life Deeply," was copied in its brief entirety on the classroom blackboard by my English instructor, and then made the text for an hour's lecture on the folly of any such writing, based as it was on juvenile ignorance, I decided to do away with myself. And I chose, as wronged maidens have immemorially done, to cast myself into a body of water. The only body of water of a size suitable for this purpose (I was a good-sized maiden) and near at hand, was the Whittier reservoir. I set out at dawn for what I intended would be my last mile. When I arrived, I found that the reservoir since my last visit had been boarded over. I was by this time tired and hungry as well as life-weary; and the only other body of water suitable for my purpose, the Pacific, was twenty long miles away. I decided, considering the facts, to postpone suicide until after breakfast.

At that time, though I did not then know it, many another person, heart-sore if not suicidal, must have stood on that hillside and looked into that pit of unrealized dreams.

"Friends' College" was never more than a dream. Whittier College grew organically out of the Quaker preparatory school.

As a student at Whittier in the twenties, none of Whittier's history was known to me. And I am amazed to find, though I played no part in its history, that I was, as a student, surrounded by those who had. I wish I could have read this book *before* I went to Whittier. Lindley, Tomlinson, Coffin, Kimber, Naylor, Hiatt, Painter, Jessup—these were campus names. C. Bevan Johnson's daughter, Johnnie, played guard with me on the basketball team. My sister Carmen married Caleb Cook's son. My roommate married an Armstrong. Thomas Newlin was the presiding minister at my wedding. (And of all the statements made about Whittier College and the education it offered, my favorite is Thomas Newlin's: "And the ultimate vindication of truth must rest on the findings of the human heart and mind in one's own experience." This is the writer's as well as the Quaker's credo.)

I was interested to see that, year for year, Dr. Cooper was able to dispose of *my* era with fewer words than those required for any other comparable span of time. Whittier was then, following World War I, at a low ebb in every way: low on number of students, amounts of available money and, with a few exceptions, talented teachers.

I went to Whittier for all the wrong reasons; or for reasons for which Whittier was the wrong choice. I think I was drawn to Whittier in the first place because "out" in Yorba Linda where I lived, a Yorba Linda girl, Marie Vernon, had been chosen as May Queen at Whittier. How Whittier ever slipped into the un-Quakerly practice of winding Maypoles, frolicking on the Green and choosing queens I know not. Nor does Charles Cooper, though the rite evidently appealed to him also, enlighten us on this point. There must have been those, at the time, to whom Maypole winding did not appeal, for Maypoles and May queens were eliminated from the Quaker celebration of spring the year I arrived. So, reason number one for attending Whittier College was eliminated.

A second ambition of mine was also destined not to be fulfilled at Whittier. When my father took me into Harry Noble Wright's office after I had graduated from high school, to discuss college enrollment, I asked Dr. Wright, "Does Whittier College give the doctor's degree?" May queen *and* a doctor! At sixteen I didn't lack ambition. Dr. Wright, a quiet and courteous man, could not resist smiling as he told me the degree Whittier gave was an A.B.

Whittier was, however, exactly *the* right choice for satisfying my third ambition. Vance Randolph, the authority on Ozark speech and folk tales, tells of the mountain girl who appeared unhappy in the college she was attending. When "the head professor" asked her the cause of her discontent she told him: "I came here to be went with and I ain't been yet."

I went to Whittier to be went with, and I was. If going steady was not invented at Whittier it was certainly practised there somewhat in advance of its time. (And I was pleased to find Dr. Cooper using a word of my day—and his—at Whittier, which I have not heard since or elsewhere. "Queening" for necking.)

No one advised me to *go* to Whittier. But my parents were strongly advised *not* to let me go. An uncle, when he heard that I was enrolled, made the trip to Yorba Linda to tell my parents that the Quaker campus was no place for an innocent young country girl. No information could have made me more eager to obtain a higher education—and on the Quaker campus.

Two teachers, of those under whom I happened to take work, I remember as outstanding, Professors Harris and Smith. I had many classes under Professor Harris, though he and I were only in simultaneous residence at the college for two years. Professor Smith came to the college in my senior year and under him I had only one class. There was no question in those days, though the campus was small (and contrary to what is now thought on the campuses of large universities) of "being friends" with your professors. The concept of a relationship between teacher and student without the intervention of desk or lectern, did not, to my knowledge, exist on the Whittier campus in my day. So Professors Harris and Smith, while friendly, were not my friends.

Charles Cooper in reporting that Herbert Harris chose (I am sure it was he who made the choice) to be married standing on a rock facing the Pacific hit upon a fact which tells as much as any single fact could about the rich, varied, and sometimes contradictory nature of Herbert Harris.

He was, as well as being a director of drama, a dramatic man himself. My first meeting with him was dramatic. I spent my sophomore year at Fullerton Junior College where former Whittier teacher, William T. Boyce was the Dean. I was on the Fullerton debating team which Dean Boyce coached. We journeyed over to debate the Whittier team on, as I remember, the question of the independence of the Philippines. Dean Boyce had ordered me to stand immediately and protest as prejudicial to the judges' decision, any mention of certain issues. They were not mentioned until the concluding sentences of the rebuttal, by my cousin Esther Milhous; this was also the concluding speech of the debate. With Boyce's eye upon me, I dared not remain silent. I rose and protested. Or began to protest. No sooner was I on my feet than an orator, more fiery and experienced than I, leaped to his feet from the floor of the auditorium and asked of heaven, the judges *and* Boyce to be told the meaning of the continuation of the debate by a non-stop Fullerton talker. Heaven and the judges did not reply. But Boyce, on *his* feet, took on an opponent beyond my powers to quell. I retreated to the Fullerton table and there, at my ease, was able to watch the performance of two remarkable men; a performance which needless to say delighted the audience: coaches taking over the fight where the teams left off.

That Fullerton won the debate speaks well for the Boyce strategy, though it does not reflect the impassioned eloquence of Herbert Harris. I was, during the next two years, to hear it often as he read Shakespeare and Browning to his classes; or as he told us in tones I shall never forget of the brilliance of the stars on a summer night over Hemet, where as a youth he had spent vacations on his father's ranch. Harris was a man of many talents and part of his appeal, I believe, lay in the communication to his students of the unresolved conflict within himself of these talents. He, like us, had ambitions, desires and capabilities not yet completely explored and never, perhaps, completely realized.

Paul Smith, young enough to be Herbert Harris' son, was able to communicate with his students by virtue of a youth he shared with us. He had also, as did Harris, the good teacher's prime requisite: delight in teaching and enthusiasm for his subject. Without these the student had as well master his subject from a textbook. Paul Smith had, as teacher, a quality which has, I would judge, played a large part in his success as an administrator. Though we were members of a class, we never felt that he was addressing us as a class: instead he was speaking to us as individuals; to Buckmaster, Ford, Sutton, West. He possessed, and has been able to maintain in fresh and running order, what Martin Buber has called the essential of *human* existence: that is a willingness to impart himself to others as he is. By this willingness he has been able to elicit from those who at other times functioned almost wholly inside the confines of teacher, financier, preacher, housewife, politician, *human* responses. This trait, this willingness of Paul Smith's, has had much to do with Whittier College's recently becoming in fact what for many years it was able only to symbolize.

For the overall conclusion to be drawn from Professor Cooper's account of Whittier College is that Whittier, like most other small denominational colleges, existed for a time chiefly as a symbol for the community. Many colleges, at many times and in many communities, functioned in this way. The community, even though what went on behind the ivied walls had only the most tenuous connection with higher learning, still declared through the mere presence of a college, that it was intellectually progressive—if not, in an educational way, fiscally sound.

It declared this, even though the small denominational college in its efforts to exclude all that did not square with its current theology was often, in some departments, anti-educational. The college, as symbol, however weakly it might be functioning in fact, stood for the deep American faith in learning. The college on the hill, of red brick or gray fieldstone, standing amidst elms or eucalyptus, was the symbol, visible to all, that the community believed that the truth, if known, would make it free.

It was a belief worth sacrificing for; and to maintain the belief sacrifices were required. Among those who made sacrifices for it, though neither they nor their alma mater intended it that way, were those students who studied at Whittier during periods when the college was longer on symbolism than performance. These students could have received better educations elsewhere. They, along with professors working for little money, and townspeople giving beyond their means, were working for the survival of a symbol.

It has survived, and the early sacrifices have been justified as the symbol has become viable. The college no longer "stands for" truth and learning: it is able nowadays to make them available. This availability is the result, as Dr. Cooper's history makes clear, of two elements: the tenacious dreaming of the founding fathers backed up by the generous benefactions of today's fostering fathers.

An idealistic people, we are sometimes loath to give the almighty dollar full credit. In the long run it may prove that Wardman dollars played as great a part in the transformation of symbol to fact as Wright scholarship, Newlin insight, or Dexter energy. It was for lack of money that gifted teachers like William T. Boyce moved on to better paying jobs. Gifted students enrolled elsewhere; or staying on at Whittier failed to develop as they should for lack of books, laboratories, competent teachers or peers in the classroom who could challenge them. The blueprints of the early dreamers were necessary. But until the benefactions of recent donors roofed, walled and equipped these dreams they were not of much use to students.

Paul Smith's work as builder is well delineated here. It may be that it is my own limitation as an edifice admirer which makes me wish to emphasize his other accomplishments. To my mind it is who goes into a building, what is said there, who listens and learns and what finally is done with that learning that is important. And Dr. Cooper's list of speakers whose right to speak at Whittier Paul Smith defended, makes me prouder of Whittier than all of the statistics of acres acquired and buildings erected. This is a time of great change and of heated partisanship. Amidst the outcries alike of those who fear change and those who wish to accelerate it, Paul Smith has had the strength of spirit to keep Whittier a center for the development of the mind rather than for the promulgation of isms; an institution where it is believed that the student who is taught how to think will not need to be taught what to think. Some truths, the Declaration of Independence held, are self-evident. For the recognition of such as these, the belief at Whittier College under Paul Smith has been that indoctrination is not necessary.

What the founding fathers would have made of a student body where Moslems outnumber Quakers, as they now do, is unfathomable. John Greenleaf Whittier, the college's patron saint, would have been unfazed. "I see good in all denominations," he said. He hoped for a people "not relying upon creed and dogma, but upon faithful obedience to the voice of God in the soul." Whittier was speaking existentially when he said, "Each life must learn the taste of truth." Though numerically Quakers have declined, Whittier is still "Friends' College" and very Quaker so long as such beliefs animate it.

JESSAMYN WEST

WHITTIER

INDEPENDENT COLLEGE IN CALIFORNIA

Fear [not] the sceptic's puny hand
While near the school the church will stand,
Nor fear the blinded bigot's rule
While near the church shall stand the school.
—JOHN GREENLEAF WHITTIER*

*Lines addressed to his namesake Quaker colony by the aging poet, adapted from his much earlier poem "Our State."

I

FOUNDING OF THE QUAKER COLONY
AND COLLEGE (1887-1900)

———

THE QUAKER COLLEGE was already latent in the minds of those mid-Western Friends who came together in early 1887 to found a colony in California. For wherever Quakers settled in their historic migration by stages westward, they had established academies and colleges for their own youth and for their new neighbors.

A head taller than the others stood Aquilla H. Pickering, commanding an easy respect and confidence. Benign of countenance, white-bearded, wearing Prince Albert and topper, Pickering was a well-to-do elder among Chicago business men, member of its Board of Trade, land and railroad promoter. On an earlier visit to the Coast, he had found many new towns without either school or church, the Sabbath "poorly observed, and on every hand intemperance." Indeed something of the Wild West still lingered in older towns, saloons and dance-hall girls, gambling and banditry—Tiburcio Vasquez hanged but a dozen years since. Would not a strong community of Friends (thought Pickering) "assist in bringing about much needed reforms?" He had raised the question with Quakers through the *Christian Worker*, and had received encouraging response. So, early in this year of 1887, he and his wife started out to find the best possible site for a Quaker colony. They had come the Overland Route by train, searched from "beyond the Sacramento to the north and as far south as San Diego" and even to Ensenada in Mexico.

Aquilla and Hannah Pickering ended their three-months' search—having viewed thirty locations and optioned twelve— and they came to rest among Friends in Pasadena and Los An-

3

geles, who had also been thinking about the proposed Quaker colony and hoped that a site for it might be found in booming southern California. Discussion of the project brought together a group of substantial Friends. Their thoughts turned to rising land values. Out beyond Pasadena in the San Gabriel and Pomona valley, now with two railroads going East, development of new towns had skyrocketed land prices. On the ocean side of the Puente Hills, however, desirable lands were yet available—for instance, the Thomas Ranch was again on the market. Although get-rich-quick speculators now asked twice what they had paid John M. Thomas for it the preceding year, this ranch of 1,270 acres was still judged a good buy at $55 per acre. It was certainly worth looking at.

These Friends drove out from Los Angeles, across the wide mesa southeast from Boyle Heights. After an hour and more of the dusty road, their team forded the Rio Hondo (the Old River) and then shortly the San Gabriel (the New River). There they passed the Ranchito of Pio Pico (last Mexican governor of California), the shacks and saloon of Jimtown, and the adjacent Strong Ranch. Then the Quakers turned left off the graded road to pull more slowly up toward the hills. They found themselves at last under the pepper trees that shaded the ranch house.

A short walk took them to a nearby knoll. There below them lay the broad acres of the Thomas Ranch. Sheltered by the Puente Hills immediately behind them, the land fell away easily to the County Road. The hillside was green and yellow with spring barley and patches of wild mustard, shoulder high. In the middle distance, the Los Nietos valley spread out with its two rivers, its verdant checkerboard of orchards and fields. Far off to the right, the branch line curved out from Los Angeles, crossed the landscape, and disappeared into the rolling country to the left. Yet more distant were Signal Hill, San Pedro harbor, and the blue Pacific.

It was the nearer prospect, however, that had brought these Friends together and that kindled their imagination and enthusiasm. Where might a townsite be platted—up by the hill here, or down by the County Road? What about water, where might it be developed? Would land costs and improvements allow town lots and acreage to be sold at reasonable prices? How might the enterprise be organized? Of mid-Western Quakers, how many would actually pull up stakes to come to California? And upon arrival, where would they live? And how would they earn a living?

But in the midst of such essential questions, surely, came at least fleeting thoughts of the college—the Friends college—so soon to be launched as a prime symbol of the kind of town they dreamed of founding. For among these men, had not Jonathan Bailey helped to start Wilmington College for Ohio Quakers? Did not Dr. Fordyce Grinnell have a bright son soon on the road to eminence in ornithology? Was not John Painter's son-in-law, ten years professor at Penn College, even now at hand in Pasadena? Was not Hervey Lindley's brother a professor of medicine, influential physician and educator in Los Angeles? Were they not *all* part of the Quaker movement westward that had planted academies and colleges wherever Friends had settled?

And what a site this very spot where they stood—overlooking the town as yet unborn and this magnificent panorama—what a site for their college!

1

LAST OF THE QUAKER PIONEERS
THE FOUNDING OF THEIR COLONY

FRIENDS, A LARGER GATHERING called together by Aquilla Pickering after the enthusiastic viewing of the Thomas Ranch, confirmed its choice as location for the colony. On April 4, 1887, the promoters, among whom Jonathan Bailey's judgment carried most weight, reached final agreement. T. Elwood Newlin, Kansas banker who had moved to California the preceding year, negotiated with the owners. Hervey Lindley's check for $1,000 bound the bargain.

The next Wednesday, in the old barn at the Thomas Ranch itself, they organized the Pickering Land and Water Company (to be capitalized at $500,000), and named directors. The following day in Los Angeles, they subscribed $210,000 in stock, of which John Painter of Pasadena took $42,000 and eight others—including Pickering, Bailey, Newlin, Grinnell, Hervey Lindley and his father Milton and Eleazer Andrews—took $21,000 each. Still

5

with business interests in Chicago, Pickering declined to serve as president of the Company. In his place the directors named Jonathan Bailey, with Hervey Lindley as secretary-treasurer. Bailey and Lindley shared the business management.

Pickering announced the undertaking at once through the Los Angeles *Herald*. Before the month was out, the *Christian Worker* carried the good news to mid-Western Quakers who had followed with such interest the Pickerings' accounts of their long search.

The money and risks involved might not have seemed great to those who ventured. For the Thomas Ranch itself, the price was $69,850—$25,000 down payment, mortgages assumed @ 9% and balance @ 10% interest, all due within a year. For the adjacent hill lands (the Turnbull Ranch of 2,450 acres needed for developing water), the price was $29,460. The total for land alone was just under $100,000, hardly too much for these nine men to carry. But Quakers of smaller means might have questioned such sums as they meditated the Seventh Query of their *Discipline*: "Are Friends careful . . . to avoid involving themselves in business beyond their ability to manage?"

The Pickering Land and Water Company moved with speed. Officers signed final papers on April 25th, and ordered the survey and blueprint for the town plat. This raised a crucial question. What should the town be called?

Obviously Quaker-Town would not do—"the worst town in Indiana," someone said. One morning Jonathan Bailey came into Hervey Lindley's office with Micajah Johnson's suggestion that the town be named for John Greenleaf Whittier, most widely known Quaker of the day. The thought had also occurred to Elizabeth Grinnell and perhaps to others. "Whittier" as name for the Quaker colony "met with unanimous approval" on May 5th. Hervey Lindley undertook to write the aging poet in Massachusetts, fully expecting his consent and blessing.

On May 11th, Jonathan and Rebecca Bailey moved into the ranch house to take immediate charge of the development—and on the next Sabbath four persons met for Quaker worship on their front porch.*

*This California ranch house, later remodeled and squared about to face Camilla Street in Whittier, was a home of charm and character for the Bailey family until the death in 1964 of Mrs. George Hunnicutt, Jonathan Bailey's granddaughter.

Jonathan Bailey, nearing seventy, was a Virginia-born Friend whose abolitionist family had moved north to Ohio in the 1820's where they had farmed and prospered. Ill health of wife and son had brought him to California for visits in the 1870's, and by 1885 he had established himself in a Los Angeles real estate office. A man of sturdy piety and humor, with Old Testament beard and luminous eyes, he set himself vigorously to the task at hand—laying out the colony on the barley and mustard slope of the Thomas Ranch.

The townsite comprised a square 160 acres, with five- and ten-acre parcels surrounding it. The four streets bounding the townsite extended from the hill down to the County Road, as did the main streets intersecting at its center. There were hundreds of survey lines to run, points to fix, stakes to drive—and streets to be named. Some were named for the Company directors and backers: Pickering, Painter, Bailey, Newlin, Milton [Lindley], and Washington Hadley—others were to bear more widely-known Quaker names: Penn, [John] Bright, and [Elizabeth] Comstock. Greenleaf, the poet's middle name, they gave to the main street north and south; Philadelphia, to the main street east and west. The next street below it they named College—and on it they reserved a triple-lot for the Friends Church.

At the last minute—no reply as yet from the Quaker poet and the map already completed—the name "Whittier" was added, in small letters at the center of the townsite, the intersection of Philadelphia and Greenleaf.

The Company set the opening sale for 9 a.m. on May 19th at Lindley's office, #75 South Spring Street in Los Angeles. To restrain speculators, no more than eight lots would be sold to any one buyer. The directors reserved certain lots, though it was mid-July before these were formally set aside. One was to be a gift for John G. Whittier. Another was the 20-acre parcel that included the knoll with its superb view—it was "donated for college purposes."*

On the advertised day, a crowd gathered beginning at 3 a.m., filling the hall and extending in a line (some said) for several blocks. When Hervey Lindley arrived with Elwood Newlin and

*The east side of Painter Avenue, between Hadley Street and Bailey, it was at once called "College Hill."

7

John E. Coffin to help him, they could reach his office only by passing through the *Herald*'s quarters next door, out a window and up over a balcony. At the appointed hour, the sale started.

Corner lots went for $250, inside lots for $200; close-in acreage for perhaps $200 per acre—a reduction from these prices was shrewdly given to those who would start immediate improvements. Terms were one-third down, an equal amount in six months, balance in a year (interest @ 10%). The first day's total —whether of sales or down-payments—was $34,000.

On into the summer of the boom, Hervey Lindley's office kept busy. John E. Coffin drove prospective buyers out from the city— Bertha Lindley, soon to be his bride, riding with him. Lindley M. Baldwin (who with Edgar Jessup had surveyed the town) brought groups over from Pasadena in his tally-ho. And William P. Cooper—who had escaped the Mountain Meadow Massacre in 1857—drove his team and wagon up from the branch line at Norwalk with passengers and freight.

Jonathan Bailey rode his gray mare about the townsite from one project to another. Up in Turnbull Canyon he directed the tunneling for water—meanwhile it was hauled from the New River and from Fulton Wells (as Santa Fe Springs was then called). Before streets could be graded and arroyos bridged, grain had to be harvested. "Uncle" Jonathan also kept an eye on the Friends Church, which the Company itself was erecting, and on other building projects.

With the town launched in the late spring, Aquilla Pickering returned to Chicago. He had been appointed "special colonization agent" by both the Union and Southern Pacific railroads. Advertising the California colony through successive weekly issues of the *Christian Worker*, he kept Friends informed of its progress. By June 9th there were already 18 homes under contract. By June 30th, the Friends Church neared completion— home-seekers crowded Whittier's large tent-hotel—the Company had piped spring water to the lots. Pickering began to organize excursions for Quaker emigrants, fortnightly departures from the mid-West.

Advertising in other journals was more exclamatory: "Whittier! Whittier!! Whittier!!! / Queen of the Foothills and Crown of the San Gabriel Valley." And another in full boom:

8

Whittier is the coming place. It will dwarf Monrovia and eclipse Pasadena. Nothing can stop it! The Quakers are coming in from all over the United States!

As a matter of fact, the Quakers could not come quite this fast.

THE WESTWARD MOVEMENT of Quakers, of which the colonizing in Whittier was a final episode, had started about 1820 when Friends like the Bailey family moved up from the South into the Ohio and Indiana country.

These "Friends," as the followers of George Fox preferred to be called, were a singular people, known for strong views and mild manners. They persisted in their Plain Talk, using *thee* and *thy* for two centuries after other folk were polite with *you* and *your*. They held to their Plain Dress, a formalized somber attire—straight-collared coat and flat-crowned hat, gray full dress with shawl and bonnet. They stuck to their testimonies, refused judicial oaths and the bearing of arms, dealt plainly in business, and concerned themselves for the welfare of their brothers, whether enslaved, imprisoned, or insane.

Generations of being "different" kept Quakers together, neighboring with their kind.

Friends were firmly established if no longer the majority in the Philadelphia area. Many of them prospered, some as brewers or bankers. They supported their schools—Friends Central, George School, Westtown, Germantown. One group established Haverford College (1833) for men and much later Bryn Mawr (1880) for women. Another group founded Swarthmore (1864) as a coeducational college. Individual Quaker philanthropists in the East endowed nonsectarian universities, Cornell in 1865 and Johns Hopkins in 1867. By and large, these urban Friends stayed put.

However, those in the areas surrounding eastern Pennsylvania were less firmly fixed, on the whole less prosperous, and subject to various economic and environmental pressures.

Never very numerous in New England states—and at first persecuted—Quakers in time made a small place for themselves. John G. Whittier was active in the Abolitionist movement and in the founding of the Republican Party. He became a member of the Massachusetts legislature and served in the Electoral College when Lincoln won the Presidency. He was an overseer of Harvard University and a trustee of Brown. It was Moses Brown, Quaker partner in the first successful cotton mill, who, with his brother Nicholas, supported the Rhode Island college that became Brown University, five trustees to be Quaker. In some numbers New England Friends crossed over into New York and then down into the Ohio country and thence by stages westward.

The larger number of Quakers went westward by another route. Many of them stemmed from Nantucket, where Quaker whalermen had settled in the mid-seventeenth century—Thomas Macy, Edward Starbuck, Tristram Coffin, Stephen Hussey, Peleg Slocum—names echoing in *Moby Dick*. A century later there were fifteen hundred Nantucket Quakers. By 1800 they had begun to lose ground on the island, separated by doctrinal differences and decline of the whaling industry. Many of them left Nantucket, sailed down the Atlantic coast, and joined Friends already long-established in North Carolina.

There near Guilford Courthouse—historic Revolutionary battlefield—Friends had started the school in 1837 that became Guilford College. The newcomers found themselves wives and settled to the business of living. But with the quickening of conscience on behalf of the enslaved Negro—and economically disadvantaged by such slave labor—many Quakers found it impossible to remain in the South. Some 25,000 of them crossed northwest into the Ohio and Indiana country before the Civil War. They farmed and traded, established schools and academies —often the only ones for neighboring children. They also founded colleges: Earlham at Richmond, Indiana (1847) and Wilmington in Ohio (1870). Then some of them were lured westward into the new farmlands of Illinois and Iowa, where they settled in southeastern counties, founding a "Whittier College" at Salem, Iowa (1867) and Penn College at nearby Oskaloosa (1873). Another surge westward took Quaker settlers into Kansas and Nebraska, where they later (in 1898) started Friends University at Wichita and Nebraska Central College at Central City.*

*Nebraska Central, never robust, was the only Quaker-college casualty of the Great Depression.

By this time transcontinental rail lines had opened up the Far West. What had been a perilous and exhausting trek of months by covered wagon, became suddenly no more than a week of swaying and cindery torment. One prong of the final thrust westward took some Friends northwest to the fertile Willamette valley in Oregon, where they founded an academy (1885) at Newberg that became Pacific College, later renamed for George Fox. At the same time a second prong penetrated the southwest, where a few Quakers had earlier settled in Los Angeles, a larger number in Pasadena, and clusters at [El] Modena (in the foothills beyond Anaheim) and at Wildomar (out near Elsinore).

This, then, was the background of those Quakers who by the emigrant carloads—the last of the pioneers—came the final stage in the sweeping movement westward that, within half a century, had surged around the Philadelphia heartland, carrying Friends to their new colony planted within sight of the Pacific.*

WITHOUT THE RAILROADS Whittier, the colony and the college, would never have been founded, nor would southern California have experienced its phenomenal growth. In 1887 it was but eighteen years since completion of the Overland Route across prairies and mountains that linked the mid-West with the Golden Gate—but eleven years since the Southern Pacific pushed its line south through the San Joaquin Valley and twice tunneled mountains to reach Los Angeles—five years since it completed its Sunset Route to El Paso and thence to the mid-West and to the South —only two years since the competing Santa Fe Railway crossed the Mojave Desert and Cajon Pass to bring its trains directly into southern California. At last in 1887, it was "Santa Fe all the way" over its own rails from Chicago and Kansas City through Pasadena to Los Angeles.

What had earlier been the $125 fare from the mid-West had already dropped to $100 and then $95 in 1885. Now, on March 4, 1887, the Santa Fe slashed its fare to $32, which the Southern Pacific matched. Then the Santa Fe cut its rate to $12 from Kansas City to the Coast. The S.P. bettered this, selling tickets for $10

*It is significant to note, therefore, that Philadelphia Quakers—Haverford, Swarthmore, Bryn Mawr and the substantial families that supported them—played but small part in the Winning of the West and the establishment of its colleges.

11

—and then for $8! And finally—out of touch with reality in its San Francisco office—the S.P. undercut itself to $6—to $4—and at last to $1!!

This, of course, did not last. But the rate settled at $25 for a mixed ticket—that is, "second class, to the Missouri River, and third class, from the Missouri River to the Pacific Coast." On these emigrant cars, such as brought the Quakers, families carried their own blankets and baskets of food. They made up bunks at night, ate hard-boiled eggs and cold chicken between train stops for coffee. And Dr. Walter Lindley (Hervey Lindley's brother) suggested that all such travellers carry "a bottle of paregoric, a bottle of aromatic spirits of ammonia, and a flask of good whiskey"—in case of need. Even a first-class ticket from New York to Los Angeles cost but $80, an additional $20 for accommodation in the ornate Palace cars of the Pullman Company.

The spectacular rate-war and the low emigrant fares that continued were a great stimulus to westward travel. Trains ran in many sections. At least 100,000 mid-Westerners and Easterners —among whom Friends were proportionately very few—migrated to California within a year, doubled the population of Los Angeles and settled new towns in the railroad valleys and coastal stretches.

Low fares were not the only factor that brought them. Driven on by the filling up of the mid-West—driven also by blizzards and cyclones, floods and drouths—Quakers too were drawn to southern California by the very real clemency of its weather and fertility of its lands, the natural beauty of its mountains and beaches, the therapeutic wonder of its mineral springs and dry-air resorts. The salubrious California climate needed no press agentry, though it got that aplenty. Those on the crowded incoming trains were ready to be welcomed with brass bands. Some 2,000 real estate agents were eager to greet them—and to sell them lots or ranches, to squire them to tourist hotels, to fill them with promises of health and wealth. Such was Los Angeles, though but few Friends settled in the City.

The City of the Angels—there were romantic touches—had become the center of a burgeoning economy, with mercantile and building supplies, agriculture and petroleum—the banks doing what they could to hold down inflation. Nor was Los Angeles without some measure of culture. In its Grand Opera House sang Adelina Patti—on occasion. In its theatres appeared Edmund Booth, Lillie Langtry, Madame Modjeska—her nearby ranch home a showplace. Commodious churches were built as far from the Plaza as Eighth Street. Landscaped estates with opulent mansions adorned West Adams.

Although the State University was firmly planted in the north at Berkeley and the new Stanford University was a-building nearby, Los Angeles already had its branch of San Jose State Normal (from which in good season sprouted U.C.L.A.). St. Vincent's College, already established (1869), had just moved way out to Washington and Grand (to become in time Loyola University). Methodists had started their own University of Southern California, now with professional schools scattered through the area. By the time Quakers arrived in any numbers, Presbyterians, Congregationalists, Brethren, Baptists were all moving toward building their own colleges in the region.

QUAKERS COMING DIRECTLY to Whittier from the mid-West did not reach the new colony until summer.

It was in July 1887 that Aquilla and Hannah Pickering returned with a tourist carload of Friends who had entrained at Chicago.* In the group were Pickering's two brothers, John H. and Jonathan E., Henry Dorland, his brother-in-law by his first marriage, and their assorted families. Their train came the Overland Route—Union and Southern Pacific—across the Sierras and south from Sacramento through the Great Valley (to which the Pickering brothers would later return), and finally through the Newhall tunnel into Los Angeles. Then their car, switched to the Anaheim branch, was at last set off on the Norwalk siding.

"Shucks," said local children to whom the Quakers were pointed out, "they just look like people!" And indeed there were few among mid-Western Friends, except older folk, who still wore the Plain Dress—or used the Plain Talk.

At the railroad siding, the newcomers were met, to be driven the six miles up to Whittier. In the two months since the opening sale, feverish activity had already created the first semblance of

*They had started with a sickly Negro orphan, whom they had hoped to restore to health, but the child died before reaching southern California.

13

a town. Wagon tracks marked out some of the streets. Tent-houses spotted some of the blocks. Carpenters hammered together the first cottages. A few business structures—and the Friends Church —neared completion. A tent-hotel and restaurant offered room and board. Such was the heartening sight.

But a distressing reality greeted the Quaker colonists. The settlement, ostensibly for them, had been largely pre-empted by others. The Company had already sold some 500 of the original 780 lots and all the parcels of surrounding acreage. Speculators had snatched up most of them, held them for resale at advanced prices. Even the Company had by July 12th raised by $100 the prices of its unsold lots. The run-away land boom of southern California swept Whittier along with it. Although the Company made good on specific promises to Quaker families, and sold Aquilla Pickering four town lots at the original price, the newcomers could only buy choice homesites, preferred business locations, and nearby farm acreage through real estate agents and at extravagant prices. By the end of the year, business lots that had been sold in May for $250, were reselling for $2,500 and more. House lots sold and resold at mounting prices. Even the Company raised its few remaining lots by $100 per week during October and November. Hervey Lindley, who had bought close-in acreage, was not alone in opening new subdivisions.

Together with C. W. Harvey, Lindley was building a $50,000 tourist hotel on ten acres up above Hadley on Painter. "Old Man" Harvey was also building a brick business block on Hadley and Greenleaf, hoping to pull the town up toward close-in acreage he was there subdividing. H. W. Sessions and Frank Wiggins (of Quaker family from Richmond, Indiana, and later the genius promoting Los Angeles as Secretary of its Chamber of Commerce) put their brick block down on Greenleaf at Penn, to pull people down toward land development there. The Company held firm at the center. Jonathan Bailey built a house and observatory at the top of Turnbull canyon to give tourists a breath-taking view of both valleys, mountains and sea.

Meanwhile came excursion carloads of Quakers—from Wisconsin, from Ohio and Indiana, from Iowa and Kansas. The Friends Church was completed in August. It was a gift of the Company, and Jonathan Bailey conducted the dedication. Its bell

—still calling Friends to church, though at a different site—was the personal gift of Hervey Lindley. By December, Friends numbered 200 and organized themselves as Whittier Monthly Meeting of Pasadena Quarterly Meeting, itself a part of Iowa Yearly Meeting and recognized by Kansas Yearly Meeting. They completed the parsonage next door and called a remarkable man as pastor—Dr. Elias Jessup. Hoosier-born and schooled at Earlham, he first taught Negro freedmen in Missouri, then studied and practiced law in Indiana. After the Civil War, he studied and practiced medicine in Iowa, where he served in the state senate and ran for governor. He migrated to Oregon, served in its state senate and helped found its Quaker college. Then, feeling a call to the ministry, he came south to Whittier, which had already attracted members of his family.

By Christmastime 1887, "the magic little city of Whittier" boasted—and boasting was the temper of the time—800 inhabitants. It had two general stores, a butcher and a milk dealer, a drug store and post office, three restaurants, three hotels, three livery stables—and twelve real estate offices. Mark Anthony, a Negro, ran a barber shop "with bathroom and everything." Tillinghast, Henry & Co. were the bankers. Dr. C. R. Dixon, the first town doctor, edited the Whittier *Graphic*, but soon yielded pen to his partner, J. C. Hiatt.

And, in the exciting immediate prospect, was the Friends' College.

JOHN GREENLEAF WHITTIER had not been able to answer at once the letter Hervey Lindley had written him, asking if it were agreeable to give the new Quaker colony his name. However, under date of October 13th, the poet wrote a thoughtful consent and appreciation, not only for the compliment but for the invitation to visit his namesake town. In speaking of "the Quaker City," he wrote—

> I use that term in no sectarian sense, for I see the good in all denominations, and hope that all will be represented in the settlement. I trust that its Quakerism will be of the old, practical kind, "diligent in business and serving the Lord," not wasting its strength and vitality in spasmodic emotions, not relying on creed and dogma, but upon faithful obedience to the voice of God in the soul.

15

This clear expression of Whittier's "reasonable faith" was of the sort that, within the year, had made him a controversial figure amongst evangelistic Quakers of the mid-West. However, he had assured them that he was "neither a Unitarian nor a Universalist" but "a Friend." This he reaffirmed in his letter to Lindley, in which he continued: "I shall watch the progress of the settlement with deep interest. . . ."

> I cannot doubt that care will be taken that the dreadful evil of intemperance shall not be permitted to fasten itself upon the young settlement, and that in *sobriety, industry, large charity, active benevolence, and educational privilege,* it may prove an example worthy of general imitation, and fulfill the fond anticipation of its founders.

Having overlooked the gift of the double lot—the northwest corner of Philadelphia and Friends worth perhaps $3,000 at that moment—he added a grateful postscript.

In the words above, those italicized as worthy a second glance, the New England poet—trustee of two universities—caught the spirit that, within the framework of their Quaker orthodoxy, animated the founders of both colony and college.

2

FRIENDS' COLLEGE
DREAM OF THE QUAKER FOUNDERS OF WHITTIER

PART OF THE PLAN and indeed the promise of those who founded the town of Whittier was "the college."

In the spring of 1888, a schoolgirl of 14 sent a letter to *St. Nicholas,* which that children's magazine published in its November issue that fall.

> Our little town [she wrote of Whittier] is scarcely a year old, although it has nearly a thousand inhabitants. . . . On clear days we can easily count the vessels in San Pedro Harbor, twenty miles away. . . .

Then she added,

> The Friends' College, to be erected on the Pacific Coast and to cost $100,000, is located at Whittier, and the grading of the grounds for

the buildings is nearly completed. The college is on quite a high hill and will be visible for miles.

With an "Adios, St. Nicholas," she signed herself "your California friend and constant reader," *Lou H——*. She was the daughter of Charles D. Henry the banker.*

Actually, the Friends' College was not as far along as it then seemed to her. Though College Street had been so designated on the original town plat in mid-May 1887, and the choice 20-acre site "donated for college purposes" by mid-July, it was not until mid-December that an organization was effected for founding a college.

On December 19, 1887—at a called meeting of those concerned —certain Friends present accepted appointment as trustees. This was the official beginning of Friends' College.** Unnoticed was the fact that this meeting followed by two days the 80th birthday of the new town's patron poet, John Greenleaf Whittier.

The trustees elected Dr. Samuel D. Coffin president of the board. Carolina-born of a Nantucket family, he had graduated from Guilford and taken medical training in Philadelphia. In 1860 he had moved his family north into Indiana, and later out to Kansas, where he had been country doctor and farmer before retiring to live in Lawrence. His son John E. Coffin had preceded him to southern California. Dr. Samuel Coffin was a man of imposing presence. Other officers of the board were Charley C. Reynolds, first vice-president; Dr. Elias Jessup, second vice-president; Willet Dorland, secretary; Dr. C. R. Dixon, assistant secretary; T. Elwood Newlin, treasurer—and Hervey Lindley, financial agent.

Articles of incorporation, filed forthwith, specified that the board was to comprise twelve members, of whom a majority "shall belong to the Friends Church." Additional trustees appointed then or shortly were Jonathan Bailey, John Painter, Cyrus Lindley (an uncle of Hervey), and Charles T. Hirt of distant Wildomar—replaced shortly by Reuben Hartley, Friends' pas-

*As Mrs. Herbert C. Hoover, she was to play a part in the later history of the college.

**No minutes of this meeting survive, but it was reported in the third issue of the new Whittier *Graphic*, January 12, 1888.

tor and one-time professor of Greek. Friends' College—always spelled with the apostrophe of possession—was to be "a school for both sexes." It was proper, therefore, that women be numbered among its trustees: Hannah Pickering, and soon Esther M. Hiatt, whose husband published the *Graphic*.

In preparation for a public meeting to launch the campaign for building funds, Prof. Charles E. Tebbetts of Pasadena spent a couple of days in Whittier "looking up the college interests." Son-in-law of John Painter, he was Iowa-born, his parents from New England. After graduation from Penn College, he had taken an M.A. at Haverford, then returned to Penn for a decade's teaching of science and mathematics before coming to California.

The meeting, called for Monday evening, January 23rd, was postponed for a week because of heavy rains.* Though recurring rain kept away certain key trustees from Los Angeles and Pasadena, the public meeting of January 30, 1888, in the Friends Church was well attended—"every chair was taken, and a number [of persons, surely] remained standing." Dr. Samuel Coffin called the meeting to order. Dr. Jessup offered prayer. Visiting dignitaries made remarks—Major E. W. Jones, Dr. William Nicholson, and Colonel Violet, who "entertained the audience with humor, sense, and sarcasm." Professor Tebbetts gave the address. "In an earnest and scholarly manner," he discussed, "the college question in all its phases." Then he made a remarkable offer, contingent upon establishment of a good college, to endow a professorship himself and to make Whittier his home.

Following Tebbetts' stirring proposal, "subscriptions were taken to the amount of $25,000," mostly from "mechanics and laboring men" who, in a scene never forgotten by those present, "promptly put down their $25, $50, $100 each, as fast as Mr. Calloway, C. W. Harvey's foreman, could call their names."

It was the will of the new townfolk to have their college. The *Graphic* proudly reported that, with the "chair" endowed by Professor Tebbetts ("nothing less than $25,000 endowment"), the gift of campus land from the Pickering Land and Water Company (worth $25,000 at that moment), and a "conditional sub-

*A copy of the handbill advertising this meeting survives in the Whittier College archives. It was a community summons, and in it the proposed College was not designated as "Friends."

scription" of another $25,000 [unexplained], the minimal $100-000 was virtually in hand. And "a number of capitalists" were expected to come forward shortly with further substantial contributions.

For the second public meeting a week later, February 6th—the dust settled and streets again dry—"about 150 earnest people met at the Church" already in the afternoon "to talk college" and to volunteer additional subscriptions. By 7 o'clock the church was crowded, everyone "in the best of humor." Again Dr. Coffin presided and reported progress: engineers and architect already making surveys, estimates, plans. Then came the speeches—the Honorable this and the Honorable that from mid-West and even New England—"after which subscriptions were taken." This time the capitalists were at hand: Hervey Lindley led off with an offer of $30,000 on condition $100,000 be raised. Old Man Harvey subscribed $6,000, then raised it to $8,500. Other non-Quakers also pledged $1,000 or more, as did such Friends as Milton Lindley, L. M. Baldwin, Eleazar Andrews and Miss Mattie B. Andrews—whose soul, then as later, was "on fire for the College." The total, as tabulated, was $137,000.

After the trustees closed the meeting with prayerful thanksgiving,

> the youthful element carried boxes and barrels to the top of "College Hill" and set off a huge bonfire that alarmed the town and countryside.

And the *Graphic* trumpeted in its next issue: "A COLLEGE SURE! / Whittier to be an educational center."

Nothing remained to be done, it seemed, except to erect the building, assemble a faculty, and open the doors of Friends' College. But it was not to be that easy.

WORK ON THIS COLLEGE HILL BEGAN. Lowering the top of the knoll by ten feet, leveling and broadening the building site, excavating the college basement—all of this involved blasting and heavy team work. Much of the labor of man and beast had been "subscribed" at that public meeting, in lieu of money, but the college board gave such workmen some cash as well as credit on their pledges. More crushed rock was quarried than needed for shouldering out the building site. Some of the gravel, hauled "by subscribed team labor," paved Painter Avenue in front of the college grounds. By early June, the grading of College Hill was completed—and Painter Avenue was paved with gravel from the Greenleaf Hotel down to Philadelphia Street. Hadley Street, too, was "piked" from the college entrance "two blocks above Painter" down "to the west line of the town" (the County Road).

Meanwhile the architect, J. E. Newsom of Los Angeles—officially engaged February 14th—hurried his preliminary work and presented two schemes and sketches within a week. The one selected was his design of a four-story structure with imposing entrance and six-story clock tower. It was all vaguely Gothic and Court-House in the style of the times, an imposing pile to surmount College Hill. The perspective sketch was sent to John G. Whittier; he pronounced it "architecturally fine." A small cut appeared with general satisfaction in the *Graphic*.

On April 13th, the college trustees directed the architect to call for bids and they contracted for a million brick, to be made locally. By May 3rd the *Graphic* reported the bid of $53,500 as accepted. This was advance news, for the authorization was not made and minuted until the following day.

To outward view and public knowledge, all went well. Yet, in the three months since the first meetings for raising funds, a variety of problems had presented themselves.

ONE WAS THE QUESTION of control. Uneasiness developed among certain Quakers lest, in the enthusiasm of local town support, the Friends' college might become merely Whittier's college.

Both the college board and Pasadena Quarterly Meeting wanted to assure "an organic connection" between the Friends' College and the Society of Friends. Therefore, agreement was reached to increase to two-thirds the proportion of trustees who must be Friends—to authorize the Quarterly Meeting to name two of the college trustees—to ask the Quarterly Meeting to recognize the college officially as "the Friends' College of the Pacific coast."

More serious than the question of control was the problem of collections. The trustees were anxious to turn the lamplight pledges into light-of-day contracts. They set up an office in "the building formerly occupied by the bank" (Tillinghast, Henry & Co.) that had already dissolved. With the office open daily "during business hours," they made an effort to formalize the subscriptions for assured collection. There was no evidence of much success.

The need for more cash money prompted an organized college benefit. The Whittier and Los Angeles Railroad (as the six-mile line was called that, at local cost, connected the new town to the S.P. branch near Norwalk) was completed in mid-March ready for inauguration of service to the City. The Dunlap subdivision, down near the depot at the County Road, was ready for its opening auction. With the help of the Los Angeles Board of Trade (certainly through the ingenuity of Hervey Lindley), a ten-car excursion train brought 800 people—including two nieces of John G. Whittier as honored guests—out from Los Angeles to Whittier in gala mood. At the auction, with Old Man Harvey crying the sale, "all over $125 per lot" on all lots up to the number of 100 was for the benefit of Friends' College. Thus were sold 75 lots "at good [but unstated] prices." The terms, as usual: "one third cash, the balance in 6 & 12 months." Guests were elegantly dined (and almost wined) at Harvey and Lindley's Greenleaf Hotel, the menu beginning with mock turtle soup and ending with plum pudding and brandy sauce.* But free rides and free lunch no longer assured overwhelming success for a land sale. No profit to Friends' College was recorded.

There was some uneasiness about the name of the college. "Friends'" seemed more descriptive or proprietary than nominative. The name "Whittier College" was never applied to it at this time as the Whittier College in Iowa (rebuilt after destructive fire) pre-empted that name. Several Quakers in Whittier had helped to found it, and the poet too would have been sensitive to usurpation of the name by the new college in California. He had contributed a small sum to the Iowa college, books for its library, and affectionate advice to its president. Friends' College could not then be called Whittier College.

On March 1st, the *Graphic* made a suggestion. Shrewdly it

* Such worldly entertainment was criticized in the columns of the Santa Ana *Blade* as unbecoming the Quaker colony, but the *Graphic* attested the propriety—and sobriety—of the occasion.

reported a new building on the campus of Earlham College: Lindley Hall. It was a memorial gift by Dr. Alfred and Eliza Lindley, he being a cousin of the Lindleys now in southern California. The editor felt confident that the doctor would "be interested in the success of our college"—and hinted that "by giving $50,000, which he can easily do, he may name this college. Lindley College would be a very appropriate name." Dr. Alfred Lindley may not have got the message—but perhaps it was intended for the Lindleys nearer at hand.

FRIENDS' COLLEGE MOVED toward a crisis, the question of name still unsettled. At the April 13, 1888 meeting of the trustees— following the motions to call for bids and to contract for bricks— Dr. Samuel D. Coffin "tendered his resignation as President of the Board." He intended to return for a visit to his old home in Lawrence, Kansas. His resignation accepted, he drew from his pocket a resolution that he read to the board:

> Whereas, Hervey Lindley . . . has, by his untiring efforts and unbounded generosity been instrumental in the founding of said College, and
>   Whereas said Hervey Lindley has done more than any other person in placing said Institution on the road to its assured future prosperity, be it, and it hereby is resolved,
>   That the College forever bear the name of "The *Hervey Lindley College*" in place and stead of the name said College now bears. . . .

There may have been a painful or embarrassed silence. The trustees postponed action on the resolution. To fill Dr. Coffin's place on the board, which he also resigned, Charles E. Tebbetts was appointed a trustee, he and Reuben Hartley then being the Quarterly Meeting representatives.

Hervey Lindley was elected President of the Board.

The *Graphic* praised the choice. "This means business." But there was no mention of the resolution—no word of "The Hervey Lindley College"—no further invitation for Lindley money. It was safer to report the contract for bricks—250,000 to be ready by June 1st—and to bleat the assurance that "everything is moving nicely." However, there were more delinquent promises than bank deposits to support the signing of the building contract authorized on May 4th. The college board resolved that in case it becomes necessary for the completion of the building we will issue bonds at a low rate of interest for the completion of the building at as early a day as possible.

The *Graphic*'s expectation was that it would be ready for use by January 1st.

But at the May 16th meeting of the trustees—held at the home of Jonathan Bailey—came a showdown. The minutes recorded fourteen of the presumed twelve trustees as present. Milton Lindley had accompanied his son Hervey to the field and was ready to vote. A resolution was offered: to put all of the assets "in legal shape" and then to complete the building contract and proceed with the construction. Put to a recorded vote, the trustees approved the resolution 8-6. A motion to reconsider passed. Then Reuben Hartley moved to postpone further consideration for two weeks "to allow the financial agent [Hervey Lindley himself] to get the assets in proper shape." This motion lost. The original resolution, again put to the vote, passed 9-5 in favor of going ahead with the building.

A second resolution was offered: "to consider [at a meeting a week hence] the question of organizing and beginning a College course of instruction next fall." Before it could be voted, T. Elwood Newlin, treasurer of the board, rose in protest.* He presented his resignation from the board, insisted it be accepted as of that date and before "further proceeding being taken in the matter of construction of the building known as Friends' College." This, from one of the project's staunchest champions, and one who, through the years ahead, continued in devoted support of academy and college!

Next day the *Graphic*, ignoring the conflict, noted that the resolution "to rent rooms and open the College this fall" had been laid on the table for a week . . . "but it will certainly pass." Four professors would be chosen, it affirmed, for the opening of the college about October 1st.

*Newlin's wife, be it remembered, was cousin to Milton Lindley there present and to his son Hervey, and daughter of Washington Hadley the Kansas banker with whom Dr. Samuel D. Coffin had doubtless already visited about current problems of the town and the college. Had Washington Hadley written Elwood urging caution upon his kinsmen?

At the May 25th adjourned meeting of the board (eleven present), Charles E. Tebbetts tendered his resignation. Trustees deferred acceptance of it, and named a committee to correspond with possible professors and to find out what it would cost to rent rooms and fit them up for temporary use. At the June 16th meeting (nine present, three of them Lindleys), the board elected Reuben H. Hartley "President of the Faculty" and authorized him to attend the Friends Educational Conference at Haverford on July 1st. The *Graphic* was enthusiastic—though calling Hartley only "temporary president," for it had opted for Tebbetts all along. But Hartley, it reported, would visit "John G. Whittier and other prominent wealthy gentlemen in the interests of the college."

The adjourned board meeting of June 25th lacked a quorum to transact business.

Then, again at the Bailey home, the board met on August 2nd. As the *Graphic* of that date announced, it was "to hear the report of President Hartley, who has just returned from the East." Ten were present and listened to his "interesting report." Then Friends' College quietly folded.

The trustees authorized Willet Dorland "to borrow money sufficient to liquidate present indebtedness." They personally accepted responsibility "for the [re]payment of the money when due." Then they authorized Jonathan Bailey

> to return the [blasting] powder and any other available property now on hand on College Hill, to as good advantage as possible and get credit for bills now due.

The board adjourned to meet again on the 17th of the month at 10 a.m.

The rest is silence—no minutes of further meetings—no more puffing reports of Friends' College in the *Graphic*, which survived but a few weeks more.

But in the September 27th issue of that weekly appeared this wistful item:

Occidental University

This university is located on the beautiful slope just beyond the city limits on the east side of the city of Los Angeles and in view of

Whittier. . . . The first term commenced, Monday, Sept. 10, 1888. The attendance is fair and the prospects good for an increase.

Rev. S. H. Weller, D.D., pres.
John M. Coyer, vice president

And another item on October 4th: "The Pomona College was formally inaugurated last week." The Presbyterian and Congregational barques were under way.

WHAT HAD HAPPENED to the founders' dream? What had gone wrong with the Friends' College in the year 1888?

The boom had burst. It was not so much a sudden collapse—the Los Angeles banks weathered it, there was no panic. The economy of southern California simply fizzled as inflated land values sagged, then settled—and finally plummeted.

Prudent Friends had been apprehensive. This was the very thing (it was later said) that John Painter, Jonathan Bailey, and William H. Coffin of Pasadena had hoped to avoid. Columns of the *Christian Worker* repeatedly warned of the "unhealthy growth of real estate in Southern California." Will B. Wickersham [Sr.], after visiting the colony in March, questioned whether Friends in the settlement would be able "to support themselves on a lot or two, or in business." In April, A. H. Hussey cautioned that "a poor man had better look well before he leaps into California." In August 1888 the *Worker* quoted Edward Taylor, returning from the Coast: "The inevitable relapse has come." Actually the boom in southern California had crested the preceding summer. Business lots in Whittier that sold for as high as $2,000 that fall—and were held for as much during the winter —were to fetch as little as $100 when the depression at last deepened in the following year.

The first anniversary of Founders' Day in Whittier honored the pioneer promoters with speeches about the town's growth, "in one short year . . . from 4 to nearly 1,000." People were still arriving—but soon many would be leaving.

Aquilla Pickering's brothers went off to farm in the San Joaquin Valley. His son-in-law, Addison Stuart and brother Elbridge Stuart—nephews of Washington Hadley—remained briefly in Whittier, then moved up into the Northwest, later to found the

Carnation Milk Company. During the second winter Aquilla and Hannah Pickering returned to Chicago. J. C. Hiatt sold his *Graphic* press to a printer in Newberg, Oregon, followed it thither, later to return.

The grand tourist hotel, the Greenleaf, soon closed. Stores stood empty. Carpenters had little or no work, though some jobs continued on the oil wells up in the hills. Fortunately the cannery, organized March 22, 1888 with J. C. Hiatt as manager, provided some employment during the summer, and continued to do so under the Vernon Brothers. Most business ground to a stop. Many persons who had bought property on contract found themselves unable to make the second, let alone the third, payment. Some of them vanished. In a number of cases, having built cottages on their high-priced lots, they simply hauled them off in the middle of the night—theft to keep a roof over their children's heads. Those from whom they had bought, in turn had payments due on their loans to others—who owed yet others—and down tumbled the house of cards. "Departing trains now had the heavier business." But "many people stayed in the new towns [like Whittier] because they could not do anything else," having no money to return to former homes. "They tightened their belts." A sort of personal scrip passed for money.

There were to be seven lean years.

Failure of Friends' College was but part of the general debacle of 1888. No record remains of the complicated affairs that Hervey Lindley was asked to put in shape. How much had been realized on lots donated for the cause? And what sums were finally borrowed by the trustees themselves to pay outstanding obligations? . . . It was later said that subscriptions for Friends' College were refunded—perhaps they were merely canceled.

Three years later this College Hill, retained by the Pickering Land and Water Company, was put to another use. Excavation for "the college" was enlarged and lined as an essential reservoir. The "campus" below it became choice residence lots.

Calamitous as the "boom and bust" of Friends' College was in 1887-88, there was one element of partial success. Rather incidentally, its Board of Trustees had set in operation a Preparatory Department.

This modest academy was the actual forerunner over the

rough road leading to Whittier College, and, as such, a separate strand in its history.

3

THE FIRST WHITTIER ACADEMY
THE SECOND—AND THEN THE THIRD

SCHOOLING FOR THEIR CHILDREN was an immediate concern of the Quaker colonists. The Evergreen public school, on the County Road, had been built in 1885 to serve the scattered ranches. In the fall of 1887 Whittier children trudged or trotted down Painter Avenue (alternately dust and mire) to attend it. The town Company set aside lots on Bailey Street for a Whittier public school, soon but not yet built. Nor was there a high school anywhere in the area. During these years, few boys and girls really expected a secondary education, and even Los Angeles High School then enrolled but 150 pupils.

The practice of Friends, however, was to establish their own academies to prepare their young people for practical vocations or for college. Pasadena Quarterly Meeting in February 1888 recommended that each Friends' community in southern California start its own academy as soon as possible. Steps had already been taken in Whittier. In January 1888, C. C. Reynolds, prosperous Pasadena undertaker, made a proposition to the board of Friends' College, of which he was vice president. He would himself build a two-story building 23' x 45' on Philadelphia Street, cornering on the alley between Bright and Washington, "to be used as school room for high school purposes until building can be secured sufficient for the purpose on college grounds." He must have made a deal with the Pickering Land and Water Company, for this site was marked "Park" on the original town map. Reynolds' proposal accepted, the *Graphic* reported work on the building "to be commenced tomorrow." This brick construction must have been rapid, for a week later: "Mr. Charley Reynolds' high school building will be enclosed this week." And J. C. Hiatt, the editor, had spotted "just the kind of man needed" as schoolmaster —young Dr. W. V. Coffin, in Whittier for a brief visit with his father Dr. Samuel Coffin; but the younger doctor returned to the mid-West.

The college board undertook to establish the Academy as incidental to its main thrust, and at once changed the name to "Preparatory Department of Friends' College." But along the street, the building was called Reynolds' Academy in March when, nearing completion, Reynolds began another brick store adjoining it, the two forming one structure. The college trustees proceeded to procure "suitable furniture, &c." and teachers, assuring salaries "for the first three months." There was to be a primary class as well as academy.

Employed as principal, Clayton B. Nordyke (Ph.B., Earlham), a young Quaker from Pasadena, was to teach the academic (high school) work upstairs. Ella C. Veeder, a young Friends minister who had arrived during the summer with her husband and family, was to teach primary pupils downstairs. Opening date for the spring term of 12 weeks was set for April 2, with "a course of study" prepared and ready for distribution. As a "subscription school," the tuitions ($9 per term for the upper grades, $4 for the primary) were expected to pay for the teachers. "The pupils were requested to bring what books they had."

It is said that 13 scholars appeared on opening day, but the number increased to some 48—or perhaps even 71 for both departments. No class records survive. An engaging photograph shows Mrs. Veeder with 15 of her primary pupils, one of whom was Mary Dell Coryell, who in 1904 was the first student to receive an A.B. degree from Whittier College. One of those in the academic department was Mattie Wood who, her education interrupted for 50 years, completed her A.B. in 1938, when two of her granddaughters were freshmen. Another student in the Prep Department of Friends' College was Lou Henry, who had attended Evergreen School in the fall term. Her essay "Camping on Clear Lake" was the first one written and read in this first Whittier academy, and was proudly printed in the *Graphic*. It concluded with seemly tact and a twinkle: "I think that, with the exception of California, Clear Lake [in Iowa] is the best possible place in which to get tanned."

Lou Henry was remembered by classmates as "a born leader." A picture shows her as captain of a "fan drill" [not dance, of course], a dozen younger girls, some of them from the primary department. Legend recalls a touching moment when one uncoordinate member of the team broke down in despair, the consoling captain putting an encouraging arm about the tearful one. Another photo, of perhaps the next year, shows her on a riding picnic with somewhat older young people. With the failure of the second bank—Ricker, Mason and Lindley—of which her father was cashier, the Henry family moved to Monterey. A decade later, after graduation from Stanford University, Lou Henry married the young Quaker engineer, Herbert Hoover.

What went on in the two classrooms of this first Whittier academy with its primary department—what courses were taught—what schoolbooks were brought from home to be studied—what religious instruction and observances—what kindling of mind and imagination, one can at best surmise. No copy of the course of study survives. Mrs. Veeder later recalled that, largely through the strength and efforts of young Prof. Nordyke, the term concluded successfully. The education committee of the Friends Church minuted the "very satisfactory results" of the school term. Certainly Nordyke expected to continue as principal of the academy, and he transferred his church membership to Whittier Monthly Meeting. He remained in Pasadena during the summer, paid occasional visits to his kinfolk in Whittier. By fall it was apparent that the Whittier academy was dead as the dodo, and that no phoenix could rise from the ashes of collegiate dreams.

DURING THE DEPRESSION that followed the collapse of colony and college, the population of Whittier dropped from "about 1,000" to a census count of 585 in 1890. Among those who remained, the greatest problem was unemployment. Any construction work for cash wages was most welcome.

Friends were among the leaders in promoting a public school for Whittier. Trustees of the district were Willet Dorland, Jonathan Bailey, and William Strawbridge (one of the first four residents). A bond issue for $8,000, presented to the voters in September 1888, passed 87-0. A second bond issue for $9,000 additional building funds was approved 101-3. Local carpenters completed the Bailey Street school during the spring and summer of 1889, bell tower and all (the bell preserved at the present City Hall).

Construction of the State Reform School on the County Road

just below the town was a far greater boon to men in the building trades. Its location in Whittier was no accident. Hervey Lindley, whose drive to establish Friends' College was thwarted—and who certainly lost a small fortune in the general ruin—turned to politics to save the town he had helped to found. His brother Dr. Walter Lindley had long advocated trade-school training for delinquent boys. With his support, Hervey Lindley secured passage in 1889 of state legislation appropriating $200,000 to set up such a school. The Governor named him to its three-man Board of Trustees. With the offer of 40 acres of free land (gift of the Pickering Land and Water Company) and option for the state to buy an adjoining 120 acres at $200 per acre, Lindley was able to out-bid the town of Pomona, which also wanted the school as a spur to its economy. The cornerstone was laid with prayer and palaver on February 12, 1890. The State School opened its doors July 1st, 1891. The first superintendent: Dr. Walter Lindley; assistant superintendent, John E. Coffin, his brother-in-law. Hard money from this "public works" helped support the stricken town. The school gave permanent employment to a number of Quaker townsfolk including B. F. Arnold, who set up the print shop and trade classes, and Lindley M. Baldwin, who served as superintendent of the State School farm.

There was also other occasional building to provide work for carpenters. The Methodists, organized in the summer of 1889, built their church the next year at the corner of Bailey and Friends (where its successor church still stands). Rev. Thomas Stalker was the first pastor. The first trustees included George L. Hazzard, Frank Wiggins, and Dr. Walter Lindley—Quaker-born turned Methodist. Orthodox Quakers moved rather easily into Methodism.

If employment was the prime problem for townspeople, the most vexing for the Pickering Land and Water Company was water. For his earlier enterprises John Painter had developed adequate water in the washes from canyons in the Sierra Madre above and east of Pasadena. But tunneling into the Puente Hills in Turnbull canyon only yielded a small flow of brackish water. C. W. Harvey found water and success to the west of Whittier. Col. Simon J. Murphy and his engineer, A. L. Reed, secured ample flow from wells in the San Gabriel River, then flumed it through the lower sections of Whittier on its way to irrigate East Whittier lands. The Whittier Water Association, separated from the Pickering Land and Water Company, had to buy water from the East Whittier ditch and pump it up to its new reservoir on what had so recently been College Hill. It was to be a decade until the problem was fully settled for the town.

Could the scant and distasteful water those first years have been the source of the most distressing social problem of the town —the saloon?

Whittier had announced itself as a Dry Town, as had certain other ones of the new communities. In its first months a mass meeting of citizens boldly affirmed "That Whittier does not need a saloon . . . does not want a saloon, will not have one and . . .," the resolution trailed off into vague threats of what would happen if one were to appear. There was not long to wait. The white tent next door to Mrs. Veeder had promised to be a meat market, but opened as a saloon. The "rough characters" who ran it began the Sunday practice of coming up to the Sabbath School, "dropping a few dollars in the collection box and then returning to the tent" to open up for the day. Citizens waited upon them, women signed a petition, the *Graphic* printed the heroic resolution. To protect themselves from the irate Quakers, the proprietors hired a couple of ruffians. Then on the Night of January 17th, 1888 the town was rocked by Foul Murder! One of the saloon keepers, returning from Los Angeles with a revolver,

> walked into the tent, and holding his gun within a few inches of Jim Miles' head . . . shot him dead. . . . Parks ran out and down to Gwin's livery stable where he tried to hire a horse [which was refused him] . . . then with revolver still in hand, he started on the run and was seen no more.

Miles, ex-convict turned bodyguard, had been too free at the bar.

The deputy sheriff arrived in due time, found the murdered man "lying on his back on the floor . . . blood oozing from his ears." Nothing much *he* could do. But next morning a hundred or so men assembled. Mrs. Veeder saw them raise their hands "in a vote to destroy the saloon." After removing the body, still awaiting the coroner, "Dr. Dixon took a pick and broke kegs. Willet Dorland tore the canvas off." One half-shaved man darted from

31

Mr. Anthony's barbershop to join the fray. Smashed tent, platform, bar, furnishings they piled high and set afire. . . . When leaders of this lawless destruction—A. Coryell and Cyrus Lindley—were sued and assessed $300 damages, virtuous citizens offered to pay their fine. There were others too, it was proudly said, who had led in the assault: L. M. Baldwin, J. C. Hiatt, Aquilla Pickering himself. As witness of this morality play—Drink, Death, and Destruction—Ella C. Veeder was within the month elected first president of the newly-formed W.C.T.U.*

It was not the end, however. "The saloon element" moved a house to the lot and started anew. The women assailed it with Scripture and vocal prayer. One after another the hired barkeeps quit, and the saloon closed. But another and larger opened down on West Philadelphia Street in that tract earlier auctioned for college benefit. This time the W.C.T.U. invaded the premises in organized shifts, to sit mutely and politely sewing and knitting from morning till closing time, refusing to leave. Their presence startled the patrons who swung open the doors, then backed out, of a sudden, quenched. For want of patronage, this saloon also closed. In July a body was found under its back porch, whether dead from thrombosis or thirst. The building was then turned into a fruit packing house.

The saloon and attendant evil were what the Quaker founders did *not* want for their town. The college and academy were what they just as desperately *did* want. The same persons who fought off the one, fought for the other.

A SECOND WHITTIER ACADEMY was organized. Whittier Friends had seen their first academy go down in the wreck of Friends' College in the summer of 1888. In the spring of 1889, Dr. C. R. Dixon proposed that a local committee organize "a Friends school of higher education" and secure "a competent and suitable Friend as principal." With him on the committee were Dr. Elias Jessup, Addison W. Naylor, and I. H. Cammack.

In August the Whittier Monthly Meeting minuted (in the insecure orthography of the recording clerk) that the committee had found "a compitant friend for principle" [*sic!*]—surely an

---

*Those who had volunteered to pay the fine were coy when it came to that action. Finally the W.C.T.U. raised the necessary money to reimburse Coryell.

academy was indicated. As the Reynolds building was occupied, the committee "secured one room in the [new] public school building ready furnished for school purposes." The Monthly Meeting pledged its "hearty cooperation," but breathed easier when "relieved from any and all financial obligation" in the matter.

As principal the committee invited a young family friend of Dr. Dixon, C. Bevan Johnson, just then graduating from Penn College. He was the son of Friends ministers and gladly accepted the call to come West. To serve with him was Miss Ida Lindley of Los Angeles, cousin of Hervey Lindley. To the committee itself were added two more members, Willet Dorland—also on the public school board—and Lydia Jackson.

It was to be a difficult year. With the public elementary school downstairs and the private secondary school above it, there were minor problems of dual authority and divided responsibility. In any case, it became apparent as the year wore on that the Grammar School would need the upper rooms for the coming year.

Times were so bad that few families could pay the modest tuition ($9 per term) that made up the salaries of the two academy teachers. The total enrollment in this second Whittier academy reached 45, "and in addition Miss Lindley taught a considerable class in piano." A later-published list of 35 names is doubtless the roll for one of the two terms. It included young people of Quaker families—Coryell, Dorland, Hiatt, Jessup, Naylor, Vestal, etc.— also the names already familiar in the Los Nietos valley: Gregg, Guirado, Moss, Orr, Pallett, etc.—and the boy who later became Mayor Porter of Los Angeles. The total income for the year, to pay incidentals as well as two teachers, could hardly have been $600.

Addison Naylor, one of the committee engaging the teachers, had a son Frank in the Academy. Naylor's small business, manufacturing brooms, failed, as the local broom corn proved too coarse. He was unable to pay his son's tuition in cash, but "he did have a fine field glass which he left with the principal as a temporary measure until he could meet the bill." By mid-April 1890 Naylor removed to San Jose with his family and thence to Berkeley where, within two years, he became cashier of the First

National Bank, which he later served as president. He did not forget Whittier.

Two others of the original committee of four also left during the spring: Dr. C. R. Dixon, to serve as physician at the Carlisle Indian School in Pennsylvania; and Dr. Elias Jessup, to serve as pastor of the Friends Church in Lawrence, Kansas. Things were falling apart—the Academy was doomed.

At the end of the second term (March 29, 1890), the young principal, Bevan Johnson—wiser for the experience—went back to the mid-West, and Ida Lindley returned to Los Angeles.*

This second academy in Whittier—like the first—was not a complete failure, however. It ran two terms, a second stage on the road toward Whittier College. It, too, provided secondary schooling for young people in the area at a time when there was no high school. But, like its predecessor, it could not be carried on into a second year.

A THIRD WHITTIER ACADEMY, started after the lapse of a year (1890-91), demonstrated the persistent will of the new town no less than of Friends to start a secondary school and found a college.

In the fall of 1889, John C. Hiatt and family had returned from Oregon. In the winter of 1890, Washington Hadley—having sold his bank in Lawrence, Kansas—moved out to Whittier to pick up the pieces of the Pickering Land and Water Company of which his son-in-law T. Elwood Newlin had been named president. By the end of 1890 Dr. Samuel D. Coffin came back to Whittier and with him his son Dr. W. V. Coffin. A few weeks later arrived Prof. John Chawner with his family from Iowa. And Dr. Cyrus J. Cook—so ill that he was not expected to live when he had first reached Whittier early in 1888—was again able and ready, busy in medical practice and in community service.**

The younger Dr. Coffin—William V[estal], to distinguish him from his elderly kinsman William H. of Pasadena and uncle William G. of Washington, D.C.—was the organizing genius of this

---

*Bevan Johnson became an attorney, returned to Whittier in 1904, and played an important part in the later history of Whittier College.

**The frail Quaker doctor (son-in-law of Dr. Elias Jessup) was president of the Whittier Rangers, vigilantes quietly organized "to rid the territory of the lawless element" after another man had been slain by an unknown assailant.

third Whittier Academy. Thirty, and as yet unmarried, he had enjoyed an eventful decade since graduation from Earlham College at age 19. First came his professional training at Miami Medical College (Ohio), M.D. at 22—then practice with his father in Kansas—medical and administrative work with the U.S. Indian Service in Idaho and Oregon and with the Friends mission in Alaska. Thereafter, he had returned to Kansas to become Clerk of Kansas Yearly Meeting of Friends.

On May 23, 1891, Whittier citizens interested in starting an academy came together at a called meeting. Washington Hadley presided, pro tem, and J. C. Hiatt served as secretary. Dr. W. V. Coffin proposed formation of a joint stock company to establish, finance, and manage a Friends academy in Whittier. On motion of T. Elwood Newlin, this was approved. Within two weeks the Whittier Educational Association was incorporated, capital stock $20,000, the shares $10 each—sold at $5 down and not more than $1 per month. The 30 shares subscribed at once brought in $150 in cash and promised $30 per month for five months. (Such was the contrast with the booming $137,000 subscribed three years before for Friends' College!) Canvassing of Friends, scattered through half a dozen communities in southern California, sold but 30 more shares of stock by the end of June. The stockholders named nine trustees, most of them from Whittier, and elected officers: Dr. C. J. Cook, president; Thomas Armstrong (the new Friends pastor), vice president; T. Elwood Newlin, secretary; Lydia Jackson, treasurer.

This academy was to be a community venture—the largest stock holder was A. L. Reed, Congregationalist, engineer and manager of Simon J. Murphy's East Whittier ranch and water company.* But, without question, the Whittier Academy was to be a Friends school. All trustees of the Association were to be Quakers, one-third of them nominated by Pasadena Quarterly Meeting (but elected by the stockholders). And it was clear that the Friends Church in Whittier would keep a watchful eye on the academy, with I. H. Cammack as chairman of the Education Committee of the church.

*He held 50 shares, first issued in the name of the company, then assumed by him personally. The stock book, prudently unlabeled but easily identified, shows that by 1900 a total of 483½ shares had been sold. Because voting on crucial matters was by shares at the annual meeting of stockholders, the stock register was of importance.

Organization of Whittier Academy proceeded at once. Prof. John Chawner and Dr. W. V. Coffiin "proposed to take charge and run the school at their own expense," accepting tuition fees as salary, provided the Association furnished a building with desks and equipment. Chawner had been principal of the Penn College preparatory department and earlier of the Bloomingdale Academy, where Coffin had been his pupil.

The Pickering Land and Water Company (which now meant essentially Washington Hadley and Elwood Newlin) offered to secure the Reynolds Block then empty (the double building) and to pay the rent for two years at $110 per year, with possibly a third year at $155. Newlin found "suitable rooms for boarding students" in the Morgan Building—15 rooms for a total of $25 per month. The trustees procured 60 school desks for $245 and a dozen chairs for $7, three tables, $11. As for library, John Chawner offered his own five volumes of Johnson's Encyclopedia in exchange for two shares of Association stock. A small brochure— four-page folder, 3½" x 6"—outlined a course of study, strong on mathematics, science, and Latin, with a dash of English, penmanship, and history. Music, drawing, and bookkeeping would be arranged at extra cost. The tuition was set at $10 per term of about 12 weeks. "Club boarding will be served at actual cost, ranging from $2 to $3 per week, including room rent." John Chawner, M.A., was announced as Principal; W. V. Coffin, A.B., M.D., Associate.

The third Whittier Academy opened on September 23, 1891 with 9 students. The number increased to 12 in a few days, and finally to 28. Including special students in instrumental music and art, the number reached 55. Ella Stalker (of the Methodist parsonage) gave the music, and Mary Trueblood added drawing and painting during the year. Prof. Chawner and Dr. Coffin shared the academic courses. Coffin also taught the commercial subjects.

Frail though such was as a secondary school, this Academy was not born to die at the end of a term or two. But regular tuition income for the three terms certainly totaled less than $800. It was shared by the two instructors. With guarantee by the trustees of 40 academic students (that is, about $1,200), they were willing to undertake another year.

36

Community support for Whittier Academy was insistently solicited by the third Whittier newspaper, the *Register*, which crowded out the short-lived *Pointer*. Publishers of the *Register* were B. F. Arnold, journalist from Des Moines, and Herman D. Williams, whose wives were sisters of J. C. Hiatt of the old *Graphic*. Dr. W. V. Coffin was for many years president of their Whittier Publishing Company. Interest of the townsfolk in such higher education as they could then afford, was stimulated not alone by full reports of Academy doings in the columns of the *Register*, but by efforts of Chawner and Coffin. In April (1892) they "gave a delightful [public] entertainment to a good audience." It included "a series of chemical experiments and an instructive discussion," in the course of which—

> The production of startling explosions, and different colored lights painful to the eye in their brilliancy, by the skillful manipulation of oxygen and hydrogen

was pronounced to be nothing less than "a good measure of how far modern chemistry has distanced the theory of the ancient Romans that water was a simple element." Yet, closer to the Romans, certainly, than to the nuclear age to come!

Concerted efforts of the trustees of the Association, of the local Friends Church and the Quarterly Meeting, assured the reopening of Whittier Academy on September 27, 1892 for its second year, with 51 pupils. The number increased to 73 by November, indeed, to 95 including special students. With Dr. Coffin as principal, at the insistence of Prof. Chawner who preferred teaching Latin and history, the faculty was enlarged. Grace M. Barnes gave courses in stenography and typewriting, the Friends pastor taught two hours of Bible a week, and diminutive Emilie V. Hadley conducted calisthenics. For the full year, a total of 110 different students could be reported, 63 of them in the three classes of the academic program and 16 in the Primary Department (Alice Miller teaching it and doubling in music and elocution). Among the special students were housewives and children of the town taking bookkeeping, art and music—including (as music pupils) Dora and George Anthony, whose father had added to his barber shop a lunch room, "meals at all hours, ice cream a specialty."

Surviving its initial year (1891-92) and carried on through a second (1892-93)—an enlarged catalog promising yet another year—the third Whittier Academy was doing good work in the usual academic subjects. Already the Athenaeum Literary Society encouraged exercise in parliamentary procedure and literary programs, and it published a 16-page *Athenaeum* in 1893 and in 1894. Each day began with Bible reading, singing, and prayer. Only such disciplinary rules were imposed as seemed necessary, but students were expected to abstain from "sinful indulgence and immoral habits," and "social parties" were reduced to a minimum.

Among those in the Third Year class of '93—corresponding to high school seniors—were J. Clem Arnold, Caleb E. Cook, Alberta Chawner, and Fred Hadley (who in time became newspaper executive, scientist, librarian, and banker). They were ready for college.

Time had come for the Academy to fulfill its collegiate promise.

4

THE COLLEGE CAMPUS AND BUILDING
THE COLLEGE PROGRAM AND NAME

A COLLEGE CAMPUS and College Building were essential if the Whittier Academy hoped to achieve its intended stature. After all, the Reynolds building was no more than a business block on the main street, and without school grounds. Nor had the room-and-board arrangement upstairs in one and then another store building been satisfactory. Already in the summer of 1892, the Pickering Land and Water Company offered to donate land for "a boarding hall for the academy." Early the next winter the Educational Association minuted that "steps be taken at once to raise funds" for a College Building.

At a public meeting in the Friends Church on March 13th, 1893, the subscriptions taken totaled $3,225—and but $3.50 expense was incurred. The trustees then employed Dr. W. V. Coffin "to make a thorough canvass" to get further subscriptions.

Within a fortnight, C. W. Harvey made an interesting proposition to the trustees of the Association. He saw a chance of ridding himself of his Greenleaf Hotel, standing empty up on Painter Avenue. Other such relics of the Boom had found academic use. Pomona College had moved from its small rooms in the town of Pomona out to the hungry tourist hotel in Claremont by the end of 1888. The Church of the Brethren bought the plush boomer hotel at nearby Lordsburg in 1891 to found what became LaVerne College. Old Man Harvey offered his $50,000 Greenleaf —40 rooms and 10 acres of land—to the Whittier Educational Association for $10,000. It looked like a bargain. Nothing was needed but the money.

If Dr. W. V. Coffin approached the Pickering Land and Water Company—that would be Elwood Newlin or Washington Hadley —for a contribution toward making up this sum, he got his answer, minuted April 4, 1893 at the P.L.&W. Co. annual stockholders' meeting.

> In the matter of Donations to the College fund it was the general opinion that the Company might if necessary [sic] donate both Lots Nos 2 and 3 Block H *but no cash donation.*

Emphasis here added was hardly needed then. It was clear that the Company had no intention of helping to bail out Old Man Harvey—but it might be willing to provide land (the word "campus" not yet used) for the proposed College Building.

These two parcels (Lots #2 and #3 in Block H) lay midway between Philadelphia and Penn Streets, in the tier of 10-acre lots east of Painter Avenue. Such lots had 330′ frontage on Painter and extended some 1,200′ up the hillside. Lot #2, however, had been reduced to about 9 acres and but 120′ frontage by the sale of the choice corner of Philadelphia and Painter, a large irregular triangle marked off from Lots #1 and #2 by the arroyo. Lot #3, with its full 330′ frontage, the Company held for $1,700— the two lots together being worth perhaps $3,000. By coincidence, this land stood at the head of College Street. Here too, happily, was a knoll—a minor Acropolis—splendid site for a College Building, though not quite up to the original College Hill, now transformed to a reservoir.

But Mr. Harvey was really very anxious to sell his Greenleaf Hotel to the Quakers. He invited the Academy trustees, with a half dozen others, to visit the premises. He was ready to make an attractive offer. He would accept one of the ten-acre parcels, the Lot #3 just then set aside by P.L.&W. Co. for the College, as part payment, plus $7,500 in dollars, for which he would take deferred payments. Indeed, Harvey said, he'd take both Lots #2 and #3 plus $6,000, and would himself subscribe $500 toward raising that sum. Or, not to seem selfish, he suggested that the Educational Association might prefer to sell off the acreage itself and thus raise cash toward his total asking of $10,000.

"It was the sense of the meeting"—minuted the trustees after returning from their tour of inspection—"that the proposition of C. W. Harvey be accepted."

But for some reason never recorded, the deal was neither consummated nor further mentioned. Perhaps Washington Hadley simply asked: Wouldn't it be better to have 19 acres and a $6,000 college building than to have the 10 acres and a hotel building of questionable stability? At any rate, within a week, the trustees resolved to erect within eight months a college building "to cost no less than $6,000" if the Company would provide the two lots for College Grounds. The Company modified its offer, giving Lot #2 and the north *half* of Lot #3 on condition the $6,000 building be completed "clear of encumbrances" within eight months from May 1st—but it further agreed to donate the south half of Lot #3 if, within three years, the trustees erected "additional improvements in building to the value of $4,000."

The offer accepted, Coffin continued soliciting building funds. An architect, Morgan by name, drew up plans and specifications. Bids were accepted for lumber ($1,500) and sash and doors ($1,350). By August, Coffin could report to Pasadena Quarterly Meeting that $6,700 had been subscribed and that work was in progress on the foundation—in fact, grading had begun in May, when Simon J. Murphy sent A. L. Reed with teams and tools to do the heaviest part of the work. Stone was already being quarried nearby, though the quarriers set to work on Mr. Worsham's land by mistake. But that good-natured rancher gave them the rock already taken "and thus saved the college from being erected on a stolen foundation."

The Whittier *Register* reported every stage of construction. Dr. Coffin himself worked at everything. Then Dr. Elias Jessup returned to Whittier—driving the 1,200 miles south from Oregon, where he had last been, Mother Jessup admitting to some weariness after 45 days—and trustees put him in charge of procuring materials and help. For the brick veneer to encase the frame structure, Dr. Jessup himself hauled sand for mortar from the river bottom. By mid-December the new College Building, exuberated the *Register*, was "fast becoming a thing of beauty."

But there were problems—beyond little boys playing and men smoking about the building. Subscribers were not paying their pledges. By mid-December it was evident that another $1,000 was needed to complete even the first floor rooms of the original north portion of what was much later called Founders Hall. P.L.&W. Co. offered $200 "on condition that $500 additional be raised."

A personal tragedy, too, darkened the winter months—the death by accident of a young workman, Edgar F. Holton, son of Quaker Dr. Q. A. Holton of San Diego county. Twice during the autumn he had fallen from scaffolding. In late January he had knocked heads in a playful scramble for a ball, falling unconscious on the gravel road, his face badly cut. Then a few days later, again at work plastering in the College Building, dizziness seized him and he "fell face forward to the floor." He died that night. After the funeral service at the Friends Church a few blocks down College Street, work resumed.

In mid-February finish-carpenters laid floor and applied wainscoting, pushing for completion in time for the spring term. Outside, workmen put the grounds in order. A community work day brought men with their teams and scrapers, picks and shovels. Promised was "a sumptuous dinner" served by the ladies. A photograph of that time showed the building still without porch and belfry—but with perhaps 150 men and a dozen teams. Honoring the occasion by their presence were "Hon. William G. Coffin, Washington, D.C., and Rev. Hiram Hadley of New Mexico." Edgar Sharpless and I. H. Cammack were among those who planted trees, and "Rev. Armstrong used the long handled shovel without any of the formalities of exegesis or peroration." And the College Building—to the extent of the first floor—stood ready for the opening of the spring term of Whittier Academy, March 28, 1894.

41

THE LONG LEAN YEARS of Depression had continued. Yet it was during the forbidding year 1893-94 that Whittier Academy transformed itself into some semblance of a college. It had achieved a college building on a college campus.

Economic conditions had actually worsened. The failure of the Riverside Banking Company in 1893 had started "disastrous runs on banks throughout the state." Farm prices dropped and wages sagged a further 25% to 50%. Robert Cleland, the California historian, writes of that year—

> Large numbers of unemployed including thousands of tramps, bums, and bindle stiffs, flocked to California to escape the cold and snow of the Eastern winter.

Discontent of the unemployed focused in the efforts of Jacob S. Coxey and Carl Browne to organize a great march on Washington, D.C., demanding a vast program of road improvement to make work. The Whittier *Register* with both sympathy and apprehension reported approach of the western unit of "Coxey's Army" that was to pass through Santa Fe Springs. The men foraged and begged as they went. Friends in Whittier took baskets of food down to them, when they encamped along the County Road—enjoining them (it is said) to sobriety. These marchers were never to reach Washington—200 arrested in Colton "for disturbing the peace," and others of the ragged company blocked by "the forbidding Colorado desert." Of the 100,000 expected, Coxey led but 500 demonstrators into Washington on May 1, 1894, himself arrested "for walking on the Capitol lawn." It was a time of violence—the Pullman strike in Chicago (Whittier travellers stranded), and Eugene V. Debs sent to jail.

And yet, at the end of the year 1894, Washington Hadley was able to organize the Bank of Whittier, thus steadying the economy of the struggling town.

Washington Hadley—the Kansas banker for whom two Whittier streets were named—had been born in North Carolina in 1817, moved with his family to mature in Indiana, then out West to Kansas where in 1865 he had founded the National Bank of Lawrence, of which he became president and his son Albert, cashier.* Together with Aquilla and Hannah Pickering, Washington and Naomi Hadley traveled to Mexico City in 1886, personally invited by President Díaz to establish a Friends mission there. They visited California on their return trip. Washington Hadley kept in close touch with the developing Quaker colony in 1887, bought stock in the Pickering Land and Water Company, invested in Whittier building. No record shows what he may have subscribed to the ill-fated Friends' College in 1888. (Could his have been the $25,000 "conditional subscription" not otherwise identified?) In 1889—perhaps in consideration of his son's health—he sold out his banking interest in Kansas and came to California. Aged 72, he said he wanted "to grow up with the country."

Washington Hadley invested substantially in the P.L.&W. Co. —$26,000 in the first year. Then, with the collapse, he invested further, buying blocks of depressed stock. With Elwood Newlin named president of the reorganized Company, Jonathan Bailey continued as vice-president. Washington Hadley was tender to the financial plight of his enterprising kinsman—"no interest to be charged on Hervey Lindley note." First, Hadley bought-in to the National Bank of California in Los Angeles, his son (health restored) an assistant cashier. Then by the end of 1894, together with his Los Angeles associates, he organized the Bank of Whittier, himself as cashier.** A short but sturdy old gentleman, with trim-cut beard, he played an important part (often behind the scenes) in church, community, and college.

THE COLLEGE BUILDING was not yet completed. The upstairs assembly hall had only rough flooring, though it could be used for calisthenics, and the two upstairs rooms to the north were put to

*Washington Hadley's son Albert and grandson Fred; his son-in-law George E. Little; and his grandson-in-law Amos C. Maple—all of them were to be bankers with him or succeeding him in Whittier.
  Other sons-in-law were Albert D. Pickering (son of Aquilla), T. Elwood Newlin, and Charles Monroe, a Los Angeles attorney.
  Two of his nephews were Addison and Elbridge Stuart—two others, Cyrus and Milton Lindley. "Those Lindley boys" [Dr.] Walter and Hervey, and their sister Miss Ida B. Lindley, were Washington Hadley's grandnephews and niece. His daughter, Emilie V. (already noted as teaching in the Academy) succeeded her father in later years as member of the Whittier College board.
  **The Bank of Whittier became the First National Bank of Whittier, and finally the Whittier branch of Bank of America.

43

use, unfinished, for chemistry and zoology. It was downstairs in the study hall, on the west side of the new building, that the third term of the third year of the third Whittier Academy opened with an assembly on March 28, 1894.

In the presence of some 50 students and numerous visitors, the exercises began at 9:15 with a hymn, accompanied on the piano (later paid for). As principal, Dr. Coffin read a chapter of Scripture (37th Psalm), which, saying something of evil-doers, speaks up for the meek and the righteous. Nannie H. Arnold "led in earnest, appropriate, and impressive prayer." A recorded Friends minister and editor of the *Christian Workman*, she was the mother of Clem Arnold, college freshman. This first meeting in the new College Building was rendered auspicious by suitable remarks from trustees and guests: Jonathan Bailey, I. H. Cammack, Dr. Elias Jessup, T. Elwood Newlin, and Mrs. H. D. Williams. Speeches concluded, the academic term got under way.

A program of college studies had already begun in the fall of that year. The catalog, published in late summer of 1893, included a Fourth and a Fifth Year, which extended the work of Whittier Academy "about two years into the ordinary college course." The intention was "to make it a full college course within two years." With the addition of Prof. B. M. Davis to fill the "chair of Natural Sciences," and teaching mathematics too, there was special interest in constructing and securing equipment for laboratories in the new College Building. Davis, who had taught previously at what was then Garfield University in Kansas, had a few eager and ingenious students, including Caleb E. Cook (brother of Mrs. Veeder). He was one of the very few, perhaps three or four, doing regular work in the collegiate department.

The number of students in Whittier Academy during this exciting year of transition to the new College Building was disappointingly small—a total of 50 in the regular three classes of the Preparatory Department, and only 12 of these in the First Year. Prof. Chawner pointed out to Pasadena Quarterly Meeting, comprising about 1,000 Quakers at this time, that the Quarterly Meeting included about 40 boys and girls of an age to begin work at the Academy. Too many children from Friends homes, he said, were simply not continuing their education beyond the grades. To increase attendance, the trustees of the Educational Association paid Lydia Jackson to canvass for funds to provide "free tuition for Friends children" of the Quarterly Meeting. By mid-August 1894 she had secured $2,500 in pledges to this end, enough to pay tuition for some eighty pupils.

Something had to be done to finish the College Building. Summer conferences of Friends, held in Long Beach in 1892 and 1893, had looked toward formation of a California Yearly Meeting—for as yet Pasadena Quarterly Meeting was in leading strings to Iowa Friends. Long Beach Quakers hoped for a Yearly Meeting Building to be built there. However, the Whittier Educational Association urged Friends to concentrate their efforts and to complete the upstairs assembly hall of College Building "with a view of using it for Yearly Meeting purposes." This the Quarterly Meeting cautiously approved, and elected Dr. W. V. Coffin its clerk. During the summer of 1894, the Educational Association, at the request of the Quarterly Meeting, released Dr. Coffin to attend yearly meetings in the mid-West soliciting funds to make up the estimated $1,600 needed to finish the college auditorium and to pay off the $600 debt incurred in putting in and plastering the stairway and hall leading to it. He met with Quaker educators at Penn College—he visited the new University of Chicago "in company with Rufus M. Jones of Philadelphia"—he appeared before yearly meetings in Indiana, in Kansas, in Iowa (where Penn College "declined to ask for any help" in order that California Friends might be given an appropriation)*. Dr. Coffin returned to Whittier in mid-October with a total of $3,500 for setting up California Yearly Meeting and for completing Yearly Meeting Hall upstairs in the College Building.

So it was that plasterers and finish-carpenters again worked, "the sound of hammers, saws, turning lathes" reverberating in the study hall below. At last "the magnificent assembly hall" was done. Wainscoted in alternate panels of redwood and pine "finished natural color," it was well lit by tall windows and dormers to the east and west. Its rostrum platform occupied the broad

---

*At Western Yearly Meeting in Indiana, "Friends balked at swallowing our stories of tomato vines twenty feet high, sweet potatoes weighing forty and fifty pounds, and two hundred pound pumpkins." When Jonathan Bailey received criticism indirectly from a remote Friend that he had strayed from Truth, he drove down into Orange County with a mischievous gleam, bought a 200-pound pumpkin and shipped it, charges collect, to the Eldering critic.

south side of the room. The Academy trustees borrowed $750 from the Bank to pay for 400 "opera seats" at $1.35 and 75 chairs at $1.25. . . . In March 1895, the north part of the Hall of Letters, as the building was occasionally called, was complete—four classrooms and study hall downstairs, two science rooms and auditorium above. And there, on Third-day, Third-month 26th, 1895, California Yearly Meeting held its opening session, Dr. W. V. Coffin its first presiding Clerk. It was a gala occasion, in a bearded and bonneted way, with much *thee*ing and *thy*ing by older Friends and visiting representatives in Plain Dress. As acting principal of the Academy, Prof. John W. Woody, appointed when Coffin went East to raise money, reported "work done during the past six months."

THE COLLEGE PROGRAM, carried on in the new building by Profs. Woody and Chawner (who were brothers-in-law) and B. M. Davis, continued but with some uncertainty. Dr. W. V. Coffin had resigned upon his return in mid-autumn to accept a more-secure position and salary at the State School, as assistant superintendent and physician. His brother John E. Coffin had succeeded his brother-in-law Dr. Walter Lindley as superintendent.*

Prof. Woody was an experienced and respected Quaker educator, first principal of the Whittier College in Iowa, with years of teaching also at Penn and Guilford. The new catalog for the year 1894-95 was more explicit about rules of conduct—the spade of "Discipline" now called by its common name—forbidding the use of profanity, intoxicating liquors, and tobacco. And during the year Prof. Woody found it necessary to dismiss one girl—her naughtiness, not of record.

Prof. Woody reported to the Yearly Meeting in 1895 that 82 pupils had been in attendance, 64 of them being Friends. Included in the total were 37 who had pursued studies "in the College department," which was giving work (he said) up through the sophomore year of the average college. Few of these, certain-

*Within two years Dr. Coffin married Sarah Nicholson, daughter of Timothy Nicholson of Richmond, Ind. Then in 1898 he joined other Quakers—C.C. Reynolds, Clyde Baldwin, and young Joseph Grinnell the ornithologist—in a missionary, mining, and bird-watching trip to Alaska aboard the small sloop *Penelope*, of which he was ship's doctor. Back again in Whittier, Dr. Coffin lived across from the campus and later served long years as trustee of Whittier College.

Portraits in Whittier College Collection.

JOHN GREENLEAF WHITTIER. 1. Portrait by Harrison L. Plummer, the poet aged 78 (1885). 2. Etching by S. A. Schoff from a painting by Bass Otis, the poet aged 30. 3. Engraving by E. W. Smith from a photo of the militant abolitionist, aged 50.

Oakknoll
Danvers Mass
Dec 4 1889

Dear Friend

I greatly regret that at this time I am not able to write a hymn or poem for the occasion referred to in thy telegram. I am gratified to know that the people of the town which bears my name will remain. on my birth-day. I watch its growth with

great interest. It has the reputation among all who have seen it that it occupies one of the loveliest sites in California, and that in a moral and religious and educational point of view, it need not

"From the sceptic's jeering hand
While near the school the church will stand,
Nor fear the blinded bigot's rule
While near the church shall stand the school."

I am truly thy friend

John G Whittier

Addressed to Dr. Walter Lindley,
Whittier,
Cala.

4. LETTER OF JOHN G. WHITTIER noted on pg. 2.

NOTICE.

❧ College Meeting at Whittier, ❧

Monday, January 23, 1888.

MEETING TO BE HELD AT FRIENDS' CHURCH AT 7:30 P. M.

ALL ARE INVITED.

JUDGE FITZGERALD. MAJOR E. W. JONES, DR. HIRAM SINSABAUGH,
Of Los Angeles.

DR. SAMUEL D. COFFIN, DR. WM. NICHOLSON, of Whittier.

PROF. CHAS. TEBBETS, of Pasadena and other prominent speakers from abroad and
at home will address the meeting.

This meeting is of the greatest importance to Whittier and the surrounding country, as it is proposed to build a COLLEGE, second to none west of the Rocky Mountains, and which will fill a long felt need in Southern California, to cost not less than
$100,000.

Other interests projected for the good of this *rapidly growing* community. Railroads and other public improvements will have a share in the discussion.

❧ COME ONE, COME ALL. ❧

On behalf of the College Trustees.

WILLET DORLAND, *Sec'y*

Reuben Haines Hartley, A.

PRESIDENT OF FACULTY.

THE FRIENDS' COLLEGE,
WHITTIER, CALIFORNIA.

FRIENDS' COLLEGE. 5. Handbill calling public meeting. 6. Architect's sketch. 7. President Hartley's professional card. 8. Preparatory Department, classes in Reynolds Block.
9. Final minutes of college trustees. 10. Reservoir in excavation for college basement.
Photos below, courtesy Whittier Public Library.

WHITTIER: QUAKER COLONY AND COLLEGE
based on the town map of 1887

The surviving copy of the town map—faded blue line on yellowed paper pasted on muslin, 36″ high by 24″ wide—is in the Historical Collection of the Whittier Public Library. Pencil markings, now faint, show it to have been used in the original selling of lots.

The legend at the top of the map reads: "MAP OF THE PICKERING LAND AND WATER CO.'S SUBDIVISION / of the John M. Thomas' Ranch, Los Angeles County, Cal. / being Section 21 and part of Sections 15, 20, 21, and 28. Township 2 South Range, 11 West. / Baldwin, Jessup & Co., Surveyors."

Presented on the following spread of pages is the central section only of the map, together with references to the points of interest related to the early history of Whittier College. The original map shows ten-acre parcels extending from what is now Beverly Blvd. south to Whittier Blvd.

TOWN MAP OF 1887 ☞

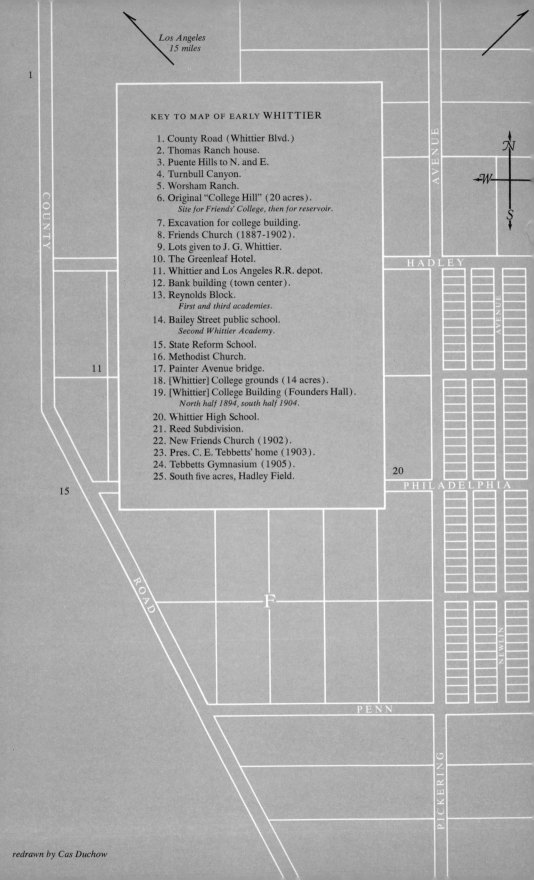

Los Angeles
15 miles

1

KEY TO MAP OF EARLY WHITTIER

1. County Road (Whittier Blvd.)
2. Thomas Ranch house.
3. Puente Hills to N. and E.
4. Turnbull Canyon.
5. Worsham Ranch.
6. Original "College Hill" (20 acres).
   Site for Friends' College, then for reservoir.
7. Excavation for college building.
8. Friends Church (1887-1902).
9. Lots given to J. G. Whittier.
10. The Greenleaf Hotel.
11. Whittier and Los Angeles R.R. depot.
12. Bank building (town center).
13. Reynolds Block.
    First and third academies.
14. Bailey Street public school.
    Second Whittier Academy.
15. State Reform School.
16. Methodist Church.
17. Painter Avenue bridge.
18. [Whittier] College grounds (14 acres).
19. [Whittier] College Building (Founders Hall).
    North half 1894, south half 1904.
20. Whittier High School.
21. Reed Subdivision.
22. New Friends Church (1902).
23. Pres. C. E. Tebbetts' home (1903).
24. Tebbetts Gymnasium (1905).
25. South five acres, Hadley Field.

COUNTY

AVENUE

HADLEY

AVENUE

N
W
S

11

15

20

PHILADELPHIA

ROAD

F

NEWLIN

PENN

PICKERING

redrawn by Cas Duchow

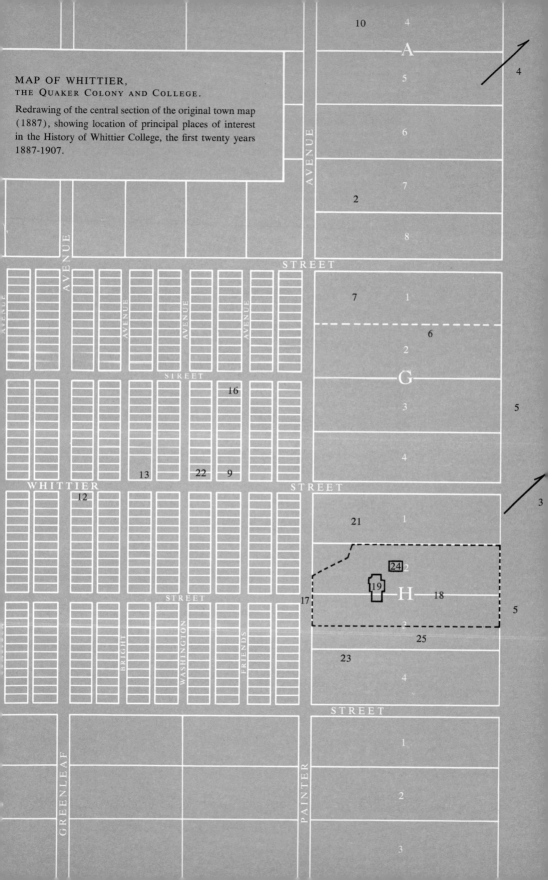

MAP OF WHITTIER,
THE QUAKER COLONY AND COLLEGE.

Redrawing of the central section of the original town map
(1887), showing location of principal places of interest
in the History of Whittier College, the first twenty years
1887-1907.

Synopsis of Events
History of Whittier College, the first twenty years
1887-1907

May 1887. Founding of the Quaker colony, planned with college in mind.

July 1887. Original "College Hill," 20-acre site donated by town Company.

Dec. 1887. Meeting to name trustees for Friends' College.

Apr. 1888. Preparatory Department (first academy) in Reynolds Block.

Aug. 1888. Collapse of Friends' College, abandoned excavation.

1889-1890. Second Whittier Academy, two terms in Bailey Street School.

Sept. 1891. Whittier Educational Ass'n., third academy, in Reynolds Block.

Apr. 1893. Conditional gift of College Grounds by town Company.

Sept. 1893. First students taking college work at Whittier Academy.

Mar. 1894. College Building, north half, lower floor rooms completed.

Mar. 1895. College Auditorium completed for first California Yearly Meeting.

July 1896. Name of Whittier Academy changed to "Whittier College."

June 1900. Whittier College tendered to California Yearly Meeting.

Sept. 1900. Charles E. Tebbetts, first president of Whittier College.

Jan. 1902. Incorporation of Whittier College, separate Board of Trustees.

June 1903. First campaign securing $50,000 for college endowment.

Feb. 1904. Completion of south half of College Building (Founders Hall).

June 1904. First graduating class of four seniors given A.B. degrees.

Aug. 1905. Tebbetts Gymnasium, largely student-built for $1,000.

June 1906. Second campaign securing $100,000 more college endowment.

June 1907. Resignation of C. E. Tebbetts as president of Whittier College.

THIRD WHITTIER ACADEMY. 11. First catalog brochure (1891), inside spread, front and
back. 12. Faculty and students (1891)—Prof. John Chawner, with beard, seated; Dr. W.
V. Coffin, standing at left. 13. First Whittier football team, 1893.

Photo #12 from Whittier Public Library.

Top row

C. Baldwin
C. Underwood
L. Healton
J. Coverly
E. Jessup

Second row

E. Coryell
H. Judson
C. Arnold
O. Ellis
E. Gregory

*First row,
l. to r.*

Tom Weed
L. Chambers
G. Hunnicutt
C. Knox
W. Dugger

WHITTIER COLLEGE. 14. College Building (early in 1894) with Academy faculty and students. 15. Prof. Davis with college students in new laboratory (1895). 16. First "Whittier College" catalog (1896). 17. Building, showing arroyos and bridge.

Photo #15 from Whittier Public Library.

CATALOGUE

OF

Whittier Coll

Whittier, California.

1895-96.

PUBLISHED BY THE BOARD OF TRUS

LOS ANGELES
CALIFORNIA VOICE PRINT
1896.

ly, were regular college students. In those still slender times, tuitions were hard to collect, and pledges to the Free Tuition Fund were easier made than paid. When Prof. Woody concluded his year's work in June 1895, he went out to collect overdue subscriptions toward making up his back salary, which had been $750 for the year. (A year later, $115.68 was still due him.) When Prof. B. M. Davis resigned that same June—to continue his teaching at Los Angeles State Normal—the Association board used the rest of its (borrowed) chair fund and Free Tuition Funds subscribed for the coming year to complete payment of his salary.

The academic structure seemed tumbling down. In June 1895, Prof. Robert C. Root of Hemet accepted appointment as principal. By September he resigned for reasons of health. Only Prof. John Chawner—widowed the preceding summer—remained, again to serve as principal. When Susan H. Johnson was elected "1st assistant" and Anna Moore "2nd assistant," the board waited a week to notify them, lacking confidence that funds would permit the Academy to go on. Finally the *Register* could announce definitely that it would open on October 1st.

The two capable women then appointed were the first on the regular academic faculty. Susan H[arrison] Johnson (A.B., M.A.), alumna of Earlham with graduate work at Bryn Mawr and Michigan, was a scholar and good teacher, with red-haired charm and wit, lover of students and nature. She had taught at both Earlham and Penn. Her husband, A. Clifford Johnson, moved by stages from Pullman conductor to bank president. She taught science and mathematics her first year, thereafter Latin and Greek. Anna M. Moore, daughter of an honored professor of science at Earlham, taught the English, Elocution, and German.

What, with the late and uncertain start, enrollment fell to 40 in the Preparatory Department, and there were but 3 regular students each in the freshman and sophomore classes of the College Department. With such a handful in numbers, it is amazing that the students could carry on an enriching collegiate life.

STUDENT ACTIVITIES were looked upon as a worthy part of the college program, and Prof. Woody commended the work of the Literary Society and of the Athletic Association in his report to the Yearly Meeting.

Collegiate athletics of a sort had begun in the fall of 1893, when "the Whittier College football team" went over to Santa Ana by train "to contest honors with the boys of that place." The State School band went along to furnish music. The victory was sweeping (as reported in the *Register*). The Whittier captain was J. Clem Arnold; the coach, Prof. B. M. Davis. Eleven of the 14 players (all identified in an old photo) were actually students in the Academy. Only three were "town boys." Of these, Ernest Gregory was son of Levi Gregory, recent president of the Iowa Whittier College. Another was George B. Hunnicutt, son of trustee William Penn Hunnicutt. A former student of Penn College, George Hunnicutt had helped build the College Building in Whittier. About 5' 11" tall and toughly muscled, he was a great athlete. Imperishable in the Whittier legend is the glimpse of Hunnicutt advancing the ball with one opponent on his back and two others dragged along, one on each of his arms! For years he played on Whittier teams, there being no eligibility rules.*

The first intercollegiate football game came the next season on December 17, 1894. This "Whittier College team" played "the Occidentals," who arrived at noon "in a hack with flying colors"— the game scheduled for 2 p.m., to be played on the vacant lots south of College Street between Washington and Bright. The State School cadets and band were on hand to cheer in force.

> The Whittier boys were admirably plucky . . . [but] the superior training of the Occidentals . . . among whom were several athletes of reputation, told in their favor.

And Occidental won, 12-6. It was a misfortune to be repeated the following season, when the game (with Occidental ahead by two touchdowns) ended in dispute, and Captain Bennick called his Whittier team off the field.**

By this time Whittier students had their yell: "Boom-di ra-da-da / Zip, boom a—h / Whittier, Whittier / Ra, ra, ra!" College colors, chosen in November 1894, were purple and gold.

*Later a building contractor, George Hunnicutt—his wife a granddaughter of Jonathan Bailey—sent four children to Whittier College, two to become prominent physicians and surgeons, one to follow him as a builder, one a trained hospital technician.
**When playing at Occidental during these years, Whittier players rode over to Los Angeles on their bicycles—and back again after the game.

48

Football was rough sport. Quaker editor, H. D. Williams—perhaps with son Harry in mind as well as nephew Clem Arnold—questioned "whether football with its present methods is a game to be encouraged." To him "swelled lips, bandaged eyes and bloody faces" savored of the arena, and he cited the opinion of President Eliot of Harvard in blaming the spectators who at heart were like "the throng which enjoy the prize-fight, cock-fight, or bull-fight."

But there were other sports, too, at the Whittier Academy up on its hill. A field day was part of the closing exercises in June 1894. The next year the events included: tennis doubles and singles, ladies' tennis, throwing baseball, batting baseball, sack race, wheel barrow race, obstacle race, running broad jump, running high jump, 100 yard dash, throwing the hammer. The day had been organized by the Whittier College Athletic Club.

This athletic association eagerly asked for the "first use of the college auditorium" when it was finished. Even before installation of the "opera chairs" for the initial Yearly Meeting, the Athletic Association invited the public to an Entertainment, given "in the brilliant light of the new Rochester [gas] burners." An orchestra—two violins, piano, cornet and baritone—performed. Dr. W. V. Coffin, in an address, reviewed the work of the Academy, not forgetting "the importance of the athletic feature." Male quartet . . . recitations . . . and the program closed with a tableau:

> "We're Tenting To-night" introduced with singing, as the curtains were drawn, by the quartet . . . while the tent and the campfire appeared on the stage beside them. A red light suddenly cast its weird colors over the lampless room and the realistic scene, and the curtains closed.*

Refreshments were served downstairs, and the art rooms opened for inspection.

The Athenaeum Society presented its literary programs. The student publication, *The Acropolis*—typed or handwritten—

---

*This was the first dramatic performance on the original "stage" in the auditorium in what was later to be called Founders Hall. Considerably remodeled a decade later, with a stage (rather than mere platform) in the east end of the hall and balcony in the west, this Chapel was further remodeled a quarter century later, then to be called Poet Theatre.

appeared, with editorials, stories, poetry, humor. A party at the home of Mrs. Susan Johnson enjoyed games, conversation, refreshments. An all-day tally-ho excursion ("four fine bay horses") took students to the Baldwin Ranch, San Gabriel Mission, Santa Anita Canyon for picnic lunch and picking ferns, sunset riding home under the weeping willows, singing. The romance of a moonlight drive up Turnbull Canyon to the Lookout —half a dozen couples properly chaperoned—was hardly dampened by the returning shower.

All, it seemed, went well up on the college hill, but the Whittier Educational Association gasped for air.

ALL OF THE COLLEGES in southern California faced crises during these years. Enrollment at University of Southern California had dropped to 192 students in 1891, all except 25 of them in the Preparatory Department—"President Bovard died of overwork and worry." Occidental University of Los Angeles reduced its name to College in 1892. Its total enrollment had been 103 in 1889-90, including prep students. Its numbers fell to 52, and then in 1893-94 to 12 collegiate students, and in 1897-98 to but 7. Pomona College, too, struggled—depended upon its preparatory department—sought merger with other colleges.

The plight of Whittier was also serious. By mid-February 1896, the trustees began looking for a new principal to replace Prof. Chawner. They tried to interest Prof. Hiram Hadley, Friends minister, who had been president for some years of New Mexico Agricultural College. On June 1st they offered the position to Prof. John J. Jessup of Pacific College, Newberg, Oregon. Son of Dr. Elias Jessup, who had died six months before, John Jessup was brother-in-law of Dr. C. J. Cook, president of the board of the Whittier Educational Association.

By mid-July J. J. Jessup arrived with his family. In a fortnight he had the new catalog ready for board approval. It was titled *Catalogue of Whittier College*. On motion, and certainly after serious discussion, "the name of the institution was changed from Academy to College." However, only two years of collegiate work would be offered during the year 1896-97.

The college building—the college program, first two years— the college name.

Although some college work was being done at the Whittier Academy, Prof. Chawner said he would "prefer to work up into a college before calling ourselves such." But young people invited to do collegiate work expected to enroll in something called "a college." To eager young Harry Williams, writing for his father's *Register*, it was the Whittier College football team from the first. And for the town it was always the College grounds and building. The trustees, in changing the name from Academy to College, asserted their collegiate intentions, the determination to develop a four-year college program.

As for the name "Whittier College," there was no longer need to defer to the Whittier College in Iowa. Though rebuilt after disastrous fire, it had never recovered. Nearby Penn College had taken its place, and the Iowa Whittier College struggled along, reduced to a Friends academy. There was no reason, then, for choosing some other name—and certainly none for reverting to "Friends' College" or reconsidering "Lindley College." But in adopting the name "Whittier College," the trustees evidenced no intention of christening the college for the venerable Quaker poet, recently deceased. "Whittier College" simply projected the name of Whittier Academy, the enterprise of the Whittier Edutional Association, which took its name from the town of Whittier—which, in turn, blessed itself with the name of John Greenleaf Whittier. Only later did the sentiment of namesake-college develop.

At last, in 1896, the name already current became official, but there was really not much to bear the name Whittier College —no more than the boxy structure and new-planted saplings on an otherwise barren knoll.

AN APPALLING ACCIDENT had occurred that winter—"the burning of the Occidental College Monday [at noon, January 13, 1896] between here and Los Angeles." It was within sight of the College Building in Whittier. But its destruction was not to be final.*

---

*Seeing another chance to dispose of his Greenleaf Hotel, C. W. Harvey showed it to "a number of gentlemen interested in the relocation of the Occidental College." But that college chose Highland Park, the Santa Fe mainline rattling through its back yard until the campus was removed to its present site in Eagle Rock in 1914.

WHITTIER, THE THRIVING TOWN
AND FADING COLLEGE—BUT NOT THE END

WHITTIER COLLEGE, thus named in the summer of 1896, was again in desperate straits. For the school year just ended, $825 was still due on the $1,800 budget for faculty salaries. This was for the three regular teachers—the special teachers of art, music, bookkeeping, even Spanish receiving simply the fees paid by their pupils. Of the $900 that the Educational Association could claim as assets in its current account, $770 was in the form of uncollected subscriptions. Resignations from the Board of Trustees seemed ominous: Dr. W. V. Coffin and L. M. Baldwin, both of them now state employees; T. Elwood Newlin, obliged to live in Los Angeles, having been elected County Clerk; Alva Starbuck, genial business man, the town's first druggist. But Dr. C. J. Cook, I. H. Cammack, Nannie Arnold, Dilwin C. Andrews, Cyrus Trueblood and others determined to push on.

The year just past—with its six in the college department and 40 in the preparatory—showed a total of 100 students, over half the number being specials. Most of these were in the autonomous Department of Music. This was the residue of a cultural scheme that had wilted on the vine. The Southern California Conservatory of Music, as it was called, established itself in Whittier in 1893 and effected an arrangement with the Academy the next year. Its faculty: Chev. Luca Fumatalli (piano, etc.), J. Bond Francisco (violin, etc.), Miss S. I. Morgan (voice), the Misses Strong, members of the pioneer family (business managers). By spring 1894, they had reduced their prices 25%. By fall they were glad to give individual or group lessons to boys and girls in the Academy—groups at 40¢ per pupil. Soon the Chevalier and Francisco dropped from sight. The Misses Strong and Morgan carried on the Conservatory as the music department of the Academy and then College.

Despite the more imposing name for Whittier College and the new leadership of Prof. J. J. Jessup as principal, enrollment for the year 1896-97 declined: 1 college sophomore and 4 freshmen, 35 prep students, a total (with specials) of 86. Only 3 carried college work through the full year, and but 4 pupils graduated from the Preparatory Department in June 1897.

Actually Jessup took hold with a competent hand. He himself taught the science and mathematics. Before long "a gift of chemical equipment to the amount of $500," the overhauling of the laboratories with installation of additional plumbing, the building of "neat and commodious cases" improved the work in this field—but wouldn't the person who borrowed the microscope the year before please return it?

The Library was less than meager—gifts of occasional volumes, a few books bought with small sums subscribed or collected. In 1898 Lydia Jackson gave a score of ancient classics. "The private library of Rev. David J. Lewis, deceased," purchased from his estate, was a dubious bargain—1,000 volumes, largely pastoral, for $700 precious cash. The northwest corner room, first floor of the College Building, became both library and college office. New books, Jessup announced, would be added in literature and the sciences.

To replace the previous three-term schedule, Jessup introduced the two semesters then usual, and adjusted tuition to $18 per semester in the college department, $15 in the preparatory. He dropped the commercial department, and outlined courses of study that looked toward the A.B. in the Classical and the B.S. in the Scientific program—but nothing beyond the first two years could be offered. No provision was made for boarding students.

However scant the course offering and small the student body, the academic work of Whittier College was worthy of recognition. A preliminary visit by a University of California professor in 1898—and by six professors the next year—brought accreditation of the Preparatory Department of Whittier College in 1900. This spoke well for the work of the three academic teachers: John Jessup, Susan Johnson, and Anna Moore.

A football team was again organized in 1896, Jessup as coach. Light in weight, it was pronounced by the *Register* as ready "to enter the arena." Especially successful was the team of 1898. Playing four games, it "was not scored against in three of them, and in the other but twice." It just missed the southern California championship. The Whittier College team still included town boys, some men in their twenties, though all but three were or had been students in the academy or college. "The playing of Hunnicutt and Chambers was up to the best varsity standards," and the other nine—for there were apparently no substitutes— "all played in first-class form." The Occidental team, reportedly beefed up for the encounter, reached Whittier's two foot line but was unable to score. Occidental was given "a sound drubbing."

The Athenaeum Literary Society met weekly, professors participating with students and young men of the town—Will Hiatt, John Coverly, Caleb Cook, Clem Arnold, and Walter Butler (who became lawyers, scientist, newspaper executive, and banker). The Athenaeum debated such timely issues as the independence of Cuba and the annexation of Hawaii, and presented a program on Africa with reports on the Boers, the Congo, and *Story of an African Farm*. The literary society also "published" the *Acropolis*—and gave public entertainments.

Baseball in season—tennis on the new court east of the College Building—the annual Field Day for track events in June. The school picnic—hikes up Turnbull Canyon, lunch "boxes and bags swung on poles"—science excursions farther afield. Chapel exercises—the solemnities of baccalaureate and commencement— the final student reception at the gracious home of Susan and Clifford Johnson.

It was all an Academia in microcosm, and . . . it was good.

THE TOWN OF WHITTIER recovered from the seven lean years of depression and enjoyed five years of remarkable growth and development to close the century.

During the years 1895-1900 the population of Whittier doubled, and during the census decade it increased 170%—from 585 to 1590, while southern California as a whole grew 47% (325,000 in 1900) against a national growth of 20%.

What had been a Friends colony, but with all denominations welcome, moved swiftly to become a secular town, though the bells of St. Mary's no less than those of Methodists and Friends assured a Sabbath awakening. The petition for incorporation of Whittier as a city was headed by the name of Jonathan Bailey. Quakers were the first city officials in 1898: Dr. W. V. Coffin, Dilwin C. Andrews, Dr. C. J. Cook (city trustees), John Chawner (recorder), B. F. Arnold (city clerk), Will M. Hiatt (city attorney), J. J. Jessup (city engineer). But the secular city at once grew restive under the leadership of the Friendly Founders. In the municipal election of 1900, a so-called "Citizens Ticket" challenged the establishment. Behind the insurgents—in the jaundiced eye of the *Register*—were the forces of evil promising "all the prosperity that a saloon brings." Friends were swept from office, but for one lone member of the library board. Of course, the City of Whittier did not succumb—no saloon swung wide its doors.* But the City had declared its independence. One measure of this was the establishment, a fortnight before the election, of a rival and secular Whittier *News*.

The vigilance of the *Register* no less than of the W.C.T.U. had indeed kept Whittier a Dry Town. A Mr. Levi Neal wanted to set up a billiard hall, viewed as next step to "the dram shop." This was opposed by others as well as Friends. H. D. Williams, the editor, bore the brunt of the promoter's frustration, for Neal finally drove to Williams' home, called him out and beat him with his hickory whipstock until it broke, then "went in with his fists." Neighbors pulled them apart. The assailant left town ahead of the sheriff. The battered Quaker continued his crusades to keep out liquor, gaming, and bad women.

The growing town needed policing beyond township constable and local Court under the venerable Judge Samuel Owens, Hervey Lindley's father-in-law. The town needed fire protection— Washington Hadley's house with invalided wife Naomi upstairs had been saved by mere chance. The town needed municipal water. Incorporation was a step toward meeting these needs, and at last, with water bonds voted, the City of Whittier bought out the water interests and distribution system of P.L.&W. Co. for $19,000, including the reservoir and old College Hill.

Through the decade that closed in 1900, the Pickering Land and Water Company played a diminishing role in town affairs. To put its own house in order, capital stock was reduced from $210,000 to $52,000, new certificates being issued at 25¢ on the dollar. The directors, Elwood Newlin as president and Washington Hadley as treasurer, tried to settle outstanding accounts, redeeming lots for delinquent taxes, canceling notes, reducing

*For forty years more, no tavern was licensed in Whittier.

55

indebtedness, pressing Hervey Lindley for some manner of settlement, tussling with C. W. Harvey over his large obligation to the Company. The P.L.&W. Co. tried for oil on its hill lands, then leased, finally sold them for $120,000 in 1900. What remained of the Company was thereafter owned solely by Washington Hadley and his immediate family.

It was the Board of Trade, rather, that came to fill the Company's place in promotion of community interests. This precursor of the later Chamber of Commerce was organized in the fall of 1893 by such men as John E. Coffin, T. E. Newlin, I. H. Cammack, and A. L. Reed. It encouraged the business interests of Whittier. The Cannery, for instance, that had helped save the town when the boom burst, employed 250 persons in its 1895 season and later as many as 600. Oil production, spurred by the Santa Fe's use of oil-burning locomotives, developed until the old Whittier field produced 60,000 bbl. of crude oil per month by 1900. The Home Oil Company, organized by B. F. Arnold with Dr. W. V. Coffin as president, had by that time six producing wells on its 80 acres above the college.* Citrus became the chief agricultural crop— I. H. Cammack prospering as citrus nurseryman. By the end of 1900, the Whittier Citrus Association was within a few months of its formal beginning, with Dr. C. J. Cook and A. L. Reed as directors. It was Washington Hadley's own effort that established the Bank of Whittier, opening in January 1895. By the year 1900, Whittier was ready for a second bank, of which A. Clifford Johnson was named cashier.

Cultivation of the mind and spirit enjoyed a comparable development during these last dynamic years of the century. By 1900 the City of Whittier had seven churches including the original Friends and Methodist—Catholic St. Mary's, Plymouth Congregational, Episcopal St. Matthias, Christian, and Baptist—with a Christian Science Society meeting in rented quarters, and other religious groups forming.

Even before a public library had been proposed by Dr. W. V. Coffin in 1892, the W.C.T.U. had coupled its anti-saloon efforts in 1888 with establishment of a public reading room—nothing

*This company was never very profitable, however. Some 3,000 shares of Home Oil Company stock became part of the Whittier College endowment. Finally the college took over the company's bookkeeping before its liquidation in 1942.

like a good book to keep boys from the bar. Prof. John Chawner chaired a general meeting in May 1895 that set up a committee to advise in starting a Public Library, which occupied various rooms about town during the next years. In 1900 library trustees were elected as city officials.

Through these years of town growth, attendance at the Bailey public school increased from 268 to 433. Quaker children—Esther Andrews, best in her class—were among the pupils. The Whittier Academy had dropped its Primary Department already in 1893. Parents and teachers of the public school met in the Friends Church to discuss perennial problems—petty thievery, obscene writing in outhouses, cheating in class work. Bailey school held its graduation exercises in the new auditorium of Whittier College.

Most important was the movement to start a public high school. Many persons doubted the wisdom of additional taxes. The proposition voted on in July 1900 was "warmly contested," but passed 170 to 133. The high school, to open in the fall using upstairs rooms in the Bailey school, was one factor precipitating the crisis on the Acropolis, for it would, of course, compete directly with the Preparatory Department of Whittier College in its bid for local students.

WHITTIER COLLEGE DECLINED, moving toward what must have certainly seemed its inevitable end, during the very years in which the town of Whittier flourished as a rapidly developing small city. Attendance at what was now properly called "Whittier College," which had risen in Jessup's second year to some 50 (but only nine of these in college classes), dropped to an average of 36 the next year—and again but 38 in 1899-1900. All but two of these were apparently prep students. However, among these few was George Anthony who graduated in 1899 and proceeded to become a medical doctor—with him Charles C. Williams, to become a dentist. Edward E. Thomas and George Willett carried on, becoming notable scientists. Cass Arthur Reed, of the prep class of 1901, was later to serve as dean and then president of International College, Smyrna—Ruth Esther Smith to serve as missionary in Guatemala. However creditable the academic work and capable the pupils, the Preparatory Department of Whittier

College dwindled—the public high school ready to give it mercifully the *coup de grâce*. As for its being a college, Whittier had become that in name only.

The incipient high school was but one reason for this. Whittier College, with at best its meager two-year collegiate program, could not attract young people who wanted to proceed directly through a four-year course. It was normal, also, for those from Whittier families to "go away to college," and strongly denominational homes supported their own colleges elsewhere in southern California. Even young Friends thought of Penn College and Earlham where parents or kinfolk had been schooled. But there was a deeper reason for the crucial lack of students for Whittier College. This was to be found within the Quakerism of that time and place.

The Quakers comprising California Yearly Meeting were part of the Orthodox branch of the Society of Friends. Their forebears had been stirred by Joseph John Gurney, the English Quaker, who in 1837 travelled in the East and mid-West, preached sin and salvation, and moved many Friends toward Protestant orthodoxy in their theology and evangelism. Already separated from them were the liberal Hicksites, Friends who followed the primitive Christianity of George Fox and his reliance, not on Scripture, but on the Inner Light. And before the Civil War, the conservative Wilburites, too, had split off, holding to the quietism of their tradition. In the decade or so before the final leap westward to southern California, these mid-Western Gurneyites or Orthodox Friends had adopted the pastoral system. They built not meetinghouses but churches—with pastors, hymn-singing, Scripture-reading, pastoral prayer and sermon in their worship. Their Protestant orthodoxy was akin to Methodism. But among these Friends were rather wide differences of view.

The members of California Yearly Meeting were far from being a homogeneous group, and they were widely scattered. One-third lived in and near Whittier or in Los Angeles (a small number only). Another third lived in Pasadena and Long Beach. The rest lived in rural areas, smaller towns, and cities from San Diego to Berkeley. For the Friends academy in Whittier that so earnestly wanted to be a college, most of the students came from Quaker families in the Whittier area. In the yearly Meeting as a whole (a fact repeatedly noted), some boys and girls of high school age were not in school anywhere.*

Even among those Quakers who valued education for their young, there was no consensus as to what kind of education it should be. Should higher education for young Friends be secular or religious? If secular, should it be practical and professional, or cultural and intellectual? If religious, should it be Biblical and evangelistic, or historical and ethical? It was not as simple, of course, as this.

When Orthodox Quakers adopted the pastoral system, they did not develop a "learned" clergy, though numbered among their pastors were men trained for other professions. Many Friends thought that Bible-school training in Scripture and Evangelism—rather than collegiate discipline in science and classics, rhetoric and history—was the proper preparation for pastor or missionary, or indeed for life itself. Differences of view in this regard came into sharp focus in 1900. Evangelistic Friends started a Bible school in Whittier, without regard to the academy-college. In March this Training School for Christian Workers, meeting in the home of Philena B. Hadley, was organized with a local board of which I. H. Cammack was president. Until 1898 he had been active on the board of the Educational Association, served as its president in 1896-97. Plans looked toward opening the fall term of the Training School "in a commodious building known as the Briggs block" on North Greenleaf, with accommodations for boarding students, Mary A. Hill, the principal.

The new Training School and the new High School in Whittier precipitated a crisis for Whittier College in June 1900. The directors of the Educational Association, after a decade's struggle to found an academy and college to serve both Friends and the community, were ready to give up. Citizens of the now thriving town had not supported it—not even to the extent of subscriptions that would total $1,000 a year as a Deficiency Fund. Nor had the Yearly Meeting wholeheartedly supported this college that it did not officially control. As consideration for completion of the auditorium and for small annual appropriations of an uncertain $700

*In 1900 there were 1510 Friends in California Yearly Meeting, including 403 "children between the ages of 6 and 21," of whom 302 were in [elementary] school, 46 in high school, and 22 in college or university.

59

or so,* the Educational Association had yielded a one-quarter interest in its campus and building to the Yearly Meeting.

In June 1900 it was hard indeed to make Whittier College look solvent, with its cash balance of $22.20. Its operating assets were $1,650—in appropriations still due from Friends meetings, delinquent subscriptions to the Deficiency Fund, unpaid tuition, and old accounts. Its immediate liabilities were $1,200—of which over $900 was owing on salaries (about half of the total faculty budget for the three professors).** The resignation of longtime trustees (J. C. Hiatt and C. E. Tebbetts in 1899) and disaffection of old Friends (Jonathan Bailey and Willet Dorland) disheartened those who remained.

With diminishing trustees, faculty, students, and funds—with the high school on one hand and the Bible school on the other— the Whittier Educational Association faced a simple choice at its June 4th meeting of stockholders: It could either *close down* Whittier College, or *give it away*. It chose the latter.

With all the pomp and circumstance of corporate legality, "it was ordered that the Board of Directors . . . be instructed to tender Whittier College to California Yearly Meeting of Friends Church." And this was duly done—with all the property, buildings, fixtures, and appliances—"for the consideration of the Yearly Meeting creating and maintaining a school creditable to the church, as an institution of learning."

Meeting in Long Beach (perhaps wisely for that year), California Yearly Meeting took up the matter submitted to it on June 21, 1900. It was no surprise, of course, as leadership in the academy venture and in the Yearly Meeting involved many of the same persons. The Yearly Meeting agreed to accept the offer and to "assume the control and management of the college."

---

*In 1898, for instance, CYM approved an appropriation of $700 for Whittier College, which would have averaged only 46¢ per member of the Yearly Meeting. But it was agreed that 70% of the total was to be contributed by the meetings making up Whittier Quarterly Meeting (two-thirds of whose members were in Whittier itself). Even these small allotments from monthly meetings were often in arrears.

**John Jessup, with a growing family, really needed the $300 due him. During the summer he moved to Berkeley, to be an assistant in engineering at the University. Thereafter he became City Engineer, first for the City of Berkeley and then for long years for the City of Los Angeles. Miss Moore needed her $150, as she was returning to Richmond. Mrs. Johnson, with $470 of her $600 salary still due, was quite willing to take a note in payment, her husband cashier of the new bank in Whittier.

Whittier College thus became officially the denominational school of Orthodox Friends in California, a religious body divided in its views of higher education and too small in numbers to support the kind of liberal arts college of which some of its leaders dreamed.

II

THE FRIENDS' DENOMINATIONAL COLLEGE
(1900-1918)

T HE PIONEERING PERIOD in the history of Whittier College had ended in collapse. It remained to be seen whether its new formulation as the denominational school of California Yearly Meeting would prove viable in the opening years of the Twentieth Century.

In the two decades from Manila Bay to the Armistice at Compiègne, the United States became a world power and the American people hurtled into Modern Times. The Age of the Railroad had reached its peak, and at last the Salt Lake Line (Union Pacific) skirted Whittier to drop transcontinental passengers at nearby Pico. The Age of the Motorcar dawned, with Dr. Levi Johnson (Quaker-turned-Methodist) driving the first horseless carriage on Whittier's dusty streets. And the *News* reported the failures and then flights that promised the Age of Air.

Trust-busters, muckrakers, and labor agitators fought Big Business, Robber Barons, and Capitalism in fields remote from Whittier—though dynamiting of the Los Angeles *Times* killed one of its sons. The Anti-Saloon League closed up the Jimtown saloon on its way to National Prohibition. The feminist movement, with Quaker women among its early leaders, pressed toward Universal Suffrage. Students up on the college hill in Whittier felt the pull of these events.

The town of Whittier trebled its population in ten years, having reached 4,500 by 1910, and it nearly doubled again in the next decade. Surrounding citrus groves came into full bearing, Friends among the leaders in co-operative packing associations. Real estate again boomed. The new banks prospered. In turn came electric lights—gas—telephones, Aubrey Wardman building and soon owning the phone lines. Then also were built the high school building, the Carnegie public library, the government laboratory, the woman's club, the Y.M.C.A., more and larger churches. Whittier was an outstanding instance of the rapid development of southern California.

Yet, as a part of the times, sawdust-trail evangelists held big-tent revivals for large audiences in Whittier. Itinerant showfolk still played out their tent-show morality of *Uncle Tom's Cabin*. The Chautauqua brought cultural entertainment of a higher cut and national speakers. But town and college were no longer dependent upon these, for the new Pacific Electric line linked Whittier to Los Angeles with the frequent and rapid service of the big red cars.

1

REOPENING OF THE COLLEGE
UNDER CALIFORNIA YEARLY MEETING

TO OPERATE WHITTIER COLLEGE the Yearly Meeting of Friends appointed a Board of Trustees in June 1900. Included among them were several who had served as directors of the Whittier Educational Association, but there were also men and women to represent the other Quaker communities: Los Angeles, Pasadena, Long Beach, Alamitos, El Modena, Berkeley. Of the twelve trustees, only Dr. C. J. Cook, Dr. W. V. Coffin, Mary T. Hadley, and (briefly) William M. Hiatt lived in the Whittier area. William E. Cox, Los Angeles attorney, became president of the board; Dr. Cook, vice president; Will Hiatt, secretary; and the First National Bank (that is, Washington Hadley), treasurer. All of the trustees were Friends, of course, and members of the Yearly Meeting.

The immediate problem was to reopen Whittier College under its new management. That meant securing a principal or president, engaging a faculty, preparing a course of study, enlisting students, raising funds. The newly appointed trustees turned to Charles E. Tebbetts, pastor of the Pasadena Friends Church, as eminently qualified to salvage the academy for the Yearly Meeting and to develop it into a college. He was well known for his part in the efforts to found Friends' College in 1888 and for his support of the Whittier Educational Association.

Charles E. Tebbetts came from the New England stream of Quakers. His parents, a merchant and a teacher—both of them recorded ministers—moved West, their son and only child born at West Branch, Iowa.* They "spared no pains" that he might have the best possible education, and sent him to Haverford (A.B., 1875). He then pursued graduate study at Iowa State (Ph.B., 1877; A.M., 1880). For ten years (1877-1887) he taught at Penn College as professor of science and mathematics. Married to Imelda A. Painter, Prof. Tebbetts brought his family to Pasadena, and served briefly as vice principal of Pasadena High School. His father-in-law John Painter, a land-developer in Pasadena and a founder of Whittier, divided his property with his grown children. The Tebbetts raised prunes on their acreage, which appreciated in value and was later subdivided. Recorded a Friends minister in 1892, Charles Tebbetts soon became pastor of the Pasadena Friends Church—"a labor of love."

In 1900, when Tebbetts became the first "president" (rather than principal) of Whittier College, he was "a heavy powerful man of middle age, with unruly black hair, bristling moustache, and a face deeply grooved with lines." He was thought of as an earnest man, "absent-minded and careless of dress," living "in the realm of mind," often with brow knit and mouth puckered, both strict in discipline and generous of heart. He was a vigorous man, striding across the campus in frock coat and bowler, playing tennis with the boys, encouraging their athletics. "A brilliant man and wonderful teacher," yet his deepest concern was for the religious life of the students, and he supported the Y.M. and Y.W.C.A. A liberal Quaker, he believed in Evolution and opposed the Fundamentalists. A great student of the Bible, he preached a "searching sermon."

During his first three years as president of Whittier College, he maintained his home in Pasadena and continued as pastor there. Early on Mondays he drove horse and buggy the 16 miles to Whittier, bringing his elder daughter Edith to cook for him

*There in 1874 Herbert C. Hoover was born of Quaker parents.

during the week. He returned to Pasadena for Wednesday evening prayer meeting, and on Friday afternoon for the weekend. When the San Gabriel river was in flood, he took the train roundabout via Los Angeles and Norwalk. But Friends in Pasadena felt they had only a part-time pastor, and Whittier College also needed "a whole man with undivided attention." In 1903 he built a home on Earlham Drive [now Earlham Hall], in the new tract south of the campus, gave up his pastorate in Pasadena and moved his family to Whittier.

In the late summer of 1900, it was not certain "until about two weeks before the opening of the college" that there would be any school at all. By September 14th, the *Register* could report that Whittier College would indeed open on Tuesday the 25th, with Tebbetts, Susan Johnson, Caleb Cook and hopefully a Miss Foella B. Hobbs to "take the chair of English"—which she declined to do.

Mrs. Johnson was, of course, well known in Whittier, as was Caleb E. Cook. He had graduated from the Academy in 1895, continued to study at Whittier "two years in advance of the curriculum" (that is, college work), then went back to Earlham to complete his B.S. degree. Thereafter he took graduate work at Throop Polytechnic Institute (forerunner of California Institute of Technology). He shared with his students his keen interest in marine zoology. It was Effine Blount, secured at the last minute in place of Miss Hobbs, who arrived in mid-October to complete the academic faculty of four as professor of English and German. Music and Art were, as previously, "independent of the regular courses." The Trueblood sisters (Mary T. Hadley, a board member, and Ruth T. Green) taught drawing and painting on velvet and china. Annie Denby gave piano lessons at her home down the street.

Enlisting students for the fall reopening of Whittier College was perhaps the most anxious problem, with the new public high school ready to receive pupils and the new Training School established in better quarters in Whittier. Except from Quaker families notably devoted to their own academic education, whence might students be drawn? For the formal opening exercises, upstairs in the Yearly Meeting Hall of the College Building (not yet called Founders Hall), there were perhaps fewer than 30 pupils present, all of them in the Preparatory Department.* If they were but a small band, they were assertedly Christians "almost without exception." All but five were Friends—all but a few came from Whittier homes.

To open the year in the presence of Friends and well-wishers, Dr. C. J. Cook presided, as he had so often done for the Educational Association. Mary H. Hill of the Training School "led in an earnest prayer." Professors Tebbetts, Johnson, and Caleb Cook spoke briefly. With forced cheer surely, Dr. Cyrus Cook spoke of "the propitious outlook and broader vantage ground occupied by the college through the recent changes." Yet he may have seen that among the prep school boys and girls there were the bright ones: Cass A. Reed and Edward E. Thomas, Anna Tomlinson and Esther Andrews who in time would serve the college well, and his daughter Loretta. These and the others were ready to troop off to class.

There must have been much improvisation during this year of transition that looked firmly toward developing Whittier as a full four-year college, though no college students were then enrolled. In the spring appeared a catalog for 1900-1901 but including announcements for the year to come.

> The first class in College work will be organized for the year 1901-1902, and only such courses will be open next year as will be required for their work [i.e., freshman courses].

Outlined, however, were two years of Greek and Latin, German, English, History, Science, and Mathematics—promising sophomore work to be added.

This school year came to its ceremonious close in June 1901: the Congregational minister preached the baccalaureate sermon—Annie Denby gave a faculty recital—eight prep-school graduates received diplomas with proper music, prayer and orations—the A. C. Johnsons entertained students and faculty at a final reception.

*No clear record survives. The only available list includes those in attendance during the two years 1899-1901. The average enrollment reported for the year 1899-1900 was 38, and the year 1900-1901 admittedly had "decreased attendance."

The sessions of California Yearly Meeting followed the next week. It was ready to hear reports on Whittier College, which it at last considered its own. President Tebbetts "earnestly recommended that the school push forward into legitimate college work," beginning with freshman work in the fall and adding a further class each of the succeeding years "until students shall be able to obtain as complete a course as is now offered at Earlham or Penn."

He presented the need for $3,000 in annual assured income. For the year just closed, Lydia Jackson—pioneer daughter of a horsetrading Quaker father who had sold Civil War mounts to the army—had secured subscriptions to cover all but $425 of the year's expenses. Caleb Cook (secretary of the board in place of Will Hiatt), gave the financial report. Only $81.65 of the year's income had come from tuitions!* But it was always expected that worthy students would receive the benefit of scholarships.

As something of a college, Whittier again got under way in the fall of 1901. Six women students enrolled as freshmen with the expectation that advanced work would be added year by year so as to permit them to receive their A.B. degrees in June 1905. Preparatory students increased to 46 in number, one-third of them in the first-year prep class, a prime source of future college students. There was at last a feeling that the Quaker college had a good start, and during the fall the trustees filed articles of incorporation for Whittier College.

Through the years 1901-1904 the academic faculty increased in number from four to six. To replace Effine Blount in 1901 came Herbert E. Harris (Ph.B., Penn College, with a year of graduate work at Chicago) to be professor of English and History. He at once impressed students with his enthusiasm and incessant labors—his encouragement of writing—his interest in athletics—his romantic appreciation of the beautiful.

The next year Helen Shelley (A.B., Stanford, graduate work at Bryn Mawr) became professor of History and Modern Languages. "A small intense woman," she also coached the girls' sports "and fairly bounced from one task to another." In 1903,

*At $30 per year, the stated charge, the tuition collected was the equivalent of only two full-pay pupils, plus a mysterious fraction.

67

Blanche Bradshaw—patient daughter of the Baptist minister—taught modern languages for the year.

There was rapid succession in occupancy of the chair of science. Caleb Cook withdrew after his second year to devote himself to his new electrical business, but continued for years as secretary of the college board.* Homer G. Rosenberger (B.S., Penn College) succeeded him but left shortly to study medicine, returning to Whittier for a practice in surgery. To replace him on short notice came another Ruth Trueblood (B.S., Earlham), both her parents teachers at Penn College. She "immediately won the good-will of all the students with her dignity and poise." Before the end of the year she looked toward a career other than teaching.

The growing attachment of Professors Harris and Trueblood could not remain unnoticed in that small world of gown and town. One Saturday a student, returning late from an afternoon hike in the hills, came round a turn in the trail and beheld two figures on a knoll silhouetted against the sunset—arm in arm, heads juxtaposed—unmistakable forms and mood. So astonished was this youth that "he went through Whittier like Paul Revere," bearing the incredibly romantic tidings from one student's home to the next. Nor surprised were they that the summer's wedding was performed upon a rock overlooking the blue Pacific.

These six professors, comprising the academic faculty in 1903-04, gave separate classes for the preps and the college students, taught up to 26 class hours per week, plus supervising study hall and much else besides. They took turns leading most of the daily chapel periods—the faculty in solemn semicircle upon the rostrum. They sponsored the student activities, chaperoned parties, engaged in church work and student recruitment. For the male professors the annual salaries were $600 to $800—for the women, somewhat less—for the president $1,000. Salaries were always in arrears, and President Tebbetts "contributed" at least as much money as he was supposed to make.

Yet, if overworked and underpaid—which could be said of

*He gave the college its first electric clock in 1907. Later he pioneered date-growing in the Coachella Valley, recovering his failing health, but died of gas poisoning in an accident at his date-packing house, aged 55.

later faculties as well—good teaching must have been done, as measured by the later lives of these pupils and students.

THE FIRST SENIOR CLASS of Whittier College looked toward graduation a year ahead of the projected completion of the four-year college course. In the fall of 1903, two students, because of previous advanced study, were ready for their senior work. They were joined at that time by two others, transferring from Earlham College.

These four seniors were Dell Coryell, who as a child had arrived in Whittier with the very first Quaker settlers; Edith Tebbetts, the president's daughter; Inez Greene and Theodore Smith, the newcomers, daughter and stepson of Dr. L. M. Greene.*

During the year 1903-04 there were actually 25 college students at Whittier, five of them men. However, the class of 11 freshmen looked well to the future. And in that year there were also 65 in the prep department, of whom 30 were boys, and that too was promising. The great majority were still from Whittier homes, as the college had no boarding facilities, and from Friends families, as the public high school attracted most of the others.

By this time sufficient courses were catalogued to allow for choice among five (very slender) group majors: ancient and modern languages, language and mathematics, mathematics and physical sciences, physical and life sciences, language with English and history. With the paucity of library and laboratory resources, it was at best a very minimal collegiate offering.

In many of the activities the younger and older students engaged as one big happy family. It took the larger prep boys to make up any sort of college baseball team, to fill out the cast of a play, to support the literary and forensic programs.

Some of these activities, nurtured by the faculty, served the religious objective of providing a "guarded education" for Quaker youth. In addition to the daily chapel and weekly Bible class, both required, there were the weekly meetings of the Y.M. and Y.W.C.A., involving almost all of the students. Promoting Christian idealism, these groups took a hand in orienting new students—chicken bake in the hills for the new boys, and a proper

*A steady champion of liberal education, Dr. Greene was soon named to the Board of Trustees (1907-23), and lived beyond his hundredth year within a block of the campus.

party with watermelon and feminine hilarity for the girls—and they looked forward to conventions at Asilomar and inspiring visitations to the campus by the college Y.M. and Y.W. secretaries. The more earnest participated in the annual series of "special services" held on the campus by a visiting evangelist—such as Harry A. Keates in 1904—or by the president himself.

The Athenaeum Literary Society was already in its tenth year in the fall of 1900. Its fortnightly meetings and occasional public entertainments were items of news for the town *Register*. Members of the faculty and former students participated with the prep and college students in the meetings of the Athenaeum as well as in these performances. Then, in 1903, pupils in the preparatory department were relegated to their own Philolithian Literary Society, and in 1904 the Iris Literary Society announced itself as specifically for parliamentary drill and public speaking.

The Athenaeum issued the first printed *Acropolis* in the spring of 1902, a literary magazine of 46 pages. Its contents included essays, stories and verse, photos of faculty and classes, pen drawings and cartoons. It summarized the year's work in athletics (croquet and baseball, coached by Harry Williams of the *Register*), the Athenaeum itself (Arthur H. Jessup, young dentist, its president), and the Y.W.C.A. and the chapel programs. Inevitably, approved jokes seasoned advertisements by faithful merchants. After three years as an annual, the *Acropolis* became a somewhat-quarterly for a decade.

Oratory was an exciting activity. The Intercollegiate Prohibition Contest aroused general interest, with speakers representing University of Southern California, Occidental and Pomona colleges. In the spring of 1904 Burtis Healton was the Whittier orator. Almost the whole school—"seventy five students," as one later recalled—accompanied him to Los Angeles on the new red cars of the Pacific Electric. In the large Simpson Auditorium, the Whittier delegation sat together, "the noisiest group in the place," to fortify Burtis with college yells and songs.

When Burtis got up to speak, he looked small and his voice seemed thin, but he was mightily earnest. This was his peroration..."With the sword of justice in our right hand, the sense of duty impelling us onward, we will wage persistent warfare on the liquor traffic, and humanity will again be victorious."

These his closing words were the signal for his Whittier partisans to cheer wildly as they tried to "shout him to victory." But he won no prize that year.

Some activities, of course, were extemporized and unsupervised. The catalog stated the expectation of "the highest standard of moral conduct" and the prohibition of profanity, smoking, and drinking. But one youth—of "handsome face, flashing eye, and fascinating cynical smile"—was unwarily admitted upon assurance that Whittier was "just the right place for him." Soon in assorted troubles, he led others astray: one was the lone male in the Senior Class, two were prep-school grandsons of prominent trustees, Washington Hadley and Levi Mills, then pastor of the Friends Church.

The four boys met one Saturday afternoon to drive off for an overnight hunting trip. The youth of handsome face, etc.—

an authority on the subject of wines—had brought several bottles of what he called "California Grape Juice" in varieties that he named Moselle, Port and Claret.

To the uninitiated he gave lessons in distinguishing flavors. It required a great deal of sampling before they could tell one from another. At last, a bit uncertainly, they drove their hired rig out the County Road past Dr. C. J. Cook's ranch home—where they were *not* welcomed by the college girls, there for a slumber party—and on toward the Coyote Hills. As night came down, they gave way to a collective impulse—stopped their nag at each farmhouse, dismounted, capered and whooped in the moonlight, shot off their guns. Then, as lights appeared in the windows, they proceeded—at last reached their midnight camp. In the morning, hunting forgotten, they slipped back to town shamefaced. Report had preceded them. The gay deceiver quietly expelled, the neophyte wine-tasters felt deeply the uneven hand of Justice that punished him alone.

Nor was this the only occasion during this early period when

71

student sons of good Whittier families were disciplined by the faculty for escapades involving drinking.*

THE FIRST COLLEGE COMMENCEMENT in June 1904 recognized its significance as "a landmark in the development of Whittier College and of the Friends church in California." The week began with the baccalaureate sermon, then proceeded with a succession of social and cultural activities and events. For the culmination in commencement exercises, Whittier merchants closed their stores and delegations arrived from the scattered Quaker communities. Speaker for the historic occasion was Augustus Murray, respected and beloved Quaker, professor of Greek at Stanford.

The college auditorium was too small and its stage too shallow for the events that had been long in preparation. Seniors and younger faculty had taken the problem to Dr. W. V. Coffin, by this time president of the board. "He found a solution," wrote Professor Harris in later years. He secured a huge circus tent and borrowed lumber. "A full-fledged stage with curtains, wings, footlights, facing backless but ample seating accommodations, sprang from the hand of a genie. . . ."

For the Class Day exercises of this commencement week, the four seniors (helped by a creative freshman) wrote and presented an original farce, *Benjamin Bean Jr*. It depicted a youth who, upon entering Whittier College, was trailed by three old-fashioned aunts, shocked by his escapades. Theodore Smith (already initiated as wine-taster) played the wayward youth. The audience of one thousand townfolk—including some Friends—crowded the tent, illuminated (as was the stage) "by a line of electric lights." Reported as hilarious beyond credence, this comic performance showed "college life" as the town, at least, thought it would be.

Next night the tent was again "well filled by a large and appreciative audience" for *The Merchant of Venice* under the aegis

*Thus, in 1906, four were expelled by the faculty. Three of these ("truly penitent") were reinstated in due course upon signing "cheerfully" and of their own "desire," pledges "to abstain from the use of all intoxicating liquor for the period of ten years" and from the use of "tobacco in any form" during their remaining years at Whittier College (including vacation time)—and their parents undertook to "guarantee" their sons' good conduct and to keep them in and at their books evenings, except for authorized lecture- and church-going. Some professors, evidently, were uneasy regarding this severity.

of the Athenaeum and direction of Professor Harris. Keenly interested in Shakespeare, he had attended the Columbia School of Oratory part-time during his year of graduate study at the University of Chicago. Preparation for this first college production of Shakespeare carried through much of the year. Harris himself undertook the rôle of Shylock. Willing prep boys filled out his college cast.

"The simple and effective stage scenery," the *Register* reported, was well executed by the students, with potted palms, smilax, and eucalyptus boughs masking the wings. "A regalia house in San Francisco" supplied the costumes. Harris used theatrical grease paint to make up his actors behind the great tent.

On stage, nervous players peeped through the curtain. Spectators (at 25¢ admission) packed the house and some were standing. The State School orchestra brought its overture to a close. Professor Harris stepped forward in costume to outline briefly the plot, "explaining some of the lessons to be drawn from the drama." The curtains parted, and the melancholy merchant of Venice, Antonio, entered—"In sooth, I know not why I am so sad . . ."—his young companions as dry-mouthed as he.

The scenes of the play moved rapidly, with no change of the simple scenery to interrupt the flow. Actors awaited their cues outside the tent, entered in various stages of fright, then warmed to their lines and business until their sweating exit into the cool night air, followed by applause or cheers or laughter. The handsome lover borrowing from his older friend—the vengeful moneylender with his skipping servant boy—the beauteous heroine, bride by the choice of caskets—the gripping courtroom scene, the disguised heroine saving her beloved—the moonlight and roses of the romantic happy ending!

The great success of this performance paid all the costs of commencement week, including fee for the speaker, and it was long remembered as a cultural achievement.

But some Friends—trustees, even a professor—did not attend it, respecting their traditional condemnation of playgoing. Criticism was voiced and echoed, especially condemning the use of theatrical make up. The play threatened to become an issue the next week at Yearly Meeting. But Professor Murray, from his respected eminence, heartily commended the performance, proclaimed it worthy of the great Shakespeare and elevating to public taste. Rev. Levi Mills took occasion in his pastoral prayer in First-Day worship to thank God "for the blessings of Commencement Week, in music and address and drama."* The more zealous Friends did not press their charges or officially "elder" the participants.

Thus, with its first commencement in 1904, Whittier College achieved a minimal collegiate program, having granted four A.B. degrees. In no small measure this was the fruit of President Tebbetts' years of determined effort.

2

WHITTIER COLLEGE—INCORPORATION, FURTHER BUILDING, ENDOWMENT

THE FRIENDS' COLLEGE of 1900 consisted of the original 14-acre campus and, on its knoll, the one boxy frame building of brick veneer.

Transfer of this college property from the Educational Association to the Yearly Meeting was the first problem the new Board of Trustees faced. There were legal questions involved, and within the year it became evident that, although the Yearly Meeting could indeed hold title to the property, its own incorporation gave it no power to conduct a degree-granting college or to handle endowment funds. It was therefore necessary to incorporate Whittier College separately as an educational institution of higher learning. The new college board reported this to the Yearly Meeting in June 1901. Friends in the Yearly Meeting approved—but with a reluctance that was never quite stilled. It seemed like "giving away" the college that they had just acquired.

The trustees filed articles of incorporation for Whittier College on December 31, 1901. The certificate of incorporation, dated January 7, 1902, gave Whittier College the right to buy, hold and sell property, to borrow and lend money, to erect build-

*Levi Mills was no ordinary Quaker—he kept theology in the pulpit, laughed aloud on his front porch, drove off for a day's fishing at Long Beach with Jonathan Bailey (behind old Polly, now white with age), and died finally a respected probate judge in Ohio. His grandson, Burritt Hiatt (later a professor at Wilmington College) performed his bit in the play and later wrote a charming Reminiscence of his year at Whittier.

ings, to establish and maintain a college, and to award "such literary honors as are granted by any college of learning, and [to] grant diplomas."

In order to "control" its denominational college, California Yearly Meeting through its nominating committee would thereafter *nominate* the college trustees (in doing which it normally consulted with members of the college board); but it was only the college Board of Trustees itself that could legally elect them, four each year for three-year terms.* It was to this separately incorporated Whittier College, then, and not to California Yearly Meeting that the Whittier Educational Association transferred its property rights in June 1902. This was "an undivided three-fourths interest" in the campus and plant, for the Yearly Meeting as such had already acquired a quarter interest in 1896. Not until June 17, 1904 did the Yearly Meeting relinquish its one-quarter property interest to the Whittier College board. And as late as 1915 Will Hiatt again had to explain this strange business of separate incorporation that had slipped Whittier College away from the controlling hand of California Yearly Meeting of Friends Church.

THE RAISING OF ENDOWMENT funds was a second problem facing the college trustees. In this matter Dr. W. V. Coffin, soon to be president of the board, took the lead. At a public meeting in April 1901, with Dr. C. J. Cook presiding and President Tebbetts speaking, the trustees presented their plan to raise $50,000 in a two-year campaign. This amount in endowment would assure $3,000 annual income, which was as much at that time as the faculty budget for the year.

At the Yearly Meeting in June 1902, Washington Hadley pledged $10,000 toward endowment as a memorial to Naomi Hadley, his wife then deceased. Before the sessions closed, the total in subscriptions stood at $25,400. A year later, on the eve of Education Day at the next Yearly Meeting, June 1903, $6,000 remained to be raised to complete the $50,000, without which none of the contingent subscriptions would have been binding.

*Already by 1906, however, the college trustees (as a self-governing body) increased their number to 15, with the provision that only 12 of them need be Friends, and they elected George L. Hazzard to membership, upon nomination by the Yearly Meeting—but Hazzard was safely a Methodist.

The evening meeting in the new Friends Church was an exciting occasion. The students sat in the center section with banners of purple and gold, the trustees in the choir loft. Washington Hadley and Levi Mills (with college colors streaming from his frock-coat lapel) especially enjoyed themselves.

When the moment came to do so, William M. Hiatt opened the subscriptions with $1,000. Others followed. Students, too, pledged small amounts. It was Charles E. Veeder whose $100 pushed the total to its goal. Joyous then was the Doxology, singing praises to God for his bounty. And Washington Hadley, to capitalize upon the high note of success, arose to offer another $10,000, provided an additional $40,000 to match it be raised within another year.

A few days later, students joined faculty and trustees to thank him at his home for his generous gift and splendid offer.

What a man this Washington Hadley! Aged 86 at this time, he had just recently purchased the 1,000 acre Pallett Ranch, rich riverlands near Rivera. He had assumed a personal debt of $50,000 to do so, and he proceeded to develop this Hadley Ranch for orange production. He carried on business from behind the old-fashioned desk in his bank, where he could keep an eye on things—an awesome sight to the little boy who happened in. When, shortly, A. Wardman came to borrow money as down payment on the Whittier Telephone Company, of which he was manager, W. Hadley interrupted Wardman's summary of his meager personal assets, and spoke up bruskly:

"No, not a cent on your assets, young man!—but as much as you need on your character and note."

Washington Hadley "conducted his affairs as though he expected to live forever." He remarried when nearing ninety, continued active until his death at age 94, a weighty Quaker of the old sort described by J. G. Whittier as "diligent in business and serving the Lord." Never failing, he trudged up the college hill to its board meetings.

ENLARGING THE COLLEGE building, however, had to come before another endowment effort.

The very next day following completion of the first endowment campaign in 1903, Dr. Coffin reported to the Yearly Meeting the urgent need for a south wing of the college building—the cost, perhaps $5,000. Such an addition was imperative if the full college course was to be given, as promised for the year 1904-05. More than that, if Whittier College was to serve the youth of the entire Yearly Meeting, dormitory and dininghall were an absolute necessity.

In June 1904 Dr. Coffin reported that the addition to the college building was to be larger than that planned a decade earlier. Furthermore, the trustees were remodeling the auditorium, giving it both balcony and stage. If the word "stage" rekindled Quaker doubts about the drama—*The Merchant of Venice* fresh in a fortnight's memory—the additional seating of some 200 persons at Yearly Meeting sessions warranted approval. Estimated cost of the addition and improvement: $10,000.

Washington Hadley had renewed his promise of the five acres lying south of the campus which he would donate upon completion of the building free of debt. Then he made a gift of $2,500 toward the work, contingent upon its completion within a year. With a further $3,000 already subscribed, only $4,000 remained unpledged.

Construction proceeded rapidly—but, again, not without accident. Walter Tebbetts, the president's fifteen-year-old son, was one of the boys who had summer jobs on the construction. He and Willis Beede were hoisting scantling from the ground to the third floor. Boy-like, they disregarded the warning: no more than two pieces at a time. Thus a 2 x 3 slipped from the rope and, after Walter had already turned away, "struck him with its end on the back of his head . . . felling him to the ground and crushing his skull." He was in conscious pain stoically endured as workmen carried him home across the field and street. Doctors summoned by his sister—their parents in the north—operated upon him at once on the diningroom table. Under anaesthetic they removed six pieces of bone and fitted a silver plate.*

With redoubled caution, construction continued. By mid-September the remodeled auditorium was far enough along for the

*Walter Tebbetts completely recovered, the plate later removed. He played basketball at Earlham, football at Haverford, proudly displayed his skull fragments fitted into the palm of his hand, and became a vice president of New England Mutual Life Insurance Company.

opening assembly, the students sitting on extemporized benches in a forest of scaffolding. During the fall term classes carried on with an accompaniment of carpentering effects from the south addition.

In early February, Professor Harris gave Harry Williams of the *Register* a tour of the new construction. Ground floor of the south wing: a new $2,000 heating plant, kitchen and diningroom seating 75, apartment of "the landlord and landlady," and physics laboratory "resting on the solid rock." First floor: president's office and general office, new chemistry and biology laboratories. Second floor: a large room for student meetings of Y.M. and Y.W.C.A., literary societies and clubs, and two new classrooms. Third floor: seven dormitory rooms with dormer windows, and a bath for the girls. Fourth floor, yet higher in the attic: six smaller rooms and a bath for the boys. Then, in the original building: the remodeled auditorium,

> increased by the addition of a balcony until 700 persons can be accommodated comfortably, and the stage [obviously Harris's delight] has been arranged to meet every demand of college entertainment, with a full paraphernalia of curtains, wings, footlights and dressing rooms.

A month later, an open house celebrated completion of the College Building. The evening program included a male quartet of young townsmen and a demonstration of wireless telegraphy by the science professor.

Removal of the laboratories to the new wing added two rooms to the second floor for other departments, making a total of eight classrooms. In fact, the new construction doubled the effective space for the academic program. Furthermore, for the first time Whittier College could offer on-campus accommodations for boarding students. The proposed rates: $3.50 per week for board; $2.25 per month for room rent in a double furnished room, but as little as $1.50 per month in an unfurnished room.

Total cost for this improvement and completion of the College Building: $15,000. It was necessary to place an $8,000 mortgage against the property—and the Hadley gift of the south five acres was not yet to be.

FACILITIES FOR ATHLETICS were still lacking, as Harry Williams pointed out in reporting the south wing of the building. The boys had leveled off a dirt basketball court and played baseball on Mr. Hadley's field, which served also to raise hay for President Tebbetts' horse and cow. Boys did their running down Painter Avenue, their athletic shirts and knee-length track pants bringing complaints of indecent exposure. The girls exercised and played ball on the leveled front part of the campus, within full view of the street. Dressed in ample middy blouses of denim and below-knee full skirts (with bloomers and hose), their attire was decried by one inflammable trustee as "a shameless leg show." It was still so close to the Nineteenth Century.

Whittier College needed a gymnasium and athletic field. The board obviously could not indebt itself further to construct them. The students decided to go ahead on their own, and the Whittier Board of Trade underwrote the project up to $2,500 in cash.

Washington Hadley made no objection to leveling off an athletic field on the south five acres, though he shrewdly kept title to it as a spur to liquidating the building debt. Scott Keen contracted to grade the ball grounds, put in a cinder track, install a cement drainage ditch. Bleachers and surrounding fence were to come later.

The gymnasium—hardly to be called that—was already under construction in the eucalyptus grove northeast of the building. At first Prof. Harris and the boys intended no more than a kind of open haybarn, mere roof over a basketball court. After this work was under way, a bright idea modified the plan by adding wall units hinged from the top so that, when raised, they would shelter removable bleachers that, in season, could be taken down to the ball grounds. When completed, the gymnasium had "a splendid basketball floor, with clear space of 40 x 72 feet." It cost about $1,000. "The boys did most of the work gratuitously" —and Herbert Tebbetts shingled the roof. Named for his father, Tebbetts Gymnasium was without dressing room or shower, but it was to serve the college well for a score of years.*

---

*Then, moved down to Washington Avenue, it became a part of the Whittier Y.M.C.A. Another twenty years later it came to useful rest behind the Friends Church.

RAISING FURTHER ENDOWMENT funds was not possible until the trustees got rid of "a floating indebtedness of $5,000," accumulated over several years. Half of each year's faculty salaries remained unpaid in June awaiting the next year's income, an uncomfortable lag.

To put the college on a sounder basis, the Yearly Meeting raised the $5,000 sum in 1905 at its annual sessions. Rufus M. Jones was the inspiring speaker of the evening. Editor of *The American Friend*, Haverford philosopher and Quaker scholar, he had given the commencement address at the college a fortnight earlier. He assured Friends at the Yearly Meeting of the great advantage that comes through education. "The evils that sometimes arise from the abuse of the power" acquired by education are not to be compared with "the baneful effects of ignorance."

Professor Rayner Kelsey of the college faculty made the financial appeal. Beginning with President Tebbetts' own pledge of $500, Friends soon subscribed the money needed to clear the deficit.

Letting the $8,000 mortgage ride, the college board announced the next afternoon a campaign for an additional $50,000 endowment. Washington Hadley renewed his offer (made two years earlier) of $10,000 toward this end. The campaign started with a show of zest. President Tebbetts and his wife Imelda were on leave for the fall term, visiting Friends in Great Britain and on the Continent and attending the International Peace Conference at Lucerne. In Tebbetts' absence, Professor Harris served as acting president and Edith Tebbetts (fresh from graduate work at Stanford) taught her father's classes in mathematics. The President was home again by the end of the year. The endowment campaign had made slow progress. During the winter, Washington Hadley agreed to double his offer to $20,000 if the other trustees would raise their sights to $100,000 as the goal and reach it. Some breathed hopes that "Eastern money" might come forth, perhaps from the Smiley family of New York Quakers or from Andrew Carnegie. At a public meeting in March, President Tebbetts himself subscribed $3,000, Dr. Coffin $1,000, and others brought the total to $6,000. In April word did come that Carnegie would give $20,000 after $80,000 in other funds had been raised. This encouraged additional efforts in Whittier. By the end of May, pledges totalled $25,000 in addition to the $20,000 offers from both Hadley and Carnegie. In mid-June the Board of Trade appealed to *all* Whittier citizens to lend a hand. However, $30,000 remained unpledged when the Yearly Meeting sessions opened on June 20, 1906.

At the Friday evening meeting devoted to Education, Dr. W. V. Coffin presided. George L. Hazzard of the Board of Trade, President Tebbetts, Addison Naylor of Berkeley, and others made their speeches. Then, Rayner Kelsey (already resigned from the college faculty) made one last appeal for funds. A number of Friends who had already given pledges, increased them in amount. But the evening closed with the total some $15,000 short of the goal—Carnegie's $20,000 and Hadley's second $10,000 therefore to be lost.

Next day the Yearly Meeting turned to other reports and business. The session nearly ended, Clara Tebbetts presented Professor Kelsey with a gift on behalf of the college alumni. Some Friends were leaving the meeting prior to formal adjournment.

Those already outside heard a round of unQuakerly applause from the church. Something had happened.

As Kelsey accepted with feeling "the beautiful chafing dish" and turned to leave, Marianna Hunt, daughter of Jonathan Bailey, rose to ask him whether the effort to raise the full $100,000 for the college was to continue. Kelsey said there were no further plans.

"Whittier College must go on," she said, "I will give thirty dollars."

The gift so small—the further need so great.

Kelsey thanked her and again turned to go. Then others stood up, pledging similar amounts. Dr. Coffin took charge of the meeting, A. C. Johnson wrote down the names and sums. Joseph Allen of Long Beach gave $500—again Friends applauded. Others followed until only $6,000 remained unpledged.

"Then," in the words of the *Register*, "came a scene that bordered on the dramatic."

After President Tebbetts had offered an earnest prayer . . . , Rev. Amos Cook, an elderly minister, arose and with tears streaming down his face pledged $500—all that he had. . . . Councilman Baldwin advanced to the center of the church and stated that Rev. Cook should not make such a sacrifice. . . . He would be one of five to take the subscription off his hands. A dozen men responded to the call.*

"Another surge of giving swept over the group," as Harris later recalled, "men and women doubling previous gifts until only $2,000 still was unpledged." With a reference to Marianna Hunt's gift that had rekindled hope, Dr. W. V. Coffin "asked everyone who would give thirty dollars to stand—and the entire $100,000 was pledged as almost everybody present responded." Someone else wrote, "It was God working when men had failed."

> All hearts were bowed in humble gratitude, while almost the entire audience wept for joy . . . singing "Praise God from Whom All Blessings Flow."

It was a magnificent achievement and brought to $150,000 the Whittier College endowment in investments, interest-bearing notes, and subscriptions. The college trustees gratefully recognized the liberality of Washington Hadley, and looked upon his gifts as endowing a professorship to be named for him and his late wife Naomi. For some reason never explained, no "chair" was ever established and so designated.

3

THE BEGINNINGS OF ACADEMIC AND
INTERCOLLEGIATE RECOGNITION

INCREASED ENROLLMENT, too, was expected to give financial strength to the young college. In the year 1903-04, the total enrollment was 89, of which 24 were college students. With tuition at $25 per semester for college and $15 for prep students, total income from this source should have been over $3,000 for the year, but it was in fact less than $1,400. However, the purpose of Whittier College was to serve the youth of the Yearly Meeting, and "No worthy student need ever miss an education because of lack of means to meet expenses."

*Thus did Amos Cook save his burial fund. Before long, in fact, he did bury his wife, but remarried in due time, prospered as a citrus rancher, and later gave the $500 *tenfold* to the college.

But Whittier did need more tuition-paying students. In the summer of 1905 Prof. Rayner Kelsey, who doubled in student promotion, looked toward an eventual enrollment of 400. Hoping to recruit some of them, he invited groups of high school seniors to visit the campus during the next spring, and he confidently expected a student body of 150 for the fall term. Such was not to to be. For the year 1906-07 enrollment was still only 87, with tuition income under $1,400.

Strengthening of the college faculty, consequent accreditation of collegiate work, public recognition of student activities—these bore fruit only later, increasing the student body in the years ahead.

THE FACULTY INCREASED at this time until it numbered nine. Most newcomers remained at Whittier only brief periods, but the strength of their work may be suggested by their later careers.

Percy II. Martin (A.B., M.A., Stanford)—fresh from a year of travel and study in Europe—served a year as professor of History and French. Dapper bachelor and "classy dresser," popular with his students, he brought a cosmopolitan culture to the Whittier campus. The college regretted his leaving—"a most loyal and helpful man"—when he returned to Stanford to become in time a distinguished professor of Hispanic-American history.

William H. Matlock replaced him. He also came with a broad European education (Ph.B., Drake, then years at Goettingen, Munich, and Paris) and teaching at Drake, University of Oklahoma, and Berkeley. Remembered as an excellent and devoted teacher, a family man and active Congregationalist, he was keenly interested in the purpose of higher education—"You are to be made intellectual men *that you may be fit moral agents*"—and he urged his students to "wear the old coat and buy the new book." Later he taught German at Pomona College until, during World War I, German was scuttled there and in most colleges.

Olney C. Albertson (B.S., Penn, graduate work at Chicago) came to Whittier in 1904 to fill the chair of science, which he dryly called a davenport, as his teaching spread across physics, chemistry, geology, biology, and physiology. After four years he joined the faculty of Whittier High School, of which he was for long years the principal.

83

During these years, others came and went. Rayner W. Kelsey taught German and history for two years, with responsibilities also in promotion and fund raising. Later he became professor of history at Haverford and curator of its Quaker collection. For two years (1906-08) Lloyd Thompson was assistant in mathematics and Physical Director, the first man so designated. He later completed his studies to practice medicine in San Diego.

Only two of those on the Whittier faculty at this time remained for long periods. Anna Tomlinson (A.B., Whittier, 1905) began her service as college librarian that continued for 24 years, doubling at first in physical education and vocal expression. Howard L. Hockett (B.S., Penn) came in 1906 as instructor in voice and assistant in history. His outstanding contribution to the college extended over a period of forty years.

With notable exceptions, this was a provincial faculty of mid-West Quakers—bright young teachers who rode the trail from one Friends college to the next, looking toward further years of study and professional work.

Whittier College began at once to assume its place among the colleges and universities of California. The preparatory department had already been accredited by the University of California in 1900. Now in 1905 Stanford University, having admitted one Whittier College graduate, placed it "on a par with other colleges in Southern California"—requiring one year of Stanford work before granting its degree. Soon the University of California accepted the lower division work at Whittier College at full credit, and in 1908 accepted a graduate of Whittier to complete his teaching certificate in a year of further work. At the time this was as high an accreditation as that of any institution in southern California.

THE WHITTIER STUDENTS were winning recognition for their own intercollegiate successes during these same years.

In the spring of 1905, the Intercollegiate Prohibition Association held its annual contest in the newly remodeled auditorium of Whittier College. Elwood S. Minchin's oration, "The Triumph of Principle," aroused "storms of applause." With the audience, reported the partisan *Register*, "it was the crowning oration of the evening." Although the Whittier rooters outdid their Occidental rivals on this occasion, the judges coolly awarded first place to Oxy's Mr. Hagerman and but second place to Minchin. However, the next spring Minchin triumphed on the Occidental campus. Then he won the Western Inter-State Oratorical contest of the International Prohibition Association held at Whittier that May.

According to the turgid report: Minchin "tossed his tawny locks like one anxious for the fray" and ambled to the center of the stage "with the attitude of one fairly consumed with a burning desire to enter the arena and slay the rum demon single-handed." He stood and looked about the audience long and hard until it reached an uneasy tension (wondering if he had forgotten his first words), and then he seized the moment and held his auditors under the spell of his flailing oratory until he "delivered the *coup de grâce*"—

> Our fathers struck the shackles from four million slaves. It is for us, the inheritors of their glory, and I trust of their noble patriotism, to rise in the strength of our young Christian manhood and deliver our beloved country from the pernicious despotism of the liquor traffic.

In the national contest three weeks later, with orators from Stanford and the universities of Washington, Oregon, and Texas, Minchin won second place—the Occidental man a close third.

Prohibition was not the only subject, nor mane-tossing the only style. For the annual Peace Oratorical Contest, Esek Perry presented "The Curse of War" in his "calm self-contained manner," and concluded:

> If the flag is so dear that a man will give his life for it, why should he not give to it his loyal service in the interest of peace and good will?

But this low key without gestures did not win him the prize.

In addition to debate and oratory, Professor Harris coached basketball, then quite a new game.

In the fall of 1904, Whittier decided to concentrate on this one sport. Of the five-man team of prep students, only one had had any previous experience in athletics. As yet Whittier had no gymnasium. Its outdoor "dirt" court was surfaced with sand and gravel. But almost all of the games in the winter of 1905 were played in Los Angeles under lights and on indoor wooden floors —the boys not getting home until often 1 a.m. But they beat the State Normal, Throop Polytechnic, Santa Monica Breakers, and Los Angeles High School. For the game with St. Vincent's, the Whittier boys spent three hours riding interurban and street cars and "walking through rain and mud, reaching the gymnasium at ten p.m." They lost that game, against a taller, heavier, better team. And they finally lost their bid for the Amateur Basket Ball League championship for the season. The next year, with the new gymnasium, the Whittier team won many of its games in that league, Aubrey Kramien of the Whittier faculty both coaching and playing center!

In 1907 Professor Harris again coached. Of his team—Paul Todd (captain), Herbert Tebbetts, Austin Marshburn, Preston Osborn, Adrian Mills—all were then college freshmen except Mills, who was first-year prep. Winning from St. Vincent's, University of Southern California (twice), Occidental, and Pomona College—all of these games by large scores—and losing only a return game to St. Vincent's 18-19, gave Whittier College its first intercollegiate championship.

Then this team went north to play the University of California for the state title. "It was a great game from start to finish . . . all our boys played well . . . [but] seemed to be out-classed in weight and strength. . . ." And Whittier lost 22-26. The University at once scheduled a second game, which the Quaker boys also lost. But theirs was a triumph, nonetheless, for the tiny Friends college with ten male students in its entire college department.

These rousing student activities—the "Alma Mater" written by Marjorie and Elwin Little in 1905, set to an Hawaiian tune— the purple and gold—the banquets with speeches and responses —the picnics, too, and tally-ho outings—workdays planting lawn and flowers—the boredom in class and dreaming out through the open window to the spring—the teasing and cheering and slights and hurts—moments of inspiration in chapel and the inner shame of inadequacy—the excitement of intellectual discovery and pride in achievement—Life and God and a pagan world unconverted, the comforting Gospel and the sweet hymns of Jesus—the overlong prayers and the impressive presence of Rufus Jones at commencement . . . these were all part of it.

These were all part of life for the young men and women, most of them Quakers, searching and studying in the academic program that brought Whittier College at last to collegiate standing as the denominational Friends college of California.

THIS WHITTIER COLLEGE was the achievement of Charles E. Tebbetts during the seven years of his presidency. Then, in the spring of 1907, he resigned.

His was a strong feeling for the ministry. Again in 1906 he took up his part-time pastoral work, serving the new Friends Church in East Whittier. He had a distaste for academic detail, perhaps thought that he had done all he could for the college. He knew, too, that some Friends wished him other than he was, more the glad-hander downtown, less the pedagogue wrapped in his thoughts. "He was misunderstood and misinterpreted perhaps by a few who [did] not know his great soul and large heart."

The college board, reluctant to accept his resignation as president, expected him to remain as professor of mathematics and Bible. This he did for a semester. Then in January 1908 he accepted the general secretaryship of the American Friends' Board of Missions, which he served for a decade in Richmond, Indiana.*

Certainly Charles E. Tebbetts contributed significantly to the history of Whittier College. He took hold of a faltering academy and made of it a college. Under his presidency, the four-year college program was developed—the faculty, doubled—the student enrollment, tripled—a permanent endowment, secured—the college building, completed—a gymnasium, built—the board of trustees, enlarged—student body, pitted against its collegiate peers. Already four small classes of college alumni were proving their worth in graduate and professional schools. Toward accomplishing all of this, Tebbetts gave his best—"broad-minded, intellectual, charitable and spiritual," beloved man that he was—

---

*Tebbetts' home remained in Whittier for the year—his sons in college, his daughter Clara (M.A., Earlham) on the faculty until her sudden death—then the family moved to Richmond. Whittier College honored Charles E. Tebbetts with a D.D. in 1916. He returned as pastor of Whittier Friends Church for an interim year (1917-18), then spent his retirement in Whittier.

and he also contributed "largely of his means" as well, his gifts a final total of $50,000.

Without minimizing the contribution of others—particularly that of Dr. W. V. Coffin—it can well be said that Charles E. Tebbets was "the founder" of Whittier as a college.

Yet when he left it in 1907, Whittier was still so young as a college, so small and weak, so dependent upon its preparatory department. Could it live and grow? Could it become fully a college and nothing but a college?

4

A CONTEMPORARY PHILOSOPHY
LIBERALIZING THE FRIENDS' COLLEGE

FINDING A SUCCESSOR immediately available, the college board accepted the resignation of President Tebbetts.

Thomas Newlin, dean of Guilford College, addressed California Yearly Meeting in June, 1907. His theme: "The Place of Denominational Education." The chief function of the church, he said, is education, and he spoke of "the open Bible"—the conscience that education awakens to all truth—and the conflict of ideas that makes for progress.

A sturdy man of average stature, thin sandy hair parted center, pensive eye, drooping moustache—Thomas Newlin was certainly being "looked over" by the college trustees as they listened to him. His presentation and the response to it satisfied them, for they duly elected him the second president of Whittier College.

Thomas Newlin came of an old North Carolinian Quaker family. One forebear was the first treasurer of what became Guilford College, and he was kin to Dr. W. V. Coffin, whose mother was a Newlin and to T[homas] Elwood Newlin, earlier of the board. Thomas Newlin went to Haverford (B.S., 1885), took graduate work at the University of Michigan in pedagogy and chemistry, thereafter returned to Haverford (A.M., 1892 in sociology and political economy). His teaching took him to the presidency of Pacific College (1891-1900). He left to become vice president of Wilmington College (1900-1902) and then dean of Guilford (1902-1907). He was one of those deans "never content to remain out of his classroom longer than overnight," and was considered a good teacher, "a preacher whose ministry was most acceptable to North Carolina Yearly Meeting," a scholar in his field. After organizing the Bible Department at Guilford, he returned to the University of Chicago for a year's study in sociology, philosophy, and systematic theology (Ph.M., 1905). Then back he went to Guilford, "a person whom everyone had liked."

Newlin was unusually well qualified, certainly, to be named president of Whittier College and professor of philosophy in 1907.

Building upon the collegiate basis already established by Charles E. Tebbetts, Thomas Newlin came with "an advanced outlook upon what the college should be." At once he published a statement of policy:

> We believe that education is mainly a moral process and the true end of scholarship is the formation of character, hence much stress must be put upon the moral and religious life . . . [and] study of the Bible. . . .
>
> We put a large interpretation on the statement made by Christ that "the truth shall make you free. . . ." But truth is much more than mere knowledge: it is culture, skill, ethics, religion.

Education he wrote of in terms of society. And he saw agreement in "geologic history and sacred history" as they trace the development of creature life. "But we now live in an age of mind," and must understand the necessity for collegiate education, not only to fit persons for personal success, but to enable them "to make success worthy." Then he called upon California Yearly Meeting to support its college:

> It is our fond hope . . . to send forth strong men and women into active church work, as pastors and missionaries. . . . Help us to establish a fully equipped Biblical department and then dedicate your sons and daughters for this work.

Such was his statement of a liberal and contemporary philosophy. He coupled with it his bid to train the future leadership of Friends in California.

"Faculty and students began to feel they were part of an institution that had attained college rank"—as Harris recalled—and supporters of the college also felt "associated with a larger, growing movement." Newlin mixed well with the people downtown, immediately interested himself in the Board of Trade. He taught a large Sunday School class of adults at the Friends Church, its socials and reunions reported in the *News*, and by invitation he preached not alone in Quaker but in Methodist churches.

FACULTY MEMBERS who carried over from the preceding years included Herbert Harris in English, William Matlock in modern languages, O. C. Albertson in science, Lloyd Thompson as physical director and assistant in mathematics.

Two places already filled before his own appointment, completed Newlin's first faculty: Hazel Howard (A.B., M.A., Penn College, with a year at Bryn Mawr), as professor of Latin; and Emory Ratcliffe (A.B., Earlham, with a year at Wisconsin) as professor of history. Ratcliffe doubled as governor of the men's dormitory and as one of the coaches. He was popular with the students, who loved to tease him—an unfeathered cockerel one morning squawked a beady-eyed greeting from his classroom vase. To raise money for athletic equipment, he and Lloyd Thompson dramatized and presented *Mrs. Wiggs of the Cabbage Patch*. He soon left Whittier, succeeded by Herbert E. White (A.B., Earlham).*

At mid-year 1908, Harry Noble Wright (A.B., Earlham) came from Pacific College to replace Professor Tebbetts in mathematics. Harry Wright was a quiet-spoken young married man—tall and spare, center-parted hair, pince-nez and high collar in the style of that day. He undertook "to build up a strong course in mathematics with application to mechanics and engineering."

To replace O. C. Albertson upon his leaving in 1908, Newlin appointed Charles E. Lewis (A.B., Penn) professor of chemistry and physics, and a second man, Lyman J. Muchmore, professor of biology. Muchmore (A.B., M.A., Williams; B.D., Drew; anatomy and physiology, Harvard) at once offered courses in Botany and Zoology, and promised other courses "if numbers will warrant."

In place of Howard L. Hockett, who returned to Penn College

*Later teaching took Emory Ratcliffe to Fresno State College, head of the department of history, campus and community leader, honored in the naming of Fresno stadium.

in 1910, came Joseph N. Whybark, and the students punned: "Why bark when you can sing?" For some reason not of record, his vocal work ended in mid-November.

These, then, comprised the early faculties of President Newlin. With them, he reshaped the curriculum, set up four courses of study, each with a good spread of requirements in what was later called general education.

I. *Course in Letters*—essentially classics, modern languages and literature.

II. *Course in Social Sciences*—"a cultural course requiring much literary, historical and economic study."

III. *Course in Natural Sciences*—with both German and French and, of course, mathematics as well as the sciences.

IV. *Biblical Course*—with Latin and two years of Greek, English and history, as well as 20 units of Biblical studies in the lower division.

All students met the eighteen-unit requirement of Bible study, spread through the four years—the obligatory two hours a week of physical training without credit—and the senior thesis, no credit.

Such courses of study and the professional preparation of the faculty were not remarkably different from those of other liberal arts colleges at this time.

THE BOARD OF TRUSTEES changed in composition soon after the reorganization of Whittier College at the turn of the century. The two-thirds of the trustees who lived at a distance from Whittier found it difficult to attend monthly board meetings and occasional committee meetings. At the end of the first year, three of these were replaced by Washington Hadley, D. C. Andrews, and Lydia Jackson, all of Whittier. The next year two more gave way for A. C. Johnson and Job Osborn of Whittier. Then Levi Mills replaced T. Elwood Newlin. By the fall of 1903, nine of the twelve trustees lived within easy reach of Dr. W. V. Coffin, president of the board.

There was a tendency to keep certain Quaker families represented on the college board. Thus, upon the death of Dr. Cook, his brother-in-law J. J. Jessup served for two terms, followed by his sister, the doctor's widow, Eva J. Cook. Will M. Hiatt and his aunt, Nannie Arnold, were succeeded by her brother J. C. Hiatt (Will's father) and then by brother-in-law H. D. Williams. T. Elwood Newlin and his father-in-law Washington Hadley were followed by the latter's daughter, Emilie Hadley. These families had supported the college from its pioneer beginnings.

The Board of Trustees of Whittier College [Inc.], with its membership increased to fifteen in 1906, was legally "a self-perpetuating body." But it thought of the college as being "the child of the Yearly Meeting," and therefore worthy of its denominational support.

When Thomas Newlin became president of Whittier College in 1907, a $10,000 debt, largely the mortgage incurred in completing the building, remained unpaid. In the closing hours of Yearly Meeting 1906 (with its dramatic culmination of the endowment campaign), Imelda A. Tebbetts had said that the Woman's Auxiliary would solicit funds to pay off this debt. Again Washington Hadley offered "the strip of ground lying just south of the College property" upon completion of this task. By April 1908 the $10,000 mortgage was at last cancelled and the gift of land secured. At Yearly Meeting that June, the trustees ceremoniously burned the mortgage, and thanked the Woman's Auxiliary and especially Imelda Tebbetts for their part in raising money and securing subscriptions—$2,500 of the total had passed through their treasury.

THE WOMAN'S AUXILIARY was already several years old. Founded in November 1904 through the efforts of Mrs. Tebbetts, Susan Johnson, and others, it started with 41 members, Clara Hiatt (Mrs. Will M.) the first president, Bertha Coffin (Mrs. John E.) the first secretary. Its purpose was to co-operate with the trustees, faculty, and students of Whittier College in their efforts to improve the buildings and grounds and to increase community interest in the college. Membership was open to all of the women of Whittier and nearby, indeed to any woman upon payment of the $1 annual dues. Auxiliary meetings monthly during the school year attended to items of business, largely carried on by committees, and heard reports on college problems, plans, and progress. Then the women got busy raising—and thereupon spending—money.

First they compiled and published a cook book. Entitled *Good Things to Eat and How to Prepare Them*—the best recipes from Quaker households—it sold for $1 a copy. By mid-January the Auxiliary discussed "how to dispose of the cash on hand, which amounts to about $190." The decision: to furnish the Association Hall in the new south wing of the college building. At Yearly Meeting time in 1905, the Auxiliary reported 351 cookbooks sold. But it had also been busy "catering for dinners, banquets, receptions and luncheons," and it announced its gross receipts for the year as $1,174.04, of which $447.10 had already been expended on college furnishings.

Through its varied efforts, the Woman's Auxiliary raised an average of more than $1,000 annually during its first four decades, and an average of twice as much thereafter by means of catering, cooked food sales, sewing bees, bazaars, rummage sales. This money the committees spent for campus improvements and dormitory furnishings, academic equipment and library books, successive pianos and (later) student loans. The personal comfort and welfare of the students was always the chief interest of the Auxiliary and earned the gratitude of successive generations.

The total amount raised by the Auxiliary and others in 1908 to pay off the mortgage and thus secure the strip of land south of the campus was over $12,500—and this was hardly too much. For the strip of land by this late date was not entirely Washington Hadley's to give; his children had acquired an interest in the lots fronting on Painter Avenue as part of the residue of the P.L.&W. Co. Therefore, when Washington Hadley placed the deed in escrow, it was with the understanding that the college would pay his son Albert Hadley $2,400 "to cover the interest of himself and others in said strip of land." Whittier College paid this sum on June 19, 1908, just prior to Yearly Meeting. At long last the south five acres belonged to the campus—fifteen years after the original offer. The athletic field, already developed on it, became known as Hadley Field.

A DORMITORY BUILDING for women was the next immediate need. Girls on the third floor of the main college building with boys on the fourth proved unsatisfactory, and in 1908 the girls were housed in the home of Milea T. Tomlinson, a half block from the campus, and the boys occupied the two upper floors unmolested.

In May 1909 the college announced the appointment of Hunt and Grey of Los Angeles as architects to develop a general plan for the Whittier College campus and buildings, the first of successive Master Plans. A college library building was to have priority. At Yearly Meeting in June, Dr. W. V. Coffin announced the board's decision to raise $20,000 for this purpose. However, later that summer, the board decided that a dormitory was the more pressing need.

The architects designed a two-story frame structure "with bungalow effect," low-pitched roof, overhanging eaves, and redwood siding. Girls' Cottage was to have a hot air furnace and electric lights—"all conveniences possible." The first floor consisted of a large dining hall seating eighty to a hundred, with ample kitchen, and reception hall for the use of both boys and girls. The upper floor, with double rooms, accommodated twenty girls. This simple building, uncompromisingly rectangular to begin with, was located along the north boundary of the original campus, on the far side of the arroyo, which was then crossed by a footbridge.* The contract price was $3,500, though with extras the cost was more nearly $4,000. It was ready for use by December 1909, and the Woman's Auxiliary furnished the rooms.

EXTRA-CURRICULAR activities developed further with the increase in enrollments. During Newlin's first year, there were 112 students, 45 of them in the college department. This was almost 30% greater than the total for the preceding year, but there were still only 15 college men.

Newlin believed in athletics; he had played football at Haverford. College men, he felt, needed more exercise than they would take "without special incentive." For him

---

*Redwood Hall, as it was later and affectionately called, occupied the southeast portion of the site of the Bonnie Bell Wardman Library. It was removed in 1961 to the tennis courts along Earlham Drive, and its redwood siding hidden by the stucco of remodeling. The footbridge later gave way to a storm drain and the picturesque arroyo was lost in the campus grading.

WHITTIER COLLEGE, INC. 18. Dr. W. V. Coffin, president of board. 19. Washington Hadley, trustee and benefactor. CHARLES E. TEBBETTS, first college president. 21. Whittier lege "charter."

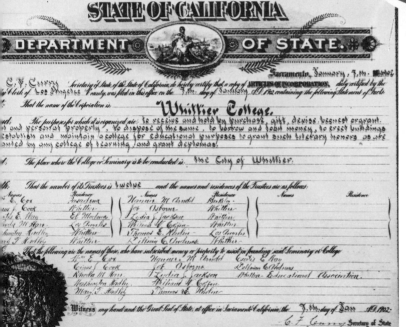

22. Profs. H. E. Harris and Susan Johnson. 23. First senior class (1904).

24. THOMAS NEWLIN, second president. 25. FACULTY-STUDENT OUTING—Dr. Allen, center, Prof. and Mrs. Ostrom, front l. and r. 26. TALLY-HO hack for student outing. 27. GIRLS' DORMITORY, faculty raid on fudge party. 28. BASKETBALL, first intercollegiate champions (1907). 29. COMMUNITY MONUMENT to John Greenleaf Whittier (1910).

1. L. Thompson, 2. E. Sharpless, 3. H. E. Harris, 4. W. Blair. 5. E. Perry.
6. A. Mills, 7. H. E. Tebbetts, 8. P. Todd, 9. A. Marshburn, 10. P. Osborn.

30. FOOTBALL, first Poet victory over Oxy (1914) on Hadley field. 31. "CHEM LAB" on ground floor of College Building, Prof. Ostrom. 32. CAMPUS MAP, senior thesis by S. C. Pickett (1911), showing arroyos. 33. WINDING THE MAYPOLE (*ca.* 1910). 34. SENIOR PLAY: *Yzdra* presented in first college amphitheater (1912).

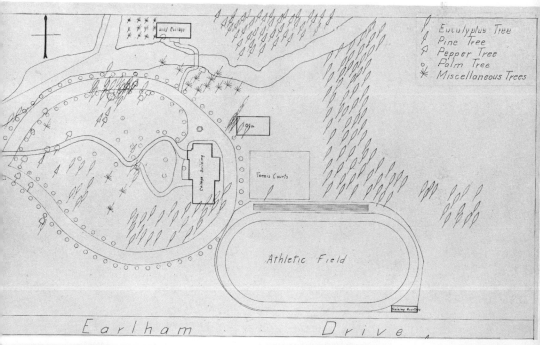

35. ABSALOM ROSENBERGER, third president of Whittier College. 36. FLORABEL ROSEN-BERGER, registrar and professor. 37. "GREATER WHITTIER COLLEGE," master plan of 1917. 38. TEBBETTS GYMNASIUM (see note below). 39. GIRLS' COTTAGE, showing footbridge (*ca.* 1910). 40. NAYLOR HALL, the new chemistry building, built in 1918.

NOTE. The above view, taken *ca.* 1920, shows Tebbetts Gymnasium after remodeling. The hinged wall units, raised above temporary bleachers, gave way to permanent installation of enclosed seating.

the aim of all college athletic work should be the development of each individual of the student body rather than, as it sometimes appears, the over-training of the few who least need physical development.

No football had been played at Whittier College for a decade. Then in the fall of 1907, some 37 men and boys signed up for the new game of American that was replacing Rugby football. It was a motley turnout as pictured in make-do outfits. Assisting Lloyd Thompson as coach was Emory Ratcliffe, who had played quarterback at Earlham, and he himself played quarter on the Whittier team in its preliminary games. That season the Quaker team lost all of its collegiate games, played against Occidental, Pomona, and University of Southern California. But after beating the San Diego Y.M.C.A. team to close the season, President Newlin cheered the boys—"had never seen such a good record made by a team in its first season." The next fall, the football team was hardly more successful. It lost to Occidental 6-25, the only consolation being a spectacular 75-yard run by "Big" Noble Renneker upon interception of an onside kick.

Basketball was the game in which Whittier teams shone during these years, continuing the splendid record begun under Professor Harris. Ratcliffe coached a championship team for the college in the winter of 1908. It overwhelmingly defeated Occidental in the opening game, then lost to Pomona and U.S.C. But in return games Whittier beat both U.S.C. and Pomona and then won the play-offs from U.S.C. (27-19) and from Pomona College (26-17). This team comprised "Little" Nolle Renneker (a steady point-maker), Rollin Holton, Herbert Tebbetts, Warren Blair, and Wendell McCaslin. They played the Stockton Y.M.C.A. for the state championship, losing by a close score. The next winter Harris again coached. His Whittier boys won the southern California collegiate championship, beating Occidental (37-24), Pomona (21-6), and U.S.C. And in the winter of 1910, Harris's team again took the college basketball championship, the fourth in succession.

Baseball was played, too, but never with such success, and there were track meets. Most of the men and boys enjoyed some form of physical activity and sport, as did also the girls.

The May Day Festival was always an occasion for the girls to shine. Inspired by a similar celebration at Earlham, the rites of spring on the Whittier campus became an annual event (1907-1919) under the direction of Anna Tomlinson. Whittier's first May Day began early in the afternoon and carried on into the evening, lighted by "gay hued lanterns suspended from branches."

> Forty dainty pink and white clad girls, winding the May pole, the crowning of the pretty May Queen, Miss Gertrude Mills, a gypsy tambourine drill by ten girls attired as gypsy maidens, the flag raising, songs, and excellent music by the State School band, were features that aided in making the affair a success.

Each year there were novelties and variations. In 1910 the Queen of May enthroned was drawn by four handsome heralds in white ducks—the music was "A Midsummer Night" cantata—and, as always, the ritual winding of the Maypole, primordial symbol of life's springtime renewal. The front campus was the scene, thus, of community festivity. Alumnae served refreshments, the Auxiliary sold homemade candy.

The previous June (1909) Professor Harris had directed *A Midsummer-Night's Dream*, staged on the front campus. He took advantage of "the tree-covered hillside" as proper setting for Shakespeare's woodsy comedy of moonlight madness, magic and mistakes. The players included those who earlier in the year had participated in football and basketball, glee clubs and forensics.*

A yet more pretentious undertaking was the commencement play for 1910, *The Sunken Bell* by Gerhardt Hauptmann, for which three of the seniors—Paul Todd, Edna Thornburg, Cora Scheurer—made the translation. (Todd spoke fluent German, having tramped Europe the previous year with Professor Harris, and all were students of Professor Matlock.) The seniors staged their play in the eucalyptus grove back of the main building. This grove was on higher ground than Hadley Field, upon which the audience sat, chairs brought up from the Friends Church to supplement the movable bleachers, one section of which crashed—

*Samuel Pickett, Albert Marshburn, Nofle Renneker, William Feeler, George H. Bell, Frank Crites, William Blount, Paul Todd—who in later life became actuary, professor, rancher, teacher, college president, business administrator, doctor, engineer.

happily without hurt. As the *News* reported, "anxious murmurs were hushed," and then—

> A sudden flash of light, and the amphitheatre was flooded with splendor. Bathed in the golden glow, our popular high brow, Professor Harris, stepped forward, and interpreted the lesson of the drama in a few well chosen words. He retired, and the enchantment of the night began—

the romantic and symbolic story of Heinrich the bell founder who left the world of wife and village for the mountain nymph Rautendelein. A worthy collegiate undertaking, *The Sunken Bell* involved most of the students in school, in one way or another. It was long remembered—the witchery of the night, the charm of the story.

The excitement of competitive forensics was also a part of these years. Burtis Healton finally triumphed on the rostrum where once as a prep boy he had seemed so small and thin of voice. In the spring of 1909 he returned to Simpson Auditorium in Los Angeles and won the Peace Oratorical Contest, honor for the college and $100 for himself.

Certainly, Whittier College was doing well under President Newlin—but there was growing opposition to his liberalizing of the denominational Quaker college.

5

FUNDAMENTALIST ATTACKS
AND REAFFIRMATION OF LIBERAL PRINCIPLES

THE DOCTRINAL CONFLICT that involved Whittier College in 1910 marked the widening differences among Friends comprising California Yearly Meeting. They shared varying degrees of evangelical orthodoxy.

The *more-doctrinaire* of the evangelical Friends held to that Bible-centered and literal orthodoxy which shortly became known as Fundamentalism. Their principal concerns were personal salvation, evangelism, church extension, missions. Their interest in education was that it should serve these ends.

The *less-doctrinaire* Friends of the Yearly Meeting held to a

97

liberal interpretation of orthodoxy that was soon tagged Modernism. They were concerned for personal fulfillment, moral responsibility, social problems, international peace. Their chief preoccupation was Education, not conceived as vocational or Bible training, but as the liberal cultivation of intelligence and character.

Within the Yearly Meeting, Whittier College under Thomas Newlin's presidency became the focus for this enlightened orthodoxy. The focus for militant evangelism became the Training School for Christian Workers, which had moved from Whittier to Los Angeles in 1901. By 1907 it had completed its new 54-room building in nearby Huntington Park, an easy car ride from Whittier.*

During its first decade (1900-1910), the Training School was unofficially tied to California Yearly Meeting through its Board of Missions, whose superintendent for five years, Irving H. Cammack, took a leading part in its development. His annual reports as superintendent of Missions kept the Yearly Meeting well informed as to its progress.

In 1907 the Board of Missions named as its superintendent a zealous young missionary, Dana Thomas, recently returned from afar and put in charge of buying supplies for the several missions in Central America and Alaska. The Board expressed concern that money entrusted to it "go as far as possible," and the new superintendent spoke up for "honest business dealings in the foreign field." The Mission Board then shortly elected him its president as well as superintendent. Within another year he was recorded a Friends minister, named co-editor (with Nannie Arnold) of the *Pacific Friend*, and appointed Superintendent of the Training School.

In the summer of 1909 the Training School under his leadership constructed a 25-room addition to its large building, doubling its dormitory and classroom facilities. It offered a three-year Biblical course to prepare ministers, missionaries, and church school teachers. Its ten or more instructors were mostly ministers, part-time or retired pastors.

*There through the years, it trained missionaries and evangelists, many of whom became pastors of the Friends churches of California Yearly Meeting. Much later it became Pacific Bible College, moved in time to Azusa and at last became Azusa Pacific College, with one or two Quaker members on its board into the 1960's.

In addition to this course, the Training School under its new superintendent provided

> secular education from the kindergarten upward, under teachers who are not only well qualified in a popular sense, but who also have a deep Christian experience, and who will not ignore nor slight their opportunity to lead their pupils to God in order to prepare them for true manhood and womanhood.

These academic classes, including the high-school grades, were "preparing [pupils] for college or for business under healthful Christian influences." And this high school work brought the Training School into direct competition with the Preparatory Department of Whittier College, which was (after all) the official denominational college of the Yearly Meeting. Furthermore, it divided the loyalties and financial support of Friends in their educational endeavors.

But the Training School and those who led it now challenged Whittier College in other ways.

By implication the college was charged with Modernism in the pages of the *Pacific Friend*. One blast against "Modern Scientific Infidelity" immediately followed the column reporting the college commencement of 1908. Some months later the new co-editor (over his initials) decried the "advanced" and shocking views on religion, morality, and marriage openly taught in colleges and universities. Later, the journal reprinted a virulent Methodist sermon on the "bold infidelity" of Charles W. Eliot, former president of Harvard.

In the winter of 1909-1910 the Training School attacked Whittier College directly. Its board members signed a lengthy resolution addressed to the Board of Trustees of Whittier College, stating:

> 1. That there is within California Yearly Meeting a relatively large number of persons . . . whose hearts are yearning for an educational institution—a college—in which there shall be much religious instruction given, and all of it from the standpoint of the evangelical faith.

Such a college, it went on, must only employ as officers and teachers persons fully in harmony with a creedal statement of the sort they then set forth:

. . . unshaken faith in the Divine inspiration and authority of the Bible . . . the creation and fall of man . . . origin and nature of human sin . . . hopeless state of man without redemption . . . Godhead of Jesus Christ . . . our Redeemer; His birth of a virgin mother . . . sinlessness . . . perfect example . . . death as a ransom for lost souls . . . His future coming to reign with His saints. . . .

Furthermore, the president and each professor "must give clear evidence of regeneration and sanctification," and evangelistic zeal for the saving of student souls.

2. We believe that such an institution . . . teaching positive Christianity . . . and breaking with the customs of the world by prohibiting all forms of immorality, and excluding competitive athletics . . .

would receive the support of Christians "of various denominations." The petitioners were also certain that such a college "would very closely unite the members of California Yearly Meeting in their educational interests."

Then came the threat of an alternative:

3. We have been urged to open such a college—evangelical in its teachings . . . and showing no leaning whatever toward that form of infidelity known as "The New Theology."

However, it concluded, *if Whittier College would hew to its evangelistic line*, the Training School would confine itself to the preparation of missionaries. In this way "the educational interest of the Yearly Meeting might be perfectly harmonized, and the support of the College greatly increased."

Those signing this communication were [Dr.] W. V. Marshburn, president of the Training School board, L. Maria Deane, secretary, and William P. Hunnicutt, William K. Green, Ervin G. Taber and others. Approving it by letter was the venerable Quaker evangelist, John Henry Douglas. As this resolution was an action of the board, the name of the superintendent of the school was, of course, not signed to it.

The Whittier College trustees received this challenge, and answered it on January 26, 1910. They pointed out that, after all, they were "under the appointment of California Yearly Meeting" and that they felt deeply their responsibility. Then they declared "without hesitation" that "Whittier College stands definitely and squarely for the Christianity of the New Testament in all its evangelical meaning." But they declared further that it stood

> for the intellectual and spiritual culture of young men and young women . . . [and proposed] that the college shall move forward along these lines in the great work which we believe God has called it into existence to do.

This letter was signed by [Dr.] W. V. Coffin and Lydia Jackson as president and secretary of the college board.

But this "ultimatum"—as the college called it—required a fuller answer, which was published as the February 1910 issue of the *Bulletin* under the title, "The Religious Situation in our College Life." It pointed out that, although "the College aims to be thoroughly Christian without being sectarian," 60% of the students were Friends and fully 95% were members of evangelical churches—and no single student actively opposed the church or Christianity.

Copies of the Training School resolution, sent by the college to prominent Friends, Quaker colleges, and other colleges in southern California, brought responses of "sympathy and sometimes indignation." There was surprise that members of the Training School board—"some who had received so much from the College"*—had been induced to sign such a "presumptuous document." And the point was not lost that the Training School had no organic connection with the Yearly Meeting.

The orthodoxy of Whittier College was affirmed. It made "no attempt to discredit any portion of [the Bible], nor to cast any doubt upon any doctrine of evangelical faith." The college found itself in harmony with other Friends colleges, and in agreement with the statement of faith set forth by the Yearly Meeting. It

---

*Indeed the Marshburn, Hunnicutt, Taber, and Douglas children and/or grandchildren had been, were then, or would soon be prominent students of Whittier College—and Mrs. William K. Green, Mrs. Mabel Douglas, Albert Marshburn, Lola and Anna Bell Taber served its faculty at one time or another.

solicited the support of all Christian people, but it did not propose "to have the standard of the College fixed by an outside institution."

Furthermore: "We expect to go to the Bible, experience, and history to find out what is correct doctrine rather than to any man or company of men."

Reliance upon "experience"—that is, direct religious experience, spiritual insight, or what other branches of the Society of Friends still termed the Inner Light—was thus reaffirmed as a guide in matters of faith and practice. It was but a small intrusion of liberalism, however, in a defense of moderate orthodoxy.

But it was scalps, not sophistry, that the holy warriors sought. The word continued to be noised about that President Newlin and the professors were "unsound." In an evident attempt to smoke out such charges so as to answer them, the college board passed a resolution authorizing each of its members

> to trace, and secure in writing, any and every charge, of which he may acquire any knowledge, against any member or members of the college faculty, and report said charges to the board that it may fully investigate, and correct anything which may be wrong.*

Such a written accusation was at last made.

William Penn Hunnicutt was a quiet and erect man, a staunchly evangelical Friend. He was a Whittier pioneer from Virginia by way of Ohio, along with the Jonathan Baileys. His sons were identified with Whittier College in the 1890's; his daughter Martha was a missionary. In the spring of 1910 Penn Hunnicutt wished to transfer his membership from the Whittier Friends Church to Huntington Park. He and Caroline Hunnicutt, wife of his last years—a fervent minister and zealous pastor —were already identified with the Training School. Some Friends in the Whittier Meeting objected, however, to releasing Penn Hunnicutt to another meeting without first trying to reconcile his personal differences with others in the Meeting. There-

---

*The only copy of this strange document is undated, but it is signed by W. V. Coffin and Lydia Jackson, and was found among college papers of Thomas Newlin's time. The minutes of the Board of Trustees for this entire period (1900-1918) have been lost for some decades, and the most persistent search has not located them.

fore his transfer was withheld unless he would first present "a number of charges in writing concerning the doctrinal views and teachings of Thomas Newlin and other teachers at the College." This he did—and in so doing he helped in a very real way to clear the air.

At a called meeting of the Whittier Meeting on Ministry and Oversight, the clerk asked President Newlin to speak to the accusations. After some preliminary remarks "concerning his experience as a student of science, history and the Bible,"

> Thomas Newlin answered the charges preferred against him in the order in which they were presented. Four vital questions concerning his doctrinal belief were . . . answered satisfactorily.

The Meeting then minuted, upon formal motion, its complete exoneration of Thomas Newlin "from all charges brought against him . . . concerning unbelief in any vital doctrine of the Friends Church," and those sitting in this embarrassing judgment extended to him "the right hand of fellowship and good will."

As for charges against the faculty, there was finally but one, and that one was leveled at Susan H. Johnson. Although she had not been on the faculty list for several years, she was a member of the student committee of the college board (though it was not she but her husband who was the trustee). The charge preferred against her was "concerning her opinion [sic] of card playing, dancing and theater going." What she responded is not of record, but she too was "entirely exonerated by vote of the meeting."

These ministers, elders, and overseers recorded a further minute on "the importance of brotherly love and harmony among members of the church."

> We sincerely deplore anything and everything that tends to disturb this love and harmony . . . hunting and watching for the faults of our fellows, or publishing them to others. . . . [This] is not in accord with the Golden Rule, or the spirit of the Christ as taught in the Scriptures, and is subversive to the welfare of the church.

With this vindication by the Whittier Friends Church, ended the doctrinal attack upon the college of 1910, spearheaded by those associated with the Training School. But the episode was not without its sequel.*

THE CHALLENGE OF THE Training School did make one thing clear. Some Friends did not feel that Whittier College was meeting all of the educational needs of California Yearly Meeting.

Back in 1899, when it was first proposed that a training school be started in Whittier, Nannie Arnold, as editor of the earlier *Christian Workman*, suggested that Whittier College should have a department or school of theology that would give "special training in Bible study for those who are to minister in the word." The college gave Bible courses—required such courses of all students —but it was only after the Training School "ultimatum" in the winter of 1910 that Whittier established and staffed a department of religion and appealed to the Yearly Meeting for funds to support it. The August 1910 *Bulletin* then featured "The Biblical Department / Our New Faculty / [and] Catalogue of David J. Lewis Library." William Raybright Lewis (M.A., Friends) headed this new work, which included Biblical History, Church History, Life of Christ, Missions, and Homiletics.

In his annual report that summer President Newlin gave his final reply to the criticism that had been directed at him and at the college. It was not the business of the college, he said, to give "superficial work in religious education," but to deal with "fundamental ideals that are eternal."

> Religion does not consist in the affirmation or denial of certain propositions, but it is a light and atmosphere that gives all propositions new meaning.

"Education," he asserted, "is the real work of the church," and added that "this includes evangelism and missionary work." Then he said:

> In college our students are taught and encouraged to analyze, compare, and dissect . . . animals, plants, rocks, theorems, philosophy, literature and creeds.

*The superintendent soon terminated his work for the Training School, his co-editorship of the *Pacific Friend*, his superintendency and presidency of the Board of Missions. His asserted mismanagement of certain mission funds led to a reorganization of that Board, and his leadership of those attacking the religious integrity of the college ended.

A creed, he said, was only valuable "so far as it has a firm grasp on truth."

> To believe that there is any conflict in the realm of truth is polytheism. The student today must be taught to believe in one God, the God of science, of history, of philosophy, of mathematics and of religion. And the ultimate vindication of truth must rest on the findings of the human heart and mind in one's own experience. . . .

This was a liberal credo, as seen in the context of that time and place. It was a far cry from yielding to the demands of a restricted orthodoxy.

Not without significance in the summer of 1910 was a movement started in the city of Whittier—and promoted with enthusiasm by the *News*—to erect a monument to John Greenleaf Whittier, and to place it "on the campus of Whittier College, as that institution bears the name of the great man." Young and old in the community contributed to build the brick memorial surmounted by a light and bearing a bronze tablet, with the poet's portrait in bas-relief and verses he had written to the new-born town in 1887.

At the springtime dedication in May 1911, President Newlin read further lines by Whittier that caught something of his own views on Education:

> Yet when did age transfer to youth
> The hard-earned lessons of today?
> Each life must learn the taste of truth,
> Each foot must feel its way.

Those present remembered the John Greenleaf Whittier centennial (December 17, 1907) when Professor Tebbetts had read the same lines, together with the letter that Whittier had written to the founders of the Friends' colony and college, hoping that their Quakerism would be of "the old practical kind . . . not relying on creed and dogma, but upon faithful obedience to the voice of God in the soul." On another and similar occasion the poet had written that his sympathies were all with "the Broad Church of Humanity."

Upon this Rock, suggested by John Greenleaf Whittier's broad tolerance, Thomas Newlin wanted to build Whittier College.

6

MOVING FORWARD WITH THE
COLLEGIATE PROGRAM AND ACTIVITIES

RESIGNATION OF FOUR professors during the springtime of doctrinal controversy may have had no direct relation to it, and the four seem to have left Whittier for assorted personal reasons. Three of them, however, were notably "liberal" members of the faculty—three of them were Friends—three of them returned to serve Whittier College again.

To replace Harris in English, came Mark Wilcox (A.B., Oberlin; A.M., Park College). Already a magazine writer, he soon married and left teaching for ranching. Following him in 1913 was Herbert F. Allen (A.B., M.A., South Dakota; Ph.D., Michigan), who came from four years' teaching at College of the Pacific. He was the first Whittier professor with a doctorate. An Episcopalian, tall and slender bachelor, he was a gifted teacher, stimulating his students' interests in contemporary ideas.

To replace Matlock in modern languages, Newlin appointed two mature women: Sareva Dowell (graduate work at Chicago as well as study abroad) to teach romance languages, and Mabel H. Douglas (A.B., Bryn Mawr) to teach German. The daughter-in-law of the aged evangelist, John Henry Douglas, her appointment may have been a conciliatory gesture toward the college critics. She was a capable teacher and, together with her two sons, Bruce and Don, came to fill an important place in the college.

To replace Wright in mathematics, the college named Russell Wilson, a solid man who in addition to his teaching coached football. To replace Lewis in chemistry and physics, Leslie C. Nanney (B.S., Earlham) served a year. Following him at the college was Gustaf E. Ostrom (A.B.,M.S., Augustana, graduate work at Illinois), who became a strong member of the faculty, continuing for nearly three decades.

Others joined the Whittier faculty to serve notably, briefer or longer periods: Esek Perry (A.B., Whittier, 1907; B.D., U.S.C.), as professor of Biblical literature and history; William T. Boyce (A.B., Guilford; A.B., Haverford; A.M., Harvard), as professor of history; Howard L. Hockett, returning to direct the School of Music.

Curricular modifications during the years 1910-1915 occurred as professors shaped their departments and courses.

Of special interest, in view of the changing times and the recent conflict, was the course in Evolution first scheduled by Professor Muchmore in 1913. Reflected in the college catalog was the care taken to forefend fundamentalist attack. Muchmore, a kindly man and former minister, lectured on the history of evolution before Darwin, as well as "the present theories and their problems with reference to variation, heredity and genetics. . . ." His purpose was "not to bolster up a theory but to learn the truth" and "to discover a reasonable and scientific explanation of God's plan for the universe."

Chemistry did not challenge contemporary orthodoxies, and by Lutheran predisposition Ostrom held scientific laws firmly within a theistic framework.

From the first he showed himself a strong department man. By 1914 he secured a change of college policy to insure the student's declaration of his major by the end of the freshman year; to place the senior thesis firmly in the hands of the department head (not the president of the college as previously); and to grant the B.S. degree for science majors. He secured ground floor rooms in the south wing of the main building—space vacated by the student dining hall—and developed improved laboratories. Soon the number of his majors increased.

Most significant of the academic developments at this time was the gradual elimination of the Preparatory Department. The trustees made their bold decision to do this in the stormy spring of 1910 when the preps still numbered 61 and college students only 47. The board announced that Whittier College would have no first-year preparatory class in the fall, and that the Preparatory Department would close with graduation of its last class in 1913. For the year 1913-14, Whittier's enrollment of college students reached 103. For the first time in the 25 years of successive academic ventures, Whittier was "all college."*

*University of Southern California, Pomona College and Occidental discontinued their preparatory departments but a few years earlier—and Occidental almost did away with its women in 1912, that disaster averted to keep the Presbyterian college coeducational. These institutions were larger and stronger than Whittier. For the fall of 1915, Pomona limited its freshman class to 200; Occidental its freshman class to 150. At that time the *total* enrollment at Whittier was but 130.

STUDENT LIFE AT WHITTIER became more collegiate with the phasing out of the Preparatory Department. There were fewer prepish pranks—as when freshmen had transferred Professor Matlock's prize rooster and some of Muchmore's hens to President Newlin's chicken coop, to his chagrin and unaccustomed anger—or when a nanny goat was hoisted to the belfry for the public kidding of Professor Nanney—or when the dignified seniors were bugled through the town in their pajamas.

During those years of transition, one of the college classes (that of '12) made two gifts to Whittier College. As freshmen they planted a California liveoak tree on the edge of the arroyo beyond which Girls' Cottage (Redwood) was soon to be built—and through the succeeding three-score years it became a magnificent spreading specimen. Then, as seniors, they decided to leave on the campus a yet more enduring gift—a great rock, largest they could transport.

Three senior men—Frank Crites, Nofle Renneker, Milton White—found the boulder they wanted up above Sierra Madre, secured permission to remove it, undertook (with the help of Austin Marshburn '10 and his team) to bring it to the campus. After dislodging the one-or-two-ton granite, they slid it down the mountainside onto the wagon, which they eased out to the road for the creaking 18-mile haul back to Whittier. Upon arrival at 2 a.m., they unloaded The Rock on the front campus—where it caused morning comment and consternation. Men of the junior class felt challenged by this heroic achievement, and that night dug a deep hole into which they tumbled The Rock, all but burying it. Next night ensuing, after the President's Reception, the three seniors used a hand crane to raise The Rock, imbedding it in reinforced concrete—the senior women rewarding them with "a delicious breakfast" as they watched the sun rise over the hill. . . .

Painting class numerals on The Rock soon came to be the accepted recognition for winning the traditional tussle between the freshman and sophomore men, which in 1914 took the form of a pole-rush.*

*The smaller of the two contending classes defended its pennant fastened atop a high pole. The larger class (limited to three additional men) had half an hour in which to remove the pennant. It was a supervised free-for-all. The invaders tried to bind and remove enough of the defenders to allow one of their own number to shinny up the pole for the colors.

With the growing number of college students and the passing of the preparatory students, the time came for reorganizing the student body. A new constitution, sharply debated, won approval in the spring of 1913. Gone were the regulations regarding behavior in study hall. The Associated Students gained the responsibility for self government, with a Joint Committee (of students, faculty, trustees, alumni) consulted "on matters of importance and general policy." The first president under this new constitution was J. Worthington Means, a slightly older married senior. He was the kind of man who, after losing his forearm in a dynamiting accident, yet turned out for football. During its first year 1913-14, the Associated Students made notable progress and prepared to establish the *Quaker Campus* as a weekly paper.

Through a span of years the *Acropolis* appeared four to six times a year, more or less as a literary magazine but with a commencement issue. With the advent of the *Quaker Campus*, the *Acropolis* appeared in 1915 again as an annual, as it had been a decade earlier. Including the usual yearbook features, it was first in a series that continued (with but one year's interruption) for the next half century.

It was through the *Quaker Campus* that the dynamics of student life and self-government manifested itself. Named its editor, Harold H. Story, then a sophomore, issued the first Q.C. on September 1, 1914. Story was an intense young Friend with Byronic tie and wavy hair. His statement of editorial policy was forthright, recognizing that as editor he was "subject to the direction of the student body," but he expected to print all the college news, columns of unrestrained student opinion, and editorials expressing his own liberal views. As the year wore on, he tried, as a Quaker pacifist, to arouse his fellow students, complacent about the fighting in remote Europe, to alert them to the propaganda that was already beginning to inch the United States toward war. Nor were his efforts confined to the Whittier College campus. He represented Whittier at a war-protest meeting in Los Angeles; he edited a Socialist page in the Whittier *News* supporting N. A. Richardson for governor; he won second place in a nation-wide essay contest on International Arbitration. But it was through his strong and at times flaming editorials in the

Quaker Campus that Harold Story dramatized Whittier's "coming of age" as a liberal arts college.

Establishment of the Acolytes was a related symbol of the changing college. The Athenaeum, as the traditional literary society, faded away during these years and died several deaths before its demise in 1915. A number of its functions—encouraging discussion, creative writing, forensics, dramatic production—were taken up by other organizations. One of these was a loosely structured but very selective society of twelve members, the Acolytes, sponsored by Dr. Herbert Allen with Albert Stone the first "Prometheus," as the presiding Head-Light was called. Although Story editorialized against fraternities in his first issue of the Q.C.—respecting the Quaker testimony against secret societies—he became one of the founding Acolytes. Upon the principle that nothing is too good or too bad to investigate in "an open, broadminded, liberal, unprejudiced manner," each meeting of the club was devoted to a paper or presentation, followed by uninhibited discussion. Topics included: Bernhardi's new book on German nationalism, the philosophies of Schopenhauer and Nietzsche, Humor, Eugenics, Socialism, Rousseau. The year ended with the informal initiation of new members after midnight on the campus—the ritual derived from Promethean legendry—the candidates led blindfold up winding paths into the hills "not far from Caucasus" . . . and it all ended with breakfast at 4 a.m. There followed a formal evening in the City (Los Angeles)—elaborate dinner, speeches, election of new Headlight (Story)—attendance at the Burbank Theatre (pre-burlesque) to see *Polly of the Circus*.

About such doings, elder Friends did not feel easy. Other student activities were more to be encouraged—the work of the Y.M.C.A. and Y.W.C.A., whose prayer meetings at Wednesday chapel time brought together most of the students. There were also annual series of evangelistic meetings. Student leaders attended Y conferences at Pacific Grove. Regional secretaries—like Harry F. Henderson, for instance, who 40 years later served on the Whittier faculty—visited the campus. And Bruce Douglas was one of three from Whittier to attend the Student Volunteer Convention in Kansas City in 1913, the speakers including William J. Bryan, then Secretary of State.

With the departure of Professor Harris, dramatic production at

Whittier College changed in character. Instead of the ambitious staging of literary classics, the campus fare consisted of recent Broadway hits such as *The Lion and the Mouse*, journalistic melodrama in the manner of the muckrakers, and the saccharine *Passing of the Third Floor Back*.

Choral music and glee clubs, started by Howard L. Hockett and carried on by others, developed with added success upon Hockett's return to Whittier in 1914. His Men's Glee Club (including the professor of Bible and the football coach) sang in Berkeley and Oakland Friends churches in the spring of 1915, and then "through the effort and influence of J. Clem Arnold," by invitation in Festival Hall of the International Exposition in San Francisco, the only college group so honored, sharing the program with Dr. Bruce Gordon Kingsley, the Royal organist.

The athletic program involved most of the men in college— there were but 25 of them in 1910 and only 65 in 1915.

Basketball, in which Whittier had pioneered among the colleges of southern California, continued to be played by Quaker teams with monotonous success. The 1910-11 team, coached by Herbert White, won two games each from Pomona and Occidental, lost one of its two games with U.S.C., but won the intercollegiate championship. The next winter, with only two of the same players, the Whittier team won all but one of its games and retained the championship. In 1913 neither Pomona nor Occidental entered intercollegiate competition in basketball—they might well have, as the Whittier team coached by Russell Wilson lost all but two of its games. Then in 1914, by defeating U.S.C. in the third of a three-game series and winning from an unofficial Oxy team, Whittier resumed its championship. And in the winter of 1915, the Quakers were again the all-round champions, beating U.S.C. and Fullerton J.C., the only academic teams willing to play. It was a great team: Lewis Cox, captain; Don Douglas, Howard Chambers, Alex McBurney, Earl Sharpless—and Walter Spicer in reserve. Invited to San Francisco, this team competed in the A.A.U. tournament at the World's Fair—won its first two games from an Oregon team and from St. Mary's, but lost in the finals to San Francisco Olympic Club, thus placing second in national championship play. It was the culmination of an amazing record for basketball: eight championships in nine years under four different coaches.

In baseball Whittier College was never so strong, though it usually fielded a team, and Everett Jordan was "one of the best intercollegiate pitchers in the south" in 1915. In tennis, Elliott Chambers was a tournament player of note during this period. In track, except for individual good runners like Adrian Mills in 1910, only in 1915 was there a creditable team centered around Walter Cammack and Verl and Earl Murray, twins from El Modena.

It was football that Whittier students wanted to play well as the accepted mark of collegiate stature.

During the 1910 and 1911 seasons there were more defeats than victories, but the games were made memorable by the playing of "Big" Renneker—Noble B., younger brother of Nofle W., "Little" Rennie, though he was hardly smaller. They were Quaker farm boys who arrived from Nebraska in 1907 with $2.50 and desire for an education. They entered Whittier College and of course played ball. Then Big Renneker yielded to poverty and temptation, "took some articles that were not his," and withdrew from the college in disgrace. But he wanted to come back to make good where he had failed. Readmitted to the college, he rewon student respect, completed his preparatory work, began as a college freshman in 1909, and became a student leader and class president. In the 1910 season U.S.C. challenged his playing, but its charge of "professionalism" was not sustained—he was, according to the (partisan) Whittier *News* "admittedly the greatest football player in Southern California." He played as part of a good Whittier team, which lost close games, one to U.S.C. (3-11) and another to Pomona (0-6). In the fall of 1911, Pomona with a powerful team (and already twice the champions) defeated Whittier badly. The next week, the Quakers forfeited their game to Occidental because of the loss from their small squad of seven men— due to injuries, sickness, and low grades. Big Renneker was "out for remainder of season [taped up] with a broken rib." Two weeks later he was dead. Trimming a eucalyptus tree for President Newlin, he slipped and plunged fifteen feet, "struck his head on the sidewalk and literally dashed out his brains . . . unable to save his head by interposing his arms." He died almost instantly. The death of Noble Brutus Renneker shook college and community. His teammates, with Nature and neighbor colleges, stood up to say to all the world, "This was a man!"*

In the next years, 1912 and 1913, Whittier continued to field strong teams but not strong enough. Then opening the 1914 season—with Europe already locked in combat—Whittier at last beat Occidental 14-7 in a terrible and weird struggle on Hadley Field that ended in confusion, protested decisions, vacillation of officials. There was strong support for the Quaker team, the Howling Hundred of downtown merchants, and the State School band. Victory jubilation included a pajamarino. Then came games lost to U.S.C. (7-14) and to Pomona (7-13), the perennial collegiate champion—small consolation in beating Throop (later Caltech) and Redlands University (the newcomer) by big scores. But this Whittier team was long remembered, with Walter Cammack and Olin "Bull" Finch named to an All-Conference team.

There was no question, now, that Whittier College (with its 65 men) was playing games with the best of them.

The games were not all on the gridiron. Besides the parlor games at the class parties—now more refined and less roughhouse—there began a sort of social intercourse among the students that came perilously close to dancing, which had been "absolutely prohibited" by the faculty in 1905. However, young people in Whittier were beginning to dance. This the Friends elders and overseers would not tolerate, nor were Quakers alone in this disapprobation. The W.C.T.U. had turned its attention to The Dance and its Evils. The *Register* reviewed a sensational new book that illuminated the dark route from ballroom to brothel.

> How many parents . . . restrict their children to parlor dancing only? . . . Dancing is too fascinating, and they who were first content with parlor dancing, soon want something else. . . . Three-fourths of the outcasts had a man's arm around them for the first time at a social dance. . . .

Dancing continued, even involved some young Friends. Public debate also continued in the *News*: "Girls of athletic tendencies

*A bronze statue—of a too-idealized youth, "The Victor," withholding dagger and extending olive branch—memorialized him for half a century in the college auditorium and then library.

are less liable to go astray", said Dr. Sargent of Harvard—Father Phelan thought it the duty of young women to fascinate men and "tango-dancing girls are engaged in God's work"—Suffrage leaders urged mothers to organize and supervise dances. Counterblasts came from pulpit and pundit. It is not surprising, therefore, that deception and ingenious euphemism screened the dancing of Whittier students at this time. In 1913 the Freshman "Hop" took place at the lovely home of Ralph Robbins, adjacent to the campus. Prof. and Mrs. Russell Wilson were the chaperons, and they helped the sophomores initiate the new students into the "social spirit" of the college,

> assisted in trying to develop poetical talent for the "Rhythmical Sway." . . . No extras were granted and the "Home Sweet Home" immediately followed the Alma Mater.

It may be added that card-playing—anathema alike to Methodists and Quakers, who associated it with saloons, gambling, and debauchery—was enjoyed in the guise of Flinch, playing cards with their faces lifted, their leprous spots changed.

THE FISCAL AND PHYSICAL development of the college should have reflected the forward movement of its collegiate activities and academic program from 1910 to 1915. But it failed to do so.

In February 1912, the trustees undertook a campaign for $115,-000—to clear the indebtedness of $15,000, to build a $25,000 library, to increase endowment by $75,000. Washington Hadley was no longer at hand to make a substantial initial gift, having died in December aged 94. But Addison and Rebecca Naylor came forward with $20,000 contingent upon clearing indebtedness and raising the rest of the $100,000. In order to do this, the trustees employed as financial secretary (Prof.) Charles E. Lewis, who had returned to Whittier; but within a week he died of an apoplexy, aged 47. President Newlin was unwilling to assume the added work of financial solicitation without increase in salary. Instead, the board named Dr. Cyrus R. Dixon, then City treasurer, but by June 1913 he had secured subscriptions only to clear the $15,000 debt. The board then asked Absalom Rosenberger, long-experienced as president of Penn College, to serve as financial secretary and to raise the funds needed. But the campaign did not go well—even though the board added its president, Dr. W. V. Coffin, as a second "financial agent in the field." Efforts to secure grants from the Peabody Fund and from the General Education Board failed. With but a few thousand dollars subscribed by the time of Yearly Meeting in June 1914, the campaign was given up, as "financial conditions prevailing" at that time were not thought "favorable" to the raising of large sums.*

These years of collegiate achievement were years of frustration in the development of Whittier College. The trustees undertook no new building. It was the Alumni Association (only 33 college alumni by then) that raised $1,500 for permanent bleachers on Hadley Field. It was the Woman's Auxiliary that built "the new banquet assembly hall at the Girls' Cottage," costing $1,000. It was the Senior Class '12 that developed a Greek amphitheater. This they built along the arroyo lying north of Tebbetts Gymnasium (between what were later Naylor Hall and Platner). "A cement conduit was placed in the bottom of the arroyo . . . and the stage [40' x 22'] was built over this." The small grove of pine trees to the north formed a picturesque background. The south bank of the old arroyo needed but little terracing to seat 1,500 persons on wooden benches built by the seniors. The Woman's Auxiliary paid for building a bridge to it across the arroyo from the end of Berkeley Way (Founders Hill Road), and by May 1912, it was ready for the senior play and then for commencement. Heavy rains the next winter damaged the conduit and stage. No adequate reconstruction was undertaken, and this first amphitheater fell into further disrepair and then disuse.

The financial picture was dismal for Whittier College in the summer of 1915. Though the accumulated deficit had been underwritten, the bank balance was only $16.77 and $1130 was owing to the treasurer.

THE RESIGNATION OF President Thomas Newlin, to take effect at the end of that year, had been announced early in February 1915, when he accepted the presidency of Guilford College, which he had served as dean prior to coming to Whittier. Guilford was older, larger, more firmly established. Newlin saw this invitation

*In the spring of 1913, Pomona College, under the skillful leadership of James A. Blaisdell, announced gifts of $415,000 and plans for four buildings.

as a call to larger service, and he gave no other reason for leaving Whittier College after his eight years as president, 1907-1915.

But there must have been other reasons contributing to his decision. One was certainly fatigue. He carried a heavy teaching load as well as administrative responsibility, and actively represented Whittier College in the local and larger communities. Another reason was probably his realization that, although "every arrow of criticism against the College has fallen harmless at our feet," he had failed to unite the Friends of California Yearly Meeting behind the college. And this failure certainly accounted in some measure for laggard growth in enrollment and lack of adequate financial support.

President Newlin's resignation was regretted by the students— 85 of them at once petitioned him to stay. They loved and respected him, appreciated his tolerance and support. The community of Whittier also regretted his going—the Bible class, the Ministerial Association, the Board of Trade, the Daily *News*. In recognition of his work and worth, the college faculty and board conferred upon him the degree Doctor of Laws at the June commencement. The day following—betokening the respect in which he was widely held—the University of Southern California honored him with the degree Doctor of Divinity.

Within his period of eight years (1907-1915), Dr. Newlin had brought Whittier College to some degree of Academic maturity. He had liberalized the denominational Friends college, nurtured freedom of thought and of inquiry, encouraged student responsibility and development. And he left with a ringing note of faith in the college and in its future.*

7

A GREATER WHITTIER COLLEGE
PROJECTED FOR THE YEARLY MEETING

THE MAN APPOINTED President of Whittier College in 1915 was looked upon as "a blessed bridge between the fundamentalists and

*Dr. Newlin's presidency of Guilford College lasted but two years, owing to unforeseen conflict within the faculty itself. He then entered wartime Y.M.C.A. service in 1917. After the War he returned to live in Whittier, to teach at Fullerton Junior College, to serve on the Whittier College board (1921-1938). He made an annuity-gift to the college and left it his library. Thereafter, Newlin Hall was to bear his name.

the liberals." His task was to unite California Yearly Meeting behind a great development program for its denominational college.

Absalom Rosenberger was already 66 and, as president, a generation older than either of his predecessors. He was no philosopher or scientist or sociologist, but a vigorous grandfatherly man of wide human experience. Hoosier-born in a log cabin, "Abbie" Rosenberger grew up with farm chores and Friends' schooling, became a young teacher and later graduate of Earlham, again a schoolmaster, then (LL.B., Michigan) a Kansas lawyer and thereafter president of Penn College for a score of years (1890-1910). Upon his remarriage he went to Palestine as missionary head of the boys' school at Ramallah. When he returned in 1913, he moved to southern California—his son already established in medical practice—and served the Los Angeles Friends Church as pastor and Whittier College as financial secretary.

Florabel P. Rosenberger, his wife, was a United Presbyterian, a brilliant woman, excellent teacher, capable administrator. Florabel Paterson had moved from schoolgirl to teacher with only normal training, taught at Penn College, then served as county superintendent of schools, honored by Penn with an A.M. degree. Soon Monmouth College (United Presbyterian) called her to its chair of history, and she taught there ten years, helping in preparation of young missionaries. Upon her marriage to Absalom Rosenberger, they went as partners to the Holy Land to run the Friends' mission school. It was as a team that they were to serve Whittier College.

The news story of April 7, 1915, announcing Absalom Rosenberger's appointment as president of the college for a two-year term, reported the resignation of Dr. Herbert F. Allen and his replacement by Florabel P. Rosenberger as professor of English. The students, startled by the unexpected news of Allen's resignation, expressed "deep concern and misgivings." They at once petitioned President Newlin and the college board. Within six weeks their efforts "culminated in an official urging of Dr. Allen to remain." With Allen's retention, Mrs. Rosenberger was listed simply as assistant to the president. In late August, however, came the resignation of William T. Boyce to accept a more remunerative position at Fullerton Junior College, and Mrs. Rosenberger became professor of history. But it was as registrar that she really "ran" the college for her husband, freeing him for its development program.

Together the Rosenbergers set to work in the fall of 1915. The critics of the liberalized program of Whittier College had been silenced in the controversy of 1910 but had not been conciliated. Withholding their approbation, they had also withheld their financial support. Now in 1915 it seemed clear that, to make the college acceptable to the entire Yearly Meeting, called for re-emphasis of its evangelical othodoxy and for de-liberalizing of its academic program and its campus activities.

THE WORK OF RECONCILIATION came naturally to Absalom Rosenberger. Everywhere were old friends. Dr. W. V. Coffin and Dr. L. M. Greene, liberal board members, had been his college-mates at Earlham. John Chawner, clerk of the Yearly Meeting (who believed that "modern thought is only old infidelity rehabilitated"), had been the friendly witness at Absalom Rosenberger's first wedding. Graduates and former students of Penn College were more numerous than Whittier alumni in southern California. Rosenberger's "mischievous good humor," his venerable aspect, his sturdy probity made him welcome in Friends' churches and homes as minister or guest.

He at once wrote a statement of his educational aims for the *Pacific Friend*. In addition to high scholarship, disciplined minds, trained bodies, high intellectual ideals—

> Whittier College believes in soul culture, and our Bible courses are intended to be more than mere methods of ethical culture, and Bible study more than a study of literature. There is a spiritual culture which the College makes pre-eminent over all its other studies. Without this all else is failure.

In mid-November a Week of Prayer at the college marked an increased religious emphasis and brought guest speakers to the campus: Morris Kimber, then studying at Los Angeles Bible Institute; Robert Simkin, missionary from China; Dr. Clotilde Pretlow, missionary from Cuba. The final program was in charge of the Student Volunteers.

John Shober Kimber (Sr.), a strongly evangelistic Friend, moved his family to Whittier from Newport, Rhode Island, in the fall of 1915. At this time Whittier had not only the Friends Church but also a tabernacle that called on the old-time Quakers and Methodists who yearned for the Old-Time Religion. The Tabernacle bid for the Kimbers' support, but they threw in their lot with California Yearly Meeting and the father became its Evangelistic Superintendent. As such he lectured at the Training School in Huntington Park, but he steered a middle course and supported the work of President Rosenberger at Whittier College. Three sons (James, Thomas, and Shober) became student leaders and in time graduates of the college. The fourth and eldest, Morris Kimber (A.B., Friends and University of Pennsylvania) was appointed professor of Biblical literature upon the resignation of Esek Perry in 1916.

Within the year, Ministry and Oversight of the Whittier Friends Church invited "the College President to sit on the platform with the Pastor at the regular Sabbath services." This, also, was fruit of Rosenberger's work of conciliation.

MODIFICATION OF THE COLLEGE program began in September 1915 as Florabel Rosenberger, registrar, "revised and greatly improved" the system of college records. And during the year there was a general overhauling of both curriculum and catalog.

The May 1916 *Bulletin* reflected a definitely more religious posture, with less emphasis on the academic. What had been phrased as "Strong Christian influences," became *Strong tides of Christian influence and culture.* The "well-trained faculty" became *exemplary in life.* The "splendid student body" became *actuated by noble purposes.* The "small classes," previously "in charge of teachers of recognized ability," became classes *under careful supervision and instruction.*

The year course in "Evolution" was dropped from the May 1916 catalog. In its place were safer courses: in 1917, *Animal Behavior;* in 1918, *Heredity.* Whether with broken health or heart, Prof. Lyman Muchmore resigned in May 1917 after nine years at Whittier College—"his plans for the future . . . not complete."* It is ironic that the new Whittier Friends Church, under construction at this very time, stood firmly upon the evidences of Evolution. Excavation for its foundation in January 1917 had

*For twenty years or so he was then on the staff of the Los Angeles Museum.

unearthed mastodon bones "several hundred thousand years" older than the Creation of 4004 B.C.

Another marked change was the firmer tone of the College Regulations, now returned to their earlier place in the front of the catalog. Whereas it had been the stated aim of the college "to help young people toward higher ideals of character," the phrase now became *high standards . . . hence the requirement of Chapel attendance.* "It is also desirable to eliminate from the college environment everything that is at variance with true Christian ideals." The tone is more paternal and presbyterian, the college prescribing the standards rather than guiding students toward establishing their own. To the previous prohibitions—drinking, smoking, profanity, and gambling—were now added explicitly *card playing* and *dancing.*

Tighter control appeared for all social functions, each requiring consent of the college president who then arranged for or approved the chaperonage. Athletes in particular were expected to maintain not only "a certain standard of scholarship" but also of conduct in order to represent the college in intercollegiate events. Furthermore, the college did not "solicit the patronage" of those who would not "yield willing compliance" with the rules. Enrollment in the college was "regarded as consent" to abide by them.

All of this, of course, was neither unreasonable nor remarkably different from the regulations current in other denominational colleges. But it was notably different from Newlin's principle that "education is mainly a moral process," the awakening of each conscience to what John G. Whittier had called "the taste for truth," and the development in students of more mature ethics and control of conduct through self-government.

Such changes as these and the more religious posture of Whittier College at this time suggested the "guarded education" (a slogan already old-fashioned by 1906) that had been the measure of Friends' academies in the 1890's.

Other modifications introduced at this time reflected the orderly mind of Florabel P. Rosenberger and the faculty strength of Professor Ostrom. The departmental major became more firmly fixed, without the earlier safeguards against over-specialization. However, the college did eliminate the Bachelor of Science degree, all courses again leading to the A.B., and it also dropped the requirement for a senior thesis. A notable omission from the catalog of May 1916 was the major in Philosophy and Biblical Studies that in some measure had competed briefly with the Training School.

Many of the changes were of a kind to conciliate the older critics of the college. Others suggested "the efficient college" that served as slogan for the development of the Greater Whittier College.

"THE EFFICIENT COLLEGE" was a phrase that President Rosenberger brought back in January 1917 from a meeting of the Association of American Colleges in Chicago, where he had heard a report setting standards for what it called the Minimum College, the Average College, and the Efficient College. Although Whittier College could not as yet be characterized as fully Average—if something more than the Minimum—President Rosenberger and the board took as their long range goal the standards for "the Efficient College" of five hundred students with a faculty of fifty, realizing that this might seem "audacious and rashly presumptuous."

They engaged Allison and Allison of Los Angeles as architects, provided them with a contour map of the campus and with standards for the Efficient College. The architects soon sketched a Master Plan for the Greater Whittier College, a formal arrangement of a dozen or so buildings

> having the dignity and simplicity of our colonial architecture [and at the same time] arcaded cloisters and tile roofs [that were] indigenous to California.

Although the Girls' Cottage worked into the plan and was to remain, the existing Main Building [Founders Hall] did not, and was to be removed after construction of a new administration-classroom building. Notably, the first building scheduled for construction was "the Chemical Laboratory." Next was to come the Boys' Dormitory, a cluster of cottages curving around the upper hill. Then, only, would come the Library. Contemplated expenditure for the buildings: about $400,000.

THE IMMEDIATE CAMPAIGN goal was $250,000—$100,000 for buildings and $150,000 for additional endowment. Professional fund-raisers came from Chicago—office in downtown Whittier—and put in motion elaborate plans under a general committee of college trustees. They set March 15, 1917, as the opening date for a campaign of eleven weeks that was to end in triumph on May 31st.

From the first, however, the campaign went badly. Even before March 15th, the nation moved swiftly toward war: Germany's unrestricted submarine warfare, the break in diplomatic relations, discovery of Germany's secret offer of alliance with Mexico, President Wilson's ominous call for a special session of Congress!

But the committee proceeded, anxious to gather in the sheaves ahead of the storm. President Rosenberger made every effort to appeal to Friends of differing orthodoxies. A letter from evangelist John Henry Douglas to more-liberal Dr. W. V. Coffin supported the campaign. Douglas was "hopeful for the future of Whittier College . . .", founded as it is on "the unchanged and unchangeable Holy Scriptures . . . holding and teaching emphatically evangelical truth." The professionals prepared endless publicity, filling columns in the *News*. The students' Q.C. was taken over with campaign ads and promotional series. The crowded issue that ironically had no space to note the actual declaration of war, reported the success of the motion picture depicting "Student Life at Whittier College," first such public-relations film on the coast.* And, as the campaign came toward its close, an alfresco dinner on the front campus brought out the town, and the *News* listed subscribers and the amount of their pledges.

However, by the end of the fifth week, only $47,000 had been raised, including $25,000 offered by Addison Naylor contingent upon the total reaching at least $100,000. (This was a renewal and increase of his previous offer.) As the weeks went on there were $5,000 subscriptions from Friends, among them Amos Cook, John Shober Kimber, Lydia Jackson, Sarah Sharpless, Eva J. Cook—and $1,000 subscriptions from A. C. Johnson, Dr. L. M. Greene, David H. White, Frank Milhous—and from non-Quak-

---

*Clyde Trout wrote the scenario, "Horace Goes to College," and himself played the Student greeted by President Rosenberger, shown the campus by a New Friend, with views of glee club, baseball, Verl Murray "flying through space on the cinder path," and the Master Plan for the Greater Whittier College.

ers, too, such as A. C. Maple and O. H. Barr. The Woman's Auxiliary teams brought in smaller gifts and pledges totalling nearly $25,000. But on May 25th, with but five days to go, the tally was still only $85,000—$15,000 short of the minimum needed—and only one-third of the set goal. Desperate efforts continued.

On the last night of the campaign, May 31st, while those at headquarters totalled the final reports of canvassers, the phone rang. It was a call from Pasadena for Dr. Coffin—Col. Simon J. Murphy (who had sent teams to grade for the original college building 24 years before) wanted to be sure that the campaign reached its minimum so as to make binding all other subscriptions so far taken. To that end he would contribute $10,000.

Without revealing this information, Dr. Coffin sent a car over to get Col. Murphy's signature before the midnight closing hour of the campaign. "Then Coffin broke his solemn silence and announced the total of $111,000"—the minimum needed, plus a safe margin. It was sufficient success to shroud the larger failure and to signal as good news to anxious Friends by prearranged fireworks. . . .

By the end of June, it could be announced to California Yearly Meeting that, as a result of the campaign, enough had been collected on the pledges to begin work on the new chemistry building. By the fall of 1918 construction was completed at a cost of $32,000. Naylor Hall, as it was appropriately called, was the only tangible fruit of this herculean effort to develop the Greater Whittier College.

The financial campaign had fallen victim to the war, declared on April 6th. At once men enlisted and were leaving campus and town—the Red Cross and Y.M.C.A. appealed for funds—the first Liberty Loan drive was on. But there were also other reasons for the failure of the college campaign. As a declared denominational college, Whittier properly looked to the Yearly Meeting for its principal support, but the financial resources of California Friends were too limited to provide it. Furthermore, they were overtaxed. Within the year Penn College had burned to the ground, and alumni living in the West had been called upon for substantial subscriptions for its $400,000 rebuilding. Then, too, within the year a campaign had raised $55,000 to build the new Friends Church in Whittier. Local Friends were pledged out.

War or no war, it was a bad time to try to raise money for Whittier College.

8

WORLD WAR I—WHITTIER COLLEGE FRUSTRATED
THE QUAKER DILEMMA

THE MOMENTUM DEVELOPED by athletics prior to 1915 carried over into the next years, though President Rosenberger's conciliation of the disaffected required the de-emphasis of sports.* Yet in the winters of 1916 and of 1917, basketball teams again won championships, baseball continued, and track improved—Verl Murray competing in the national meet of 1916 and winning both the high and low hurdles of the Western A.A.U. meet in Fresno the next year.

It was in football, however, that this momentum was most obvious. The 1915 team lost a close game to Occidental, won decisively from Redlands, then met Pomona College on Hadley Field. The Huns (now in wartime rechristened the Sagehens) were the team to beat. "Finch caught Dahlem's opening kick and ran the entire field for a touchdown." It was not luck, for his teammates gave him perfect interference. The game, with its irresistible line plunges, was a 23-0 victory for the fighting Quakers. The metropolitan sports writers (among them Harry Williams) were ecstatic, looking forward to the Whittier game with U.S.C.

University of Southern California had pulled out of the Conference the preceding spring—Coach Glaze was through competing with small colleges that played "prep school football." A good back-East high school could beat Oxy, Pomona and/or Whittier, Glaze said. He wanted real competition. And he got it, for in mid-December 1915, the Poets "vanquished the U.S.C. varsity by a 19-2 count at Washington Park." The mighty Glaze did not resign. Five Whittier players were named to the All-Southern-California eleven: Olin Finch, Howard Chambers, Morris Bogue, Joe Siemon, and Robert Robbins.

The next season for Whittier opened at Berkeley. In a brilliant game the Poets outplayed the Bears—with "a bewildering exhibition of forward passing." As the end approached, the Quaker

*The ultimatum of 1910 specifically called for an end to competitive athletics.

team was leading 17 to 14. Then, as the San Francisco *Examiner* reported,

> Under cover of darkness the football team of the University of California snatched victory from the Whittier College boys . . . in the last minute of the game that was as full of thrills as a Drury Lane melodrama.

The play that brought down the curtain: "Bull" Finch—unaccountably, unless he was dazed—threw a forward pass from deep in his own territory, and it was intercepted for a touchdown. Time has embroidered the legend, deepened the shadows, hidden the ball under a jersey!

The defeat of Arizona, of Redlands, of Pomona and of Throop followed. Then came preparation for the Oxy Tigers on Hadley Field to decide the championship. The Week of Prayer and the Y.M. and Y.W. "nut party" paled in the excitement of the Big Rally and the game itself, which ended in a 13-13 tie. Occidental retained the championship.

During this year of triumph, the *Quaker Campus* editorialized on the "many evils" of college athletics, including "a tendency to give time to athletics which should rightfully go to literary societies, mission circles, Y.M.C.A." In his annual report in 1917 President Rosenberger made but a passing reference to "the usual interest in forensics and athletics." He did not even mention the resignation in mid-year of Russell T. Wilson, professor of mathematics and athletic director, who left to accept a coaching position at Stanford University.

But the de-emphasis of athletics—which may indeed have usurped too great a place in the life of the college—was brought about, not by administrative slight or by Wilson's resignation, but by the War, which soon drained most of the men away from the campus.

OTHER STUDENT ACTIVITIES, too, were carried forward by the momentum of the preceding years. The Associated Students took an important step in the fall of 1915, voting to accept a Code of Honor developed by a committee of which Harold Story was chairman. It was an agreement entered into by the students themselves "to co-operate for the honorable maintenance of order and propriety" in seven particulars that included: refusal to give or receive help in course work, and respect for the property of others. President Rosenberger commended this and other efforts to improve student government. But he spoke cautiously of the new College Council—of trustees, faculty, and students—"to give counsel in all matters pertaining to the college as a whole."

With the Athenaeum forgotten and no literary society or debating club of any sort, Harold Story led in a student body request for instructional work in forensics, asking for a department of oratory and debate. In 1916 Eugene Knox, "an impersonator of sixteen years' experience upon the best Chautauqua and Lyceum platforms," and for years also a teacher of oratory, was added to the faculty, and a School of Expression appeared in the catalog. Professor Knox' work included coaching the plays—the Senior Play in 1917: *The Servant in the House*, a deeply moving religious drama then popular—and coaching debate. Interest in forensics increased, and students formed a new society, Agora, to promote it.

The controversial men's society, the Acolytes, of which Dr. Herbert F. Allen was the sponsor, carried over from the year 1914-1915. Whatever the action taken against the Acolytes in the spring of 1915—or what relation this may have had to Dr. Allen's "resignation" at that time—this "loosely organized but nonetheless durable organization" continued quietly without any word about it in the student publications. Then in mid-February 1917, just as the financial campaign was about to be launched, articles again appeared in the Q.C. The purpose, sponsor, and activities remained what they had been. The dozen members, leading students, met to discuss "in a broad-minded, liberal, unprejudiced manner" topics of contemporary interest. The Q.C. reported on May 31st that the Acolytes would hold their initiation in Los Angeles, with a dinner and theatre party. It was the night of solemn vigil closing the trustees' financial campaign. That was the end of the Acolytes. "A positive order" disbanded them. And—without public announcement or explanation—Dr. Allen was quietly dropped from the faculty.*

*For the next quarter century he was a popular professor at the University of California at Los Angeles, kept in touch with former Whittier students and, in his later retirement during World War II, tried to find a place to live in Whittier.

Six new faculty members were announced in the spring and summer of 1917, while the nation was mobilizing its war efforts.

In place of Russell T. Wilson came Dr. Harry N. Wright, brought back from the faculty of the University of California as professor of mathematics and dean of the faculty, which was then looked upon as a step to the college presidency. Wilson's work in athletics was taken over by Herbert White, who again coached a winning basketball team, and by I. H. Van Cleave (Y.M.C.A. College, Springfield, Mass.). Van Cleave was soon named director of athletics and professor of physical education. With but five lettermen from the preceding year, the valiant football team of 1917 lost all but one of its games. The other colleges, with military units, were markedly stronger.

Upon Professor Muchmore's resignation, Howard E. McMinn (A.B., Earlham, M.A., University of California) came to Whittier as professor of biology, but left at the end of the year.* . . . Mlle. L. J. Setchanove (M.A., Geneva; diplomas, Paris and Jena), "a brilliant, intense woman," became professor of romance languages. Her French classes presented Molière's *Le Bourgeois Gentilhomme*, "splendidly staged and costumed," in the spring of 1918. . . . To serve as the first Adviser to Women, and to fill out in Latin and history, came Miss Ida B. Lindley (A.B., M.A., Wesleyan College, Cincinnati), who had taught in Los Angeles schools and at University of Southern California. She was a sister of Hervey Lindley, cousin of the Ida Lindley who had taught in the second Whittier Academy. She was a sociable member of the older community.

Maxwell Anderson (A.B., North Dakota, M.A., Stanford) received appointment as professor of English literature upon the dismissal of Dr. Allen. Anderson had been teaching in San Francisco, where he had contributed editorials to the *Bulletin* and sent poetry to the *New Republic*. At Whittier College he at once scheduled courses in advanced composition and short story, in verse-writing and modern poetry. He and his students also experimented with playwriting.

Heralded as "a man of very strong personality"—football

*He married President Rosenberger's daughter Helen, became an eminent California botanist, professor at Mills College. His sister, Lillian McMinn, came to Whittier in 1923 as wife of Paul S. Smith, young professor of history.

player as an undergraduate—Maxwell Anderson was a large man of beetle-brow and unruly hair, reserved and soft-spoken son of a Baptist minister. But he soon became known as one of the campus liberals. In the sequence of daily chapels, Maxwell Anderson took his first turn to read the parable of the Good Samaritan and to urge wartime tolerance. "Patriotism for us is not hurling invective at the German people, but extending to them our sympathy."

However, Scriptural love for the atrocious Hun did not quite catch the current temper. But, then, he was no Billy Sunday.

FOR A SPECIAL CHAPEL program the preceding week, Professor Kimber had secured the popular evangelist and ex-ballplayer, Billy Sunday. He was the most dynamic, flamboyant, and slangy preacher of the day. To accommodate the interested townsmen, the college chapel was held in the new First Friends Church, which seated 1,800. Only with difficulty were places saved for the students.

> Ten o'clock. . . . Every seat in the house was full . . . people were standing in rows all about the room.
> A slight confusion at the east door, a cheer, and "Billy" was with us. Then another as the crowd realized that "Ma" Sunday had come, too.

And up the aisle she swept like "a ship under full sail. . . ." There was a hymn—a brief introduction by Dean Wright—and the celebrated revivalist took over with a laughing reference to "the quiet Quakers." His sermon (full of wise saws and modern instances) he spiced with jokes.

> The real purpose of education is not to become a cold storage of facts. . . . Be better men and women because of your education. . . . Have faith in yourself. . . . Be well rounded. . . . Always have to unbutton your collar to take it off. . . . If you get it in the neck, be thankful you aren't a giraffe. . . . Get the best the world has to offer. Come home to God a winner.

It was a spell-binding hour. At the end, "Ma" Sunday moved in "majestically" to protect Billy from the crowd, then whisked him away. . . . Much campus discussion followed.

But this Sunday chapel on Tuesday did not touch the agony of the world at war or sense the anguish of the Quaker dilemma.

THE PEACE TESTIMONY of the Society of Friends had been a part of Quakerism from the beginning. But during World War I, as in previous wars, there were "fighting Quakers" as well as conscientious objectors, among the young men in Friends meetings and colleges. Whittier College did not train a military unit—nor did it train men and women for humanitarian war work—but President Rosenberger made an effort to keep men in college in preparation for "a consecrated world-wide service for mankind when the noise and din of battle are over." And this meant, in large measure, carrying on college without much reference to the war.

With the coming of war, some college men enlisted at once—Joe Buckmaster and Will Fawcett the first to do so. By July, Elliott Chambers '16 was among those training at Haverford for the Friends Reconstruction Unit. He and Lowell Chawner '19 were in France by fall, and Chambers' letters home were printed with interest in both the Q.C. and the Whittier *News*. But patriotic Whittier—Quakers now outnumbered seven to one—may not have thought of him as a conscientious objector, for the town showed no sympathy for pacifists. Nor was the Whittier Friends Church united in its peace witness.

During the year 1917-1918, the college men from Friends' families faced multiple questions. First, whether they indeed were conscientious objectors or not. Second, if they *were*, then—whether to volunteer at once for Friends Reconstruction work or for Y.M.C.A. or Red Cross or ambulance service—or to await the draft, hope for exemption, refuse induction, or accept noncombatant service in the army. If they were *not* conscientious objectors, then—whether to go into the army or navy at once—or await the draft—or hurry into marriage and farming. Through the months, the Whittier College boys made their choices, or, in a case or two, broke down with dilemmas unresolved.

Whatever they did, however, the Friends churches and Whittier College for the most part stood by them. T. Elwood Newlin gave the college a service flag in March 1918. By the end of March, there were 36 stars for students and alumni in the armed services, and 20 some men were in Friends Reconstruction and Y.M.C.A. work. By June, there were 69 stars on the military flag.

Harold H. Story '16 was a militant Quaker pacifist, chairman of a committee to aid conscientious objectors.* He was arrested in Los Angeles in October 1917 while addressing a group of Christian Pacifists. The charge—

> discussing, arguing and preaching certain thoughts and theories ... calculated to cause any American citizen then and there present hearing the same to forthwith proceed to assault and batter the persons so uttering same.

Tried and found guilty—unlawful assembly, failing to disperse, and disturbing the peace—he was fined and given six-months' sentence. He lost his appeal in Superior Court. Imprisoned in May, he was drafted in June. He refused the uniform, and the Court sent him to Leavenworth, where he was a model prisoner.

His brother Donald G. Story became editor of the *Quaker Campus* in the fall of 1917. He maintained the policy of an Open Forum column. Two days after his brother's arrest, but with no mention of it, Donald Story ran an editorial under the title of "Judge Not," in which he regretted the growing intolerance in the nation—a public demand for Senator La Follette's arrest for treason, even "his immediate execution!" "Yes," wrote Story, "this intolerance is found also on the Quaker campus. . . ." Whatever the past days' talk about alumnus Harold Story, the buzzing now was that Donald Story was unpatriotic and even disloyal. One of his staff resigned. Next day Harold Story, awaiting trial, came out to the campus to see his brother.

The following issue of the Q.C. reported the troubles of another student pacifist—troubles that soon involved a member of the faculty.

THE MAXWELL ANDERSON AFFAIR showed the new professor of English to be an uncompromising man of principle. In that time of war hysteria in the community, he stood up for the right of a student to a respectful hearing as a conscientious objector.

*During the war an active peace movement continued, with such notable members as David Starr Jordan, Henry Wadsworth Longfellow [II], Scott Nearing, ex-Senator John D. Works of California, and Victor Berger.

The Q.C. (10/25/17) reported that Arthur Camp had received notice "that his exemption had been denied." Camp was a senior student, manager of forensics, summer employee in the U.S. Government citrus laboratory. He was drafted and called—he failed to report for induction—he was arrested as a deserter and taken before the United States Commissioner. While under detention he wrote a statement for the Open Forum of the Q.C. and sent it to the editor. Learning of this, the Executive Committee of the Associated Students refused (as publishers of the *Quaker Campus*) to let the paper print it. Donald Story, standing by his editorial policy, resigned.

In place of Camp's statement, however, appeared a letter by Professor Anderson. While not knowing Arthur Camp well, Anderson wrote, he had "formed a high opinion of his ability and of his motives."

> It takes a brave and high-spirited man to take the stand which he has taken. He deserves to be heard . . . And where can he be heard more naturally, where should he be more welcome, than in the columns of the paper of his college?

Then Maxwell Anderson went on to say:

> If there is criticism of the government in this college it should be represented in the paper. It is a weak and shaky government that cannot stand criticism, and it is a weak and shaky intellect that never has any criticism to offer. If our colleges are to stifle thought, where is the thinking to be done?

As champion of this pacifist student, Anderson came under community pressure. In the absence of President Rosenberger, Dean Harry N. Wright tried to mediate. But Maxwell Anderson —who had written of the timorous student executive committee: "there is always something to run from if you are coward enough to run"—was in no mood to back down or to adjust himself to the temper of the time and town.

His resignation was a foregone conclusion, though it was not announced until mid-April. Then it was reported that Maxwell Anderson had resigned in order to return for further study and teaching at Stanford University. The Q.C., which from time to time had published Anderson's verse, regretted his leaving, wished him well, and predicted that as a poet his name was destined to live.

As it happened, however, Maxwell Anderson did not return to Stanford, but went to San Francisco and shortly thereafter to New York City as a writer. He soon found success in the theatre, first with *What Price Glory?* (1924), then with such verse dramas as *Elizabeth the Queen* (1930). For thirty years he was one of the two or three leading playwrights in the first great flowering of the American Drama.*

As for Arthur Camp, he accepted induction, visited the campus in uniform to preside as "our soldier-chairman" at an intercollegiate debate. Later (Ph.D., Washington) he became an agricultural scientist of some note.

COMMENCEMENT AT THE END of May 1918 was to be a grim time. The date had been set early by order of President Wilson so as to hurry young men into uniform. The college invited Dr. E. P. Ryland, already well known in Whittier, to be the commencement speaker. A prominent Methodist minister and strong pacifist, he had resigned his pulpit in Los Angeles when the Bishop directed all Methodist preachers to speak out actively in support of the war. The announcement that Dr. Ryland was coming to Whittier blew up something of a storm, though no protest was actually presented to the college itself.

The township constable as much as forbade Ryland's appearance. "As a peace officer," he deemed it unwise to bring to Whittier such a notorious "champion of pacifism." He said, "Blood is running hot in Whittier . . . I believe it would be unnecessarily inciting mob violence." The same day the *News* reported formation of an American Protective League—Gen. [and Judge] Madison T. Owens as "Chief"—to root out all pro-Germanism in the town. Dr. W. V. Coffin and Dean Harry N. Wright acceded to the community will and told Dr. Ryland he was not acceptable. In his place, Dr. Hugh K. Walker, Los Angeles Presbyterian pastor, addressed the dozen graduates, four of them men. His subject: "Vic-

*Anderson was not bitter about his experience at Whittier College. When, during World War II, permission was asked for producing one of his plays at Whittier College, he wrote: "I cannot help envying the present generation of teachers and students."

tory." His wartime sentiment: "All things work together for the good of those who love the Lord." The college awarded honorary degrees to John Shober Kimber and to Edwin McGrew, Whittier Friends pastor recently named president of Penn College.

Upon his resignation as president of Whittier College, Dr. Absalom Rosenberger (granted the honorary D.D. degree in 1916 by both Penn and Friends) became a trustee of Whittier College and its treasurer. Dr. Harry N. Wright, already carrying much administrative responsibility for the college, became its fourth president.

THE SUMMER OF 1918—time of crisis on western campus as on Western Front—ended a period in the history of Whittier as the Friends' denominational college. Charles E. Tebbetts had founded a minimal collegiate program; Thomas Newlin had enlarged and liberalized it; Absalom Rosenberger had tried to unite the Yearly Meeting behind its substantial development. In some measure all had failed.

At Yearly Meeting that second summer of World War I, Levi Gregory and his cousin Evelyn Almond Withrow presented to the college a portrait of John Greenleaf Whittier that she had painted. The presentation was an occasion for Levi Gregory, John Shober Kimber and others to give "interesting reminiscences of the poet." These could not but remind Friends of the dilemma John G. Whittier himself had faced as an avowed pacifist and militant abolitionist during the Civil War*

Dark as was the wartime hour that summer, there were those who saw in the friendly countenance of the Quaker poet a ray of Light for his namesake college.

*By the time of World War II, this portrait was to look down upon another generation, challenging its passing youth with the eternal question then lettered below it: "What and where is Truth?"

III

A FRIENDS COLLEGE
FOR THE WIDER COMMUNITY (1918-1934)

WAR-TORN SEPTEMBER 1918 brought Whittier College to its knees. Enrollment dipped to a dangerous minimum of 50 students, of whom only 15 were men. Friends of California Yearly Meeting, who had by no means united behind their denominational college on the eve of the War, were now divided by a different cleavage.

For the city of Whittier, however, the war year had been a good year—but for the tragic toll of local boys lost in France or dead in training camps. If there had been food rationing, there were also vegetable gardens on vacant lots. If all prices were going up, so were wages. If building of new houses declined, bank deposits rose, and further savings poured into Liberty and Victory bonds. Patriotism, brandished in song and oratory, and zealous witch-hunting for slackers and pro-Germans were coupled with this general prosperity.

The Quaker college shared neither the prosperity nor the fervor. Except that it honored its boys who served, it stood largely aloof, and thus separated itself from the rest of the town—and even from the militant Friends in the local church. But if Whittier College survived the wartime ordeal, might it not find new strength and support in the enriched town and the wider community?

1

THE END OF THE WAR AND
THE SETTING OF NEW ACADEMIC STANDARDS

THE NEW PRESIDENT of Whittier College faced problems doubly compounded in the opening weeks of the fall term. Added to the war itself and the drastic reduction in student body, was the

134

dread Spanish influenza that had struck in the spring. In the fall came its second wave, bringing swift death—killing in army camps half the number of American boys who died in France. In Los Angeles, bodies were removed from the Ascot army hospital at night to avoid civilian notice and panic. In Whittier, the college had been lucky—no more than serious and debilitating attacks upon faculty and students—but, in compliance with Public Health directives, the college closed its doors for three weeks. Students came singly to get assignments and to leave reports—all wore gauze flu-masks.

For President Harry N. Wright, these final days of October were surely a testing time: the campus was deserted but for occasional faceless figures. And the handful of men still on the college roll—such as Donald Story, senior now and chemistry assistant—were receiving draft notices to appear for induction. Could Harry Wright have looked but a fortnight into the seeds of time, he might have seen the Armistice signed at Compiègne, draft calls cancelled, and Donald Story dead. Stricken by influenza on the Thursday set for his induction, he succumbed at home in Bellflower over the weekend.

The community of Whittier celebrated wildly at the end of the war. Singing and cheering college girls mounted a hayrack that Professor Kimber pulled through the town with his old Cadillac. Except for the continuing epidemic, Armistice Day brought some immediate relief to Whittier College. Arthur Beede and Eldred Ferguson took the Pacific Electric into Los Angeles that morning to report for army induction, returned to Whittier that night to continue their college courses. Early release of students from the army camps promised well. Some men who had transferred from Whittier to colleges and universities giving military training would soon return. But for the spring semester of 1919—with masks optional, though a third wave of influenza struck—the enrollment was still no more than 65 students, only 25 of them men.

"AS IS THE FACULTY," said President Wright, "so is the college." It was his conviction (perhaps also his rationalization) that "A good college can be housed in poor buildings, but it can never be made by a poor faculty."

135

Although he himself was the only professor with a doctorate—
the Ph.D. less common then—he may have felt in 1918 that his
faculty of a dozen mature and experienced teachers was at least
competent to reach toward the academic standards that he set
for Whittier College: Gustaf Ostrom and Ruth Merrill (M.A.,
Berkeley) in the sciences, Mlle. Setchanove and Mrs. Douglas in
modern languages, Miss Lindley in Latin. It had been announced in the spring that Herbert E. Harris would return to
replace Maxwell Anderson, but instead Harris resigned to serve
the Y.M.C.A. in an army camp. President Wright secured Anna
Painter (A.B., Earlham; M.A., Columbia) in his place. She was
a sensitive interpreter of literature and ideas, later took her doctorate at Yale. Earl L. Shoup (graduate work at Yale and Chicago, teaching at Earlham and Stanford) came to Whittier as
professor of history, and Mrs. Rosenberger shifted to education.

Looking toward the year 1919-1920, with anticipation of increased enrollment, Wright urged the college trustees to improve
the fortunes of the faculty. They raised the two top professors'
salaries from $1,500 to $1,800—the president himself to $2,500.
Women's salaries were lower than men's on the theory that men
supported families, and the Spanish instructor was hired for
$600, then raised to $800 "owing to the fact that her work is
heavier than anticipated."

The early form of tenure or continuous appointment for the
professors, introduced by President Newlin in 1911, had fallen
into disuse. Now in the spring of 1919 the board issued formal
contracts to be signed annually. In 1920 the college granted
Prof. Ostrom a year's leave on salary to pursue further graduate
work. In 1922, it regularized payment of salaries, checks issued
the first of each month beginning September 1st.

As anticipated, the student body did grow in size after the
war, from 116 in 1919-20 to 208 in 1922-23. This allowed for
some enlargement in the faculty. There were also resignations
and replacements. Herbert E. Harris did return to Whittier in
1920, making a second professor in the English department. At
the same time, Esther Andrews '05 began her long service as
professor of German, and Esek Perry '07 returned half-time as
director of athletics. The resignation of Morris Kimber had al-

ready brought W. Carlton Wood (Ph.D., Hartford) and his wife Alice C. Wood in philosophy and religious education.

In history a succession of appointments was followed in 1922 by Paul S. Smith (A.B., Earlham; M.A., Wisconsin). Tall and shy, as yet unmarried, he was an earnest and enthusiastic teacher, at once a favorite with his Whittier students. In mathematics a succession of men led in 1922 to the appointment of Marcus Skarstedt (A.B., Augustana; M.S., Iowa). After teaching at his alma mater, he had taken library training (B.L.S., Illinois), served as city librarian at Evanston, then taught at California Polytechnic, San Luis Obispo. In biology and in romance languages, also, there were successive professors, none of them serving long periods. But the faculty developed a stable core, and salary raises approved by the college board in the spring of 1923 brought three professors to $2,700—not unreasonable at the time—and the president to $3,000.

In 1918, Wright had shifted Mrs. Rosenberger from history to education. The department that she set up, in line with the growing practice in liberal arts colleges, began the systematic preparation of teachers at Whittier College. At that time she succeeded Miss Tomlinson as secretary of the faculty.

Viewed in the context of that time, this was a solid faculty, with "teachers of maturity, ability and fine Christian character," as President Wright could assure the Yearly Meeting in his annual report.

CURRICULAR AND ACADEMIC modifications made by the faculty under Harry N. Wright's presidency were gradually changing the character of Whittier College. It was becoming *less* the denominational Quaker college and *more* the nonsectarian liberal arts college for the wider community.

It was not easy to alter the set patterns. Mrs. Rosenberger had reworked the catalog but a few years earlier when she had assisted her husband in reshaping the college. It was not until 1921 that the opening four pages, which had been notably emotional and promotional in style, were cut down to a spare two pages or so of statements more restrained and direct. The 1916 regulation for student conduct was also modified, though this did not mean abandonment of the established norms of social conduct, rather, a difference in administrative approach.

Some of the faculty, however, favored an authoritarian control, particularly as regards class and chapel attendance. A committee (Professors Ostrom, Rosenberger, Shoup) re-worked the regulations, requiring their colleagues to keep meticulous attendance records, submit reports to the registrar, and leave excusing of absences to a special committee—tardiness to count as one-third of an absence, overcuts to be penalized, etc. This disciplinary system, which seemed more Presbyterian or Lutheran than Friendly, was debated long in the faculty, advocates of the scheme carrying it after some parliamentary maneuvering. The resulting problem—how to police the faculty itself in enforcement of the regulation—provided further parliamentary exercise for several seasons. The effort to force the students' fidelity to their academic business continued through the succeeding decades.

Other regulations also tended to raise the academic standards of the college: a new curfew for the Girls' Cottage and for social events, a closer check on student eligibility for participation in intercollegiate activities and public events, a common effort by the entire faculty to raise the level of the students' oral and written English, and exacting regulation of departmental majors.

Again the door opened to more intellectual inquiry, as viewed within the framework of that time and place. Successive professors worked with student debaters upon questions of pressing interest. The *Quaker Campus* reflected divided concern for the League of Nations and other questions of national policy. In May 1922 the Whittier catalog once again announced a course in Evolution, Heredity and Genetics to be offered in a later year. There was evident student interest when the fossilized femur of a giant sloth (mylodon harloni), unearthed in nearby Eastridge, came to the college for its collection. This creature had been

> about ten foot two if he cared to stand up, with a chest like a [World War] sausage balloon, a tail like a kangaroo, a head about the size of a football and legs extremely small compared to the rest of his make-up.

Had it not, the Q.C. reporter speculated, "lain down to rest" where the Senior Bench then stood?

RECOGNITION OF THE creditable work being done at Whittier College under the quiet and purposeful leadership of President Wright, came in the form of accreditation.

In 1919 he announced that the state boards of education of both Arizona and Oregon had put the college on their lists of approved colleges. Whittier graduates, having taken specified courses, were then certified to teach in the high schools of those states without examination.

Whittier students had already been transferring credits to other colleges at full value when, in 1921, the University of California placed Whittier on its list of "accepted colleges of the graduate school." As the University was then "one of the four generally recognized standardizing agencies of the country," this approval was tantamount to general accreditation by all colleges and universities.

Whittier College alumni, though still few in numbers, were already doing well in their graduate and professional studies.

2

RESURGENCE OF STUDENT ACTIVITIES AND
SOCIAL LIFE AT WHITTIER

STRONG TIDES OF CHRISTIAN idealism marked the immediate post-war years on the Whittier campus. Winning of the war had made the world safe for democracy. The parliament of nations promised to keep the peace. Prohibition had driven out the iniquitous saloon. Universal suffrage recognized woman as equal partner with man. And Christ's army of disciples stood ready to carry salvation (and sanitation) to the pagan world! Something of this spirit moved across all the denominational campuses of the land and pervaded Whittier, too.

To enlist young Friends in this great effort came a Deputation Committee in 1920: Clarence E. Pickett, Quaker pastor formerly of Penn and Earlham and now of the Five Years Meeting; Willis Beede, former Whittier student and assistant superintendent of Friends missions; and Ellison Purdy. They explained the Friends Forward Movement, the part Quakers would play in the Inter-Church World Movement that planned to recruit 100,000 young people within the five years to go out as gospel missionaries, doctors, and teachers. It was a time for personal commitment, for the giving of life to the highest purposes. A fifth of the Whittier student body became Life Recruits, "consecrating their lives to Christ." It was the high resolve of these 20 students and one professor to train for Christian Life-Service "either at home or abroad."*

With this Deputation Committee came Howard H. Brinton, publicity secretary of the American Friends Service Committee, who told the Whittier students of another dimension in Quaker activity overseas: work of the Friends Reconstruction Unit during and after the War, in France, in Siberia, in Vienna, in Poland, and in Germany, where child feeding had been carried on at the special request of Herbert Hoover. Calls for Friends workers still came from many countries, "pleading for the gospel of good will through deeds of Christian love and Brotherhood of man." Half a dozen and more Whittier students and alumni had already served in this work.

Supporting such idealism, the daily half-hour chapel presented a wide range of devotional and occasional programs. The Y.M. and Y.W.C.A. continued their weekly meetings and annual Asilomar conferences. The Student Volunteers led among the Life Recruits, and reported their national conventions to the entire student body.

It was a heady time in which to be young and to feel the call to high endeavor.

EXUBERANCE ALSO RETURNED to other phases of student life. Restored was the freshman-sophomore brawl and the painting of the winners' class numerals on The Rock for the rest of the fall semester. Then at mid-year came the ceremonious repainting of The Rock with the college "W" in purple and gold. It proved to be a bit difficult to keep some of the returned soldier boys "down on the farm / Once they had seen Paree." Misapplication of what one of them called "christening fluid" led the local police to lay

---

*And most of this number did go out as pastors, missionaries, or teachers to serve in Alaska (William and Maria Henley), Belgium (John and Grace Winston), Syria (Furnas and Helen Trueblood), or to serve as pastors, physicians, Y.M.C.A. secretaries, or teachers nearer home.

Forty years later, the Peace Corps and VISTA programs challenged students in much the same way.

stern hands on college delinquents from prominent families. But President Wright's approach to malefactors was suasive rather than punitive.

Queening, in the phrase of that time, occasioned faculty disapproval. But in June 1921, after a particularly ardent spring—and "in view of the social conditions, not approved by the Faculty"—

> a motion prevailed that social visiting between men and women shall not be permitted during the hours regularly set apart for class work . . . unless authorized by the proper faculty authority.

By fall, however, after a spate of summer weddings, the president reported to the faculty that the Student Body was taking the initiative, in "correcting some of the most objectionable features of the social life on the campus." And the noxious ordinance was suspended. The next year the no-nonsense faculty tried again: put the girls to their studies at 7:30 p.m. and lights out at 10:30 Sunday through Thursday—made the proctor of the men's dorm responsible for proper conduct—adjourned all college functions at 10:30—and underscored the required chaperonage of college parties and trips. Queening somehow prevailed in this age of comparative innocence and, by and large, student conduct was notably proper.

Shenanigans, of course, there were in the dormitories: the pranks of perennial sophomores, the stacking of rooms and water fights, the serenading of the girls and surreptitious fudge. As a lark, some sophomore men ran their own candidate for Beauty Queen in the contest held by the W.A.A. in preparation for its Carnival. The male candidate was "Percy" (Harold Cunningham, gifted singer but short on stature), who enjoyed the frolic. Leading students and faculty declared for "Percy."* Local and metropolitan papers joined in the sport. The Percy Club bought votes recklessly, expecting to recoup at their carnival sideshow. They stuffed the ballot box; they won. But "Percy" was not crowned. The joke had been carried too far—hearts were broken—and the W.A.A. called off the Carnival. In the excitement of

*Among them, Bill Jones, Tom Bewley, Vernon Hanna, Albert Behnke, Roy Votaw, and Professors Smith and Hockett.

the contest, no one had given thought to preparation for the Carnival itself!

LITERARY, DRAMATIC, AND FORENSIC activities—all were stimulated by the return of the men and increased enrollment after the war.

The *Quaker Campus*, which had dwindled to a small three-column fortnightly in 1918-19, resumed its larger format and weekly publication. With its ups and downs of successive editors, who struggled with more-or-less faithless staffs to fill its columns, the Q.C. again fulfilled its avowed purposes. It carried the usual flow of campus news—editorialized for more pep at games, less complaining, and improved student behavior—predicted athletic victories and detailed every play of the games—featured Dorm Life, exchanges, joke fillers, local ads. An occasional item of note: A Modern Parable by Jessamyn West fabled a cruel tyrant entombed alive by his slaves while inspecting his monument built by their toil. A chapel talk by Frank G. Swain '11e detailed his experiences as a Rhodes scholar. An Outburst by W[illiam] C. J[ones] lamented "the glaring, unapologetic anti-Japanese propaganda" in a current movie. An editorial by Leighton R. Stewart (a veteran) foresaw dire results from rejection of the League of Nations. And the Q.C's razzberry edition, *The Durham Deacon*, was neither worse nor better than other such festive folly of the boy-bishops.

The *Acropolis* had failed to appear in the wartime spring of 1918. A year later it resumed its annual summary of student life. Predictable in scope and content though it was, yet, through the narrow and stilted format, shines forth the student life of Whittier College during these years.

Dramatic productions, the Junior and Senior plays, had for a decade been largely the popular Broadway shows of past seasons. Then in 1920, with the return of Herbert E. Harris, they again became more literary, such as *The Romancers* by Rostand. But the principal undertaking of this time was the development of a new amphitheater for outdoor productions, the earlier one having fallen quite into decay.

It was Professor Harris's idea. The site he chose was the south slope of Fire Hill in a natural cirque lying high above the rest of the campus and overlooking the valley as far as sea and island. In the spring of 1921 he won over the seniors to the project. As he himself later wrote:

> Given permission by the board, they hired a team of horses, which they kept stabled near by, and took turns when out of classes at grading the site. They planted temporary shrubs, constructed rough board seats, staged the dramatization of *The Scarlet Letter* with every student in college in the cast.

It was Harris's own dramatization of Hawthorne's classic, which he had directed the preceding year at Penn College, where it had been commended for the delicacy with which it portrayed "the consequences of sin." The Whittier production, promoted by Gerald C. Kepple, senior class president, was hugely successful. The one night's performance cleared $1,600, which with some special gifts paid for the amphitheater as then developed. Later senior classes improved it. The Herbert E. Harris Amphitheater, as it was later called, was to be the setting for successive commencement exercises through the years.

In forensics, the days were gone when Prohibition and Peace were the principal subjects for oratory and debate. Other topics of national interest became the whetstone for sharpening the wits of future legislators, lawyers, teachers, preachers, and other professional and business men.* Coaching them, with the help of the history professors, were successively Eugene Knox, Herbert Harris, and Victor F. Deihl (A.B., Michigan) who taught public speaking and then economics for several years.

The expressed need for a men's literary society led to the organization of a group in the fall of 1921 that elected Warren Mendenhall as its president and chose as its name: Franklin Literary Society. Its aim was to cultivate its members in the art of public expression. The meetings mixed a large ingredient of parliamentary horseplay with prepared and extemporary speeches on "any subject whatever, be it pathetic, sublime, or comic." Other principal activities were the taking in of new members, devising discomforts for their initiation, and the election of offi-

*Gerald C. Kepple, Tom Erwin, Tom Bewley, Arthur Corey, Oran Cosand, Joseph Wright, Teauey Hawley, Furnas Trueblood, Herbert Lund, John Winston, Raymond Janeway, Albert Behnke, Merritt Burdg, Wilfred and Clifford Haworth.

cers. The Franklin Society, which soon dropped its middle name, was a far cry from the earlier Athenaeum, but it was not quite the fraternal Acolytes with Promethean ritual.

The women students were not far behind. In mid-May of the same college year, they organized their own literary club, the Palmer Society, of which Ida Crum was the initial president. The Palmers' exalted purpose was "to promote appreciation of English, both in Literature and in its common usage." They exchanged ideas and ideals, broadened outlooks and cultivated "a taste for the better things." For their first full year, they elected Jessamyn West and then Louise Hollingsworth as successive presidents. What their mysteries, no man knew.

With all of these literary, forensic, dramatic, and journalistic activities—dormitory life, stepping out, and queening on the front steps—there was still time for many of the same students to sing in the women's and men's glee clubs, each of them giving a dozen or so performances, including a home concert, and taking an eventful if exhausting spring trip.

ATHLETICS AND SPORTS revived at once at the end of the war. In the spring of 1919, the basketball team lost only to Redlands, and won from Throop (soon to be Caltech), Pomona, and Occidental by substantial scores. Three of the same men made up a tennis team. Most of them also played a late season of baseball. But in track Whittier was represented at the intercollegiate meet by only one man—Verl Murray, "possibly the best hurdler in the world"—who won both of his races.

Now women's sports received a new emphasis. In the fall of 1919, the faculty approved interschool competition, but restricted the entrance of Whittier College women to "such games only as are played without gate receipts." As assistant instructor in history, social sciences, and girls' athletics "at a salary of $300," Edith Logan advanced their sports and games by long strides. In 1920, they organized a Women's Athletic Association, and this W.A.A. held its first carnival to raise money for equipment, as the girls were fielding baseball and basketball teams. And, above all, the girls wanted the fellows to take it all very seriously, which it was evidently difficult for them to do. At Bovard Field in the spring of 1921, the Whittier baseball team "trampled on the coeds of U.S.C." The score was 43-39. An *Examiner* photo caught an action shot of B. Smith swinging a hefty bat. In the return game, "after playing havoc with Pitcher B. Smith," the U.S.C. team was treated to "a sample of the real thing" in pitching at the hands of Gladys Foster who pitched "a mean ball." But B. Smith came through at the plate,

> slamming out two home runs and a double and a couple of singles, then Gladys Foster helped out the score by hitting the pill for a home run with two on base.

Others, too, had their innings—as reported in the Q.C.—but the Whittier girls lost the game. Miss Logan complained that the attending crowd was "too busy razzing the umpire to give much attention to encouraging the team." The student editor assured her: "The boys are for girls' athletics strong!"

It was football—for men, of course—that caught up the student body with a driving unifying purpose. And Whittier again fielded a team in the fall of 1919. With but 50 men in the college, Coach Van Cleave had 25 out for football. There was only one veteran player, Joe Siemon, whom the others elected captain. They lost every game played that season, totalling but 20 points against their opponents' 94. But the unanimous verdict of students and townsmen was that "the Quakers died game."

In 1920 Esek Perry replaced Van Cleave as coach, bringing with him some championship players from Coronado High School. He developed a strong fast team that took the other colleges by surprise. For the first game of the season, played on Patterson Field, the Occidental coach was so confident of a pushover that he went off for the afternoon to see U.S.C. beat Stanford, while his frantic assistants watched the fighting Quakers tear the stripes off the Tigers 21-7. The Whittier students and town rooters went wild with excitement. Next came victories over Redlands and Caltech. Only Pomona stopped the Poets (14-0), thus retaining the championship. As comic antimasque for the season, the Poets "completely annihilated" the Southern Branch (as U.C.L.A. was known when first born from the brow of the L.A. Normal). The score was 103-0, and as the *Times* reported, it revealed "the ability of the Whittier team to keep running up and down the field without getting tired." Altogether it was a year to breathe new life into the Howling Hundred.*

For the next football season (1921) most of the same players were on hand, and Whittier College, because of its small enrollment, was allowed to play freshmen on its varsity. The season opened with a close win over Oxy on Hadley Field before a crowd overflowing the stands. At Redlands the next week, the Poets won the hardest fought game of the season. Next came Caltech, opening with Ed "Puss" Thompson's squirming through tackle for thirty yards and a touchdown, but, when Ed Suggett received the second-half kickoff, he

> fumbled it, picked it up and with perfect interference, made straight down the center of the field . . . ninety-five yards . . . third touchdown.

Against Southern Branch, Whittier again won handily (63-0), and Perry played most of his men from the bench. And finally on Armistice Day at Claremont, the Poets beat the Sagehens 42-9, "winning, for the first time, the Southern California intercollegiate conference championship." After that, it little mattered that the Whittier boys lost to U.S.C. (0-14) and to University of Arizona (0-7). Three of the Poets—Suggett, Joe Buckmaster, Albert "Mick" Madden—received All-Southern-California honors. Walter Camp honorably-mentioned Suggett for All-American, and seductive scouts from U.S.C. and Stanford made offers that he rejected.

The football championship of 1921 was the high point in the postwar life on the Whittier College campus.

---

*This loose gathering of town boosters was first called into being by the piping voice of little Mel Rich, five-year-old son of Walter G. ("Bill") Rich, manager of the Gas Company. At a game back in 1914, when Whittier faced defeat and the stands sat dispirited and still, little Melvin cried out, "Yell, Daddy! Yell, Whittier!" and next day Rich *père* and others formed the Howling Hundred, which, through the years, supported the Poet teams and their coaches, raised money to send championship teams on trips for intersectional games, provided part-time jobs (real work, not subsidies) to deserving boys who needed them.

It worked both ways. Of the Whittier boys thus helped with part-time and summer work, the Southern Counties Gas Company retained a number for permanent employment, six of them from these years rising to positions of responsibility and divisional management, three of them retiring after 40 years and more of service.

3

PROBLEMS OF THE WHITTIER COLLEGE BOARD
FINANCE AND DEVELOPMENT

THE BOARD OF TRUSTEES changed in character during the years immediately following World War I. The Old Guard passed; New Blood came in. Denominational ties lessened, though most of the new trustees were Quakers. Relationship to the wider community increased, as most of the new board members were business men. As a matter of form, California Yearly Meeting still nominated the trustees, at least 12 of the 15 drawn from its membership.

Dr. W. V. Coffin was the outstanding old-timer, closely identified with the college since its permanent establishment as an academy in 1891. Now, in 1920, he resigned from the board after serving 18 years as its president.* Lydia Jackson, owing to illness, had already given over as secretary of the board in 1918. Absalom Rosenberger took her place briefly. His minutes, on typed numbered pages, are the first ones to survive since the records of 1888-1900. Older Friends who passed from the scene during these years were Curtis E. Way, A. W. Naylor, and H. D. Williams—J. J. Mills, Dr. L. M. Greene, and Mary H. Lewis. D. C. Andrews, after 20 years on the board, resigned to make room for a younger man. Founding families continued to be represented by Emilie V. Hadley and Eva [Jessup] Cook—and A. C. Johnson remained active as a college trustee.

New names appeared. Virgil J. Trueblood, elected to the board in 1919, served as its secretary and then president before becoming treasurer and business manager of the college. Albert N. Chamness, named to the board in 1920, succeeded Trueblood as president in 1922. Herman L. Perry (banker son of a Friends pastor and brother of Esek Perry) came to the board in 1921, later to be its president. C. Bevan Johnson (also a banker and attorney, schoolmaster of that second Academy) was elected to the board the same year, at once becoming its secretary and later its presi-

*Dr. Coffin went to Richmond as director of the College Endowment Campaign for all the colleges of the Five Years Meeting. Within a year, he returned to Whittier seriously ill, and the death of his schoolboy son Samuel was followed next day by the death of his centenarian mother. Upon Dr. Coffin's recovery, he continued his interest in the college the remainder of his long life.

dent. C. C. Barr (Methodist lumberman and banker) and Cass A. Rees (pioneer grocer and realtor) began their terms of service at this time, as did Thomas Newlin. Bailey Howard '13 and then Edward E. Thomas '07 were first among the alumni to share the direction of their alma mater.

Such, then, was the shifting pattern of the Board of Trustees, with three successive presidents within the five years of Dr. Wright's presidency of the college faculty.

THE FINANCIAL AND DEVELOPMENT needs of Whittier College were clear: expendable income, productive endowment, additional buildings, expanded campus. Having weathered the war, the college had to move forward. It was the business of the board to push ahead.

Despite the postwar increase in enrollment, the college was running an annual deficit of about $10,000. The endowment was little more than $150,000; double that amount was needed to forestall further deficits. As for buildings, little Naylor Hall was the only new building since the south wing of Founders Hall (as it was now called) and the Girls' Cottage—Tebbetts Gym being hardly more than a barn. And the campus itself—less than 20 acres of knobby hillside!

The trustees proposed a $200,000 campaign for the year 1920-21, $75,000 of it for endowment and $125,000 for buildings.

Again there was master-planning by the college architects, Allison and Allison, who dusted off their old campus map. They prepared sketches for a cluster of men's dormitory cottages below Fire Hill, and for an additional dormitory cottage to accommodate fifty women. The college board asked Esek Perry to devote half-time to fund-raising. President Wright suggested that he solicit the Friends churches throughout the Yearly Meeting. There was hope, too, that the Friends Forward Movement would yield support for the endowment portion of the campaign, particularly as Dr. W. V. Coffin now headed that larger effort for Friends colleges. But growing opposition among some California Friends to the averred liberalism of the Five Years Meeting led the Whittier College board to withdraw cautiously from the Forward Movement. However, Friends of the Yearly Meeting churches were still not moved by Perry's appeal for substantial support for their denominational college.

Therefore in April 1921, the trustees reshaped the objectives of their campaign for $200,000. All of this amount, they decided, should be earmarked for endowment; and they petitioned the General Education Board (a Rockefeller benevolence) for a grant of one-third of this amount. In addition, the college board solicited funds to pay off current indebtedness, and asked the General Education Board for $5,000 for each of the next two years to help sustain the college pending the increase of endowment income. In May, Rockefeller officials visited the Whittier campus and agreed to grant the $66,667, contingent upon the college raising $133,333. They also agreed to grant the requested sustaining funds.

With these assurances, the college board proceeded to set up its campaign. Subscriptions would be in the form of five-year notes, the subscriber to pay interest to the college at 7%. Albert N. Chamness undertook direction of the campaign, with Gerald C. Kepple '21 in charge of publicity. They announced an intensive eight-day drive. This time they directed their appeal, not to Friends meetings, but to the wider Whittier community. The Chamber of Commerce cooperated in sponsoring an invitational Civic Dinner at the First Friends Church on September 23, 1921. Chamness outlined the need—$133,333 plus $20,000 to clear indebtedness.

The goal was not met in eight days. Indeed, after a fortnight, the college board put Chamness on salary. Then, after six weeks' further work, he reported substantial progress: subscriptions totalling $125,000. And the college needed only $30,000 more to clear itself and secure the matching grant of $66,667. By March 1st—without tear-jerking finale at Yearly Meeting, or climactic midnight with fireworks—the campaign quietly reached its goal. Then the General Education Board signed the final contract, in which it agreed to make its payments to the college *proportional to the amounts actually collected on subscriptions*, that is, year by year as the notes were paid off.

The endowment campaign of 1921-22 exemplified the pattern of support for Whittier College at that time. Of the $200,000 pledged and promised, approximately $100,000 came from non-

Friends: $66,667 from the Rockefeller grant and about $33,333 from Whittier townsmen who were not Quakers. Of the $100,000 or so subscribed by Friends, only $10,000 came from members of Yearly Meeting churches scattered beyond the Whittier area, and about $90,000 came from members of the Whittier Friends Church and from other Friends nearby.

A year later (February 1923), the college still had less than a total of $200,000 of *actual* endowment funds invested, for the fruits of the recent campaign were still largely in promissory notes. But at this time the college did have $300,000 endowment (*including* the notes) producing interest or income at about 7%. And it had some $90,000 more of anticipated endowment funds, including the Rockefeller grant yet to be received. Therefore, the total endowment in hand, in pledges, and in contingencies added up toward an uneasy $400,000.

However, there was no money at all for building. The students themselves had financed and built the Harris Amphitheater in the spring of 1921. It was as much as the board could do to put in a storm drain where the old amphitheater had been, and later to fill the arroyo to level off a woman's athletic field north of Tebbetts Gym. The need continued, not only for dormitories, but for an auditorium and fine arts building, a library, and a main classroom building "to replace old 'Founders' Hall."

EXPANSION OF THE CAMPUS, urged by Addison Naylor right after the war, seemed the imperative need.

There were but two directions in which the campus could be extended without crossing a street. North of the campus was the ten-acre Lot #1 Block H of the original town plat, but this had long since been subdivided by A. L. Reed, with houses built along Painter Avenue and Philadelphia, Berkeley and Stanford Way. East of the campus, and outside the original town limits, was the Worsham Ranch, consisting of 133 acres of hill land broken by ridges, arroyos and one broad canyon.

Originally the Worsham Ranch had been a quarter section of government land taken up and dropped by several homesteaders between the years 1875 and 1885 when southern California was opening up. Then William G. Worsham of Los Angeles filed on it under the Homestead Act. He expected to commute his obligation in six months by paying the Government the usual $1.25 per acre ($200 for the 160 acres), but a neighbor contested his claim, and Worsham was obliged to meet the standard homesteading requirement of five-years' residence and minor improvements.

In 1886 the Worshams started to live in the little ranch house (built on the site later occupied by Wanberg Hall) and planted pepper trees to shade it. In time they put in olive trees around on the western slope of the ridge and oranges in the bottom of the broad canyon. But for the time being, Mr. Worsham continued his business in the City (Los Angeles), doubtless driving out to his ranch on weekends. When the Worshams had proved up their claim, the Government issued them a deed (14 August 1893), signed boldly by Grover Cleveland as President of the United States.* As it happened, the Worshams' only access to their ranch house was across land soon to become the campus of Whittier College. They asked and secured permission to drive in and out across the college grounds. Some years later the Worshams sold the north 20 acres of their quarter section to the Home Oil Company, and then five acres on their southwest corner to Dr. Fred Robbins. For themselves, the Worshams built a new ranch house up at the head of Philadelphia Street. Soon thereafter, Mr. Worsham was killed in an accident—his horse took fright up at the oil drilling and backed his rig off the embankment. His widow continued to live on "the home place" and held the ranch together, refusing to sell any further part of it.

The dreamers of dreams—Professor Harris certainly one of them—saw the Worsham Ranch as the natural extension of the college campus. But it was not available. Then, suddenly, in the spring of 1923 Mrs. Worsham indicated her willingness to sell—but only if the buyer took the whole property. Her price was $230,000. "The College did not need the entire ranch, and had no money to buy any of it." But the trustees got wind of "other interests" considering its purchase. This would have foreclosed future expansion of the college. Realtors Gurney Maple and Cass A. Rees secured an option so as to let the college see what it might be able to work out. . .

*Mailed to W. G. Worsham (Los Angeles Furniture Company, Los Angeles) this deed now rests in the college vault.

But there were other problems for the trustees to work out at this same time.

PRESIDENT WRIGHT had already handed in his resignation on February 27, 1923. In doing so he felt relieved of a great burden, and he was in good spirits when he left that board meeting and greeted one of his faculty colleagues crossing the campus.

There was apparently but one question that separated Wright from his trustees: the function of the college president. Should he devote himself largely to administration of academic affairs and student life? Or should he give himself largely to outside promotion, fund-raising, and campus development? In what must have been a showdown, President Wright presented his letter of resignation. As then reported, "He did not feel able to assume the responsibility of looking after the finances of the college as was expected if he remained." There was evident surprise among the trustees, but they promptly accepted the president's resignation—with no recorded minute of regret. Then they moved at once to "outline a financial policy to be followed in the matter of raising funds for the college."

Harry N. Wright's resignation came as a surprise also to Friends in the Yearly Meeting and to the college community. The faculty being informed, at once passed a resolution of sincere regrets and appreciation of his "unswerving integrity," his high educational standards, his fair dealing and sense of democracy. The Q.C. editor wrote that it was

> largely due to his efforts that the college has taken rapid strides in the advancement of its standards which have placed it in the scholastic position it occupies today. . .

It was only then, the first of June, that the college board passed an appropriate resolution to "assure Dr. Wright of our warm appreciation" and to hope for him "great future success" in whatever field he entered.

Harry Wright did not yet know what he would do next.*

---

*By August he had two positions: a lectureship in mathematics at the University of California at Berkeley for the year, and the deanship of Earlham College to begin in the fall of 1924. Subsequently he went to City College of New York, soon assumed administrative duties there, and served eleven years as its president before his retirement.

A tall spare man, unassuming but friendly, with a tight voice but a twinkle, precise of mind and firm of convictions—Harry N. Wright was the first president of Whittier College who was not a recorded Friends minister—the first to come from a university professorship—the first to have a Ph.D. In fact, he was the first Ph.D. among the presidents of the denominational colleges and universities of southern California, for it was still the era of academic divines, when good churchmen with D.D.'s served (and often served well) as college presidents.

What Harry N. Wright had done for Whittier College in his six years as dean and president was evident. He had guided it through World War I and into the postwar period. He had altered its character from being a denominational Quaker college to being a Friends college for the wider community. He had changed its academic goals in line with standards then established for undergraduate colleges.

Upon his resignation in the winter of 1923, the college trustees at once sought his successor. By mid-April they were in touch with Dr. Walter F. Dexter, professor of education at Earlham College. By mid-May they offered him the presidency, and he accepted it, perhaps not quite knowing what he was getting into. For Dr. Wright felt so uncertain about the financial future of Whittier College that he said to a young colleague before leave-taking,

"I hope the college doesn't have to close its doors next year."

4

A FRESH APPROACH——THE WHITTIER IDEA
FOR A "FUNCTIONAL" COLLEGE

DYNAMIC OPTIMISM was the posture of the new Whittier College. It characterized the new president. It marked the breath-taking occasion: the John Greenleaf Whittier Banquet—December 17, 1923—the Grand Ballroom of the new Ambassador Hotel in Los Angeles.

At the speakers' table stood Dr. Walter F. Dexter as toastmaster. He was short, clean-cut, boyish. Notable guests sat to his left and right: Governor Friend Richardson, Speaker of the Assembly John C. Merriam, civic officials, past presidents of the college, presidents of the student body and alumni, presidents of other colleges and universities in southern California . . . the main speaker, the extraordinary concert artist! With the poise of an accomplished after-dinner speaker, which he was, President Dexter faced the sea of colorful tables and the guests in all shades of Sunday-best and formal attire! To celebrate thus the birthday of John Greenleaf Whittier and to support thus the college bearing his name, these friends of Whittier College had paid $100 a plate for their dinner.

But the essential feast was one for mind and spirit. Even the long long trail of introductions proved tolerable: the honorable this and distinguished that, with responses, greetings, and congratulations. Striking a cultural note of the highest order, Madame Ernestine Schumann-Heink—beloved the world over as contralto and mother-image—sang a full recital of arias and German Lieder (her fee a handsome $2,500). And her listeners would not let her go until, for the Christmastime, she sang "Stille Nacht, Heilige Nacht."

At last, William Gibbs McAdoo, upon gracious presentation, towered above Walter Dexter for the moment, then addressed himself to his subject: "John Greenleaf Whittier, the National Idealist."

> Whittier was the American poet of freedom, faith and the sentiment of the common people . . . The inward voice was his inspiration, and of all American poets, he was the one whose song was most like a prayer . . .

So the speaker began—McAdoo, genius of the New York subways, wartime Secretary of the Treasury, post-war leader of the Democratic Party. And he continued in moving eloquence his eulogy of the Quaker poet. "No other poet has sounded more native notes . . . so much of the American legendry . . . so patriotic, clean and true." And so he continued. . . .

But who was this young college president now seated beside him? (Walter Dexter impressed people as boyish, though now 37.) Who was this dynamic optimist who, in a matter of months, had swept the faltering college toward what seemed assured success?

154

Son of an English horse dealer, an immigrant, Walter Friar Dexter was born in Chicago. When their home was burned out, the family moved to a farm in Missouri. After a boyhood and one-room schooling there, Walter set out on his own, "working his way through the West as a farmhand." Aged 19 he found himself in Oskaloosa, Iowa. There he was encouraged to get an education. Already in his twenties, he started high school work at Penn Academy. He graduated, married Ethel Smith (Howard Hockett singing at their wedding), and at once entered Penn College. He was an active student, "undefeated debater during his under-graduate days." A frequent speaker in Friends meetings, he was soon recorded a minister. In his junior year, Pres. David Edwards called upon him to head a financial campaign for endowment funds and new buildings. During this, Penn College was utterly destroyed by fire, with the loss of two lives, college records, valu-able collections. It was the courage and determination of young Dexter that led older Friends in the fund-raising for rebuilding. After graduation (A.B., 1916), Dexter went to New York to raise money for Oakwood Seminary. Then he studied at Columbia, coming under the progressive influence of William H. Kilpatrick of Teachers' College (M.A., 1918). Next he moved to Boston, served as a Friends pastor, and studied at Harvard (Ed.D., 1921)—the *first* among the first granted that new degree by its Graduate School of Education. Thereupon, David Edwards called him to be professor of education at Earlham College, of which he had become president.

It was as a proven fund-raiser and educator that the Whittier board invited Walter F. Dexter to visit Whittier College in mid-April 1923 as candidate for its presidency. He came early in May. The trustees took him up the hill to look over the Worsham Ranch, already optioned for purchase. They told him of the proposed Syndicate of 50 business men, each pledging $3,000 to finance the purchase, to subdivide parts and thus pay for the ranch, and to give the central 50 to 100 acres free of cost to the college. And as Dexter and his hosts stood there on Fire Hill, they looked out upon the inspiring spread of citrus lands in the valley and the forest of oil derricks newly sprung up at Santa Fe Springs. (And they heard just behind them the panting of gas-engines pumping wells in the old oil field of the Whittier hills.)

In the few days of his visit, Dr. Dexter talked with the college faculty—addressed the student body—preached in First Friends. Everyone found him winsome and youthful, with a contagious and friendly outreach of personality.

Would he accept the presidency of Whittier College?

Dexter's answer was Yes, at $5,000 (which was double his Earlham salary and $2,000 more than that of President Wright). Provided also, that Whittier moved forward with the Syndicate purchase of the Worsham Ranch. These conditions stated, Dexter entrained for the East.

The college board and the Syndicate acted promptly, met his conditions, and wired him en route. Dexter then accepted the offer—but with one more proviso: As he would be devoting himself largely to college promotion and fund-raising, he would need as dean, Dr. J. Herschel Coffin, then professor of psychology at Earlham. The board agreed but boggled at the proposed $4,500 salary for him as likely to cause difficulty with the $2,700 top professors. Then, too, Dexter wished to bring two office secretaries. The board reminded him that he would have to raise the money to support these expenditures.

Dr. and Mrs. Dexter and son Walter reached Whittier by midsummer. And on August 14th, Dexter presented to the board his immediate plans for the development of Whittier College:

1. *First Goal.* Attempt to raise one million dollars in the shortest possible time.

2. *First Event.* Build an organization around what might be called "The John Greenleaf Whittier One Hundred Thousand Dollar Banquet of Southern California" to be held . . . December 17th. . .

3. *Nature of Banquet.* (a) Sell one thousand plates at one hundred dollars per plate making a total of $100,000.

(b) Secure some national or international speaker . . .

(c) Arrange for fifty tables of twenty plates each . . .

(d) Appoint an executive secretary for each table group . . . responsible for selling tickets . . .

(e) An effort will be made *"IMMEDIATELY"* . . . to secure several large gifts . . .

(f) *Purpose of Banquet* . . . interesting citizens of Los Angeles and Whittier . . . giving publicity to the college . . . collecting a large number of small gifts . . . securing a sum of money for immediate use.

On motion of A. C. Johnson, seconded by H. L. Perry (both of them solid bankers), the board adopted the young president's plan.

But to many persons it seemed a preposterous proposal!—more grandiose than the Greater Whittier College scheme of 1917. Strong members of the college board, however, having now launched the Whittier College Syndicate, were caught up in the booming spirit of the times. What—with the phenomenal oil production down at the nearby Springs, the expanded agricultural economy, the steady rise in bank deposits in Whittier, the fortunes being made in southern California real estate!—Dexter's financial program was not overbold, was indeed modest compared with current development programs for other colleges.

An *"IMMEDIATE"* and substantial gift was too significant to await announcement at the banquet.

A week after Dexter outlined his plan, Aubrey Wardman, a new member of the college board, walked into the president's office with his own offering of $100,000 "to be used in any way the Board of Trustees sees fit." This good news—Dexter was in ecstasy—was at once released to the Los Angeles *Times*: "the largest individual gift which the college has as yet received." It was a tremendous boost.

A. Wardman was an extraordinary man, self-made and self-educated. He was a Canadian farm-boy who grew up with the telephone industry. In 1903 he had superintended construction of the Whittier Home Telephone lines. At age 32 he controlled the company, shortly became its owner, a substantial community leader. In 1921-22, while recovering from serious illness, he risked all he had to buy up options and make down-payments on townsite lots in Santa Fe Springs, and leased them for oil production. The first well on his land proved a gusher. In the spring of 1923, he had a first-month's royalty check of $100,000!

The day after the Whittier board offered Dexter the presidency, its executive committee (with Dexter present and discussing "certain matters") recommended Aubrey Wardman for board membership. Three months later, Dexter announced the gift that Wardman had made before he had yet had time and means to clear his own investments, to secure his own future, to travel the world, or to build himself a new home. It was an extremely generous gift, coming from a man whose net wealth lay still in the future. But Wardman sensed his new rôle as an enlightened capitalist.

> All of us who have been fortunate [he then said], owe more to society at large than the mere building up of a large fortune . . . There's a duty we owe to society in general . . . to help worthy institutions.

He was happy to help the local college, and hoped (with the further blessing of good fortune) to do more "for the community which has been so kind to me."*

At the great banquet, President Dexter proudly, and again, announced the Wardman gift and the imminent construction of a men's dormitory to be named for him.

But "Gus" Wardman (as he was called) had made more than this gift. He had worked hard throughout the fall of 1923 to insure the success of the banquet, and urged others to join in the effort. In all, 100 influential citizens sponsored the occasion, these divided into teams of ten each. The college students themselves undertook to sell 200 places, promised that then the entire student body of 200 would be guests without charge. With parades, posters, and playlets—and an assist from parents and friends—they fulfilled their quota. And Dexter promoted an essay contest in the high schools of the state—"Why a Christian College is a Fitting Memorial to John Greenleaf Whittier"—the prize winners also honored at the banquet.

But even while the drive was going on to sell the 1,000 tickets at $100 each—against a dead weight of skepticism—the Syndicate pushed ahead with the College Hills subdivision. On Decem-

---

*The public announcement of Wardman's gift precipitated a strike of his nineteen telephone operators. "They held that if he could afford to give Whittier College $100,000, he could well afford to increase their wages." This, then, he did. He had already proposed a raise, but was awaiting a ruling from the State Industrial Welfare Commission. A friend of labor, and his Whittier Telephone Company considered a good place to work, Wardman felt personally hurt by the strike.

ber 1st the lots went on sale. And on December 17th, Walter Dexter announced confidently to the assembled banquet guests the greatly expanded Whittier College campus.

The thousand and more guests at the Great Banquet, having heard such announcements, the introductions, the inspiring music, were now still listening to the celebrated Mr. McAdoo extolling John Greenleaf Whittier, the Quaker poet,

> revered by the people because he was a spokesman of the people . . .
> He possessed a pure and simple heart. He was a man that his people understood and one that understood his people.
> In his life can be found no better example of a national ideal.

The professors present were caught up with pride in the whirlwind of the occasion. It was exactly *one hundred days*, no more and no less, since the new college president had outlined to the faculty his plans for the year! And in that 100 days, this $100,000 banquet—the $100,000 Wardman gift—the 100 acres of additional campus!

There seemed no end in sight. And why not $1,000,000 for development of the New Whittier College!

THE NEW WHITTIER COLLEGE, however, was not essentially conceived in terms of campus and buildings. Rather, it was to be an idealistic experiment in higher education.

A strange team of opposites were Dexter and Coffin, whose common bond was a dream.

J. Herschel Coffin, a bit older than Walter Dexter, was a mild and slender man, already balding, refined of feature, tense as he spoke. But when he wore his hat, as he did in crossing the campus with a springy step, he always seemed more youthful than he was. Herschel Coffin, kinsman of Dr. W. V. Coffin, also came of the long family line that had made the Quaker progress from Nantucket to North Carolina to Indiana to Iowa. After graduation from Penn, he proceeded to the Quaker-founded Cornell Unversity (Ph.D., 1907), then settled down as professor of psychology at Earlham College. Besides his thesis, he published two other books during the next years: *The Socialized Conscience* (1913), a psychological and sociological textbook on Ethics; and *Personality in the Making* (Houghton Mifflin, 1923), a substantial contribution to the psychology of personality. However, it was not so much as a scholar but as a philosopher that J. Herschel Coffin made his noteworthy contribution to higher education.

The dream that Coffin and Dexter shared was an educational philosophy for the redevelopment of Whittier College as a "functional" college. Later, in his *Story of an Educational Adventure* (1928), Dr. Coffin wrote of the birth of what they later called "the Whittier Idea."

Over a cup of tea brewed in Coffin's tiny office at Earlham, he and Dexter questioned the value of "lectures, quizzes, examinations, and academic machinery in general" and noted the obvious "hiatus between 'education' and life."

> Would it be possible to construct an educational program . . . based upon the native tendencies and interests of young men and women . . . [and] actually correlate it with the concrete needs of life?

Could they utilize "the tremendous content of the traditional curriculum" in fashioning such a college program? Or, would they have "to junk the whole works and strike out on an entirely new line"? Oh, for the chance to conduct such "a holy experiment in education"!

Little did they think that, within three months, way would open.

Whittier College seemed to Dexter a perfect setting for what he and Coffin wanted to do. It was a Friends college young enough to be flexible, and already accredited by the state university. Furthermore, it was located in a Friends community and a rapidly expanding area of great natural wealth.

When Walter Dexter arrived back in Richmond in May 1923, it was with Whittier College in his pocket.

Tea-drinking now went on in dead earnest. Of course he and Coffin needed no detailed blueprint to begin their new work. The new president at once assured the Whittier faculty that "an institution must grow upon its past" rather than being changed abruptly from without. But he and the new dean had certainly thought out in advance the *goals* toward which they would strive in remoulding Whittier College to their hearts' desire.

The Whittier Idea, as they conceived it, was threefold:

First, education must be functional. That is, education should prepare young people "for the exercise of the major human functions." Coffin and Dexter saw these in terms of five life-situations: the home-life situation, the vocational, the social, the avocational, and the religious or life-philosophy situation. They agreed that knowledge of sex and marriage, spiritual attitudes and life values, enriching hobbies and interests, participation in social and community life were quite as important in education as the wise choice of vocation and preparation for it.

Second, complete education must be religious education. They did not mean "religious education" in the usual sense. Rather, higher education should

> attempt to throw into the foreground of science . . . history . . . philosophy and every other subject the spiritual interpretation that by our best insight we believe Jesus would give.

Higher education, even in most so-called Christian colleges, was essentially pagan: behaviorism in psychology, mechanism in biology, materialism in physical sciences—determinism in history, imperialism in government, capitalism in economics—and skepticism in philosophy! Why could not a definitely Christian point of view, based upon the simple teachings of Jesus, pervade the entire curriculum and college?

Third, education must be democratic. It would have to be "real democracy," they agreed, "not simply lip service." For, democracy was an organizing principle, deriving not alone from their Quaker faith and practice, but from the heritage of American idealism and constitutional history. And they dreamed, as Coffin later wrote,

> of a 'community of will' which shall include every student, every faculty member, and the administration . . . based upon a spirit of friendship and good will.

Its objective should be the highest group welfare, "that each person may have the greatest opportunity for self-realization."

Such, in essence was the Whittier Idea, deriving from Dexter's training in educational theory and Coffin's in personality development. It also derived from their Quakerism, for they were sensitive to the implications of the Friendly tradition: simplicity of life, inner authority, respect for individual differences, spiritual reality. But neither of them, be it added, had any experience in college administration when they came to take up their duties in the fall of 1923 as president and as dean of Whittier College.

It is one thing to conceive a philosophy of higher education, and quite another to put it into effect. Committed to democratic procedure, Dexter and Coffin could not impose their educational philosophy, but had to win over the faculty to the Whittier Idea and its implications. For in the tradition of Friends colleges, the faculty itself was essentially the "authority" in academic matters.

In explaining to the faculty his hopes for a truly greater Whittier College, President Dexter used all his forensic gifts, and Dean Coffin spoke earnestly to his faculty colleagues, with diagram and example, of the Whittier Idea that would remould the curriculum and reform the entire pattern of college life. The imagination of younger professors was quickened by the prospect of educational adventure. But there was skepticism in the academic establishment.

After one enthusiastic exposition by Dexter of his educational philosophy, a mature professor stopped him to say:

"That was a good talk, Walter . . . but I didn't understand a word of it!"

Who comprised this faculty, whose understanding and support the new president and dean needed if they were to realize their dream of a functional, religiously-oriented, democratic college?

THE TEACHING FACULTY during Dexter and Coffin's first year at Whittier (1923-24) was, with but one exception, held-over from the preceding year. Of these professors something has already been said: Harris in English, Ostrom in chemistry, Skarstedt in mathematics, Mrs. Rosenberger in education, Smith in history, Esther Andrews in German, Hockett in music, Esek Perry in physical education. All told, it was a faculty of 21 full-time persons. Dean Coffin was the only one with a Ph.D., except for the professor of Biblical literature and philosophy, who was to be replaced at the end of the year.

It was certainly the desire of Dexter and Coffin to strengthen and stabilize the faculty, and to enlarge it by adding capable professors sympathetic to their views.

During the next eight years (1923-31), the faculty increased in numbers from 21 to 35, twelve professors with doctorates. Ten were given leaves of absence during these years (on approximately half salary) for further study, and of these six returned for extended periods of teaching, three of them with Ph.D's. By the spring of 1931, six faculty members had worked together with Dexter and Coffin for the eight years. Five others with Ph.D's had served the faculty for as many as five years; for example, Dr. Mary Hill (Ph.D., Stanford), an experienced teacher and accomplished Chaucerian scholar.

But the mere doctorate, important as that was becoming, was not a restricting criterion—as, for instance, in music and languages. A succession of instructors in piano included Ivan Knox and the brilliant young artist Arthur Hitchcock; and in 1929 Margaretha Lohmann came, fresh from extended European study. In French Dr. Jessie Smith (Ph.D., Liége) was followed by Dorothy Mead (A.M., Stanford and further study at Grenoble). In Spanish Alma Mozelle Anderson (M.A., Berkeley, with years of study in Spain and Mexico) began her thirty years of teaching at Whittier. Several other professors of unusual breadth of experience were added specifically to work with Dean Coffin in the curricular development that was under way.

It was this faculty—especially the weighty nucleus—that had to be won over to the Whittier Idea by Dexter's dynamic optimism and Coffin's quiet dialectic.

THE NEW CURRICULUM, as projected by Coffin, called for new types of instruction: the Correlation Course and the Project Method. And it also called for other changes, the further development of science courses for general education, and the modification of requirements for graduation. But the crux was to be the Correlation Course, and the key to orderly change was the curriculum committee of the faculty, which for 1923-24 comprised Professors Ostrom, Rosenberger, and Andrews. By May 1924, the new college catalog could do no more than promise that Whittier College was "earnestly seeking" to remedy notable defects of higher education:

to 'functionalize' the curriculum . . . building it around the Christian idealism of the great apostle of friendship . . . John Greenleaf Whittier.

It would take Coffin another year of work with the curriculum committee (now, Ostrom, Andrews, Smith, Williams) and with the faculty to secure approval of the new curriculum on April 3, 1925.

But with consent of the president, the dean then withheld publication of the catalog and postponed for another year the Correlation Course. He may have sensed that weighty members of the faculty had given their ayes to the noble experiment but not their hearts.

The year in which the New Curriculum remained in abeyance was not lost. Dexter had become the most widely-sought speaker in southern California, averaging 20 major speeches a month, and he never failed to touch upon the underlying themes of the Whittier Idea. At the same time Coffin placed three articles in national publications: *Religious Education, The Survey*, and *Social Science*. Thus Dexter and Coffin brought their educational philosophy to a wide audience and developed *outside* approval and support for it. Others joined in their effort. Paul Smith addressed a gathering of the alumni of Friends colleges on "The Modern College Curriculum," and appealed to them "not to join in the general criticism, but to stand back of their alma mater." By the time college opened in the fall of 1926, the Q.C. reported with undergraduate enthusiasm that "the attention of prominent universities and colleges of the country has been focused with approval and great interest" on the Correlation Course then to be launched. Certainly there had been encouraging letters from a good number of prominent educators.

The Correlation Course was a four-year sequence, the core of each student's program, three hours per week for a total of 24 units of social science credit.

The freshman course, *Human Issues*, oriented the student to college work, to his own abilities and powers as a student, to "that orderly body of knowledge touching the physical and social world in which he lives." It confronted him "with the major practical problems of modern life, such as war, poverty, race relations, etc., that are to-day demanding solution." It served to guide him in the selection of his vocation and course of study. Coffin brought Dr. Louis T. Jones from Earlham in 1925 to set up this course and to serve as Director of Correlation. Jones had an unusual breadth of training. His B.S. degree was in physical science, his M.A. in economics and sociology, his Ph.D. (Iowa) in American history. Dexter had been one of his students at Penn Academy. Jones had drunk philosophical tea with Dexter and Coffin at Earlham.

The sophomore correlation course, *The Psychological Aspect of Human Issues*, considered

> forms of conflict between traditions and customs on the one hand and new forms of mental response to new inventions and discoveries, to new desires created by economic and political progress on the other.

The human issues included questions of democracy and war, sex morality and industrial conflict. This year course included the equivalent of one-semester in general psychology. The first to undertake this course was John R. Wilkie, an older professor who first taught French and German, then history and classics. His training was varied (A.B., Centre College; M.A. and B.D., Princeton) and his interests wide-ranging. He was the archetypal college professor, beloved by his students, with kindly indulgence, easy grades, and wisdom that they appreciated.*

The junior correlation course, *The Basis of Social Progress*, was not to be given until the year 1927-28. Dealing with the forms of social organization and institutional life, the practical problems of human welfare and public health, it was taught by the new professor of sociology, Constantine Panunzio (A.B., Wesleyan University; Ph.D., Brookings). An Italian immigrant and a social economist, he had already become widely known for his writing on the national problem of immigration. When he left Whittier for university teaching, David E. Henley, sociologist and Friends minister, followed him in teaching this course.

*A story that he himself told with a twinkle: A burly football boy arose to translate the day's assignment in classics. After a moment's hesitation, he came halting forth—"A group of horsemen ... galloped swiftly ... over the plain."

"Excellent," said the professor. "Very good. Very good indeed! But would it not have been yet better to have said, 'A shower of stones, thrown from the battlements, struck them from afar'?"

The senior correlation course, *Philosophy of Christian Recon-struction*, was to be the capstone of the four-year sequence. Coffin's own course, it was not to be given until 1928: "An introduction to philosophy, including an effort to correlate the important findings of science." As later expressed more explicitly:

> The thesis of the course [was] that the religion of Jesus furnishes the only finally workable philosophy of life . . . based upon sound sociology.

Such, in essence, was the Correlation Course that was to be at the very center of the New Curriculum. But the faculty, whatever its approval in form, was not fully won to this educational adventure.

Within a month after the freshman and sophomore correlation classes began in 1926, this faculty skepticism was expressed in the Q.C. by a professor. He was pleased to note but few students expressing strong disapproval—or, for that matter, strong approval —for the new courses. He felt sure that, with the aid of the more thoughtful students, the faculty would be able to eliminate from the new curriculum "whatever undesirable features it may contain." The critics of established curricula who say that they should be reorganized so as to "prepare students for life" bear a terrible responsibility. And he concluded his editorial by saying,

> We are trying out some interesting things at Whittier College . . .
> into our new curriculum has been injected not a little of daring . . .
> but I think we have safe hold on things that are, while we are
> reaching for new things that might be.

Thus encouraged, the faculty renewed its firm grip upon things that were and had been.

But beyond the lack of whole-hearted faculty support, the Correlation Course certainly faced other problems. New courses of this kind demanded professors of broad education and maturity of experience. They called for special gifts and techniques in handling lecture-size classes in required courses in such a way as to maintain contact with the individual students. Furthermore, for trail-blazing courses of this sort, there were no textbooks, and the professor had to create materials or cull appropriate readings.

If the professors in some ways failed their task, it is notable that they in some wise succeeded.

THE PROJECT METHOD, science courses for the non-science students, and changes in graduation requirements were also important aspects of the New Curriculum.

The Project Course was of particular interest to Dr. Dexter, and reflected his studies under Kilpatrick at Columbia. In the Whittier scheme the student's project (which accounted for a third of his upper division work) was planned by the student and his professors so as to involve him in some form of meaningful work in the community under competent professional guidance. Coordinated with this were wide reading, study, and reports.

The Project Course also presented its own special problems. There were never more than eight students enrolled in this work —this peak reached in the spring of 1930. Most of the projects were in the general field of applied sociology.

Developed "as a basic part of the Correlation program" were four humanized courses in the natural sciences and mathematics: Applied Biology, Pandemic Chemistry, Applied Physics, and Elementary Mathematical Analysis. Ostrom had long given his popular course in household chemistry, with Mrs. Ostrom demonstrating cookery. This he transformed into a year course in Applied Chemistry and Physics. These were all designed for the non-science students, and they may have served well the purposes of general education.

Modification of the requirements for graduation, called for by the general concept of the New Curriculum, was a matter of great importance to the faculty. To achieve the aim of a broadly liberal education, a new formula was developed to assure adequate distribution of the student's studies, taking into account the high school work that he had had.

During his junior and senior years, the student had the option of taking a group major or the more rigorously prescribed departmental major. If he fulfilled the requirements of one of the eleven departments offering a major—with B or better in 75% of his departmental grades—he would be eligible for recommendation for graduate school.

This, in summary, was the New Curriculum, the curricular expression of the Whittier Idea.

5

STUDENTS AND FACULTY AS PARTNERS
IN THE EDUCATIONAL ADVENTURE

AN ESSENTIAL PART of the Whittier Idea, as Dexter and Coffin conceived it, was Democracy, with students and faculty united in "trying to get hold of human life as an experience of the human spirit." At Whittier College not only the curriculum but the extracurricular activities were to be so ordered as to accomplish this. All of college life was to be viewed as a joint undertaking. Democracy, friendliness, and co-operation (which Dexter pronounced with emphasis and a long e) were to be more than mere slogans.

The student body increased rapidly in size during the first years of Dexter's presidency. For the first year enrollment remained what it had been the year before. Then it jumped 30% (from 217 to 281 regular students in 1924-25), which certainly reflected Dexter's popularity as speaker for high school assemblies and commencements. This level of enrollment held for a second year, then again it jumped 35%, remained steady for another year, and finally increased 12% to reach 437 in 1928-29, the high mark of the decade. This 100% increase between 1923 and 1929 was certainly one measure of approval for the Whittier Idea.

It was also a measure of the place Whittier College was assuming in the wider community. In Dexter's first year, 52% of the students were from Whittier homes; the rest (except for 13 from out of state) came from communities and rural areas largely in southern California. A full decade later, 37% of the students were from Whittier homes; the remainder (but for 15 from out of state) came from the wider community, largely the southern part of the state. This was a 175% increase in the number of non-Whittier students. The college was becoming noticeably less local.

In another way, also, the student body changed. The number of young Friends decreased from about 100 in 1923 to only 67 a decade later. Proportionally Quaker students dropped from 44% of the total to but 17%.

The students of these years were rural and small town boys

and girls from public high school. Most of them came from middle class homes of mid-Western culture and average means, and belonged to Protestant churches, with Methodists about 25% of the total. The number of Roman Catholics, Episcopalians, and Christian Scientists increased. The proportion of "church young people," however, decreased gradually from 90% to 60%. But most of the students professed to a belief in God, attended church if irregularly, and were in process of making up their minds about religion, authority, evolution, and politics.* There was notable freedom from snobbery and from racial prejudice.

In general these young people were healthy, fond of sport and full of life, loyal and co-operative, willing to study hard enough to stay in college if not always to excel. They were idealistic. The majority looked toward vocations and professions offering opportunities for humanitarian or social service rather than for social status or riches.** And they chose to come to Whittier, somehow paying their tuition, rather than to attend the public institutions already then available in southern California.

Such, then, was the student body during these years.

How to introduce the practice of democracy into the full college community, both Dexter and Coffin realized, was as much a problem as the reorganization of the curriculum. There was already, of course, the Associated Students that managed the usual range of student activities with faculty advice. But something more was needed.

Dean Coffin devised a new instrument for furthering campus democracy.

THE JOINT COUNCIL OF CONTROL, organized in 1925, consisted of six students appointed by the student body and four faculty members appointed by the college president. Its duties were "to define standards of conduct on the campus and to recommend penalties in cases of violation." The Joint Council was also "to formulate policies and initiate public opinion." For its first year,

---

*Generally Republican, they were strong for Herbert C. Hoover throughout these years. In the 1932 Q.C. straw ballot, Hoover won, and Socialist Norman Thomas "nosed out Roosevelt by two votes," for second place.

**A survey of the alumni in 1926 showed that 74% had entered "character-building work," half of these being "mothers in homes," that is, raising families.

Randolph Pyle was chairman; the faculty members included Dr. Louis T. Jones and Prof. Paul S. Smith.

The Council undertook its new task with general support. Specific problems immediately raised important questions. Whittier students had burned a "W" on the Occidental campus prior to the football game. What should the Council's jurisdiction be over students when off campus? Then, there occurred a flagrant case of cheating. Should Whittier again institute an Honor System comparable to that in nearby colleges and universities?

The Honor System proposed by the Joint Council received the approval of the Associated Students and the commendation of the faculty.

> We, the students of Whittier College, agree that only individual work in examinations, regard for the property of others, and proper campus conduct are in accord with the ideals of Whittier College and resolve to abide by these principles.

Responsibility for student conduct was to be borne by the students themselves. "Any student who may witness a serious transgression" was duty bound to talk with the offender and then, if he felt it necessary, to report the violation to the Joint Council.

But a certain amount of cheating continued, as evidenced by comments in the Q.C., and Whittier students were much interested in lapses of honor on other campuses, as rationalizing their own corporate failure. The Associated Women Students considered the problem at their southern California conference, and placed their hope on social pressure of the student élite—among whom, however, there were also cheaters! The Q.C. editor wrote in 1932 of "the abysmal failure of the honor system in examinations" at Whittier. And, as for the "regard for the property of others," he cited a good number of things actually taken: books, gym clothes, money—even a purse from the Y.W.C.A. room. However, the Whittier tradition continued—a book left on Senior Bench in April was usually still there (spattered by sprinklers) when needed for late-May study.

The older prohibitions against smoking and drinking, profanity and gambling, card playing and dancing had already been softened. Now, in 1927, the new and democratic approach to campus discipline found expression in the Whittier catalog. All the elements composing the college were attempting to achieve at Whittier College "a community of will," instead of one "community of authority" (faculty) and another "community of obedience" (students). For college should be "a place of intellectual adventure and personal growth" in an atmosphere of friendship and co-operation.

The Joint Council and Honor Pact were instruments to this end.

When Wardman Hall was so new that the room doors were still without locks, Dr. Dexter wandered up to see how the boys were getting settled. In one room that he entered, he startled three freshmen—George Outland, Eddie Guirado, and another—being introduced to the mysteries of poker by Byron Deshler, experienced junior, son of a Quaker pastor.

"What's the game, boys?" asked Dexter to break the ice.

"Cards." Then feebly after a strained pause, "Draw."

"Well, any time you're in trouble, just drop into my office—the door is always open."

And the scared boys listened to the beating of their hearts as the president walked out and down the hill.

"Love is now the motive of school discipline where force once ruled," Dexter said in his report to the Yearly Meeting of Friends.

COMPULSORY CHAPEL ATTENDANCE seemed strangely inappropriate to the democratic aims of the college in which a "community of will" was to replace the traditional faculty authority and student obedience.

Required chapel came under fire on many campuses at this time. At Whittier in the mid-'twenties, the college required attendance at three chapel exercises per week. Usually only one of these was a religious service, such as a talk by a local pastor. Faculty members and guest speakers were more likely to give purely secular chapel talks. Some of these were effective and well received. Others certainly were sad and dreary. Student inattention was embarrassing—slumping, drowsing, whispering, scribbling, or study. Even so distinguished a guest as William Allen White— the sage of Emporia but no great shakes as speaker—was treated with outrageous discourtesy.* It took Count von Luckner, dash-

*A sophomoric prankster came to chapel with alarm clocks to wake up the audience!

ing German sea raider of the war, to arouse a united and attentive student response.

In the spring of 1927, Dean Coffin proposed that chapel programs be arranged by a joint committee of students and faculty, and that a trial be given to voluntary attendance. The faculty agreed to this experiment, but set 60% attendance as the measure of success. A joint committee went to work with a will, provided a variety of devotional, dramatic, and musical programs as well as speakers. Even in the inviting face of spring, voluntary attendance started off well above the requisite 60%. But during the fall semester, it slipped and averaged only 46% for the term.

The faculty restored compulsory chapel. Students wailed, but blamed themselves. One professor editorialized on the virtue of compulsion—lots of things you are compelled to do are really good for you. The community of authority thus restored, the faculty imposed fresh sanctions—expulsion from college for the student whose chapel cuts exceeded nine in a semester. And the faculty expected the Dean to carry out its will in the matter.*

But the Joint Council continued its efforts to achieve the friendly co-operation of students and faculty striving towards campus democracy.

STUDENT ACTIVITIES, always engaging the interests of most Whittier students in one way or another, were now viewed as an integral part of their educative experience.

Lively interest centered in a radio contest sponsored by Desmond's Men's Store in Los Angeles. It was open to all of the colleges and universities in the area. Whittier's variety program won the first prize of $700 in the fall of 1926. For its entry the next fall Wally Wiggins the Q.C. editor served as announcer, the Whittier students presented a "Dorm Life" skit, musical numbers, talks by the A.S.W.C. president and football captain, college yells and a final singing of the Alma Mater. It was "an all-student enterprise," and again won over six other colleges.

*A year later one mischievous student, knowing that attendance was required also of the professors, kept his own tally of faculty noses for some weeks. He reported in the Q.C. that "less than one-third" attended chapel. He asked impishly whether this meant that "the Profs are staying away for fear they might learn something?"

In addition to the Men's Glee Club—Mr. Knox's impersonations, a star attraction—and the Women's Glee Club, in gayer costumes now and with marimbaphone specialty, there were other musical activities. Repeated efforts were made to hold a band together beyond the rally-demands of football season. A small orchestra developed, and in 1929 (with Vera Barstow directing) gave a "first annual symphony concert" sponsored by the Woman's Auxiliary.

Dramatics continued much in the pattern already set, with plays sponsored by the junior and senior classes. Literary dramas such as Barrie's *What Every Woman Knows* alternated with sure-fire farces like *Charley's Aunt*. Professors Harris, Knox, and Deihl shared the direction. The Franklin Society began a sequence of "Stag Follies." The first, managed by Bill Jones, sophomore class president, consisted of good one-act plays and musical numbers. These Follies never again aspired so high, and descended by way of classical and popular farce with female impersonations, to an original musical in grass skirts.

The forensic activities also had their ups and downs, with Deihl and Knox coaching. In the fall of 1924, Roy Votaw won the conference extemporaneous contest held at Whittier. Now for the first time Whittier women regularly debated other college teams —no-decision contests, to spare feelings. In 1927-28, however, the Whittier debaters (male) won the conference championship —their first. The question:

> Resolved that the practice of armed intervention by the United States in the internal affairs of Latin American countries should be condemned.

Societies and clubs flourished as normal and useful sorts of educational activity. The Franklins promoted quasi-cultural activities as well as their annual round of pledging, initiating, electing, partying, and banqueting.

The Palmer Literary Society faded in 1923 and revived in 1924, with Ethel Koontz and Helen Fé Haworth as the semester presidents. And in that year was organized its great rival, the Metaphonian Society, with Frances Hunnicutt and then Dorothy Trueblood as presidents. By the end of the decade these sororal societies were joined (1928-29) by two more, the Athenians and the Thalians.*

With these were arrayed numerous departmental and special interest clubs. The Chemistry Club was looked upon by Professor Ostrom as quite enough of this sort of thing for his students. To him it seemed thoroughly democratic: he himself appointed a different student each meeting to preside. But for the students this was not enough. In 1926-27 a group of nine men from the Quan class organized the Foundation. Not restricted to chem majors, it was looked upon as one of the men's societies. With various professors as advisers, it held serious meetings, took scientific field trips, even enjoyed a social evening now and then. The sheer number of these clubs—"at least twenty"—concerned the faculty, and in 1928 the Q.C. editor also wondered whether Whittier students weren't making a fetish of extracurricular activities. But perhaps the phrenetic campus served as schooling for the hectic after-life.

Student publications at this time included *The Student Handbook*, originally put out by the Y.M.C.A. and then jointly with the Franklin Society. As the Frosh Bible it served a useful purpose. Perhaps the *Al-maniac* served none. A somewhat humor magazine, it was another Franklin effort, and lingered for several years.

The *Acropolis*, published annually by the Junior Class up through 1929 and thereafter by the Associated Students, included among its editors during these years Vernon Hanna (talented maverick)** and Howard Baker, novelist later and instructor at Harvard. But the *Acropolis*, though serving well as summary of the year's activities, was entirely traditional in format and contents at this time.

The *Quaker Campus* provided the running comment, and played an important rôle in the furthering of campus democracy. It helped to shape student opinion; it supported the efforts

*The Palmers bore the name of Alice Freeman Palmer, the distinguished educator. The Metaphonians (averred the Q.C. 4/24/31) coined a pseudo-Greek name: from 'meta'= *among*, 'phon'= *to talk*—"figure it out for yourself." The Athenians, obviously from Athena, though the Q.C. doubted the goddess of wisdom. Thalians—Thalia, muse of comedy and bucolic poetry.

**Dr. Coffin excused his numerous overcuts, gave him his A with "God forgive me" in the margin of the grade sheet.

41. DARK DAY for Whittier College—wartime student body and faculty in flu masks.
42. HARRY N. WRIGHT, Ph.D., fourth president. 43-45. LONG-TIME FACULTY MEMBERS:
Herbert E. Harris, professor of English; Gustaf E. Ostrom, professor of chemistry; Anna
Tomlinson, instructor and librarian.

46-48. PROFESSORS beginning long service in 1920-22: Marcus Skarstedt, mathematics/librarian; Esther Andrews, German; Paul S. Smith, history. 49. FOUNDERS HALL as it was before 1924, unchanged since the addition of 1904. 50. FOOTBALL CHAMPIONSHIP in 1921, the first for Whittier College (continued).

Perry, Wingert, Shaffer, Latson, E. Pickett, Weaver, Frampton, P. Pickett, Frazier, Kramar, Compton, Gammon, Madden, McPh

51. DEED TO WORSHAM for his 160-acre ranch homesteaded in 1885. 52. PRINCIPALS AND PRESIDENTS of Whittier Academy/College: Chawner, Coffin, Tebbetts, Newlin, Rosenberger, Wright, Dexter. 50 (cont.) Esek Perry, head coach (l.); Carl Breuchner, assistant coach; Leland Johns, team captain.

er, Jessup, Rayburn, Woodward, L. Johns, Suggett, Morris, G. Reese,

——————, Brownson, Thompson, R. Johns, Rohrbough, Sheldon, Breuchner

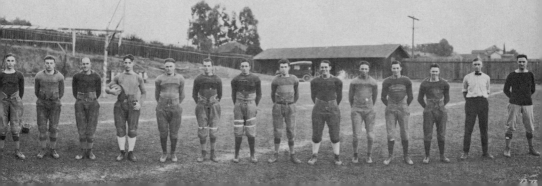

53. WALTER F. DEXTER, fifth president (aged *ca.* 50). 54. COLLEGE HILLS subdivision, Whittier College Syndicate. 55. JOHN G. WHITTIER Birthday Banquet, December 17, 1923, Ambassador Hotel, Los Angeles—Mme. Schumann-Heink, world-famed contralto for the program (continued).

Banquet photo by We

56. J. HERSCHEL COFFIN, second dean of Whittier College. 57. MONTAGE of title pages and covers of earlier and later books by Dr. Coffin. 55 (cont.) THE $100,000 BANQUET, as it was called—1,000 guests at $100 per plate—William Gibbs McAdoo, the nationally-prominent speaker.

58. WARDMAN HALL (1924), view taken later. 59. WALTER F. DEXTER *ca*. 1923, aged 37. 60. AUBREY WARDMAN, whose $100,000 gift built these buildings. 61. WARDMAN GYMNASIUM (1925), view taken later. 62. BASKETBALL TEAM of 1924, coached by Esek Perry, winning eleventh championship for the college.

1. A. Jones
2. M. Dozier
3. E. Perry
4. R. Ranzon
5. D. William

6. C. Reese
7. R. McWhi
8. C. Eckels
9. R. Johns
10. F. Ferguso

63. PLATNER HALL (1928), the west entrance. 64. MRS. HERBERT HOOVER and President Dexter (1928), awarding her an honorary degree. 65. BROADOAKS in Pasadena, the seven-branched liveoak. 66. MISS ADA BROOKS, founder of Broadoaks, portrait by Mannheim. 67. RADIO CONTEST, Whittier's winning team.

row, l. to r.
. Turner
  Starbuck
  Painter
  Tomlinson

le row
  Harris
  Johnson
  Smith
. Wiggins
  Myers
  Young

row
Sanders
  Hadley
  Foster
  McRae
  Woodard
. Loughman

68. Herbert E. Harris, vice president, acting president (1931-34). 69. Howard L. Hockett, comptroller, business manager (1931-47). 70. J. Gustav White, director of the Y.M.C.A. School (1931-49). 71. Women's Glee Club (1930), Pauline Terpstra, director. 72. Caricatures by Richard C. Harris, *Acropolis 1934.*

of the Joint Council; it reflected the co-operation and friendliness characteristic of the Whittier Spirit. The Q.C. was indeed one of the chief instruments for developing that "community of will" which Coffin and Dexter—but not the traditionalist professors—sought to achieve. Inevitably the Q.C. ran afoul of the faculty, which in the winter of 1928 had just restored compulsory chapel.

Leonard McCorkindale was a facile student journalist, associate editor of the Q.C., and president of the Historical Society. He wrote clever pen-portraits of faculty members (always a risky business) and occasionally trod quite directly on professorial toes. In his RED-INK column, "Corky" touched lightly, often pointedly, sometimes sophomorically on an endless variety of items. Specifically, he urged students to welcome C. T. Bau, a Chinese student brought to Whittier College through the efforts of Dr. Louis Jones and the Men's Bible Class of First Friends.

Corky hoped that Mr. Bau would return to China with a better understanding of the American people. A week later he added the hope that Mr. Bau—A Christian Chinese of the highest culture—would be able to give Whittier students

a good enough impression of the average Chinese person to allow us to disregard all the facts of the scum and what-have-you of the lower elements of the Chinese race.

This tactless last line—sprung from historic California prejudice, tales of tong wars and opium dens in Chinatowns, current jingo and Oriental exclusion—triggered an explosion next day in faculty meeting. Resentment had been building against "the questionable spirit" of Corky's columns in the Q.C. Now the faculty found itself "greatly humiliated" by what he had been writing about Mr. Bau. In a lengthy motion unanimously carried, the faculty declared these paragraphs

a serious breach of courtesy and good breeding . . . an affront to Mr. Bau . . . a slap at the effort of the College to develop the spirit of socialized good will.

Accordingly, the faculty requested the Dean to convey these sentiments to Mr. McCorkindale. Also the Dean was directed to ask

175

Corky to withdraw permanently from the Q.C., and to allow him to remain in the college only if he demonstrated a "satisfactory attitude." The action was, of course, a slap at Dean Coffin, at the Joint Council, at the Whittier Idea itself. In anger, acting as "a community of authority," the faculty meted out arbitrary penalties upon an immature student.

In the event, the Dean did less than directed, Corky's student editor pleaded his cause, the faculty withheld execution of its sentence subject to the culprit's good conduct. But the manifest differences of view regarding campus democracy were not resolved.

INTERCOLLEGIATE ATHLETICS were expected to trumpet the new Whittier College throughout the Southland, though Dean Coffin himself was not much in favor of this sort of thing.

Esek Perry had coached that amazing championship team in 1921. His next teams were less successful. In 1924 Russell Wilson returned part-time to coach the backfield for Perry. This Poet team played hard fast ball, was able to beat Southern Branch and then Caltech in a close tough game that precipitated a hassel and the breaking of athletic relations. The Los Angeles newspapers had a field day. By the time peace was declared and play resumed a year later, both Perry and Wilson had been replaced.

For in January 1925, Whittier trustees were concerned about "the football situation." They were not concerned about the averred roughness of play, but about losing teams. Theirs were long thoughts of Big Time Football. Esek Perry stepped aside, to serve another year as director of physical education, thereafter to devote himself to his insurance business. In his place the board hired Leo Calland, who came with a splendid record of playing and coaching at U.S.C.

Calland's first season at Whittier, with Perry assisting him, was not outstanding.* The next season (1926), Calland's team did better. But again the Poets were beaten both by the Tigers and the Sagehens. The great game of the year was with the U.C.L.A. Bruins. The Quakers were "doped to lose by a big score." But they opened with successive gains before the Bruin line stiffened, and

*By this time Whittier College, with increased enrollment, was no longer allowed by the Conference to play freshmen on its varsity.

Tom Denny dropped back and place-kicked for 3 points. The Bruins again kicked off,

> and Tommy Denny . . . received the kick on his own 3 yard line, and aided by wonderful interference, squirmed and dodged and ran 97 yards down the field for a touchdown.

It was, in fact, the second longest run in the entire country that season, did much toward winning the game 16-6, and won Denny honorable mention for All-American. This was the seventh and last gridiron victory of Whittier College against the University. But Leo Calland moved on to other fields of play at the end of the year, to be succeeded by George Philbrook, who entered the lists with fanfare in the fall of 1927.

Philbrook came from coaching at University of Idaho, and had played at Notre Dame under Knute Rockne. His 1927 Whittier team finished third in the conference. The next year his team lost to Oxy, Pomona, San Diego, Arizona—stood fourth in the conference—and Philbrook moved on. To succeed him in 1929, Wallace "Chief" Newman came from high school coaching in nearby Covina, and began an extraordinary career in college coaching.

So much for football at this time. Basketball did somewhat better.

Esek Perry coached a great basketball team in 1924. From the beginning of the season it was expected that the Whittier duel with Southern Branch would decide the conference title. The college five met the university team in old Tebbetts Gym. So crowded was it that boys climbed to the roof and pulled away shingles to see the game. With "the packed-in rooters howling throughout," the brilliant shooting of Charles "Chili" Eckles and Russ Ranzona won the game for the Poets 22-20. At once attention focused on the return game, with build-up in the city papers. Expecting a large crowd, the University shifted the game from its little old gym on North Vermont to the vast U.S.C. Pavilion, which gave the Cubs the advantage as they had practised on that floor. The game was hard-fought and close, with the University ahead at the half. Then Whittier's "stonewall defense and long shooting" evened the score, which stood at 21-21 with but 45 seconds to play. Finally, Ranzona got off a spectacular shot, and the Poets won 23-21. The *Times* called it "a hair-raising contest that left some 2,000 frenzied spectators limp and exhausted with the final gun." It gave Whittier its eleventh basketball championship, adding (as the Q.C. put it) "prestige to the institution."

There were to be other good basketball teams, too. That coached by Leo Calland in 1927 tied U.C.L.A. for the conference championship. The 1928 team, coached by Ray Johns, tied Occidental for the championship—and had the pleasure of beating U.C.L.A. 31-24, though the University had withdrawn from college play to try conclusions with its university peers in the Coast Conference.* Soon Verne Landreth came to Whittier to begin his coaching of basketball.

Baseball continued to be the game that Whittier men played on spring afternoons simply because they liked to play it. During these years (1924-29) George "Rube" Ellis from nearby Rivera coached the college team. An old pro—outfielder and pinch hitter for the Angels and the Cards—he was admired by his men and idolized by the neighborhood boys. He fielded good teams, but it was not until 1928 that Whittier won its first baseball championship.

In track during these years, Whittier had one outstanding athlete, Nathaniel George, a sprinter who won the 100 yard dash in 9 4/5ths at the A.A.U. Relay Carnival at the Los Angeles Coliseum in the winter of 1929. He was duly honored in the Negro community of Los Angeles as well as in Whittier. Nat George, a student leader, graduated in 1931 to enter Y.M.C.A. work.

The women, too, were enjoying their sports—basketball, tennis, hockey, and now archery.

> The above girls [pictured in the *Acropolis 1927*] are sixth-class archers. Before the school year ends it is probable that some of these will have advanced to the fifth class of archery.

They were still at it the next year—"It is not easy to stand at a distance of thirty or forty yards and hit the target." But, by a system of points managed by the W.A.A. and Irene Palmer, the women's coach, they won their honors.

*By this time U.C.L.A. was thirteen times the size of Whittier.

By and large, this *was* the good life for students—not merely
what promised future riches.

6

DEVELOPING CAMPUS AND RESOURCES
FOR THE NEW WHITTIER COLLEGE

GREAT PUBLIC SUCCESS had climaxed the first hundred days of
Walter Dexter's presidency. The net profit of the John Greenleaf
Whittier Banquet was just short of $100,000; the announced gift
of A. Wardman was a round $100,000.* On that memorable night
in December 1923, the $1,000,000 goal really seemed attainable,
and there was just a possibility that even greater riches lay in
store for the little college guided by the Christian idealism of the
Quaker poet.

An enlarged campus, a succession of new buildings, an increased endowment—these were called for by the dream of a new
curriculum, strengthened faculty, student body of three to five
hundred. The first of these, the greatly expanded campus, was
already assured.

THE WHITTIER COLLEGE SYNDICATE, which so stirred Dexter's enthusiasm, had as its sole purpose acquisition of the Worsham
Ranch lands for the expansion of the college campus.

The Syndicate itself formed on June 8, 1923 with the following as its trustees: C. Bevan Johnson, A. Clifford Johnson, Cass A.
Rees, Charles C. Barr, Albert N. Chamness (all of them trustees
also of the college), and Amos C. Maple (banker), Alphonzo E.
Bell (Santa Fe Springs rancher with new oil wealth), and Herbert F. Harris. Without assuming liability (such as A. C. Johnson
proposed), they signed a trust agreement naming Whittier College as beneficiary.

The price of the 133 acre ranch was $230,000, one-third in cash
payment ($76,700), the remainder secured by a five-year mort-
gage at 7% interest. To pay for this property, the Syndicate proposed to subdivide one or two portions of it at once, and thus
(within six months or a year) to make enough from the sale of
lots to pay both for the ranch itself and for development and sale

*The net from the banquet was $97,000 in cash and promises to pay for tickets;
but as of 3/1/24 $49,000 of this amount was still uncollected. Of Mr. Wardman's
gift of $100,000, he found it necessary to borrow back $30,000 for the time being.

of the subdivision. To swing the deal, the Syndicate needed something like $200,000 in cash. It proposed borrowing this from banks using the personal notes of a large number of guarantors as security.

Some 68 persons subscribed $3,000 each in the form of a short-term personal note, which established a line of credit in the amount of the $200,000 needed. With this arranged, the Syndicate proceeded to borrow the money necessary for the down payment and for the development of the College Hills subdivision.

The total costs of the ranch and development would finally amount to about $350,000, including the $150,000 mortgage due to the Worshams. But the sale of, say, 100 lots at an average of $3,500 each would allow the Syndicate to come out on the deal even without financing the second possible subdivision of choice view property on the southeast edge of the ranch. And Whittier College as beneficiary would receive without cost 100 acres of land for campus expansion.

As General Manager of the enterprise, the Syndicate trustees employed Professor Harris. In him they saw a practical man, who had long served and loved the college, an experienced rancher, knowing well the manage of horse and man. He worked with the landscape engineer in planning the picturesque subdivision of hillside homesites: concrete streets in sweeping curves and contours—sidewalks, curbs, ornamental lights—all utilities underground—streetside plantings of red-flowering eucalyptus.

During the hundred days in which Dexter pushed the sale of banquet tickets, Harris urged on the survey teams, construction crews, the "fifty mules and attendant skinners." On November 8th, a well-publicized meeting of the Syndicate guarantors heard reports on plans and progress. Harris announced the opening day for the sale of lots, ranging from $2,000 to $6,000 in price, "at least a thousand dollars per lot under value."

> In fact Mr Harris intimated that if anyone desired to make $100,-000 clear profit he could purchase that amount of lots on opening day, December 1, and within two or three months sell at an advance for the profit.

No one was to be that greedy.*

*The subscribers of the $3,000 personal notes were permitted to select one lot, but no more, a week in advance of the sale.

A large ad in the Whittier *News* showed the plat, with 117 lots and the assurance that all utilities would be installed and ready for building by February 1st. The realtors of the town were to serve as agents. Successive ads assured the public there would be no dickering from the published price list. Terms were to be an easy one-fourth down, the remainder in three annual payments— at 5% discount for cash.

Whether any lots were firmly spoken for by the guarantors before the public sale, is not of record. On December 1st, the streets were not yet ready for travel owing to unavoidable delays in grading. But the big display ads of the Syndicate and the classified ads of individual brokers brought out interested visitors on Saturday (and Sunday!) December 1-2. They came to view the "new high class addition to Whittier"—East Philadelphia Street curving up past the Worsham homesite and the olive-tree hillside, the gentle grade up the old arroyo and swinging around to follow the ridge with its spectacular views...

On Monday the Syndicate blazoned success of the opening sale: 14 lots sold for a total of $49,800! The *News* reported one-eighth of the available lots disposed of—J. Clem Arnold well advanced with building plans and A. C. Johnson not far behind—others anxious to begin construction shortly. During the week a half-dozen different real estate offices ran small ads offering College Hills lots. Then, during the week just preceding the big Banquet, the number of ads dropped to two, then to one, and to none. But on December 14th a full-page display by the Syndicate faced the extra section of the *News* devoted to final promotion of the banquet itself: 300 plates to be sold in a photo finish.

That was the last ad and the last mention for the time being of the College Hills subdivision.

What happened may be summed up in the one word "OIL!" Or, rather: prospect of oil, which was not quite the same thing.

The week following the opening sale of College Hills lots, an oil company (as Harris later wrote) "spudded in a well to try out the deep sand immediately north of College Hills subdivision." There opened a new vista. If Standard Oil really did prove the lower sands under the old Home Oil Company's land, then the Syndicate might indeed become the very rich benefactor of the college—and of those few who had their names securely inscribed as owners of College Hills lots.

No further lots were sold. No further work was done on the streets and improvements. Oil fever ran high along the Puente Hills. By the end of December a new well was flowing 5,000 bbl. a day on Rideout Heights a couple of miles to the west, and Standard was redrilling on its Murphy lease a mile or so to the east. The *News* carried the daily petroleum drama of Santa Fe Springs and the entire Los Nietos valley.

At the end of January 1924, the Syndicate confirmed its decision to wait and see "owing to the unsettled and uncertain conditions in regard to the prospect for oil." Harris suggested that he was no longer needed as General Manager, but continued for a couple of months at reduced salary. The sale of lots was definitely blocked. As Harris later wrote, "a high type residence section could not be developed adjoining an oil field [newly activated]." It might take eight months more for Standard to complete its test well.

Meanwhile the six-month notes of the guarantors were running out. A change in the money market made it impossible to borrow the $77,000 still needed to complete the subdivision improvements. But somehow $23,000 *had* to be borrowed to meet the interest coming due and to repay those who, having made down payments on lots, now wanted their money back. What had started as a sure thing for Whittier College turned into a nightmare of continuing anxieties. And at long last the test well proved unproductive.*

The trustees of the Syndicate now looked to the college trustees for help. They were largely the same men, of course, but the two enterprises were kept scrupulously separate at this time. By the fall of 1925 conditions bettered sufficiently so that the College Hills improvements could be financed and completed. The sale of lots resumed. And by fall of 1926 President Dexter's home

*Had each of the guarantors simply agreed to buy and pay cash for one or more lots instead of merely lending briefly of his personal credit, all or most of the College Hills lots would have been sold by the Syndicate. Then the guarantors who hadn't wanted the lots for their own use might have sold them individually on their own initiative. Many or perhaps most of the guarantors would have been able to do this, but such was not the original or even later scheme.

neared completion on Hillside Lane. Professor Harris's home, high up above Fire Hill at the end of Worsham Drive, at last gave him the panoramic view he loved so much. What he daily saw from his great picture window evoked one of his most charming essays.*

A few other fine homes were built in College Hills at this time. Aubrey Wardman built one as an encouraging investment. The restrictions called for Mediterranean style, the various shades of off-white stucco and red-tile roofs sorting well with the sad green of the olive trees.

But only thirty lots were finally sold—or remained sold—during the next two or three years. Beautiful as the properties were, and reasonably priced as of that time, they simply did not sell. For all the booming prosperity and the annual influx of a million and a half visitors and newcomers to southern California, there were soft spots in the economy of the mid-1920's, and more lands were subdivided than could be sold.

The Syndicate continued to be in trouble. The carrying charges for the various bank loans and for the mortgage amounted to something like $25,000 a year. Street bonds on unsold lots added perhaps $5,000 more. And there were taxes. Unable to find money elsewhere in January 1927, the Syndicate borrowed $9,500 from the College itself at 7%, giving 4 lots as security. But worse yet: the entire balance of the $150,000 mortgage was coming due in June of 1928.

On January 27, 1928 the Syndicate trustees appointed a committee of three "with full power to act in regard to the disposition of the property." The committee was authorized "to enter into any sales agreement, fix the terms, and do anything necessary for the *complete disposal of said property* [emphasis added]."

What the Syndicate trustees did on June 18, 1928, was to transfer to Whittier College itself all the unsold lots in College Hills and the 110 acres or so of Worsham ranch lands—together with the accumulated financial obligations—and closed the Syndicate books with a final balancing entry: "credit of $230,000 from Whittier College."

*"My Window" in *Teamwork: Pertinent and Impertinent Parables* (1950), by Herbert E. Harris, with frontispiece of the window by his son, Richard.

Thus the college acquired a staggering debt as the price for lands largely impracticable for campus expansion.*

To refinance the Syndicate obligations, the college borrowed $10,000 at 7% from a local bank, for which it pledged not 4 but 28 of the College Hill lots! To borrow $225,000 from a Los Angeles bank at 6%, the college mortgaged 59 more College Hill lots and the rest of the Worsham ranch—*plus the college campus itself with its buildings!*** To borrow a further $30,000 from a Pasadena bank, a college property in Long Beach was given as security.

The Stock Crash of 1929 was still over a year off in the unseen future. It still seemed possible that the college might indeed sell its 87 unsold lots for enough to pay the land debt; that is, with a favorable change of fiscal wind. For the Q.C. readers, the transaction was glossed over: the college finances were so much "improved" that it was at last able to "purchase" the Worsham ranch "held for five years by the Whittier College Syndicate." Nothing was said of the blood, sweat, and tears.

But to return, now, to the second phase of Dexter's development program.

BUILDINGS FOR THE NEW Whittier College were expected to arise in stately succession. Allison and Allison prepared a fresh Master Plan by updating the previous one. Something of the sort was displayed by projection at the great Hundred-Thousand-Dollar Banquet.

In early January 1924, the college board ordered definite plans for a men's dormitory to cost about $100,000. But Dexter suggested a larger building program to make the most use of the Wardman gift. He proposed building only the central portion of the dormitory, to be followed at once by construction of a new gymnasium. Furthermore, he said: remodel old Founders Hall, even if for only a couple more years of use, and spend a few thou-

*The Worsham land, particularly the broad canyon, was by no means valueless in the future development of the college. But it was to be 13 years before the debt was cleared, 20 years before a college building could be built on any part of it, 35 years before the final development of Memorial Stadium would clear the inner campus for construction of the new science building.

**The adjoining lot, upon which Platner Hall was being built, was excluded from this commitment because of a special covenant with the donor-annuitants.

184

sand dollars to improve the appearance of the campus. To this the board agreed.

First came Wardman Hall, located high on the shoulder of Fire Hill and close to the new amphitheatre and with a magnificent view. By mid-April ground was broken with photographed ceremony interrupted by a shower. Under the beaming supervision of President Dexter, Aubrey Wardman handled the plow and Bonnie Bell Wardman drove the mules for the first furrow of the grading. Soon the sturdy concrete building in Mediterranean style with red-tiled roof took shape on its imposing site. All but completed and furnished, it was ready for the fall term 1924. The cost was just under $50,000, the furnishings $5,000 more, and it accommodated 50 men. To left and right of the triple-arched entry were apartments for faculty resident and for guests. The ample lounge had an ornamental stair and great fireplace.* What a splendid building to start the redevelopment of the college campus!

During the spring and summer of 1924, Founders Hall was somewhat remodeled, repainted, and redecorated at a cost of about $10,000. Lost to view and tradition was the red-brick of the original college building. It was stuccoed over in the belief that this would make it less conspicuous among the buildings soon to rise.

At the same time construction of the new gymnasium began. Located at the southwesterly corner of Wardman Hall, it was pushed to functional completion (at a cost of $40,000) in time for the spring semester 1925. The last game in old Tebbetts Gym had been played and won (from Pomona 34-11) on January 19th; the first game in new Wardman Gym was played and lost (to Oxy 15-23) on February 6th. Outside, this concrete building was unfinished and roughhewn. Inside, it was sturdy and simple (stronger than necessary, as steel supports that blocked the view were later removed)—unexcelled basketball floor— seating for 2,000. The east end of the building was a concrete proscenium filled by a wooden wall, to allow for a stage beyond the building if it should later be used also as an auditorium. But

*At a later date Richard Harris '34 painted an historic mural for above the hearth, depicting William Penn with the Indians, Levi Coffin and a runaway slave, and Quaker relief work in France.

185

essentially, this was a gymnasium, with locker rooms and showers for men and women in the spaces beneath the bleachers.

Wardman Gym, Wardman Hall, and Founders Hall refurbished—the $100,000 gift of Mr. and Mrs. Wardman had been well spent. Unfortunately, no other such generous donors came forward to further the building program. But Dexter thought up a good scheme for getting the next building that he wanted.

Iowa Memorial Hall! In 1924, the board agreed to hire a financial agent to raise funds from among the retired Iowa farmers still swarming to southern California. Iowa Hall, to be built on the front campus, was to include an auditorium and music department rooms, an Iowa Historical Library and "Iowa Hall of Fame," etc. Clarence Schouboe was employed as solicitor—salary, percentage, and furnished office—with the expectation of a $250,000 harvest. But within six weeks he gave up. Then the board took on another fund-raiser at higher retainer and 8% of the take. Again, failure. And Iowa Memorial Hall sank without trace, except for two architects' renderings of the proposed façade that floated up to the college attics.*

More pressing than the need for an auditorium was that for a college library. For a moment it seemed that this might be quickly realized. Professor Skarstedt—on leave to complete his doctorate at Berkeley—employed as his substitute a retired mathematician, Anna L. Van Benschoten (Ph.D., Cornell). She became good friends with Anna Tomlinson, the college librarian, who impressed upon her the great need at Whittier for a library building. Already in frail health, Miss Van Benschoten became ill. Having some means and no immediate family, she decided to leave her money to the college for a library. On Friday afternoon she told Miss Tomlinson of her intention and called her attorney to come, please, to change her will. He couldn't very well make it until Monday morning. Sunday night she died.

The college still needed a library, and in 1926 the board declared it would build one within the year at a cost of $35,000. A committee determined the site. But funds for this building were not found. In 1928, the Library took over and remodeled the first

---

*The net result of this fiasco was $515. Realization of the building, with its commitment to the Iowa Association, with its suite of rooms for entertaining eminent Hawkeyes, and with the proposed annual Iowa picnic, would have been a mixed blessing.

floor of Redwood Cottage. Dr. Skarstedt, newly appointed librarian, planned the transformation, and, trained in carpentry as a youth, himself constructed the book stacks.

Lacking further substantial gifts for buildings, there was still one way for Dexter and the college board to push ahead with campus development. That was by "selling" annuities. An annuity gift to the college—in money, securities, or property—assured the donor a life income of a fixed amount per month or quarter. Beyond its obligation to meet these contractual payments, the college was free to reinvest the money. This could be prudently done in building dormitories, the income from which would more than provide for the college payments to the annuitant.

In 1926, Dr. Fredrika Bolte, a Swedish masseuse who had moved to Whittier during the War, deeded her home on Philadelphia and Berkeley Way [Founders Hill Road] to the college. In exchange for this property, valued at $15,000, Dr. Bolte and her companion received $1,500 a year while both lived, and $1,200 to the survivor. The college used her home as a dormitory, and moved to the same lot another substantial old house, the gift of A. Wardman in 1927. Thereafter, the Woman's Auxiliary connected them with a lounge, and Bolte Hall continued to serve as a women's residence until 1964.

In the fall of 1927, David H. and Jennie M. Platner gave $56,000 to the college largely in the form of trust deeds, receiving a life-time annuity of about $300 per month. The college then built Platner Hall on Berkeley Way, adjacent to the campus. When completed in September 1928, this dormitory housed some 50 women students at $75 per semester. Half of the gross income sufficed to pay the annuitants. Platner Hall took the place of Redwood Cottage as a dormitory, and Platner lounge—furnished and refurnished by the Woman's Auxiliary—became the social center of the campus.*

There was no further building on the Whittier campus at this time, except for construction of the U.S. Government Entomology Laboratory, built by the Whittier District Fruit Exchange

*For 25 years, prudent little Mrs. Platner (in her black cotton stockings) faithfully attended meetings of the Auxiliary held in that lounge and sat under the photos of the donors.

on a two-acre plot of the Worsham land east of Hadley Field. The college received ground rent on a 25-year lease, extended until 1961.

BEQUESTS, FURTHER ANNUITIES, and gifts added to the college resources during these years.

The will of Curtis E. Way provided the first considerable bequest for the college in 1924. Curtis Way was a Hoosier-born Friend who came to California in 1885. Without much schooling, he "spent almost half a lifetime as a hired man on the farm." He gradually acquired his own ranch at El Modena, then other property. He served on the college board for 18 years. Widowed and childless, he left the bulk of his estate for scholarships and student loans as a memorial to his wife Charity Way. This bequest of $47,000 included a large house on Painter Avenue, which became "residence quarters for needy students." Way Hall, moved twice to make way for much later building, continued in use until 1962.

There were also bequests from other Quakers: lands in Merced County from John H. Vestal; properties in Indiana and Long Beach from Amanda Whitson valued at $44,000, establishing a loan fund for needy students; the $10,000 estate of Eliza E. Hockett of Illinois, specifically for aiding women students; a gift and legacy of $18,000 from Robert L. Gifford for an Eagle Scout scholarship; $10,000 from Olive Naylor of Berkeley; and lesser sums no less welcome.

Meanwhile Dexter sought annuity gifts from elderly Friends: In 1925, Charles E. and Imelda Tebbetts gave another $20,000 to the college in this form. At the same time William and Frances Milhous made the first of successive annuity gifts that by 1931 totalled $50,000. Another Quaker annuitant was Joshua Stanley, crippled as a boy in a mowing-machine accident, who exchanged Montebello land valued at $25,000 in 1927 for an annuity contract. That same year, the college accepted a $100,000 business lot in the heart of booming Long Beach for an annuity to Samuel C. and Ella W. Peasley. On it the college built and leased a bus depot. Annuities in lesser amount also looked toward the future development of the college and its endowment, but they were of limited immediate help.

THE CHIEF FINANCIAL PROBLEM was to carry forward the adventurous college program in the face of annual operating deficits.

Student enrollment bore an immediate relation, of course, to the total tuition income of the college. In 1923, the tuition was $150 a year. With an enrollment of 200 students this meant $30,000—less the amount of free tuitions granted as scholarships. Raising the rate $50 per year in 1925 and again in 1927 brought the tuition to $250 a year.* With an enrollment of 400 students, the tuition income totalled $100,000—less scholarship grants. This, in 1928, was approximately equal to the faculty budget, but no more, and that was only three-fifths of the total annual expenditure. The difference was expected to come largely from endowment. But the Endowment Fund was quite inadequate for this.

In 1923 the actual endowment in invested funds was only $200,000, with interest-bearing pledges for another $100,000, plus other subscriptions and contingencies for about $100,000 more. In May 1925 the General Education Board paid a second installment of about $25,000—that is, the college had then been able to certify that an additional $50,000 had been paid in on the 1921-22 pledges. But the General Education Board still withheld $35,000 of its promised $66,667 awaiting further collections by the college on $70,000 in notes and pledges still unpaid. Despite various efforts made by the college board, it was the end of May 1928 before it could claim and receive the final payment on the Rockefeller gift—and that only on the eve of the Syndicate debacle.

Throughout this decade the endowment income was between $12,000 and $25,000 a year, which bridged less than half the gap between tuition income and the total costs of operation.

To meet the operating deficit the college had to look elsewhere for sustaining funds. Might the answer be an annual John Greenleaf Whittier banquet?—not at $100 a plate, but perhaps at $25. The second such banquet, held in 1925 at the Hotel Maryland in Pasadena, was a beautiful occasion with 800 persons in attend-

---

*Tuition at Occidental was $250 until 1931. A survey of thirty private colleges in 1927 showed an average tuition of $329 for men and $343 for women, an increase of $200 over the tuitions of 1907.

ance—but the Governor sent last-minute regrets, and Carrie Jacobs Bond fell ill, her singing intended as "the end of a perfect day." But the net income was little more than $15,000. . . In 1926 at the Breakers Hotel in Long Beach, with 1,200 seated at the tables, the net result was hardly better. . . In 1927 the college board tried to farm out the "rights" to the banquet. . . In 1928 the question of a banquet was raised and dropped. . . In 1929, a John Greenleaf Whittier Banquet was again held, this time at the Los Angeles Biltmore. Of the 737 persons present, many were students and their girl friends or escorts at $2.50 per plate. Again, it was a delightful evening—but it made up less than $10,000 of the annual deficit that was then $30,000. And there was already gnawing anxiety lest the New York stock crash of October 24th send shock waves rolling west.

Efforts to develop the Whittier campus and resources to match the brave New Curriculum were in trouble from the start. And it is notable that the financial crisis at the college *preceded* the economic collapse of the nation.

7

DEVELOPING PROFESSIONAL TRAINING:
BROADOAKS AND Y.M.C.A. SCHOOL

TRAINING YOUNG PEOPLE for lives of service was the dream of Dexter and Coffin from the beginning of their educational adventure. It seemed natural that Whittier should prepare students for vocations in youth leadership and education.

It would also seem natural to add: religious education and the ministry. But efforts to do this were in large measure frustrated by the uneasy relationship existing between Whittier College and California Yearly Meeting. Young men and women who felt called to evangelical-fundamentalist ministry and missions found what they sought in the Training School for Christian Workers. Fewer among the liberal young Friends chose these vocations and came to Whittier.

With no intention of developing a professional school of theology, Whittier nevertheless did give courses suitable for pre-ministerial training and for directors of religious education. With the latter in mind, Dexter brought Walter J. Homan (A.B., Penn;

190

M.R.E., Boston) to the faculty as professor of religious education. A personable young teacher with administrative ability, he soon served as dean of men (1926) and later as registrar (1931). A second man was added as professor of Biblical literature—Clarence G. McClean (A.B., Penn; M.A., Chicago)—and he took a turn as dean of men. With these two Quakers—Homan a recorded Friends minister—Dexter hoped to make some contribution to the pastoral ministry of the Yearly Meeting. In 1930 "a special course for ministers and those planning to enter related vocations" was announced. It had been worked out in co-operation with the Pastors Association of the Yearly Meeting. But this effort, thwarted by both doctrinal and economic problems, was notably unsuccessful as far as the Yearly Meeting was concerned.*

The number and proportion of young Friends at Whittier College continued to drop during these years. More Whittier students found their way into the ministry and religious education of other denominations than into such work in Quaker churches.

PUBLIC SCHOOL TEACHING was another service vocation open to idealistic young people. Whittier had already gained recognition as a teacher training institution when Dexter, a professional educator, set about enlarging this department. Within a year the college offered the courses required by the State of California for both the elementary and the junior high school teachers' certificates. Joseph T. Williams (Ph.D., Columbia), experienced college and university teacher and author of textbooks in educational sociology, succeeded Mrs. Rosenberger in education. Mrs. Jane W. McKee was borrowed from the University of Southern California to supervise the practice teaching given by the college in the Whittier public schools. In close touch with the State Department of Education, professional work at Whittier developed rapidly during the next few years.**

*The evangelical fervor so strongly felt on the Whittier campus immediately after the World War, seeped away with the changing times. Although Mrs. Rosenberger could look back in 1930 and list 37 former Whittier students who had served "in some form of mission work" overseas, most of them were alumni from earlier years. Of the pastors serving Yearly Meeting churches in 1930, only two out of 24 were alumni of Whittier College. Many if not most of the rest were from the Training School.

**In June 1927 William John Cooper delivered the Whittier commencement address and the college gave him an honorary LL.D. He was State superintendent of public instruction, and became the first commissioner of the Office of Education in the Federal Government.

In January 1928 the State of California accredited Whittier College for the general elementary certificate and for the special secondary certificates in music and physical education. When Williams resigned after six years' teaching at Whittier, Harry H. Vannorsdall (Ph.D., Ohio State) succeeded him for a year (1930-31). Then Jane W. McKee (A.B., M.A., Southern California) returned to Whittier after two years' absence. She brought with her the Broadoaks Kindergarten Training School of Pasadena, of which she was then the director.

The Broadoaks School was the property of the Brooks sisters, Miss Ada Mae and Miss Imelda. In 1906 Miss Ada Brooks, a public school teacher in Pasadena, had undertaken the care of a child about to be orphaned. Within three years she had a "family" of five children otherwise without a home. So she built them one on La Loma Road, not far from beautiful Arroyo Seco, adapting her house plan to the magnificent seven-branched live oak, one of several on the property. Miss Ada then gave up her teaching to run a private kindergarten in her home. Within a year Miss Imelda resigned her public-school work to teach the primary grades. Soon the Brooks sisters discovered themselves teaching kindergarten teachers as well as the youngsters, and expanded the grounds and school through to California Street. Owing much to the pioneer work of Montessori, Pestalozzi, and Froebel, the Broadoaks School became widely known, and graduated large classes from its two-year normal course. Miss Ada retired in 1925, Miss Imelda in 1929, at which time Jane McKee became the director.

Jane McKee—a solid, mature woman, with big brown eyes, a ready smile and quick mind—had the same sort of dynamic optimism that characterized Walter Dexter. She was an early alumna of Broadoaks, kindergarten and primary teacher in public schools, university professor of elementary education, author of two textbooks for teachers.

Broadoaks faced a crisis in the spring of 1929. The State Department of Education announced that after September 1931 teaching certificates would be issued only to persons holding a four-year college degree. Obviously little Broadoaks could not suddenly provide a baccalaureate curriculum. Mrs. McKee suggested transforming Broadoaks into a small Graduate School of Child

Research, reorganizing the children's school as a research laboratory and adding a nursery. Recognition was sought and granted for the Broadoaks degree Master of Education in Child Research, and the two-year normal course was eliminated.

But in the year 1929-30, when the depression was only beginning to be felt, the Broadoaks enrollment dropped to a dangerous low, and the number of graduate students was quite insufficient to support the venture. An upper division course of study was therefore added in 1930-31, leading to a Bachelor of Education degree; it was intended for transfer students and junior college graduates. But to assure accreditation of this work, it was deemed necessary for Broadoaks to affiliate with a well-established academic institution. Dr. James Huntley Sinclair of Occidental College was already directing graduate research at Broadoaks and his colleague Dr. Martin J. Stormzand had just collaborated with Mrs. McKee in writing *The Progressive Primary Teacher* (Houghton Mifflin, 1928). It was natural for Broadoaks to think of affiliation with Occidental, less than three miles distant.

But it was with Whittier College that the Brooks sisters at last came to terms in the winter of 1931. Their contract was a trust agreement, giving the Broadoaks School and sustaining resources (securities valued at well toward $100,000) to Whittier in return for an annuity, and Miss Ada and Miss Imelda were duly elected to the enlarged college board. Mrs. McKee continued for another year (1931-32) as director of Broadoaks, also professor of education and head of the department at Whittier.*

There was a genuine effort made to integrate the Broadoaks School of Education on its Pasadena campus with the college in Whittier. Soon the college unified the administration; popular Whittier professors gave a few academic courses on the Pasadena campus; the Q.C. printed Broadoaks news; the *Acropolis* published a Broadoaks section. Much was made of the Broadoaks alumnae, already numbering some 800, at the John Greenleaf Whittier Banquet held in Pasadena on December 17, 1931. It was a great occasion, combined with the football banquet to assure a large attendance of Whittier students and alumni. A skit depicted the union of Broadoaks with Whittier in the guise of an old-

---

*She then retired from academic work to prepare for another vocation as a Christian Science practitioner and teacher.

fashioned Quaker wedding. During the next years Broadoaks maintained its traditions on its picturesque campus: student organization and social program—professional sorority Delta Phi Upsilon (the founding chapter)—baccalaureate, the seniors in formals descending the stairway curved around the great oak.

The merger, absolutely essential to the faltering Broadoaks, was a good thing for Whittier, increasing its capital assets as well as expanding its professional program in education. And the operation of the Pasadena campus was at once budgeted to show a small operating profit. Mrs. McKee's salary was reduced—said Dexter: "It wouldn't look good, Jane, for your salary to be $1,000 higher than mine"—and her successors were paid no more than other Whittier professors.

The immediate adjustments worked out in the spirit of general goodwill, and Broadoaks School of Education of Whittier College continued for another fourteen years on the Pasadena campus.

THE Y.M.C.A. TRAINING SCHOOL, affiliated with Whittier College at the same time in 1931, prepared young men for vocations in youth leadership.

The Pacific Summer School of the Y.M.C.A. arranged in 1930 to use the Whittier campus. That fall Dexter reported to the college board the possibility of developing at Whittier a special school, like those in Chicago and in Springfield, Mass., for the training of Y.M.C.A. secretaries. This might be done, he said, by forming an alliance with the state organization of the Y. It would provide an additional kind of professional education appropriate to the Whittier Idea.

Thus, the Pacific Southwest School of the Young Men's Christian Association, which had been developing at the Los Angeles Downtown Y under the guidance of J. Gustav White, was established on the Whittier campus as an integral part of the college under his part-time direction. As professor of applied sociology he continued his teaching on the campus until his retirement in 1949.

A Dane by birth, Gus White went directly from his undergraduate studies at Berkeley into Y work. During World War I he served in a camp for German prisoners, then as chief of the Y.M.C.A. educational work with the A.E.F. in the British

Isles. After the War he became director of education in the Los Angeles Downtown Y, developed the summer school for further training of Y.M.C.A. secretaries, and then specialized in counseling. A man of restless energies, he published small volumes on his *Educational Work Among Prisoners* and his *Present-Day Hymns* —developed a mnemonic and memorandum system—and became a popular public speaking coach for the Toastmasters clubs.*

In the affiliation of the Y.M.C.A. School, there was no property involved. It was expected, however, that special contributions from the Associations and from those supporting the Y.M.C.A. programs would help to finance the training school. Otherwise, tuitions paid by students enrolling in the college especially for this training would hopefully make it pay. Within the first year (1931-32) there were 22 students in the program and it was anticipated that student interest would increase. Few special courses were needed, for the certificate requirements were largely met by the established liberal arts courses. Thus started, the Y courses continued through the succeeding years as an important adjunct to the department of sociology. In it a significant number of young men (and a few young women) prepared themselves for careers in the Y.M.C.A. and in related forms of youth leadership.

Development of these professional curricula for service vocations during 1930-31 was a significant corollary to the New Curriculum.

8

FUNDAMENTALIST REBUKES—TRADITIONALIST
REBUFFS—FINANCIAL CRISIS

THE COLLEGE FACED REVERSES of several sorts during these same years. They did not arise suddenly but developed from the beginning of the Dexter and Coffin administration and simply culminated in 1930 and 1931.

One of these was the final concerted assault of religious conservatives upon the college. Though the attack a score of years earlier had been repulsed, the Training School in Huntington

---

*After his retirement from Whittier College, he continued his professional work as a rehabilitation counselor for the State until his second retirement, then carried on in private practice as a psychologist until well into his indefatigable eighties.

Park continued the focal point of disapproval, ameliorated but briefly during the War. In the spring of 1923, however, the Huntington Park Friends Church withheld its "proportionate share of the Yearly Meeting budget to Whittier College" and called upon others to do likewise. The funds thus denied were negligible, but their refusal was an effort to force the college to conform its teaching to evangelical-fundamentalist orthodoxy.

Even before the Scopes "monkey trial" in 1925, Whittier students expressed interest in the wider conflict over evolutionary theory. Local ministers watchdogged the college teaching at this point. One arose after monitoring a class and accused the professor of atheism. It was noised about town that the college was "a hotbed of infidelity."

The Wilkie affair was the climactic incident in this Fundamentalist attack on the Evolution front.

Guy Fitch Phelps, itinerant Methodist preacher, came to Whittier to conduct revival meetings at the Nazarene Church. The Monday *News* (February 24, 1930) reported his first meeting. The same issue carried a long article on Prof. John R. Wilkie of the college, just elected vice-president of the Southwest Archeological Federation. By the end of the week, Phelps had sized up the town, worked up his audience, and chosen his antagonists. On Saturday he published a CHALLENGE calling upon Judge A. Wray, Prof. Harris, Prof. Wilkie or Dean Coffin to debate him on the question: "Resolved That the Theory of Evolution is Unscientific and Absurd." Next day "full and overflowing houses" greeted Phelps. He announced as his subject for Tuesday night "Some Questions to an Evolutionist" and promised to review Coffin's new book, *The Soul Comes Back* (Macmillan, 1929).

By this time the revivalist's insinuating, incidental, and invidious attack upon the college and the good name of its students was the talk of town and campus. Students, eager for the Great Confrontation descended to the arena, accompanied by dear old Professor Wilkie and young Dr. Albert Upton. Every seat was taken. After due formalities of prayer and praise, Rev. Phelps launched his assault upon the college.

> He seethingly rebuked the modernists . . . teaching evolution and anti-fundamentalism when they draw their salaries from fundamentalists [*sic!*] and are supposed to preach and teach the Bible . . .

Wilkie—red-haired but benign of mien—stood up to defend the college and set straight the facts. Two burly ushers closed in, grabbed him by the arms and hustled him out treading air. There was a stir and scuffle of defensive activity on the part of the college students in the back of the church.

Quiet restored after removal of this antichrist, Phelps breathed deep, fluttered his nostrils—fleered: "Now things smell better!"— and proceeded to lambaste Dean Coffin's book as "unorthodox and contrary to the teachings of the Bible."

Next day, representative students, duly authorized, invited Phelps to the campus to speak his mind about the college, the students then to ask questions. Rejection of this invitation, they said, would be interpreted as "complete denial and apology for all insinuations thrown at professors and students of Whittier College."

Awaiting Phelps' reply, Dexter spoke constructively of the incident as a shared experience bringing students and professors closer together, and announced a public lecture on Evolution to be given shortly by the new head of biology, Dr. S. Arthur Watson. A competent scientist and devoted Quaker, Watson was a theist who believed in evolution "as an honorable and legitimate means of creation." He said, "it is the nearest I have ever come to an understanding of how God in infinite wisdom and power created the Universe."

Guy Fitch Phelps did not reply to the students. But he did address a virulent epistle to Professor Wilkie, whom he had had to "arrest" for disturbing "a religious meeting." Phelps thanked him profusely for sending his "paganized gangsters" to the church. Their behavior showed well the "degrading fruits in human character and conduct" borne by "your sewer theory of evolution" and "modernist reek." In turgid fulmination, the spell-binder continued to his peroration:

> When the church of Peace has fumigated you infidel vermin out, and put real scholars in your stead . . . then I will work for Whittier College . . . Till then, professor, it is war to the hilt!

But Pastor Phelps withdrew to attack in some further vineyard. And other questions were already drawing the Fundamentalists' fire.

In *the Coffin affair*, the charge was doctrinal "unsoundness"!

Even before Phelps reviewed *The Soul Comes Back*, it was being widely read and roundly condemned. Perhaps the perky title (the editor's) or the jaunty style (Coffin's own) or the subject itself (Modernist) struck some readers as irreverent. Coffin opened his book with brilliant portraits of the student agnostic, materialist, idealist, fundamentalist, and modernist. Then he introduced his concept of Personality, and led the reader to his special definition of *soul* as "the self-conscious level of personality." It was his contention that "to be a soul means to be self-conscious of relations between itself and the cosmos, other selves, and God." A soul is not something one is born with, he said, but something to be achieved. Here is where religious education (in his special sense referred to earlier) came in. And Coffin faced the question whether the soul thus acquired and cultivated did indeed survive death.

This was in truth a disturbing book to the orthodox of the time, and Coffin had treated lightly the Fundamentalists and their stereotypes. He had taken *their* word "soul" (quite out of fashion in unorthodox circles) and defined it in terms already familiar in science and philosophy. "To be saved," he wrote, "would mean to be in the enjoyment of the maximum of psychosomatic health —physical, mental, moral, and spiritual." This sounded nigh unto hedonism—nay, heathenism!—despite what he said about the religion of Jesus.

Phelps' assault had come in March 1930. In May, the Friends churches in Bell and Montebello sent communications to Quarterly Meeting taking exception to Dean Coffin's book. Inadvertence or a friendly hand "mislaid" these letters, but the scandal of dancing and card playing at the college (of which more presently) threw the fat into the fire. The letters were found, and the Quarterly Meeting referred them to the local meeting "for investigation and care." The Whittier meeting on Ministry and Oversight appointed three (Dr. L. M. Greene, Esek Perry, and Sara V. Sharpless) to read the book and "to act on the charges" according to their best judgment. These Friends met with "the author" (tenderly avoided minuting his name) about his motives and meaning "regarding the matters in question." Failing to discover "heterodoxy as charged," they recommended that "the author be exonerated." This, then, was notified to Quarterly Meeting.

However mild and embarrassing this "heresy trial," it humiliated Coffin, upon whom other and heavier blows were soon to fall.

The Dexter affair was the third assault upon the college at this time. The question was student dancing.

Evangelist Phelps had chilled his audiences with insinuations of student misbehavior and immorality. The Fundamentalists looked upon dancing—nay, stared at it in fascination!—as the first steps toward sexual delinquency and that fate vaguely "worse than death." The "passionate crooning and wailing" of the barbaric saxophone—the "syncopated embrace" of the fox trot—*Dancers in the Dark!* It was "impure, polluting, corrupting, debasing, destroying spirituality, increasing carnality."

The post-war years were a time of rapid social change marked by the failure of Prohibition, increased mobility by automobile, and the questioning of traditional values on college and university campuses. Dexter and Coffin knew that willy-nilly the majority of Whittier students danced at their off-campus and private parties. It would be socially healthier, they thought, to recognize dancing as a college activity and encourage well-ordered dances on campus.

In 1929 the Joint Council conducted a survey of all segments of the college community, and discovered opinion quite evenly divided among trustees and faculty—with older Friends generally opposed and younger students generally in favor of dancing. The college administration reluctantly reaffirmed the previous regulation: no college dances either on or off campus. And the *Pacific Friend* reassured its distressed readers: there was "nothing to fear," the matter was settled.

But in explaining the decision to the students, Dexter pointed out that those who wished to dance certainly had a right to, and suggested that parents might well arrange private dances at the Woman's Club "to which the college students might be invited" as individuals. That fall the student societies began having formal dinner dances in place of their previous theater parties and banquets. These college social affairs were properly chaperoned, with faculty couples in attendance, and not uncommonly Dr. and Mrs. Dexter themselves went to parties at which the students danced—this to the expressed "grief" of Bell and Montebello Friends.

In September 1930, the students asked President Dexter whether they might trip the light fantastic at the annual Student Body Reception. Perhaps he hesitated a moment. Then he took it upon himself to say: Yes.

Beautifully decorated, Wardman Gymnasium was "mellow in the glow of colored flood-lights" . . . a bit of Hawaii with its palms and gay lanterns . . . leis and flowers as favors. It was a memorable reception and well attended by trustees, faculty, and older students welcoming the incoming freshmen.

> At the close of the formal program, the orchestra struck up the grand march, and the colorful column of guests, led by Dr. and Mrs. Dexter, wound up and down the floor until all had found partners. Delicious refreshments of ice cream and cake were provided.

Found partners! And then the Q.C.—whether through accident, excision, or ecstasy—skipped the next fateful steps, reported happily in the *Acropolis*: "The rest of the evening was spent in *dancing, bridge, bunco and other games*" [emphasis added]!

The students, for the most part, fox-trotted off and about. Others resorted to the gaming tables. Professors in a quandary faced the music stoically or hovered uneasily about the bridge and bunco. Some few danced an enjoyable evening. Dr. Louis T. Jones, himself a Friends minister, stuck by the dancing—but, then, as an anthropologist, he knew the Navajo wooing dance. Edna T. Nanney '11, newly appointed to the college board (and recording clerk of the Whittier Monthly Meeting), swirled about with her husband, earlier of the faculty.

But—"After the ball was o-ver, / After the break of morn"— outraged elders telephoned Edna Nanney, waited upon Louis Jones, and assailed Walter Dexter. The Whittier meeting on Ministry and Oversight addressed a formidable petition to the college Board of Trustees, in which it asserted that the college was subject to California Yearly Meeting, which "by its policies, traditions and doctrines has regarded dancing and card playing as improper social amusements for students of its college" [sic]. Permission for the dancing and card playing had been granted in violation of the college By-laws in that the trustees had not been consulted.

Continuing failure in this matter might well call into question their right to control the college property! And the irate petitioners closed by reiterating their stand against dancing and card playing "being permitted in the social life of the students on the territory over which the College has control."

What heat this petition generated at the next board meeting was damped down by the bland minutes of the secretary. "A number of letters" had been received regarding the dance at the reception. "Considerable difference of opinion" divided the trustees on this question. A committee of five was named, including A. Wardman (who favored dancing) and Thomas Newlin (who opposed it).

This committee duly met and tried to find some solution to the problem. The most telling point against dancing on the campus was quite irrelevant to the issue: Repeated waxing and then scouring of the gym floor would ruin it for basketball! The committee recommendation and board decision followed: "Dances as social functions [will] not be permitted on the College Campus." That is, "not on territory over which the college has control." The last words of the protesting elders had inadvertently suggested a compromise solution.

The next Freshman Reception, held at the fine new Woman's Club, had "dancing in the spacious ballroom" for those who wished and unspecified games downstairs in the reception hall— safely three blocks *off campus*.

These rebukes by the religious conservatives and fundamentalists were the last of their sort. They were a far cry from the kindly simplicity, friendliness and large charity that John Greenleaf Whittier had bequeathed to the Quaker town and church that had founded Whittier College.

THE NEW CURRICULUM, quietly resisted by the traditionalist professors from the beginning, came "under direct fire from all directions" in 1929-30. The Correlation Course was in its fourth year of operation, and the seniors of that year were the first to take Dr. Coffin's own course and thus to complete the four-year sequence. It is certainly true that Coffin himself did not "reach" all his students, doubtless bored some, perhaps evoked inner conflicts in others. It may also be true that, in his course and new book, he challenged fundamental assumptions and value systems of some of his faculty colleagues.

Whatever the subconscious motives and the outward pressures, the New Curriculum faced a crisis on March 17, 1930 when Dean Coffin called a special meeting of the faculty "to consider some of the problems growing out of the present educational and financial situation."

The financial situation, briefly, was the weight of indebtedness, the growing deficit, and the first shock waves following the Stock Crash. Specifically, the college board hoped to trim $10,000 from the budget for faculty and administration and hold it to $97,000 for the year ahead.

The educational situation was certainly the growing opposition to the New Curriculum.

The faculty minutes blandly record, "A general discussion followed," with no hint of a confrontation of opposing educational philosophies. The matter was referred to the [departmental] Advisers and Curriculum Committee. Their detailed and devastating recommendations, presented to the faculty on May 5th, were considered and tabled, to be taken up item by item a week later.

First (the constructive note!), the faculty approved "the principle of Correlation" and resolved to make a special study of it and "determine how the Faculty as a whole can best cooperate to this end." Then the faculty approved naming a committee—the department heads with the Dean as chairman—to lead in making this study. Next the faculty approved item 3: "That English and Correlation courses be made optional for graduation." This, of course, was it—a shrewd move to couple English (which most advisers would insist their freshmen take) with the Correlation sequence (which many of them opposed) and make both "optional." For to make the new courses optional, effectively removed them as the core of the students' programs. It had been the Whittier Idea that *all* the students should be led toward maturity of personality and the correlation of their growing knowledge with the human issues of modern life—not just such students as might elect these courses or take them upon the insistence of their advisers.

Whatever might have resulted from the faculty study of

Correlation, not yet begun—however unanimous the faculty approval of "the principle of Correlation"—the sequence of Correlation courses was doomed before any single student had completed it.

The special committee met—dean and a dozen department heads—but it was impossible for it to report "a week hence" as directed. In fact, the study then undertaken continued through the summer and next year. With the curriculum in disarray— the old New Curriculum in part dismantled and the new Old Curriculum not yet installed—the college could not publish the expected May *Bulletin* announcing courses for 1930-31.

In August 1930 came a skeletal catalog—without statement of college aims and philosophy of education. Faculty members, degrees listed in full, were arranged under department heads. Admission requirements and college expenses followed, but no statement of graduation requirements. Next came the departments of instruction, with course offerings and class hours scheduled (but without course descriptions)—then the departmental requirements and those for teaching credentials.

"Correlation," in the alphabetic sequence of departments, listed only the freshman course. Cross-references indicated that the former sophomore, junior, and senior Correlation courses were to be found under departmental headings and traditional titles.

This make-shift catalog, reissued in February 1931, was prefaced with a Note. "The Faculty of Whittier College is making a thorough study of the problems of the college." The study was including a re-evaluation of

> the statement of aim and objectives, the means and methods most effective in the achievement of these, together with the type of organization best adapted to the aims and methods.

Modification of graduation requirements and some "shift in emphasis" were announced in the May 1931 *Bulletin*.

However, no catalog was issued at that time. With the curriculum in uncertain flux—and other drastic changes already public knowledge—it was Dean Coffin's distasteful task to assure the student body that all was well, the Whittier Idea remained unchanged, and "four new features" would be added in the curriculum in the fall.

But all was not well either in the college or in the country at large. The shadow of the Depression had crept across the land to darken the gloom on the Whittier campus.

In March 1931, while the faculty was wrestling with the curriculum, the finance and faculty committees of the Board of Trustees met jointly to consider the increasingly desperate condition of college finances. They recommended that the faculty and administration budget for the coming year be cut to $80,000, and added: "It will be noted that this requires changes of place [sic] for the following persons," and there followed a list of twelve persons to be eliminated and/or replaced. Of these, three were withdrawing anyway; nine others were simply to be let go.*

But in the reorganization of the faculty and administration someone had to assume the *functions* of most of those who were thus dropped—except for teaching the freshman correlation course and project work that were eliminated. Certain courses could be omitted from the schedule, asterisked to be given another year, and there was some doubling up. But in a number of cases assistants and instructors had to be hired to carry on essential work of the departments. Administrative duties were added to professors' teaching loads—for additional pay. In fact, after the faculty "purge," reorganization and adjustments, the budget for faculty and administration for 1931-32 actually amounted to $94,000—a saving of only one $3,000 salary over the budget for the preceding year! However, the number of Ph.D.'s on the faculty was reduced from 12 to 7. And four or five members of the remaining faculty enjoyed increases in salary!**

*Of the twelve, Clarence G. McClean (dean of men) continued his teaching at Los Angeles Junior College, Mary Mendenhall (dean of women) served long years at San Diego State College, Dr. Louis T. Jones joined the high school faculty, Dr. Mary E. Conrad (in biology) taught later at Catawba College. Others dropped were Dr. Roy Van Deman (visiting professor of sociology), Dr. S. M. Hadley (visiting professor of mathematics), Peggy Baum (in French). Rosa McKusick (registrar) and Esther Wilkie (assistant librarian) were leaving anyway, as was Dr. Harry H. Vannorsdall (in Education) who was returning to Wilmington College. Esther Andrews and Eugene Knox were also on the list of twelve, but by June were issued contracts for the next year. Professor Wilkie asked for a leave of absence to teach a year in Turkey, and Irene Palmer resigned, so that the final count continued to be twelve fewer members of the faculty and administration.

**There seems to have been no suggestion at this time that the entire faculty share in the misfortune and take an across-the-board salary cut so as to save the positions of those to be released.

This radical shaking out of the faculty in the spring of 1931 eliminated three of the professors who were then giving optional remnants of the Correlation sequence. And the fourth, Dean Coffin himself, was to be repudiated before the reorganization of the faculty and administration was completed.

FINANCIAL TROUBLES were the accustomed state at Whittier during the decade of economic growth and booming prosperity that crashed to a close in 1929-30. The crisis came for the college in June 1931.

From the very beginning of Dexter's time, Whittier College ran in the red. Within a year of the Great Banquet of 1923, the Board of Trustees "resolved" to borrow up to $50,000, and the indebtedness for current expenditures was up to $86,000 before the landslide of the Syndicate overwhelmed the college in 1928. Then it was borrowing money to pay interest on money already borrowed and then borrowing to pay interest on *that*! The college surely was being drawn into the whirlpool of bankruptcy.

Then the board freed Dexter from campus responsibilities to devote his time to college finances. Beginning in 1929, the trustees also employed the first in a succession of four fund-raisers. With "fees as high as $1,600 a month," they scarcely brought in more than their own costs. And Dexter himself seemed to have lost the secret of his youthful success—frankly disliked asking people for money to support Whittier College.* Yet sustaining funds were the crying need, and the operating deficit was some $25,000 annually.

In the spring of 1930—doubtless distressed by inadequate efforts to control the budget in the downward spiral of college finances—A. Wardman offered his resignation. At the April 2, 1930 meeting, he was urged to withdraw it and did. Thereupon H. L. Perry tendered his resignation as president of the board and A. N. Chamness as secretary-treasurer and comptroller of the board and business manager of the college—these resignations to take effect as soon as successors were chosen. At the May 6th meeting, the trustees elected Wardman to be treasurer of the Board of Trustees—and Howard L. Hockett to be comptroller

*One well-to-do Whittier business man, who rode horseback with him on the hill trails, wondered why Dexter never suggested that he contribute to the college.

and business manager. In the reorganization, C. Bevan Johnson became president of the board to succeed Herman Perry.

The year 1930-31 that lay ahead of them was to be a year of mergers, mad schemes, and mounting deficit.

The merger of the Broadoaks School with Whittier College was one of the deals worked out by Dexter and his financial associate Mr. Wills—and this was a good thing for all concerned: the school itself, the Brooks sisters, and the college. The affiliation of the Y.M.C.A. School also proved to be successful. But some of the other efforts seemed little short of frantic.

In the spring of 1930, Dexter got the idea of developing Whittier as a "Radio University for the United States" by alliance with a Los Angeles radio station. This scheme did not work.

Then in the spring of 1931 came a prospect of another sort. A Dr. Patrick of Orange proposed that a portion of Whittier's expanded campus be turned into an Avicultural Gardens. What gave piquancy to this mad scheme was not the strutting peacock —or even nicker of Arab stallion—but "a possible connection with Mr. W. K. Kellogg" and his breakfast-food millions. This came to naught.

However, there was the possibility of affiliating other horses— leasing part of the more remote campus to a riding academy. But this southeastern edge of the Worsham ranch faced the Eastridge development of fine homes. Alphonzo E. Bell protested the proximate horseflies. His objection was heeded. The Whittier board nayed the riding horses. And this scheme, too, came to naught.

But by the end of the calendar year, the college did get a clutch of stuffed ducks, a gift of the Whittier Ornithological Society. Thereafter they looked down in silent comment from the science cabinets in Founders Hall.

However diverting these prospects, they in no way stopped the circling drift of the college toward the vortex of disaster.

The moment of truth came at a meeting of the college board on June 1st, 1931. The question was: how to meet the payroll of that date. In the course of the trustees' discussion, "the following facts were brought to light, namely—that *we were without funds and unable to borrow*." No emphasis beyond the bare statement was needed in that meeting of bankers, businessmen, ranchers.

Dexter, too, must have realized that his report to the meeting on the possible Avicultural Gardens was irrelevant to the immediate need.

Whittier College was not bankrupt—nor had it ever been, nor was it ever to be—but the financial crisis was no less real. The stark question was: how to meet the June payroll. To do this, the trustees did, what as trustees they were most loath to do: they borrowed $10,000 from the Endowment Fund, assigning to it pledges in that amount secured in the 1928 drive for funds. But it was clear that the college simply could not continue on the course it was following.

"In this emergency," as Professor Harris later wrote, "a quiet, secret session" called together three professors and three trustees. "A full discussion of proposed remedies" brought forth no panacea for the dire financial predicament. Then, "Herbert Harris was asked to study conditions and plan a reorganization which would make continuance possible." After "searching analysis," Harris again met with members of the board and proposed a sharp scaling down of expenditures, cutting the budget by $16,000, and he proposed "another provision which would insure continuance of the college" if approved by the board and accepted by the faculty.

The board had lost confidence in President Dexter as it had in Dean Coffin. Without terminating the contract of either one, it created a new office, that of Vice President of the college. Answerable directly to the board, this executive officer was to be "in charge of all internal administration except finance and physical properties," which were the province of Howard L. Hockett as comptroller and business manager. The board action, thus reorganizing the administration, was completed on June 29th. Dr. Herbert E. Harris—for he had been honored by Penn College that June with an LL.D.—was named Vice President of Whittier College, to assume his new duties at once, July 1, 1931.

President Dexter had lost control of the administration, as Dean Coffin had lost control of the curriculum. It was the end of their educational adventure in reshaping a liberal arts college. Yet neither Walter Dexter nor Herschel Coffin was personally repudiated, and it remained to be seen whether their Whittier Idea in its broad principles was dead beyond recall.

9

NEW ADMINISTRATION—NEW ECONOMIES
AND THE OLD CURRICULUM

As VICE PRESIDENT of Whittier College, Dr. Harris was without question the man in charge. Dexter was confined to fund-raising, public lecturing, and ceremonial occasions.

In the summer of 1931, aged 56, Herbert Harris was tall, with a slight forward stoop, bald and a bit craggy, acerbic wit shielding a sensitive nature.* He had first taught at Whittier 1901-1910. In 1920 he returned after a decade that included ranching, writing, war service, and teaching for a year at Penn College. He loved teaching, especially his Shakespeare course, and directing outdoor dramas. His courses in journalism and short story were coupled with his own writing—in all, some thousand pieces for the Whittier *News*. A Quaker from college days, Harris had a strong calling to community service. A member of Rotary, he was an intimate of business men in the community. His vision had inspired the ill-fated Syndicate.

Achievement of widest influence was Harris' initiation of the Sixth (later Fourth) Object of Rotary,

> the advancement of understanding, good will, and international peace, through a world fellowship of business and professional men united in the Rotary ideal of service.

This practical pacifism, first proposed in the Whittier club, was accepted in 1927 by an international committee representing 38 nations. Harris, given a two-months' leave by the college, lectured across the land and attended the convention of Rotary International in Belgium. After his return to Whittier, he became District Governor of Rotary, relieved of two classes to perform this service. He was then named chairman of Rotary's five-man international committee on International Relations.

The position in which Harris was placed as vice president of the college in the summer of 1931 was a delicate and difficult one. With the continuing presence of both the president and the

---

*A splendid portrait by his son, Richard C. Harris '34, is among the portraits he painted of the Whittier College presidents. The collection was hung for many years in the college Library in the O. T. Mendenhall building.

dean, it was not easy to clarify for campus and town just what his rôle was to be. The immediate task was completion of the reorganization of the college and publication of the catalog. With the deans of men and of women both dropped from the faculty, it became evident that Harris would serve as dean of students. As the year moved ahead, it also became evident that he was expected to serve as dean of the faculty—and to continue teaching "as many classes as reasonably possible."

Word spread that Whittier College might close its doors. Mr. Wardman suggested as much to the students in a chapel talk and to the community as well. Some trustees asked Mr. Hockett to determine just what steps would be taken if the college were to be liquidated.

An "undercurrent of uncertainty," felt by the faculty during the fall of 1931, prompted the appointment of a joint committee "to appraise the entire college set up."* This committee reported to the board on February 23, 1932.

Before proposing specific "entrenchment in the budget," the committee suggested some points of general policy, in substance:

Whittier College—a four-year liberal arts college of high standards, built around Quaker idealism of Christian spirit and practical service.
Faculty—small but of high type, permanent, largely younger men.
Departments—only those central to a liberal education.
Administrative staff—small, with faculty sharing in the work.
Salaries—equitable, based upon training, experience, ability to teach, and service to college and community.

Then came the suggestion: cut the salary budget by $10,000, but keep the heads of departments at their current level.** It followed that "Any cut, then, must be made in administration and in secondary positions."

This joint committee further proposed that the financial re-

*The committee comprised two professors (Skarstedt and Smith), two administrators (Harris and Coffin), two trustees (H. L. Perry and Ashton M. Otis), and the presidents of board and faculty (C. B. Johnson and Dexter). With Harris as chairman, it met repeatedly.

**This was then $3,000 for Ph.D. heads of departments; $2,500 for other professors; $1,800 for instructors—with extra pay for coaches and those with added duties, i.e., librarian, registrar, etc.

sources for operating expenses be increased. (This, in the Depression trough of 1932!) And that a million dollar endowment "be secured through a period of perhaps five years." (This, exactly what President Dexter could not do!)

At the same time the college board offered Dean Coffin a year's leave of absence (at $100 a month) with the privilege of returning to the college as professor of philosophy but not dean in the fall of 1933. This he did after a year as acting professor at Swarthmore and lecturing at Pendle Hill, new center of Quaker studies nearby.

All of this was a tightening of the institutional belt.

The undercurrent of uncertainty went far beyond the campus. Bustling Rumor had it that Whittier's time was up. Smith received condolences from historians on other campuses. Upton, thrice asked if the bad news was true, replied that, like his reported drowning when becalmed off Huntington Beach, the rumor was somewhat exaggerated.

Taking this occasion, Upton then wrote an editorial for the Q.C. (his title: "And the Rain Descended and the Floods Came—") and said to the students:

> When the world approaches you with the question, 'Is Whittier College on the rocks?' answer, 'Yes, high and dry! Ever since the Quakers founded her there in 1901.'
>
> Tell them she's founded on the rock of integrity, the integrity of the trustees who recognize the high seriousness of their trust.
>
> Tell them she's founded on the rock of service, the service of faculty members who seek something more lasting than dollars in the rich recompense of their high calling.
>
> Tell them she's founded upon the rock of the spirit of youth, the youth of a splendid succession of young men and women whose frank questionings are an eternal challenge and whose loyal friendship is a treasure.

The college was sustained by this kind of confidence in the long future, and cheered by its spirited display.

THE NEW COMPTROLLER of the college, Howard L. Hockett, was indeed an exceptional person. Joining the Whittier faculty in 1906, he had served 25 years as director of music and professor of voice, continuously at Whittier except for six years at his alma mater, Penn. But before committing himself to a career in music, he had taken two years of professional training in law. The college board had already given him occasional business assignments before naming him comptroller in the summer of 1930. Increasingly hard of hearing, he gave up his teaching in 1932 to devote himself to his heavy responsibilities as business manager.

Howard Hockett had the ungrateful task of *not* spending money. He had the unwelcome job of collecting tuitions, fees, rents. He bore the brunt of figuring out how to meet the fixed obligations of the college: huge interest payments on what finally was $412,000 indebtedness, land taxes and assessments, annuity payments.* He also had to meet the payroll. After a difficult first year—some trustees fearing his appointment had been a mistake—he developed an amazing talent for working things out. If at times he seemed penny-pinching, a man to drive a hard bargain, this was born of necessity out of the money-starved economy of hard times. And through his tight control of finances, he helped save the college to serve another day.

When on that June 1, 1931 the college found itself "without funds and unable to borrow" it had been forced to dip temporarily into its Endowment Fund for $10,000 to pay the faculty. Within two months a second $10,000 had to be transferred to the hungry General Fund to get through the summer. This is how it was done:

That spring Aubrey Wardman had made an unrestricted gift to the college of the house he had built as an investment in College Hills. Valued at $10,500, it was not marketable during the Depression. His gift had been part of the unsuccessful end-the-debt campaign. Now its value was badly needed to meet current expenses. Therefore the house was "sold" to the Endowment Fund by the General Fund. In order to "buy" this property as an endowment investment, the Endowment Fund had to sell one of its mortgages for $10,000 cash. This $10,000 was thereupon "paid" to the ravenous General Fund, and thence to the professors as salaries.

*During the Depression there was never a default in payments to annuitants, though their contracts were based upon values inflated by the prosperity of the later 1920's. And Hockett himself felt secure in swapping his home adjacent to the campus for a college annuity as part of his and Mrs. Hockett's retirement income.

This sort of horse-trading was what Wardman himself enjoyed in his own wide-ranging enterprises. Hockett learned and practiced it in his artful management of the college. Not always involving real estate, it could be as simple as crediting sacks of potatoes against a boy's room rent, or accepting a father's labor as painter in partial payment of his daughter's tuition. So it was dickering and dealing, rather than philosophic vision and dynamic optimism, that withheld Whittier College from ultimate disaster.

The decimation of the faculty in the spring of 1931, and the drastic cut in the faculty budget in the spring of 1932, left untouched the professors who were heads of departments. At the end of March 1932, the faculty committee of the board suggested a salary budget of $71,000 (exclusive of Broadoaks). The administrative costs were cut by over $4,000: a net saving of $1,500 from Coffin's salary and decreases of $500 for Dexter, of $750 each for Harris and Hockett, of $400 each for Skarstedt and Homan as part-time librarian and registrar. The professors and instructors were to remain at the salaries previously set, except there was reluctance to pay Upton $3,000 as he was still a bachelor and only acting head of his department.

But this budget was still too high. Fiscal salvation was to be wrought only by a sterner measure.

On May 9, 1932 Harris proposed to the faculty that, instead of cuts from established salaries, *only 75% be guaranteed* for the coming year 1932-33. This came as a sobering shock, and a committee (Smith, Ostrom, Henley) was appointed to consider the matter further with the administration. As approved by the faculty, administration and trustees, contracts were then issued in which the trustees pledged themselves to pay full salary checks for the first nine months of the year. Then—

> If there are insufficient funds available for payment in full the last three months of the year, the available funds shall be prorated among the faculty members in proportion to their regular salaries.

And in lieu of the unpaid balance at the end of the year, the faculty agreed to accept credit toward payment on College Hills lots.* Or the faculty might prefer to accept prorata rights to "the current unpaid tuition accounts which shall be set up in a special fund under the control of a committee." A long hungry summer was in prospect for 1933, without the usual salary checks. But, as Harris later wrote with satisfaction, "after the critical fall of 1932, the college ran every year within its income."

For the following year (1933-34) some of the trustees wanted to lower the guaranteed percentage to 60% or even 50% of the nominal salaries. But with Skarstedt negotiating for the faculty, the 75% was again agreed upon. To ease the next summer for faculty families, checks in the amount of 75% were to be paid each month throughout the year "if and when funds from the current income of 1933-34 are available." Which was something less than a guarantee.** The remainder of "the net operating income"—carefully defined—was to be impounded until the end of the summer, then to be prorated to the faculty according to their share in the faculty budget.

Summers were still difficult. Under the "if and when" clause, salary checks were delayed a week or ten days or more during the last months of the year.

Actually these professors' salaries were livable, as the cost of living had decreased 25% since 1925, and the prorata payment of whatever was available beyond the 75%, coming at it did at the end of the summer, was a welcome "bonus," and was so called. Even 10%, as in 1934, meant a $250 to $300 check for a professor (no deductions in those days), to add prudently to rainy-day savings (no Social Security or pension plans as yet), or toward a car ($750 for a new Ford or Chevy). And, through the careful management of Howard Hockett, the non-guaranteed 75% was assured. The "if and when" gave way in a couple of years to "as and when," and the bonus of 10% soon increased.

In the bottom of the Great Depression, the land debt of $230,000 was the largest, but by no means only, millstone round the neck of the struggling college. There was an additional $180,000 indebtedness from accumulated deficits. The annual

*Six or more professors did accept lot payments instead of summer salaries, and two or three later built upon them.
**Salaries of less than $1,000 per year were paid in full.

213

interest charges amounted to more than $20,000. A campaign in the fall of 1930 to clear $150,000 of this debt (one-third in each of three years) was unsuccessful. From 1929 on, efforts had been made to sell "all or any portion of" the Worsham Ranch—*without any regard for its intended future use as part of the campus*—simply to get out from under. In 1931 the trustees proposed to sell 88 acres of Worsham Canyon to the City of Whittier for only $100,000! But the municipal bond issue for this recreational park failed at the polls. Then, in 1932, Dexter proposed that all the remaining lots in College Hills be sold for as little as $75,000 (less than $1,000 per lot)—but this also failed. Had these efforts succeeded, almost all of the land would have been disposed of to clear only 40% of the total debt! As it was, the college *had* to hang on. Gradually lots sold, the banks renewed mortgages (and at the reduced interest rates then current), and small payments of principal were undertaken.

On February 27, 1934, the board looked ahead and decided that, in the case of the termination of annuities, the direct saving to the college should be applied to reduction of the debt. And at that time, student enrollment increased 5% and collections ran 10% better than for the preceding year. Within another month, the college felt the direct benefits of the New Deal: "the first monthly payments from Federal Aid for worthy students had been received." It was some satisfaction to partisan Republicans that Whittier College had already pulled itself clear of the economic maelstrom.

By this time, in the spring of 1934, there was again the solid feeling of solvency.

CURRICULAR CHANGES for the year 1931-32 and the related changes in faculty and administration were fully revealed in the college *Bulletin* of August 1931, the first full-scale catalog since May 1929.

As Dean Coffin had assured the students, the principle of Correlation was reaffirmed. But the Correlation courses were now indicated as optional, and that for freshmen was dropped. This catalog described the promised "four new features" for achieving Correlation: The faculty continued its study in conferences. Professors lectured occasionally for each other. One course was given jointly by professors from two departments—Foundations of English and American Civilization, Smith and Upton. Some professors made a conscious effort to keep the great human issues and problems of modern living in relevant focus in their various courses and in the requirements for their majors. Three former correlation courses were still available under department headings, and the Project Work continued *in the catalog* much as it had been before. There was no desire to lose whatever magic the words "correlation" and "project" might have in public relations and student promotion.

The structure of the curriculum and the requirements for graduation showed marked changes. The faculty had reduced the requirements in general education and placed all this liberal arts work in the lower division, facilitating the transfer of students from junior college. The cultural values of general education were to be assured by a new formula of distribution. Compared with previous formulae, it decreased by 30% the proportion of general studies required of Whittier College students: 28% less in English and languages, 48% less in history and social sciences, 14% less in mathematics and natural sciences. As a result, the lower-division student had greater freedom of election in his college program—or so it seemed. But actually, the "augmented major," as it was now called, included a more-clearly defined set of departmental prerequisites and suggested courses in related departments. And this prepared him for a more concentrated upper-division major, with supporting courses in allied fields— *all of it prescribed by the department head or adviser.* Thus it was that the old order was restored: the strong, if "augmented," major with no minors, and the authority of the faculty adviser. Even the "group major," which antedated the New Curriculum, was virtually eliminated.

So it was that Whittier College opened in September 1931 with a considerably revised curriculum and with a considerably reduced faculty. Including the Broadoaks staff and part-time lecturers, the faculty didn't *appear* smaller as listed. But the faculty available on campus was reduced from 34 to 25. Nor was the administrative reorganization such as to disturb academic procedures and student traditions.

Survival and solvency were the twin objectives that united the faculty and students with a spirit that triumphed over adversity. And when in the spring of 1932 Upton wrote his editorial for the Q.C. to quash the rumor that the college was about to close, he said that he had

> hastened to boast of the striking morale of our growing student body and the steadily improving quality of both our academic and extra-curricular programs.

10

STUDENT INITIATIVE—COLLEGE VITALITY— AND NEW STABILITY

THE WHITTIER STUDENT BODY had doubled during the first six years of Dexter's presidency. It fell off 10% in the year of the Stock Crash, but recovered the next year, 1930-31. Even the rumor that Whittier was closing lost but a few students for the college, and the newly-acquired Broadoaks added 50 students in 1931-32, making the total 469, the highest enrollment to date. Energetic recruitment held the student body to about this size for several years. Whittier had become "the largest Friends college in the Five Years Meeting."

Those were hard times for college students. Even before the Depression closed in, a good proportion of Whittier students had "worked their way through college" in whole or in part. Now, the parents of many students were impoverished—unemployed, savings wiped out, property values deflated. During the year 1930-31, some 50% of all Whittier students were partially or wholly self-supporting. Of the men 83% earned at least part of their expenses, 30% earned all of them. (However, only 2% of the women were thus fully on their own.) The college helped as many of these hardworking students as it could with scholarships, tuition grants, loans, and on-campus jobs. By the spring of 1934 N.Y.A. funds paid for student help (at 25¢ or 35¢ per hour), and earnings from such work on the grounds, in laboratories, and in offices were credited toward the students' tuition.

Working as much as many of them did, it is a wonder they found time and energy, not only for classes and study, but also for the wide range of college activities that they carried on.

216

MANAGEMENT OF CAMPUS undertakings by the students themselves, in close association with the faculty, had been a vital part of the Whittier Idea. But traditionalists on the faculty had shown impatience with democratic fumbling, inefficiency of co-operative control, and non-authoritarian discipline. In the reorganization of faculty and administration, the Joint Council was shorn "of Control," and the idealistic statement regarding a student-faculty "community of will" dropped from the catalog. However, the Joint Council continued, reduced in size and in function. And a strong bond of loyalty to common ideals and purposes united students, faculty, and trustees during these difficult Depression years.

It was the Associated Students (A.S.W.C.) that constructed a pair of new concrete tennis courts, with approval and $100 assist from the trustees, using $500 of the Radio Contest prize money that they had saved for such a purpose.* In the spring of 1933, the A.S.W.C. and Joint Council took up the question of a much-needed Student Union. They remodeled rooms in the Music Building, to which the first Campus Inn had been adjoined in 1928. This large old house had been moved south on Painter Avenue from the corner of Philadelphia to make room for the new Elks lodge. Then in June 1933, the A.S.W.C. placed its surplus $500 in trust, looking toward later building of "a permanent student union." This was the only building reserve fund the college then had.

The vitality of student enterprise and life shows through the student publications of these Depression years, not only in their contents but in their style and spirit. The *Quaker Campus*, with a succession of capable editors, provided good reportage of campus news, sports and society, features and columns, caricatures and editorials. The Q.C. seemed keenly aware of the larger world beyond its microcosm, and for the first time won All-American honors as judged by the National Scholastic Press.

The *Acropolis* showed a new exuberance in its paragraphs. The *Acropolis 1934*, edited by Robert Cole, was stunningly modern in design, typography and tone—Marjorie Hildreth and Ed Breitkreutz doing much of the brisk writing. Its opening picture was a

*Located along Earlham Drive, with a third added later, they became the site for relocating Redwood Hall in 1962.

doublespread: Prof. Paul S. Smith lecturing, chalk in his firm grasp. On the blackboard (for whatever lecture in American history) was a list of key words, reading up from the bottom: "New Dispensation of the Holy Spirit / Original Society / Eclecticism / Syncretism / Transcendentalism / Vice-President." In the front row sat an intent student, his gaze fixed at the top . . . Another double-spread: a campus cartoon crowded with students and faculty, sharp caricatures by Dick Harris. . . This *Acropolis* deserved the high praise and honor it received.

The "fraternity question" had been with the college off and on since the numbered days of the Acolytes. Although the Foundation society maintained its professional character, the literary societies established during the 'twenties had become essentially fraternal and sororal. In 1928 the faculty had ruled firmly and the board concurred in refusing to allow a Whittier chapter of a national journalism "fraternity," and reaffirmed the traditional Friends' testimony against secret societies.* They boggled at the word but blinked the reality. To the Franklin Society was added the Orthogonian Society in the fall of 1930, with Albert Upton as sponsor and Dick Nixon (then a freshman) as its first president. This "spirited group of men" developed a close feeling of "unity, good fellowship, and college loyalty." By 1933, the Lancer Society was being formed and the William Penn Society submitted its constitution for approval. Upon recommendation of the Joint Council, the faculty now drew up certain regulations regarding pledging, and forbade the secret ballot, the blackball, and first-semester rushing. But ostensible ground rules hardly inhibited these brotherhoods, each with its secret initiation, ritual, and mystique.

The student body as a whole, however, needed an enlarged social program, and that meant more student dances. Running for the A.S.W.C. presidency in 1933, Dick Nixon made this a campaign issue and won. Thereupon he arranged to meet with the college board "to present the social situation on the campus from the student's viewpoint." Because of the ruling against having dances on the campus, he said, the student body had to go elsewhere and rent places that were always expensive, often

*No objection was raised two years later in accepting Delta Phi Upsilon as part of Broadoaks.

remote, and sometimes undesirable. Wouldn't the trustees help the students solve their problem? By the end of summer, the board approved a Joint Social Committee to encourage social activities for all the students. Furthermore, "since there is no building on the campus which is equipped and suitable for large social functions," the board (carefully avoiding the word "dance") appropriated up to $200 a year for rental of the Woman's Clubhouse for such functions. With this help, the A.S.W.C. proceeded to schedule monthly dances.

It was not lost on the students that *in principle* dancing was no longer prohibited on the campus, and informal dancing in Platner lounge raised no stir. It was a score of years since the first furtive "rhythmical sway" of record.

DRAMA, MUSIC, AND ATHLETICS reached a new high point of student involvement and achievement during these Depression years following the college crisis of 1931.

Dramatic activities had been a mixture of warmed-over Broadway hits, hilarious farces and Stag Follies, with occasional outdoor production of literary classics. Such was the Senior Play in the spring of 1931—Shakespeare's *The Tempest*, tenth anniversary production in the Harris Amphitheater. And with this presentation, Prospero abjured his rough magic and broke his staff, for it was the last of the college plays directed by Professor Harris.

Colleges and universities were beginning to feel the exhilarating stimulus of the New American Drama. In the 1920's, Eugene O'Neill, Maxwell Anderson, and others had achieved a place as worthy successors to Ibsen, Hauptmann, and Bernard Shaw. Community and "little" theaters (notable among them, the Pasadena Playhouse) were changing the collegiate taste in theater art. A new sort of development in drama at Whittier College was the combined effort of students and faculty in 1931-32. A Joint Drama Committee and a dramatics club sought to improve the quality of plays selected for campus presentation and encouraged reading of good modern and contemporary plays. With Albert Upton as faculty mentor, a group of unusually gifted and eager students, among them Herschel Daugherty and Marjorie Hildreth, sought to improve the quality of the acting and stage production. The student body (Daugherty running for A.S.W.C.

president) voted a student assessment of $1 per semester as a drama fee, collected at registration. For this, students received tickets to the four major productions of the year, and the drama board secured a dependable income. During the summer of 1932, the students—with Upton helping at every turn—enlarged and remodeled the stage and auditorium. Opening production in the new Poet Theatre, as it was thereafter called, was John Drinkwater's *Bird in Hand*. Later in the season came Martin Flavin's strong social drama, *The Criminal Code*, and Philip Barry's social comedy, *You and I*. For several years the drama students collaborated with the music department in the production of a Gilbert and Sullivan operetta, but this began as a constructive alternative to the Stag Follies.

In May 1932, the Franklins "assisted by the men's and women's glee clubs," presented *H.M.S. Pinafore* in the new high school auditorium before an audience of 1,700. Pauline Terpstra [Spencer] directed the music. The Savoyards included Manville Saxton, Josephine [Whistler] Dockstader, Gordon Berger, and Edith McDonald. A large segment of the student body was in the production or sold tickets, and the Franklins contributed the net profit of $443 to the remodeling of the Poet Theatre stage.

This performance served a further purpose as the evening entertainment for 600 high school seniors and junior college sophomores—who had already enjoyed a high school music festival that afternoon in Wardman Gym, a women's physical education Festival of Nations in the amphitheater, a science demonstration in Naylor Hall, intramural football on Hadley Field, and picnic supper!*

At Whittier, as in other small colleges, many of the same students participated in these various activities, enjoyed wide-ranging experiences that contributed to their later success as civic and professional leaders. And a large portion of the student body enjoyed recreational activity, intramural team sports, or intercollegiate athletics.

During these trying Depression years, football and basketball

---

*This Spring Festival in 1932 was first in an annual succession. *The Mikado* was second in the series of operettas, and brought Mr. Hockett from his desk in the business office to assume musical direction upon Miss Terpstra's illness. An important part of student recruitment, these Festivals were wholehearted undertakings of faculty and students under guidance of the Joint Council.

were important foci for student spirit and co-operation. Wallace "Chief" Newman and Verne Landreth were both excellent coaches and good educators, highly regarded by their colleagues no less than by students and townsmen.

Football started off well in the fall of 1932, with 60 men (including freshmen) "out" for the teams, 30% of the male students. After two early season wins, the Poets met the Tigers at the Rose Bowl in the 24th game between the two colleges since 1895. Of these Occidental had won 15—and it won this one, too. But during the next weeks Newman's team won five games in a row, and on Thanksgiving Day, it met the unbeaten Redlands team on Hadley Field. After a scoreless first half, the Poets came back to "march the ball down the field," and with an end-around play went over for a touchdown. Then Redlands, taking the kick-off and completing a series of pass plays, was able to even the score. At the end, it was a 23-yard run by Bill Brock, a 20-yard pass to Glover, and "the Quakers smashed over for the deciding score."

Thus, the 1932 team won the conference football championship, the first for Whittier since 1921. The next year, the Poets had the pleasure of beating the Tigers on Hadley Field for Homecoming—overcoming Oxy was always enough to make it a good season—but Whittier only tied for second place in the conference.

In the winter of 1933, following that football championship, Verne Landreth's basketball team hit its stride. First came a heartbreaking loss to Redlands in the opening game. But the Poets won *all* their games against the other conference opponents by substantial scores. Then, again, came Redlands. The game was played in Wardman Gym, Saturday night March 11, the day after the destructive southern California earthquake.*

Paul Bixby, whose home in Long Beach was destroyed by the quake, had little sleep Friday night, but next day led the Poets to a brilliant victory over the Bulldogs 35-24, which gave Whittier "undisputed championship of the Southern conference for the first time since 1924." It seemed anticlimactic the next week to beat Santa Barbara 63-19 and 60-24.

In that pivotal year 1932-33, Chief Newman's baseball team

*It harried Bill Brock from his lonely room high in old Founders Hall, as it rolled with the shocks, creaked and stood firm, "high and dry—on the rock." The new high school auditorium was damaged beyond repair for safe use, except later as a library.

also won its conference title—Whittier thus dominating its peers in three major sports. The Poet tennis team lost everything—final count, 35 matches lost, one won.

As VICE PRESIDENT of Whittier College, Harris was the executive officer but not the skipper.

President Dexter, with strong support from some of the trustees, devoted himself to public relations. He made no bones about his desire to engage in other interests. Already serving as president of the fourth district of Lions, he had his sights set on some form of public service.

Lou Henry Hoover continued to have Quaker friends in Whittier from the time of her girlhood. In the election summer of 1928, Dexter had taken the lead in conferring upon Mrs. Hoover an honorary Litt.D. degree before an enthusiastic community audience of 2,000 in the Friends Church. The Whittier students dedicated the *Acropolis 1929* to her, and in 1930 A. Wardman completed the six-story Hoover Hotel in Whittier, named not for the President, but for the First Lady.

As election-time approached in 1932, Walter Dexter wanted to play some part in the Republican campaign to re-elect President Hoover. He wrote a substantial book, *Herbert Hoover and American Individualism* (Macmillan, 1932), tracing elements of Hoover's political philosophy to their Quaker roots. Following its publication in July, Dexter spent a memorable weekend with the Hoovers at their hide-away on the Rapidan River. In November Hoover was defeated. Dexter's plans for the future, in so far as they may have hinged on Hoover's re-election, had to be revised.

During the weeks of suspended animation between the election of Franklin D. Roosevelt in November and his inauguration in March 1933—with banks closing and the stirring of grave discontents—the college board tried to settle its own problem of the presidency. Should the trustees at once choose a successor to Dexter? Or should Dexter be continued for one more year "with the definite understanding" that his contract terminated as of September 1, 1934? If so, should not Dexter agree to devote full time to the work of the college? And if not, and he remained as president in an advisory capacity, who should be held responsible for the administration of the college?

Dexter did not resign the presidency; he did accept reduced salary for a final year, with "freedom for outside activities." Though relieved of all administrative duties, he insisted that when he was present "on all public occasions," he should be recognized as president of Whittier College. Harris was continued as vice president with all administrative duties and responsibilities. But for Harris this was hardly fair, and he addressed a letter to the board regarding his designation and responsibilities for the coming year 1933-34. In considering this letter at their August meeting, some trustees wished simply to define more clearly the office of Vice-President. But the motion carried "that Dr. H. E. Harris be elected Acting President of Whittier College."

There was no consensus that Harris should succeed to the college presidency.

The board had already appointed a committee to proceed with the selection of a new president. "After considering a number of men," the committee corresponded with Dr. W. O. Mendenhall, president of Friends University. In November 1933 he was invited to Whittier to meet the trustees, faculty, students. He spoke in chapel, preached in church. Then the board "called him," and he accepted before the end of the year. In January 1934, a special committee began planning his inauguration. Within a month the same committee was also planning a community reception to honor Walter Dexter, and he was granted an LL.D. at his final commencement as president.*

In the flurry of farewells to Dexter and welcomes to Mendenhall, it seemed hardly to be noticed that Harris was bringing his own administrative services to an end.

---

*For some time the Dexters maintained their home in College Hills. Walter Dexter ran for the Republican nomination for U.S. Senator, but was defeated in the primaries. He then served as assistant to Governor Frank C. Merriam, who had attended the Great Banquet in 1923. Merriam appointed Dexter State superintendent of schools in 1937, and he was then elected and re-elected to that office, serving well the State until his death in 1945. He had been named a Whittier College trustee in 1943.

IV

WHITTIER COLLEGE IN SEARCH OF
A CONSTITUENCY (1934-1951)

———

THE DEPRESSION CRISIS marked the end of one stage in the history of Whittier College and the beginning of another.

During roughly a decade, the nation worked its way out of economic troubles, troubles that were in fact global, only to move step by step toward a second and greater World War. Then, after only brief years of postwar peace, came involvement of the United States in Korea. Through seventeen unsettled years the Friends college in Whittier made its way. Ideological and personal conflicts on the Quaker campus played themselves out against this wider background as the college made successive efforts to define its rôle in the changing times.

What constituency should it serve? From whom should it draw its students and its support?

They were such obvious questions that, in 1934, no one quite bothered to answer them, unless it was the man who drove out from Kansas that summer to take up his new work in California.

1

INAUGURATION OF A NEW ADMINISTRATION
FOR WHITTIER COLLEGE

THE GREAT PROCESSION was colorful. Gay academic hoods and dresses set off the black gowns and business suits. Thus robed and marshaled were college trustees and faculty, student and alumni representatives, Quakers and civic leaders, college presidents and other educators, scholars and assorted delegates. Past old Founders Hall, they wound up the hill to the Harris Amphitheater, there ushered to their seats by handsome and charming students and the orchestral strains of Schubert's "Marche Héroique."

This inauguration of W. O. Mendenhall was the first and, as it happened, the only formal induction into office of a new president for Whittier College.

Invocation by the local Friends pastor—lively movement from a Haydn symphony—audience singing of J. G. Whittier's beloved hymn, "Dear Lord and Father of Mankind." Then the honored guest, Lou Henry Hoover, spoke briefly of the *first* Whittier Academy, forerunner of the college. Dr. Robert L. Kelly, executive secretary of the Association of American Colleges, gave the main address. He challenged his listeners with the pressing problems of the day—"new frontiers," he called them, to be explored and settled in the spirit of pioneers. Then C. Bevan Johnson—who had been schoolmaster of the *second* Whittier Academy and who was president of the college board in 1934—formally inaugurated William Orville Mendenhall as the sixth president of Whittier College.*

President Mendenhall responded with a short address, "The Search for Truth." He saw progress being made "in the conflict of ideas," and hoped that students would develop "an inner poise and the way of life which will enable [them] to move steadily amidst confusion." He made a plea for tolerance, invoked the spirit of the Quaker founders, and pledged himself to hold before the students "a belief in God and faith in humanity."

The ceremony concluded with the Alma Mater—benediction —recessional. Thereafter the special guests banqueted at the Woman's Clubhouse, Dr. Walter F. Dexter as toastmaster, with speeches by other college and university presidents of southern California. It was a lively and festive dinner, but not without incident. During a lull, there was a sharp report and a thud. The distinguished Huntington librarian went down on a collapsed chair, pink cheeks and white Vandyke soughing up from the floor! No

*The continuity of the college was well represented for the occasion. At hand were Dr. W. V. Coffin, principal of the *third* academy, and John J. Jessup, under whom it became Whittier College. Of the five successive presidents, only Charles E. Tebbetts was deceased; Harry N. Wright of New York City College (soon to become its president) was not free to attend. Thomas Newlin and Walter Dexter were both present; and Absalom Rosenberger, too ill and frail to join the procession, was driven up to the shoulder of the amphitheater to view this inauguration of his one-time Penn College student.

commotion, hardly anybody laughed, and a nervous host restored the portly presence to a firmer seat.

Then, in another pause, the bumptious wife of a visiting dean asked her Whittier hostess an audible question.

"What reason is there for a little old college like Whittier?"

W. ORVILLE MENDENHALL was a long-experienced college administrator when, aged fifty-five, he became president of Whittier College. He was tall and slender, proud of his Rees portion of Cherokee blood, dignified but with a ready smile. Although he was easy to approach, Dr. Mendenhall was somehow aloof from the hurly-burly. He was a trained mathematician, a man of reflective mind and spiritual gifts.

Orville Mendenhall was born of Quaker parents at Ridge Farm in Illinois, where his father's family had pioneered. His mother, Almeda Rees, came of a North Carolinian family that had moved up into Indiana in the westward sweep of Quakers already noted. Orville Mendenhall graduated from Penn College, went East to Haverford for his A.M., taught in Portland and at Stanford, and then joined the faculty of Wilmington College in Ohio. There he met Lucy Osgood, professor of English, whom he married.

In 1907 W. O. Mendenhall went to Earlham College as professor of mathematics and "governor" of the men's dormitory. In due time he completed his Ph.D. at Michigan and became dean of men at Earlham. He developed a special interest in the Y.M.C.A., and came into sharp conflict with Elbert Russell, professor of religion. Russell opposed President Robert L. Kelly, who he believed was leading Earlham away from Quakerism, and resented Mendenhall's intrusion into the work of his department—for the professor of mathematics began to give some work in the field of religion. But more than that, Russell charged that discipline was lax under Dean Mendenhall whose theory (Russell said) was that "you cannot compel students to observe regulations they do not approve." The effect (he wrote) was that they came to feel "morals and religion" less important than "scholarship and athletics." But the Earlhamites loved and respected "Guv" Mendenhall. He had "an impressive way of reminding [them] of the straight and narrow path without even mentioning it."

In the larger controversy, Russell resigned from the Earlham faculty in 1915, later to serve Duke University as dean of the School of Religion; Kelly resigned in 1917 to become founding secretary of the Association of American Colleges; and Mendenhall resigned in 1918 to become president of Friends University in Wichita, Kansas.

There he entered into the life of the community, became district governor of the Lions clubs of Kansas, and was honored with an LL.D. by the University of Wichita. His interest in the work of the Y.M.C.A. led him to become national chairman of the student division. His Quaker concerns led him to become presiding Clerk of the Five Years Meeting of Friends—of which California Yearly Meeting was a part—and vice-chairman of the American Friends Service Committee. He was often called to address conferences and national meetings. In 1926 he had visited Whittier—house guest of his cousin Cass A. Rees of the Whittier College board. During his sixteen years at Friends, its enrollment increased from 153 to 360, its endowment from $200,000 to $600,000.

With this training and experience, W. O. Mendenhall undertook the presidency of Whittier College in 1934.

AT THIS STAGE WHITTIER was somewhat older, larger, and stronger than the Friends college from which Mendenhall had come. So, at least, it may have seemed to him during his brief visit to Whittier the preceding December.

Certain things were obvious enough. The campus itself consisted of only 19 acres, but there was the adjacent 100 acres of ranch land around the hill and up the wide Worsham Canyon. Three permanent buildings—two dormitories and the gymnasium—were new, and Naylor Hall for chemistry and physics seemed sturdy and modern. But, except for the library and faculty offices in Redwood cottage, all other college offices and classrooms, auditorium and biology laboratories crowded old Founders Hall, a frame structure 30 to 40 years old. However, the campus had natural beauties: eucalyptus trees, palms, and lawns—winding paths and encircling roadway—green playing fields and amphitheater—magnificent view of the agricultural and industrial valley and its cities.

The Whittier student body of about 400, of whom one-sixth were Quakers, was augmented by some 85 women on the Broadoaks campus in Pasadena. By and large these students were country and small town young folks, much like those Dr. Mendenhall had known so well in Kansas, Indiana, and Ohio. They were healthy and outgoing, proud of their achievement in sports, their resourcefulness, their idealism.

The college faculty of about 40 included few old professors and a good portion of young men. Ten professors had doctorates, several were gifted artists. Ten were rounding out a decade or so of service, eight more had been at Whittier at least five years. Eight were Friends, most of the rest were Protestant church-members. These were competent teachers, doubtless, but none except J. Herschel Coffin had made himself known in scholarship or higher education much beyond the narrow limits of the campus and southern California. There were no sharp "differences" presently dividing the faculty, but scars remained from the conflict of the late 1920's.

The curriculum and courses of study, which Dr. Mendenhall could well examine in the current catalog, were traditional enough but with vestiges of the previous daring. He noted with approval, certainly, the training program for Y.M.C.A. leaders, no less than the curriculum for teacher training—recognition by the State Department of Education—accreditation by colleges and universities—the A.B. degree with a dozen majors, and a modest graduate program in Education.

The Board of Trustees that named Dr. Mendenhall to the presidency of Whittier College was a self-perpetuating body of 30 persons of whom a majority were members of California Yearly Meeting of Friends.* Actually two-thirds of the trustees were Quakers. Two-thirds had Whittier addresses, seven more lived within a further radius of 20 miles, and only two came from as far as northern California. Of the 30, eight were women—six were alumni—four were benefactors to the extent of $100,000 or more in gifts or annuity-gifts. Composing the group were orange ranchers and their adjacent town bankers, businessmen, doctors, teachers, widows, and housewives—a few others—but only two or three were men with wider interests or influence in business or

*Until 1932 there was a gesture of their being nominated by the Yearly Meeting, and throughout this period (1934-51) the Trustees of Whittier College were listed as one of the Boards in the Yearly Meeting Minutes.

industry. Such were the trustees—local, Quaker, mid-Western, conservative—idealistic, concerned for youth, devoted to the interests of Whittier College.

The total assets of the college at this time were $1,300,000—based, certainly, upon pre-Depression evaluations. The total liabilities were $450,000—owing, just as certainly, in hard-to-get Depression dollars.* But the college was operating in the black, with even a modest operating surplus for the fiscal year just closed.

How realistic Mendenhall's appraisal was of the small Quaker college he came to lead, it is difficult to judge.

UNLIKE HIS PREDECESSOR, Mendenhall did not come to Whittier with an educational program, a developmental plan, or an articulated policy to put into effect by vigorous leadership. "Let performance exceed promise" was his repeated slogan. But he did come with a philosophy of college administration. He felt that, as president of a Quaker college, he should be free to pursue as he felt led his wider interests in the Society of Friends and in the Y.M.C.A.—to leave largely to others the direction of faculty and curriculum, management and development, student guidance and promotion. He therefore needed an administrative team.

Within a fortnight of his inauguration, President Mendenhall left for the East to attend the annual meeting of the Y.M.C.A. student division, of which he was chairman. On his return he stopped at Wichita, where he "renewed many acquaintances" (as the Q.C. reported) at Friends University. Although Whittier had no Dean of the college, or even dean of men, Mendenhall again went East in January for three weeks to attend college, Quaker, and Y.M.C.A. meetings—and again in the spring for three weeks in Richmond, Philadelphia, and New York in pursuit of his various interests. In the meantime he was gathering together those whom he expected to form his administration at Whittier College.

His personal secretary had come with him from Friends University. For financial secretary in college development, he at

*The 1934 Audit shows the Land Department as still owing the bank $211,500 on its mortgage, plus $173,000 owing to the Endowment Fund of the college proper. In addition, other bank loans totaled $65,000.

once recommended B. B. Wilcox, many years in such work for the Y.M.C.A. In 1935 he brought O. B. Baldwin (Ph.D., Kansas) from his deanship at Friends to be professor of education and psychology—but with the expectation (it was thought) that he should become Dean of the college. At the same time he brought Louise Pfuetze (A.B., U.C.L.A.) from Y.W.C.A. work and student counseling at College of the Pacific, to be dean of women—and Lucille Verhulst (earlier at Friends) as director of physical education for women. In 1937 he brought Esther Hoff, also from Friends, to be Registrar. And Clara Dallas became secretary of the General Office. In their several ways, these were all good and capable persons. But they were lumped together (in some faculty minds) as "the Kansas gang," and their group loyalty—even their theater party with the Mendenhalls—was somewhat resented, though really without personal animus. And the Whittier board did not name Dr. Baldwin to the deanship.

CHAPEL WAS PARAMOUNT in importance for President Mendenhall. In his first talk to the faculty in September 1934, he stressed "chapel exercises as the center of unity of the college." It was in chapel, he felt, that "the college becomes integrated." In his inaugural he pledged himself to a religious emphasis. He looked upon his presidency, it seemed clear, as a form of Friends ministry.

Strangely, some thought, his first faculty appointment was of a Baptist to fill the chair of religion in the Quaker college. To replace Walter Homan, who resigned to go to the University of Hawaii, Mendenhall named Herbert F. Evans (Ph.D., Chicago) who came to Whittier from Pacific School of Religion in Berkeley. Evans was a scholar not only in religious education but also in church architecture. He was not a Friend, but Mendenhall made it clear at once that he himself "consented to assume personal direction of chapel arrangements"—assisted by a committee.

Mendenhall felt himself to be the college chaplain. As a recorded Friends minister, his gifts were widely recognized. In his quiet way, with a string of homely anecdotes and touches of humor, his gravelly voice hushed or questioning, he was able to inspire students, whether with a chapel talk on the mystical experience and prayer or on some current problem set in its larger context. He made a profound and life-enduring impression on many students. Some came to his office for pastoral counselling or accepted his invitation to brief worship at 7 a.m. on Mondays at his home.

Upon his arrival in Whittier, President Mendenhall announced at once through the *Quaker Campus* that the new chapel program would be scheduled for three full class periods during the week. But this arrangement did not seem possible to the faculty (or perhaps even desirable)—it blocked the scheduling of two double-period laboratory sections in the forenoon. Therefore, only a Tuesday and Thursday morning hour was given over to chapel. For the next year, a 35-minute period was worked into the schedule mid-morning, for three short chapel exercises and varied talks per week.

But despite Mendenhall's interest in this student ministry, chapel was hardly more successful than in previous years—and the chapel committee, with Dr. Evans as chairman, worked hard to improve the programs. Students were restive under compulsion. Some students and faculty felt that the old auditorium in Founders Hall (Poet Theatre) was not conducive to an appropriate chapel atmosphere. It was neither a Friends meetinghouse (Dr. Mendenhall's preference) nor a churchly chapel (envisaged by others). In the fall of 1935, the new Lancer Society "presented to the faculty a project for the building of a small chapel building." With encouragement of the college board, the Lancers began raising money. But their dream was of an intimate chapel, something for June weddings, and not of an auditorium to hold the student body. Nor would the proposal and first steps in any way solve what had become the "chapel problem."

In 1940 compulsory attendance was again abandoned. President Mendenhall himself suggested that there might be a *15-minute chapel period* on three mornings a week for devotional meetings—and longer assemblies on Tuesday and Thursday, which students would be required to attend. It had been a notable retreat from the three required 50-minute chapel periods announced in September 1934. The short voluntary chapel exercises drew together but a small portion of the student body and faculty.

However moving or illuminating were those occasions when Mendenhall addressed the entire student body at one of the convocations, chapel as such had not become "the center of unity of the college."

Older patterns of college life had already begun to change, and not only at Whittier. W. O. Mendenhall, as a Quaker liberal, was open to new ideas that he felt made for progress.

2

DEPRESSION MANAGEMENT, CAMPUS DEVELOPMENT,
ENDOWMENT AND DEBT

THE BUSINESS AFFAIRS of the college President Mendenhall left in the capable hands of Howard L. Hockett, the comptroller, who was answerable directly to the college board. To one professor's question that involved expenditure, Mendenhall responded,

"Oh, that has to do with budget—who am I to tell Mr. Hockett how to budget?"

The budget was the key to survival during the 1930's. Though the national economy was to be saved through the liberal policy of deficit spending, the college was at the same time saved by the conservative policy of balanced budget. For the college this simply meant restraining expenditure and cultivating sufficient income to equal it. It was easier said than done.

The chief source of income was tuition. For the year ending August 31, 1934, tuition income had totaled $97,000, with tuition at $250 per year. Three-fourths of all college income was from this source, and it equalled the expenditures for instruction and administration. As enrollment increased, so did tuition. The college board raised it slightly in 1937 and again in 1940, when it was $300. The enrollment reached 591 on the Whittier campus during 1939-40—and that meant a 40% increase in tuition income within five years. The New Deal brought $6,000 to $10,000 a year in Federal funds. Under the National Youth Authority (N.Y.A.) the college hired students at minimal hourly rate, and credited their government earnings against tuition.

Endowment at this time was woefully small. The assets and debts of the Land Department of the college—essentially the unhappy College Syndicate of the 1920's—were "transferred, assigned and set over to the Endowment Fund of Whittier College," in the fall of 1934. Mr. Hockett further proposed that endowment funds be used to decrease indebtedness, "provided that no endowment contracts be violated." The Security bank of Los Angeles still held a $211,000 mortgage on the college campus and Worsham ranch land. It offered to renew the college note at lower interest if the college would undertake payments on the principal. Thus to reduce its debt—and to carry the $1,000 a month interest load—the board sold all property it could that was not needed for college use. To the city, for instance, it sold 25 acres in Savage Canyon for $13,000. Some endowment funds remained in securities, rentals, and citrus grove—but net income from all of these amounted only to $15,000 a year.

Current gifts and subscriptions at this time seldom added more than $5,000 a year to the operating budget.*

A further source of income was, hopefully, the traditional John Greenleaf Whittier banquet. This was intended to gather support for the college from the community. The banquet on December 17, 1934 combined with the football banquet to assure attendance—net income, $5,700. In 1936 the biennial banquet in Los Angeles did hardly better—about $7,500. The 1938 banquet, for which Thomas E. Dewey was invited as speaker, was postponed (with Dewey's regrets) to become a Founders Day dinner scheduled for April 21. The college cancelled its 1940 banquet in deference to the local Y.M.C.A. drive. And the banquet scheduled for December 19, 1941 was the first college casualty of the War. It was a dismal record.

The only way to balance the budget, it seemed, was by husbanding well the regular sources of income (tuition, fees, dormitory rents), by raising tuition and fees, by increasing enrollment, and by collecting a higher percentage of the outstanding student accounts. And by keeping down expenses. In doing these things Howard L. Hockett was something of a genius.**

Only the most necessary maintenance work was done. Stan

---

*President Mendenhall reported in August 1940 that "income for the year from outside sources totalled nearly $140,000." He explained that this included the Brooks Trust of $83,000, released to the college by the death of the Brooks sisters, an anonymous gift of $50,000 already announced the preceding year, an annual gift [of $3,600] previously pledged. *New contributions*, therefore, *totaled no more than some $4,000* for the year 1939-40, when the national economy had recovered from the Depression.

**Representatives of nearby colleges came to find out how he did it.

Lewis lived in a campus cottage and took care of the grounds, with the help of the *deaf* Mr. Cooper who raked leaves and often tended sprinklers by the light of the moon or lantern. Heavy-set Ben Hamilton Sr., superintendent of buildings, lugged the mail from the post office, smoked a cigar in his hideaway near the furnace (noxious fumes venting up into classrooms), and raised gladiolas to beautify the offices. And old Elias Hansen, cared for Menden Hall, left anti-nicotine tracts on library tables, lectured boys on the weed, even snatched a cigarette from the lips of an astonished freshman on the street corner! . . . These and the rest of the staff served with devotion and helped keep down expenses.

The biggest item of expense in the college budget was faculty salaries. The formula, earlier set, carried on through the decade. Professors received 75% of their *nominal* salaries in twelve monthly checks, with a hoped-for 10% bonus at the end of the summer. Then in 1937 the percentage was raised to 85%—and the board was still able to pay a 5% bonus. For the year 1940-41 the bonus was 15%—that is, the salaries totaled 100% for the first time since 1931-32. It was Mrs. Hoover who "pointed out the necessity for striving for the 100% basis of salary payment." In 1943-44 the 100% was at last guaranteed and to be paid in regular monthly checks.* The total (nominal) salary budget remained virtually unchanged during the Depression decade— and with it the net size of the teaching faculty.

In this way the "operating budget" was kept balanced by Mr. Hockett while he quietly inched the college out of the hole.

DEVELOPMENT OF THE CAMPUS was hampered, of course, by this debt no less than by the Depression. Upon President Mendenhall's arrival in 1934, the board expected him to go right to work in raising money. He reported "through Mr. Hockett" (for he was in the East) that "this is not an opportune time for an old fashioned campaign for funds," though of course there should be constant solicitation. And he recommended (as earlier noted) the engagement of a financial secretary.

*However this was contrary to the conservative inclination of some trustees who still wanted to hold down the guarantee (and the college liability) to 90%.

At the same meeting of the trustees, Marcus Skarstedt, professor of mathematics and librarian, reported the great need for a library building. Adjacent to the campus was the imposing new Elks lodge. It was available.

Steel-framed, this tile-roofed structure, built but a year before the Crash, occupied a choice triple lot at the corner of Philadelphia and Painter. Building and site had been valued at $125,000. The Elks lost their property to the Depression.

In 1935 Bank of America owned it. Herman L. Perry, the bank's Whittier manager, was a trustee of the college, as was his brother, Esek H. Perry, chairman of the finance committee. The only question was the money. The bank had $52,000 tied up in the lodge. The college finance committee offered the bank $30,000—*not in cash of course* (there was no cash) but in "guaranteed notes"—and asked the bank to "subscribe" the additional $22,000 to the college. The bank wasn't that anxious to sell.

Another plan developed, a swap deal showing the master touch of Mr. Hockett. A widow, Mrs. Lena May [England] Mendenhall—no close kin of Dr. Mendenhall—could no longer manage her La Habra ranches and Whittier properties valued at $50,000. On February 29, 1936, she agreed to deed these to the bank— the bank agreed to deed the Elks building to the college—the college agreed to pay to Mrs. Mendenhall or to her sister Lura England $3,000 a year for at least five years or as long as Mrs. Mendenhall lived. In addition, the college agreed to pay the bank $5,000 (*cash*), making the total consideration "$55,000"— depending upon what the bank might realize on the depressed properties. Mrs. O. T. Mendenhall lived but a few years, so that the cost to the college of this valuable building was hardly more than $25,000, with payments spread over seven years.

Remodeling and furnishing were to cost another $15,000. The large upstairs hall with picturesque ceiling and high windows was transformed into an excellent library reading room. The mezzanine held the (old) book stacks for 50,000 volumes. On the ground floor was the Great Hall (as it came later to be called), surrounded by the administrative offices.

The Woman's Auxiliary undertook to help furnish this hall— paid for the high drapes and half the cost of an excellent 20' by

50′ used Oriental rug.* Above the (false) fireplace Dr. Mendenhall placed the Withrow portrait of John Greenleaf Whittier. Upon the mantel below it, the poet's lines:

> Early hath life's mighty question
> Thrilled within thy heart of youth,
> With a deep and strong beseeching:
> What and where is Truth?

Securing and adapting of the Elks building was a major achievement during the Depression. The only unhappiness in the whole matter was naming the building.

Although Mrs. O. T. Mendenhall looked upon the deal "as a business proposition, and not a charity affair," the agreement stipulated that the building be considered "a memorial to Mr. and Mrs. O. T. Mendenhall"—that it be known as the *Mendenhall Building*—and that it be marked with an appropriate bronze tablet. Nevertheless, the college shortly announced that—in honor of the donor, Mrs. L. M. Mendenhall—the new building would be called *Menden Hall*, the name of the ancestral home in England. Repeated protests of Mrs. Mendenhall herself, of her sister, and of her attorneys were disregarded or evaded. It was not until after President Mendenhall's resignation—and more than eight years after the agreement—that the bronze plaque, "O. T. Mendenhall Building," was placed over the entrance.**

A second permanent building came to the college soon after the beginning of the War—a virtual gift from Standard Oil Company. Four blocks west of the campus on the corner of Bright and Penn stood the company's district headquarters, no longer needed. The two sturdy buildings on two good lots had cost over

*The Auxiliary spent $1,000 on the Mendenhall lounge at this time. In 1951-52 it paid $3,000 (plus tax and trade-in) for a Steinway concert grand piano, as the Great Hall was a beautiful setting for recitals for a score of years.

Through sixty-odd years of its history, the Woman's Auxiliary contributed a good $100,000 and more to Whittier College. It furnished dormitory lounges and administrative offices—bought pianos (8 or more), sewing machines, instructional aids—set up a student loan fund—served the college in countless ways. It was a link between faculty women and wives, trustees and wives, mothers of students and alumnae, and the community.

**Perhaps Dr. Mendenhall was sensitive about presiding in a building bearing his surname. Or it may have been one of those "delicate matters wherein he relied upon Mr. Hockett's careful judgment"—lingering memory of Oscar Mendenhall's youthful folly, for in the lively pioneer days the husky young rancher had run afoul of the Whittier elders!

$30,000 in 1914 and 1922. The company sold this property to the college for $5,000—$500 down and $500 a year, interest at 2½%. Converted into a very satisfactory dormitory for 44 men at a cost of $10,000, the combined structure was named Newlin Hall in honor of Thomas Newlin, second president of the college and trustee for 18 years. His bequest of property valued at $10,000 had just come to the college.

At the time when the college acquired the Elks building, Mrs. Ruth Kerr—identified with the manufacture of glass jars for home canning—contributed $5,000 for the remodeling of Redwood cottage to establish the "Alexander Hewett Kerr Laboratory of Home Economics." She agreed further to support a (new) department of home economics with annual gifts of $3,600 for six years. Prof. Maude D. Evans set up an academic program in foods and clothing, preparing dieticians, secondary teachers, and housewives. Whittier College honored Mrs. Kerr with a doctorate in 1937.

Throughout the Depression decade, development of the campus was painfully slow. New money of consequence was not found. Further debts dared not be incurred. Trading, moving, remodeling were the best that could be done. In 1937 the college traded a house and lots for the home of Dr. W. V. Coffin on Earlham Drive, originally built by President Tebbetts in 1903. As Earlham Hall, it housed women students. . . . In 1938 Dr. William F. Kroener gave his large home to the college for $125. Moved to the campus on Earlham Drive, it became the Music Building. . . .* In 1939, the college bought the William K. Green property on the north side of Philadelphia for $9,000, "a part of the purchase price being a lot in College Hills." This fine old pioneer home—up a curved driveway by the verdant arroyo— occupied a sightly knoll surrounded by orange trees, an acre and a half in all. As Crestwood Hall it was a dormitory for women . . . And through this time the college was able to buy a number of the properties within the campus block now cornered by Bolte Hall and Menden Hall.

Even small campus improvements were main efforts at this time—a new Senior pavilion under the trees, a further remodeling of Poet Theatre in Founders Hall to reduce fire and panic

*Used 21 years for this department, it thereafter housed students.

237

hazard, construction by W.P.A. of a proper storm drain through the campus, costing the college but $4,000. Mr. Hockett secured some four thousand truckloads of free dirt to fill the arroyo above it. The front campus thus leveled, the once-deep arroyo was lost to view and to mind.

The proposed Lions Club gateway, a president's home on Fire Hill, the Lancer chapel—these were dreams not to be realized as then planned.

As for endowment funds, Whittier received but one substantial outright gift during this decade.

Elbridge Stuart and his brother Addison had been Whittier pioneers, though they soon moved away and in time established Carnation Milk Company. They were nephews of Washington Hadley, cousins therefore of Emilie Hadley, who continued the family place on the college board until her death in 1937. Elbridge Stuart quietly made a gift of $50,000 in 1940, establishing the Amos and Matilda Hadley Stuart Fund, honoring his parents, the purpose being "to assist worthy and needy individual students of Christian character in their educational program."

Annuity gifts from Bessie Davis McClelland in 1939 and 1943 amounted to some $42,000—she was a friend of Mrs. Ella Peasley.

A one-seventh interest in 1,000 acres of Utah land was willed to Whittier College. Appraised at $2.50 per acre, rented for grazing at 10¢ an acre, this yielded no more than trouble and a wistful hope of oil!

Was there *no* concerted effort to raise money for Whittier College during this decade of economic recovery?

Early in 1939 the college engaged professional fund raisers—Ketchum, Incorporated. Their Mr. John Cromer came to Whittier—at $300 a week and expenses—and President Mendenhall cleared his calendar to pitch in. Esek Perry and Howard L. Hockett were optimistic. But some of the citrus trustees were "reluctant on account of local conditions and others on account of past experiences with professional money raisers."

The Half Century campaign was to start in 1939, celebrating vaguely the 50th anniversary of the Whittier Academy. It was to "climax" in 1951, the 50th anniversary of the college chartering. In March, Mr. Cromer outlined yearly objectives: $100,000 new endowment by June 6, 1939 plus $100,000 annually to 1951, and one "essential campus need" (that is, new building) each year. In April Mr. Cromer sounded cheerful, but the "victory" dinner was postponed.

Beatrix Farrand, landscape gardener, and her architect associate prepared a new Master Plan for the campus. It showed a new Founders Hall, a new Academic building, a new Library, a new Science building, a new Music building and Auditorium, and a small Chapel with churchly steeple. It was all very pretty, and the Q.C. looked forward with high hope to the Founders Banquet scheduled at the Biltmore for June 6.

On that occasion, Dr. Mendenhall did announce $95,000 as raised during the preceding months: an anonymous gift of $50,000 (Elbridge Stuart's expressed intention), an annuity gift of $22,500 (Mrs. McClelland), and "about $17,000" in miscellaneous contributions during the year. The college alumni had raised "between four and five thousand dollars" by means of $100 notes. Net income from the banquet itself was but $4,890.

The apparent success of this campaign was largely illusory. Nothing like $100,000 was actually added to endowment. The Comptroller reported a total of $40,500 in gifts for the year ending in August 31, 1939—*only $4,000 specifically "endowment."* The splendid $50,000 gift from Elbridge Stuart, whose interest Dr. Mendenhall had so carefully cultivated, was actually received during 1940. Ketchum, Inc. faded quietly away—after collecting $5,500 expenses.

But if there were no further financial gifts to report, interesting items can be noted: the massive desk and the papers of Washington Hadley, most substantial of the early benefactors, came to the college from the family in 1941. It proved more enduring as a memorial than either Hadley Field or the sundial bequeathed by his daughter.

Another item of personal interest came to the college in 1940 —rather, to the Friends Historical Association, whose effects became a part of the Quaker Collection in the college library. This was the ceramic teapot that had belonged to John Greenleaf Whittier. It was the gift of Dr. Charles Elmer Rice of Alliance, Ohio.

239

A more valuable gift was an original portrait of Whittier painted by his friend, Harrison L. Plummer, the artist. They had been schoolmates at Haverhill Academy. Then in their late years (in 1885, the poet nearing 80), the retired artist painted Whittier's portrait for the Haverhill town library. He painted another for George C. Wadleigh, who willed it to Whittier College after his death and that of his wife. Charmed by a visit from Professor Romer—then spending a post-doctoral year of study at Harvard on the history of atomic science—the widowed Mrs. Wadleigh decided to send the portrait to the college forthwith in the spring of 1942. The Plummer portrait depicts, not the passionate liberal whose fiery verses lashed out against Slavery— nor the Wordsworthian versifier of barefoot boy and "What might have been"—but the venerable bard in his ailing age, snow-bound in his whiskers. It showed him just as he looked in the very years when his namesake town and its college were founded.

These interesting mementoes of the past, however interesting, did not further the development of Whittier College, maintain the educational program, increase the endowment, or build any of the new structures sketched on the Master Plan. They did not even whittle away at the Great Debt.

Perhaps it was this burden of indebtedness—and preoccupation with its elimination—that blocked the college through this decade.

3

REORGANIZATION OF THE CURRICULUM,
ADMINISTRATION AND FACULTY

As THE NATION EMERGED from the Depression, President Mendenhall saw, as did so many others, the oncoming of World War II. In the fall of 1935, his second year at Whittier, the American Friends Service Committee asked him to head up "a vigorous nationwide campaign" of peace education. Would the college board release him for eight months (from January 1, 1936 to August 31st, without loss of salary) to perform this national service in the great emergency?

The trustees replied that there was also some emergency at Whittier, particularly with no Dean of the college and the Dean of Broadoaks on leave. However, they did free Mendenhall for the first weeks of January and again for three weeks in February. And he was actually away part of each month during the winter and spring of 1936, either helping to organize regional groups for this peace effort or attending national meetings of Y.M.C.A. and Quaker groups.

His absence created a sort of administrative vacuum in academic affairs. Into this stepped Dr. Albert W. Upton.

RECONSIDERATION OF THE CURRICULUM was precipitated by an academic crisis. Rumor had it that, unless the college modified its course of study, its right to recommend for State teaching credentials might be withdrawn. New methods of instruction in the schools called for a new sort of teacher training. To consider this, the faculty seminar committee asked Upton to prepare a paper for its evening meeting in November 1936. This was to look toward an all-day faculty conference in January.

Whittier College (Upton said in his paper) had been "struggling toward a modernized curriculum" for a dozen years. He outlined sympathetically the educational philosophy of Dr. J. Herschel Coffin, and his four-year Correlation sequence. Its failure had not been caused by faculty intrigue, Upton thought, but by its inherent structural fault—"its *vertical* organization." In his view, "the kind of integration we seek may be achieved for the average student only by means of a high degree of *horizontal* correlation," with several professors "in intimate cooperation" giving, say, the freshmen orientation course and with student discussion "in small tutorial groups." And this sort of instruction, he felt, would meet the demands placed upon the college for teacher preparation. Any new educational adventure, Upton realized, could only be undertaken with full recognition of existing handicaps—the college debt, poverty, poor facilities—the faculty underpaid, overworked, "disgruntled and confused by frequent reorganization and wholesale replacement."

"Education for citizenship in a Christian democracy" and "development of well-rounded personalities" were established objectives for Whittier College. Accepting these, Upton asked two questions: What should a graduating senior *know*? And what should a graduating senior be able to *do*? First, Upton

241

thought he should have critical definitions—that is, his own definitions significantly oriented to others'—of key terms in at least some fields of knowledge, and the capacity to use their functional categories. Second, he should know "how to analyze a problem of conduct from the standpoint of a theory of value, . . . how to pray, . . . how to vote." And, then, Upton asked:

> Should he not be equipped with library, laboratory and field techniques of research and a functional knowledge of such sciences as concern his daily well-being?
> Should he not be able intelligently to go about the art of interpreting the past?
> Shouldn't he be able to demonstrate the process of logical definition and the simpler forms of deductive analysis?
> And finally, shouldn't his study of psychology have provided him with a conscious technique of communication with his fellow men?

With a charming informality quite lost in summary—and a shrewd eye to the predilections of his colleagues—Upton then proceeded to "the problem of method." He favored "the historical approach" as being "the current scientific method of attacking present day problems." He spoke for "a considerable degree of specialization in a chosen field," but with "a considerable body of first principles in other fields."

First, he advocated a strong block of work for all students in the sciences,

> two well integrated courses [totaling 20 units], one in the physical sciences and mathematics, one in the life sciences including individual psychology.

Their intention should be "pandemic" but "solid enough to serve as introductory to any of the science majors." Second, he proposed a comparable 20 units, two courses, one in Western Civilization and one in Anglo-American Civilization. These—with a 4-unit "service course" in English and the statutory course in the Constitution—were the gist of Upton's scheme for a new curriculum.

EVENTS MOVED RAPIDLY. The all-day conference in January generated a certain excitement. The faculty explored a new frontier in the spirit of Robert L. Kelly. A special committee undertook to devise a class schedule that would make the new curriculum workable. In mid-February, at the suggestion of the curriculum committee, the faculty approved in principle the new plan. Two weeks later, Upton presented the enabling class schedule, the brilliant work of Alfred Romer and Charles B. Spaulding. April 5th, the faculty approved outlines for the required freshman and sophomore courses in the social sciences and the natural sciences. A committee began studying techniques for teaching such courses. May 17th, upon motion of Coffin himself, the faculty abandoned the traditionalist group-requirements that in 1931 had blotted out the brave New World of Correlation!

The March issue of the college *Bulletin* described briefly "A New Program for Whittier College." The June catalog gave the rationale of the New Curriculum, with full description of the new lower division courses. A four-page supplement, addressed specifically "To the High School Graduate," contrasted conventional college curricula with the new departure at Whittier.

A rousing class of 142 freshmen enrolled in the fall of 1937, an increase of 40% over the preceding year and the largest class to date.

The content of these new courses cannot be detailed here, nor can the development of each be traced through the successive years. More important than the mere subject matter, was the development of interrelationships, insights, understandings, attitudes—the integration of courses into a whole, of faculty into an academic fellowship, of students into an intellectual and social community, and of the inner life of the student as a personality!

Even limited success of this venture, the faculty realized, would depend upon discovery of appropriate methods of instruction. Team-teaching was at the very center of the new program—each divisional course under an interdepartmental committee. . . The use of "student coaches" was part of the scheme—seniors and graduate students were closer to the lower classmen than professors and could serve as intermediaries through small-group discussions* . . . Two large classrooms, remodeled on the first floor of

*With an eye to the Quaker constituency, Upton pointed out that Joseph Lancaster, Friends schoolmaster in London (dead a century), had taught a thousand boys in his school by training and overseeing the older boys who passed on their modest learning to those who had less—foreshadowing the world literacy program of Dr. Frank Laubach.

243

Founders Hall, had up-to-date film and sound equipment for the use of audio-visual materials, and one of them (with gradient seats) had a laboratory table for scientific demonstrations.

Remarkable textbooks distinguished the two social science courses, books that in themselves were notably integrated: John Herman Randall's *The Making of the Modern Mind*, Esmé Wingfield-Stratford's *The History of British Civilization*, and Vernon Parrington's *Main Currents in American Thought*. Each in its way was a cultural history, calculated to help the thoughtful student understand himself and his society. Each was "too hard" for lower classmen—but when Randall was set aside, students petitioned overwhelmingly to have it restored.

The English service course developed a unique method—Basic English (then new) used as a tool for improving the student's skill in interpretation. Upton's own textbook, *Design for Thinking*, grew slowly as a "first book" in semantic theory, interpretation, problem solving. He acknowledged his special indebtedness to I. A. Richards, English scholar at Harvard.

Other original work was also done. The freshman began his Physical Science course with "the history of mathematics, based on the development of scientific reasoning." Then came a simplified presentation of "modern physics," for which Romer prepared his own syllabus. The scientific principles already presented served as basis for considering what chemistry is and what chemists do. For the Life Science course, the staff at once brought together an experimental textbook. The course began "with a brief summary of the geological phenomena which have created the habitat for life." The student then studied "the life process through the various levels of organic structure," prehistoric man and man himself—anatomy and physiology, sensitivities and learning.

Fine Arts was added for sophomores, at first "a series of experiences with the beautiful," illustrated by lectures on architecture, painting, music, household arts and, soon, also literature and drama. The staff developed some elements of a general art theory, and enriched the campus itself by hanging a collection of paintings and fine prints.

This complete reorganization of the lower division was an ambitious undertaking. That it succeeded, even in some measure, was an academic triumph. It was a response to the challenge of crisis—favored certainly by President Mendenhall's liberal attitude of inquiry. It was rooted in Professor Coffin's Quaker view of education, developed by the cooperation of some twenty participating members of the faculty. But, in no small degree, the success of the venture was due to the peculiar genius of Albert W. Upton—his insights, resourcefulness, pertinacity.

Through the winter of 1937 Upton rode up and down the wagon train, urging on the laggards, quelling mutiny, promising rewards in the Golden West! He spent earnest hours with his colleagues—philosopher in tweeds, shrewd pedagogue, maverick intellectual. He could be Machiavellian, tenacious, exasperating —artist, sentimentalist, generous friend. He was not a Quaker— and his ubiquitous leadership in the new program was suspect to some of his Friendly colleagues.

"Perhaps we'd just better call it Upton College!"

No danger of that—the matter was being taken care of.

THE WHITTIER FACULTY had been described by Upton in 1936 as "disgruntled." The most disgruntled at that time was Dr. Herbert E. Harris, "dean" of the faculty in seniority.

When Mendenhall became president, it was presumed that Harris would again head his old department. But Upton, acting head for five years, stood in the way. To fit Harris back into the English department as head at $3,000 (par), the faculty committee of the board proposed cutting Upton's salary, reducing Eugene Knox to half time, and dropping Don Evans. However, Upton worked backstage to keep his friend Evans (liberal journalist, eager historian) and to save Knox. Harris agreed to be part-time head, but took a leave of absence to visit the Orient in the interests of Rotary International. For the next year (1935-36), Upton was chairman of the department again at full salary. Harris (part-time) was assigned his choice courses, Shakespeare and Life and Literature of Today. But these had lost their old fervor. Harris had become edgy and sharp. Students avoided him. Hurt by his small enrollments, Harris resigned in the spring of 1937. To mollify him, Mendenhall named Harris "professor emeritus"—but, aged 62, this further embittered him. The disaffection of Harris saddened his old friends on faculty and board.

The college lacked a Dean—this was increasingly apparent.

In the winter of 1937, President Mendenhall reported to the board that he needed either a "field man for outside solicitation" or a "Dean on the campus." As trustees had already lost confidence in his administration, they voted unanimously to "liberate" him for fund raising (for which he was not gifted) "by the appointment of a Dean from our faculty to carry out the details of the president's program." Evidently by prearrangement, Mendenhall then recommended and the board approved appointment of Dr. S. Arthur Watson as Dean of the College—and of Dr. O. B. Baldwin as Dean of Men.

Arthur Watson was tall and big-framed, with firm features, soft voice, and quiet humor. He had been on the faculty nine years, devoted teacher of biology and chairman of the curriculum committee. He respected Coffin's philosophy of education and supported the New Curriculum. As a Friend, Watson was a recorded minister, sponsored the gospel teams on campus. A determined personality—sure of himself when he felt a clear leading—he proceeded to gather the academic reins of the college into his hands.

A number of faculty members came under fire at the February board meeting in 1938 because of "certain disturbing rumors, complaints and charges." Three persons in particular—David E. Henley, head of economics and sociology; Don Evans, instructor in journalism and history; Louise Pfuetze, dean of women—were under suspicion as supporting the socio-economic policies of the New Deal. Trustees also questioned reappointment of Dr. Evelyn Gentry as instructor—she was returning from a year's post-doctoral study in Europe. These and three other appointments were referred back to the faculty committee of the board. After lengthy meetings—What would happen if the college *dismissed* the persons in question?—the committee finally recommended that all of them be reappointed. But with provisos: Henley to be restricted to teaching sociology, Evans to be advised to complete his doctorate, Gentry to be questioned regarding her "Christian, social and political beliefs," and Pfuetze to be told plainly "to show due respect" for others associated with the college and "to make promise of cooperation." The board approved.

Watson's duties as Dean now needed more precise definition in order to implement the will of the board. A specific committee—C. Bevan Johnson, Mendenhall, and Watson himself—spelled this out. Watson was to have charge of curriculum and academic standards. He was to counsel the faculty in educational matters, to appoint faculty committees, and to preside in the absence of the president. He was to propose changes in faculty personnel—and to *report directly to the board!** The board thus transferred to Watson the academic responsibilities and authority that had been Mendenhall's. It was a humiliating delimitation of the office of president.

But Mendenhall was still the administrative head of the college—and of the deans of men and of women. It was *his* painful duty, therefore, to communicate to his charming and vivacious dean of women the displeasure of the trustees. In the fall of 1938 she resigned, effective June 1939, but President Mendenhall withheld announcement of her resignation until late in February.

Meanwhile Dean Watson began to reshape the faculty and strengthen major departments, replace "controversial" with more "acceptable" professors. For the fall of 1938 he brought back Dr. Harold F. Spencer '31 from Michigan State to be professor of biology, and Dr. Charles W. Cooper '25e from Fresno State to be professor of English and director of Poet Theatre. At the same time Miss Elva Brown (M.A., Berkeley, in history) came from high school teaching to be professor of secondary education. During that same fall, trustees asked Watson to outline a more comprehensive reorganization of the faculty. In February 1939 he listed 16 faculty "problems" for which he suggested solutions—and he tallied the effects to show that they kept within the budget. To strengthen chemistry and physics, he proposed adding an instructor—[Dr.] W. Roy Newsom '34 was soon appointed. To strengthen history, he suggested a new full-time instructor—[Dr.] Harry W. Nerhood was shortly named. To unify all professional work in Education, he recommended that Coffin be named Director of Education, eliminating the separate deanship for Broadoaks.

Other changes Watson proposed according to his principle of "teaching-administration." As Dean he continued teaching, as

*These specifications, when approved, were *not* to be incorporated in the By-Laws "as the duties of any Dean who might [later] be appointed."

did the Dean of Men and the Librarian. So Watson recommended that Dr. Spaulding double as Registrar—in place of Esther Hoff; and that Prof. Elva Brown double as Dean of Women —in place of Louise Pfuetze.

Then, there was another problem: the headship of the English Department—though the board had confirmed Upton as chairman only three years earlier. But Upton had antagonized some members of the faculty by his leadership in the New Curriculum. He was thought responsible for the disaffection of Harris. He was even suspected of enjoying a pipe and an occasional sherry. And he championed Don Evans. Watson felt that if Cooper were head of the department, Harris would come back and harmony prevail. But Cooper said he had *not* returned to Whittier to replace his friend Upton—even to reconcile his friend Harris—and Dean Watson tried another tack. Don Evans was out, so he brought Harris back as director of publicity and set off Journalism as his separate department.

The various changes in faculty approved by the board on February 27, 1939, screamed forth on the front page of the Whittier *News*: REORGANIZATION OF ALL DEPARTMENTS OF COLLEGE. Three days earlier it had reported Mrs. Pfuetze's resignation. Now it was apparent that the college had dropped Evelyn Gentry, Esther Hoff, and Don Evans. And the students assumed that two others who had resigned had also fallen under the axe. They petitioned the board (135 signatures), demanding an explanation. The faculty, too, communicated to the trustees its sincere concern "for the welfare of Whittier College."

The college was again in crisis.

To restore faculty confidence, the board set up a new Advisory Committee, consisting of the president of the board and chairman of its faculty committee, the president and dean of the college, and three professors appointed by the board. Its function: "to advise . . . in matters pertaining to faculty appointment." With this forward step in policy, the faculty was not inclined to fight for those already lost in the shuffle. To answer the students, Dean Watson prepared a careful statement, quashed rumors that all departments were to be reorganized and that Baldwin would be removed from his deanship. The students accepted things as they were.

What did this "reorganization of the faculty" mean in the life of the college? Was it really a purge of the liberals, as some felt, a violation of academic freedom and tenure?* Or was it a repudiation of President Mendenhall by the removal of some of his appointees and friends?

Certainly all liberal members of the faculty were under scrutiny by conservative members of the board. But of the professors who might have had "tenure" in any usual academic sense, only David Henley had his "academic freedom" infringed: he was crowded over in his department to teach Sociology (the field of his doctorate), leaving Economics to his more conservative junior colleague, Spaulding. Of the four persons dropped, two were strictly administrative personnel and two were part-time instructors. They would not, therefore, have had "tenure" even if there had been such a college policy at that time, which there was not.

The relationship of board to faculty was thought of by many trustees as simply "employer and employee." A special committee of the board—Glenn Lewis '15, chairman, Herman L. Perry, Ashton M. Otis, C. Bevan Johnson, and W. O. Mendenhall—was working earnestly at this very time to develop a full statement of Policy for Whittier College. Section by section this was studied by the board, revised, approved—though the final sections on academic freedom and tenure, which were liberal and professional in substance, were not finally approved until the fall of 1943.

The reorganization of administration and faculty in 1937-39 surely weakened the position of the college president, but it strengthened the position of the faculty. Fruits of the furor were the Advisory Committee and the policy statement on academic freedom and tenure.

Other changes followed in the spring and summer of 1940. In mid-April Dean Watson resigned to accept the presidency of Wilmington College. After brief uncertainty, the board named Dr. Harold F. Spencer '31 to succeed him as Dean and head of biology. A young man of thirty, quiet and unassuming, he was the first

*Edward R. Miller '32 was researching his alma mater during this year as a basis for a doctoral dissertation, *The Educational Program of a Church-Related College: A Study of Whittier College* (Yale, 1942). He wrote that "on several occasions" there had been "dismissal of a faculty person on grounds of 'liberal activities' without any previous definition of what such activities might be, official investigation, or review of the case" (MS p. 115). He gives no names or details.

alumnus given a major administrative post. Within a fortnight, came the resignation of Dr. Marcus Skarstedt to become director of the library of San Francisco Junior College. To replace him as professor of mathematics came Dr. H. Randolph Pyle '26, who had served Penn College as president in its Depression crisis and then Earlham College as dean. Skarstedt's assistant, Benjamin G. Whitten, became acting librarian and then librarian. At the end of the summer of 1940, Dr. Gustaf E. Ostrom resigned to become director of research for a newly-formed corporation. His assistant, Dr. W. Roy Newsom '34 assumed his place as head of chemistry. By the following spring Dr. Harris again resigned; it was forty years since his first appointment.* He lived another decade in his aërie overlooking the campus. Edwin B. Bronner '41 replaced him briefly as director of publicity.

The resignation within a year of four senior professors—strong members of the faculty, conservatives all of them—might have seemed a second crisis at Whittier during the year that saw the darkening War in Europe, the fall of France, the isolation of Britain. But the younger men who replaced their seniors—four of the five were alumni—showed their own strengths. Four of the five were to serve the college 25 years or more;** two were in succession Dean, another chairman of the graduate committee.

There was no crisis, there was but transition.

With the curriculum, administration and faculty as reorganized, Whittier College proved itself sufficiently strong to ride out the storm that was rapidly making up in the Far East.

4

STUDENT LIFE, ACTIVITIES, AND CAUSES— GOOD YEARS IN TROUBLED TIMES

THE STUDENT BODY on the Whittier campus increased 44% in size during the first six years of Mendenhall's presidency. The total in 1939-40 was 591. Then in the next three years of peace-time draft, Pearl Harbor, and war, the number dropped back to what it had been a decade before.

*The trustees asked him to write a history of the college, and published his *The Quaker and the West: the First Sixty Years of Whittier College* in 1948.

**Edwin B. Bronner, the fifth, his career interrupted by the War, became professor of American history and curator of the Quaker collection at Haverford College.

If these students seemed boisterous boys and giggling girls at times, more interested in sports than studies, they were in the main idealistic, serious about their purposes in life. More than half studied to become teachers. Others were drawn to such service as Y.M.C.A. and youth leadership, religious education and the ministry. A good number prepared for the professions of law and medicine. And for the decade 1936-45, Whittier stood second among the small colleges of California in number of alumni who proceeded to doctorates in the sciences. In fact, it was the only one sending students on (three of them) to the Ph.D. in genetics.

Oldsters in the community who were concerned for the welfare of these students, need not have worried. They were healthy, friendly, well-adjusted young people, maturing as persons while preparing for useful careers in society.

A questionnaire, answered by about half of the student body in the spring of 1939, reflected their attitudes. As for Whittier College, they "liked it" (16 to 1); they thought old Founders Hall should be kept "due to tradition" (3 to 2); they were against smoking on campus (7 to 3). As for personal behavior, 30% of those answering this question said they drank (3 to 1 these were men); 35% said they smoked (2 to 1, men); 60% owned to "petting" (2 to 1, men—but half the girls modestly declined to state). As for God and Family, 96% believed in Him; 95% wanted to have children; 93% expected to get married.* Finally, they believed that Hitler was *not* crazy; they would *not* vote for Roosevelt for a third term; they thought professors did *not* give too heavy assignments. And only half of them saw their dentists twice a year!

These were good years, the later 1930's, full of fun and frolic. From Freshman Week in the fall through Senior Week in June was an endless round of student body, A.W.S., A.M.S., class, and society affairs and events: informal and formal dances, rush parties, banquets, picnics, mountain and beach parties, dates for games, movies, theatre and music. The Wild West Day, with whiskerino and kangaroo court—spring Carnival, with booths, side-shows and concessions—small wonder the faculty decided in 1940 "to study the problems of interference of the extra-class-

*The shocking disparity in these last items reflected no more than a slight difference in percentage of those responding to the questions.

251

room activities of the students with their academic work." But the departmental clubs, service organizations, dormitory groups and the Peppers for off-campus women served their purposes. The William Penn Society—Paul S. Smith the first sponsor and Frank Alexander the organizing chairman—added to the Franklins, Orthogonians, and Lancers as men's societies, and balanced the Palmers, Metaphonians, Athenians, and Thalians for women. Two-fifths of the students belonged to one or another of these local fraternities and sororities, which evidenced no racial or class barriers to membership. They all filled a strongly-felt social need.

ATHLETICS DURING THE DECADE 1934-44 was a unifying interest in the student body. By no means were they mere spectator sports. Some 20% of the men went out for football, another 20% participated in other intercollegiate sports, and a good share of the rest joined in the intramural program. For the most part, students and faculty believed in physical fitness and health, the values of team play and recreation. The physical education staff—particularly Wallace "Chief" Newman, Aubrey Bonham, and Lucille Verhust —were respected members of the faculty. Together they trained a large number of very successful high school and junior college teachers and coaches, many of whom became school principals and superintendents.

Track was never a strong team sport on the Quaker campus, though individual men occasionally shone as Randy Carter did in 1937, setting a conference record of 20.7 in the 220 yard sprint. And in that season Bonham sent a team of seven to the Drake University Relays. These men won the 880-yard relay ("on a muddy track and in the face of a driving rain") and the mile relay, bringing "glory to themselves and to their college and city." However, the Whittier student body wasn't much interested in track.

It was even less interested in baseball, though "Chief" Newman coached five championship teams in his first 13 years at Whittier. In 1939 the Purple Sox (with Gold trim) won "the undisputed championship"—the 1941 team was undefeated in conference play—the Poets retained the championship in 1942 with players "versatile enough to play every position." These were extraordinary baseball years.

Basketball, however, always attracted more student support. During the decade 1933-42, Verne Landreth, then Newman, and (from 1938) Bonham coached. Whittier won five conference championships and placed second three other years. The teams tended to be "nonstar." The 1935 champions were big men; the 1938 champions were mostly slight and fleet. The 1940 team went undefeated in conference play; the 1942 team lost but one of its conference games. In 1943, in a brilliant non-conference season, the Poets once more defeated U.C.L.A. As perhaps "the greatest small school team on the Coast," Whittier was invited to represent the West in the A.A.U. tournament at Kansas City. It could not do so because of the loss of key men to the armed forces. Aubrey "Bonnie" Bonham had become an outstanding coach and teacher of basketball fundamentals, the fast-break offensive and man-for-man defensive play.

The record in football was just as impressive. "Chief" Newman coached five championship teams and two second-place in a decade (1932-1941). In 1934 the spectacular passing of John Arrambide helped defeat Occidental, and the Poets won all their conference games—also beat Pomona 50-6 "to the delight of a large Homecoming crowd." That year Whittier men filled five of the eleven places on the so-called All-Conference team. . . The 1935 season opened with a heroic defeat at Berkeley. The California crowd sat "in amazed silence" as the valiant Poets held the Bears scoreless for 51 minutes. Then in the fading moments, the University team turned "a Quaker mistake and blocked punt" into a winning touchdown. In conference play, Whittier again won the title, and the Victory Bell in Founders' tower peeled forth the glad tidings!. . . The next three teams were strong if not champions, with Myron Claxton named "Little All-American" in 1938 by the Associated Press. . . The 1939 champions, one of the highest scoring teams on the Coast (with "slippery-hipped" Gene Wineinger totalling 60 points), had six of their 22 players named All-Conference. . . The 1941 team again won its conference title. Two days after the Football Banquet honoring it, the nation was plunged into war—and things were then to be different.

Part of football was the razz-ma-tazz, rooting section, Howling Hundred, pep band, rallies, serpentine downtown—and the bonfire on Fire Hill to work up enthusiasm for the big games. Freshmen roved the town alleys and countryside gathering combustibles, often snatching away some farmer's privy as pinnacle for the mountainous pyre. In 1940 it was well toward morning when the exhausted builders returned to their dorms, leaving some men to stand watch. Toward dawn, several attractive girls (it is said) approached the stalwart guardsmen—fresh enough to be interested—lured them aside. From concealment sprang villains, who applied the torch and then escaped with their shills! Up went the flames, a magnificent fiasco.* It was all to do again that day with frenzied zeal—classes dismissed (to be rescheduled on a Saturday)—and the Homecoming game, stubbornly fought, ended in a scoreless tie.

THE FULL RANGE OF STUDENT and curricular activities, with no sharp line dividing them, engaged a share of the energies and interests of a large portion of the student body.

The Pep Band was a purely student venture. Men's and women's glee clubs, under faculty direction (Frank Pursell, then William H. Wright), were transformed into an A Cappella Choir. In 1938 a Bach Festival—the first of its four concerts nationally broadcast with a greeting from Mrs. Hoover—began an annual sequence under the direction of Margaretha Lohmann, with Ruth Haroldson directing instrumental ensembles. Through the years, the Festivals performed a great part of Bach's voluminous literature—for piano, organ, voice, chorus, strings, brass, and orchestra. Music majors and others participated, and the student body always appreciated chapel hour performances by faculty and gifted students such as Frances Copeland, Marjorie Lewis, Herbert Nanney.

Drama also enjoyed a thriving decade. Winn F. Zeller (Ph.D., Iowa) brought a liberal university spirit to the production of a wide range of provocative plays—the Soviet farce, *Squaring the Circle*, Capek's *R.U.R.*, and Ibsen's *Ghosts*—whose themes of wife-swapping, robots with soul and sex, and degenerative syphilis brought rumbles of community opposition and Zeller's resignation. Dr. Cooper was brought back as director of Poet Theatre. With trained assistants (Paul Camp and others) from Pasadena

*At the same hour "parties unknown" fired the Redlands pile sixty miles away—an inexplicable coincidence.

Playhouse—and Theron Ashby teaching radio drama—an enlarged program developed. Stage classics such as *The School for Scandal* and Molière's *The Would-Be Gentleman* (in Basic English) balanced contemporary dramas like *The Petrified Forest* and *Our Town*. In *Green Grow the Lilacs*, singing cowboys a-horseback serpentined down from Fire Hill into the Amphitheatre, holding their girls saddled in front of them—LeRoy Hughes (all conference end) singing Curley.* The farmhouse setting, haywagon and bunkhouse, rowdy hoe-down and shivaree, suggested with nostalgia the pioneer days of Whittier's founding. In 1938-1943, a fifth of the student body participated on the Poet Theatre stage annually, many others backstage, and most of the students and faculty attended the performances.

Journalistic activities utilized the varied talents of almost a tenth of the student body. The *Acropolis*, which had shown such marked originality in 1934, continued to be an excellent summary of the college year in picture and paragraph. *Acropolis 1936* (Barbara Todd [Kennedy], the editor) was judged the best college annual in the country—first among five "pacemakers." And *Acropolis 1941* (Norfleet Callicott, Jr., editor) was rated All-American, "easily one of the finest books" of those years, thought the judges.

The *Quaker Campus*, weekly and then biweekly, had as many as ten students on its editorial staff and thirty as reporters, also a succession of original cartoonists. Faculty advisers in succession were Don Evans, Herbert E. Harris, and Edwin Bronner. Administrative restraint was seldom necessary. Notable student maturity, usually if not always, balanced traditional freedom of the press. In 1936 the Q.C. (Roxie Willis, editor) received a First Class, if not All-American, award as judged with other small college papers. Through these years, news coverage was good, editorials tackled student problems, and columns touched on cultural and campus doings. And the Q.C. kept in view the ominous events in the larger world scene.

"THE TIDES OF FASCISM and Communism sweep in upon us from all directions," said President Mendenhall in his annual report of

*This folk play by Lynn Riggs was soon turned into *Oklahoma!*, first of American musical comedies.

255

1938 to the college board. "Emotions are running high and people are growing severely critical of one another." It was his aim

> to maintain on the campus a clear idea of the meaning of democracy, to bring the students into the habit of looking at issues objectively, thinking seriously and without fear, to apply [a] scientific approach to our social and economic problems.

Difficult as this was to do, he felt it might be "the salvation of America." He had faith that "our religion which we so glibly call Christian will take us far in extending brotherhood among men, without taking us into experiments based on violence and hatred." The trustees accepted his report "with favorable commendation" and directed that it be printed for wide distribution.

Fascism was certainly viewed with alarm on the Whittier campus. As early as 1935, Don Evans predicted Franco's victory in Spain because of Hitler and Mussolini's intervention. In an effort to understand the forces that had shaped Mussolini, Roberta Forsberg (then a senior) reviewed Pareto's *Mind and Society* in the Q.C. Il Ducé's cub, Vittorio, on his shocking visit to southern California, extolled the "beauty" of bombing Ethiopian villages. In his novel *It Can't Happen Here*, Sinclair Lewis fancied a fascist coup in peaceful Vermont. Howard Scott, crusading Technocrat, addressed the Whittier student body advocating government by *self-appointed* engineers and technologists, ready to "take over" with the "inevitable" breakdown of Capitalism. Accompanied by husky bodyguard, opening his talk with a smart paramilitary salute—was not Scott a fearsome harbinger of native Ducé or Führer?

If to the students the greater danger was from the Right, to the college trustees the real menace was from the Left. Many of them tended to "regard socialism, communism, and the New Deal as synonymous." All liberals were suspect. The hand of Communism —the Party, comrades and secret cells, espionage and subversion—appeared to them in every demonstration of discontent. Rioting of 3,000 students on the U.C.L.A. campus in the fall of 1934, protesting suspension of four student officers, seemed Communist-inspired. In the fall of 1939, Whittier College received a solemn letter from the Associated Farmers of California warning of the Communist propaganda in schools and universities of the

State. Martin Dies and his House Un-American Activities Committee were already at work. Mused Carl Hanson in his Q.C. column:

> I wonder just what kind of Red or Communistic goings on he would find here at Whittier. . . Surely he won't begrudge a few students (few is the correct word, I believe) doing a bit of advanced thinking and research. . .

Certainly there were no Communists on the Whittier faculty or in the student body—though on one occasion (it was rumored) an "organizer" appeared briefly, left shortly, frustrated by student "apathy."

In his history of *The American College and University*, Frederick Rudolph writes that " in the great urban centers a small number [of students] even signed up with the Communist party," but adds

> Very few students, it is true, were red, and many certainly were green, but most in any case were party to that spirit of change, social protest, and repudiation of the past that was one of the most significant characteristics of the American campus in the 1930's.

However, on the Whittier campus *most* students were really not deeply stirred by "that spirit of change, social protest, and repudiation of the past," and on other Western campuses, too, protesters were a minority. But activists there certainly were.

The Student Peace Movement at Whittier was part of the national effort—and overseas, Oxford dons and undergraduates also foreswore war. The historic peace witness of Friends and President Mendenhall's leadership in peace education made quite natural the All-College Peace Observance in the spring of 1936 as part of "the national student strike for peace." The guest speaker was Jerry Voorhis, running for Congress as a New Dealer. The student body as a whole was not much stirred; the town and trustees were. In 1937 Bill Schmitt, dynamic student liberal, organized the STUDENT STRIKE AGAINST WAR, which he announced as "a DRESS REHEARSAL of the action we will take the moment our government seems likely to declare war." A respected Whittier pastor, member of the American Legion, was prudently chosen to introduce the speakers. But when the program was over, the Q.C. lamented the students' "indifference to the whole question of peace action." Or was it their dislike of the word "strike"? Peace Emphasis Week the next year—no "strike" this time—went by "without causing even a ripple in the sea of [student] complacency." Only 25% responded to the "peace poll"—and the Q.C. added that liberal Jerry Voorhis had voted for Big Navy! In the spring of 1939, Bob Schostag's editorial—"Will Pacifism Suffice?"—commented on the students' peace pledges and resolutions of the preceding four years. He honored the churches for their condemnation of warfare, but said "we certainly deceive ourselves if we think that [such pacifism] is in itself enough to keep us out of war."

Various other student causes and activities during these years also disturbed the Establishment. Bill Schmitt was drawn into several off-campus youth organizations. In 1937 he helped plan the Emergency Youth Assembly in Los Angeles. It proposed State legislation, a California Youth Act to provide "wages for all youth from 16-25" administered by a Youth Commission comprising representatives of youth and labor unions. This was heady stuff—frightening to conservatives. If it came to naught, Gordon Foster's championing of this cause in the Q.C. was a challenge.

That fall Foster threw down another gauntlet. The Student Christian Association filed an entry blank for the 1937 Armistice Day parade sponsored by the American Legion. The Legion approved the form. The students began building their float—a scene from *Bury the Dead*, the stark anti-war play that Zeller was producing in Poet Theatre. On second thought, the Legion canceled the entry. Foster blasted the Legionnaires in the Q.C. for their blind militancy—and drunkenness at conventions. Controversy ensued. Foster gamely printed an anonymous response that called him "a little fellow who has made an ass of himself." The youthful crusader plunged on.

In the Easter issue of the Q.C.—next to three columns of Passion Week features—Foster printed a robust editorial: STUDENTS DEMAND FREE WASSERMANN TESTS, and the next week reported that Mrs. Pfuetze's S.C.A. class in Men-Women Relations volunteered to take the test. There was never a dull issue—Foster commended Harvard for taking a "forward step" in appointing an avowed Communist to its faculty. But this journalistic activism reached a *buffo* crisis in the fall of 1938. It was incidental to "Ham and Eggs" for the old folks.

This fantastic scheme—Thirty Dollars Every Thursday for (unemployed) persons over fifty—was placed on the California ballot as an initiative measure. In a bid for votes Culbert Olson supported it, running against Republican Gov. Frank Merriam. A tremendous effort was made by almost all responsible groups in the state to defeat this funny-money pension plan. Interested students took a straw vote at a football rally. Gordon Foster gave the results directly to the town paper. The 317 students voted 2 to 1 for conservative Merriam and rejected "Ham and Eggs" 6 to 1. That was safe enough. But the 19 faculty votes were 2 to 1 for Olson—and *half* the faculty wanted Thirty Dollars Every Thursday! The community was stunned. The *News* was good enough to print at once the comforting word that the college trustees utterly condemned the ruinous pension plan.

But all hell broke loose. Next morning the faculty, in unprecedented emergency session, opposed Ham and Eggs unanimously. Only seven faculty members had voted at the student rally—the ballot box had been stuffed by some jokester. Henley, already suspect of Keynesian heresy, reaffirmed his stand against the measure. The *News* set the record straight, and the editor wrote in his column, "Heard in the Barber Shop"—

'I was shocked by the story of the straw vote . . .,' said the Man Who Was Reading the Paper.

'You were no more shocked than the faculty itself . . .,' said the Man Who Was Waiting for a Chair.

On campus the student editor came under pressure because of his gaffe, which brought about his resignation effective at the end of the semester. Commented the *Acropolis* in the spring: "Compromise was no part of Gordon's scheme, and the truth was printed more than once."

The student activists and their causes were symptomatic if not characteristic during the troubled times of the late 'thirties, as the contention of alien "isms" drew college and country inexorably into World War II.

WARTIME—CHAPMAN COLLEGE ON CAMPUS
CO-OPERATION AND RESIGNATIONS

EVENTS IN EUROPE moved swiftly—the partition of Poland, the fall of France, the isolation of Britain. Step by step the United States became involved—destroyers, lend-lease, war orders convoyed across the Atlantic. And at the same time in the Pacific— embargo of war matériel, with provocative freezing of Japanese assets. Those on the Whittier campus were fully cognizant of all this, as "preparedness" waxed and "peace movement" waned.

The Selective Service Act, first peacetime draft in American history, came in the fall of 1940. At a solemn convocation, two Whittier professors (both of them Quakers and pacifists) outlined the bill and its provisions. They spoke briefly of the Friends' faith (underlying the college) that there is "that of God" in every man. They pointed out how diverse were the practices of Quakers in wartime, some remaining conscientious objectors, others serving in hospitals or fighting with the armed forces. They advised students to comply with the law (which provided for alternative service), to hold fast to their convictions, to exercise tolerance and understanding.

Student deferments kept most men in college during the year. Registration in the spring of 1941 showed no appreciable decline, and there was a slight increase in the fall, when the enrollment reached 556, the highest ever.* But there was general uneasiness about the future. A Q.C. survey in February 1941 indicated that a majority of students "expected to see this country in active fighting within a year." The college town was strongly militant—the local paper showed concern when Friends set up a forestry camp for c.o's in nearby San Dimas.

Whittier continued much as usual through the college year and into the fall: scholarship honor roll, All-College Picnic, Religious Emphasis Week, *Acropolis* making "All-American," Homecoming with *Pygmalion* and the trouncing of Oxy 14-7 before a wild crowd, football championship and banquet December 5, 1941.

*A decrease in enrollments was expected everywhere for the fall of 1941, and U.C.L.A. reported a drop of 700 students.

Then, Pearl Harbor—Sunday, December 7th—America at war and momentarily stunned.

WHAT EFFECT WOULD WAR, actual war, have upon the Quaker campus? The Pacific Coast was wide open for a hit-and-run attack by Nipponese carriers. There were measures for Civil Defense, but no panic. At a special Monday convocation, President Mendenhall urged students to remain calm and continue their college work. On Tuesday, Eleanor Roosevelt addressed student leaders from the Southland colleges assembled at Occidental College. She also urged students to stay with their studies as long as they could, but to enlist for civil defense. Several days of classes remained before the three-week holiday. Dress rehearsals of Maxwell Anderson's *Journey to Jerusalem* prepared for its West Coast première. A handful of townfolk made their way up to Poet Theatre by flashlight, through the first blackout, to experience the story of the boy Jesus, who had never borne pain but realized that he must suffer and die.

For the Christmas convocation, the music department presented Handel's *Messiah*. In a special issue of the Q.C., the editor featured a photo: the Japanese friendship lantern, long a fixture on the campus.* Beneath it, the caption: "The Light Went Out." But Japanese-Americans must be fairly treated (the Q.C. insisted), and the white-gift Christmas spirit must not be forgotten. "Let's not blackout our hearts."

By the end of Christmas vacation, 25 college men had already withdrawn to enter military service. The spring semester 1942 opened with a 12% drop in enrollment, but 208 men were still on campus, winning basketball and baseball championships. Then, with insufficient men in prospect for fall football, Whittier withdrew from the conference.

Military evacuation of all Japanese-Americans from the Coast touched Whittier at once. Roy Harada and Dorothy Fujuita arranged to transfer to Earlham College. Sam Ishikawa stayed with his people to help them, and Whittier students collected books and recreation equipment to send him.

*Placed there in 1930 by Lydia Cammack, a gift of Professor Yasuma of Okazaki, it was dedicated to Friendship between the children of the two lands. Because of vandalism, the college removed it for safekeeping during the war.

Against the background of desperate war news—Singapore, Bataan, Corregidor—the uneasy college term drew toward its close. Chuck McEvers resigned as A.S.W.C. president, expecting to be assigned to a Civilian Public Service camp—he wanted his successor named at once to prepare for the fall. *Acropolis 1942* (Jean Moore Webster, editor, upon Callicott's leaving) was distinguished for its beauty, again rated All-American, one of the best in the nation. On its dedication spread was a dramatic photo by [Japanese-American] Midori: a pair of peaceful gulls soaring against stormy sky—and the poetic caption by Ruth Walker:

> THERE IS
> YET A MAN
> WHO CARRIES
> A GUN IN
> HIS HAND
> AND PEACE IN
> HIS HEART

Already there was a casualty to report: Lieut. Lowell J. "Tod" Mulcahy '39e, varsity fullback when a Whittier student, killed in action in the Pacific. In the anti-war play, he had been one of the Dead *who would not be buried* until he had had his say. . .

CHAPMAN COLLEGE in Los Angeles—the denominational college of the Disciples of Christ—faced institutional problems that were at once compounded by the war. Already in the spring of 1940, the trustees of Chapman College explored the possibility of a merger with Whittier College, though the matter was then dropped. Shortly after Pearl Harbor, the Navy leased the Vermont Avenue campus of Chapman College, whose trustees made a definite proposal in March 1942 that Chapman merge its student body with Whittier's at least "for the duration." With its own decreasing enrollment, Whittier College welcomed its Christian brothers.

A carefully-drawn agreement between the two colleges guarded against campus rivalries. Chapman set up a skeletal administration—Rev. George N. Reeves as president; Rev. Rush M. Deskins, local Christian Church pastor, as dean—and released its faculty in Los Angeles. The residue of its students, Chapman brought to the Whittier campus. There was to be essentially one student body. Chapman students paid Whittier tuition, met Whittier requirements, accepted Whittier regulations, participated in the full Whittier program, curricular and extracurricular. However, Prof. Bert Williams gave Chapman's own denominational courses in religion, and these were open to Whittier students. The initial agreement was more restrictive than later deemed necessary; and the Chapman students maintained their identity and loyalty to their own college and traditions, while at the same time contributing greatly to the life and activity—sports, drama, and social events—of the Whittier College campus.

As part of the Whittier College commencement exercises in June 1943, seven Chapman seniors received their academic degrees from their own college. And, according to their custom,

> They participated in their impressive ivy-ring ceremony in the Herbert E. Harris Amphitheatre in the waning light of the afternoon. . . Joined in fellowship by an unbroken ring of ivy, they bowed their heads in prayer.

President Reeves then cut a portion of the "ivy ring" for each, and "these symbolic tendrils were planted this year on Whittier's campus, Chapman's temporary home."

Although Chapman never mustered the 100 students it hoped for, indeed hardly more than 50, the group included many fine students.* They were heartily welcome in the Whittier classroom and on the Poet campus. With no discernible friction, and with great mutual respect and satisfaction, this close co-operation continued for the three war years, after which Chapman College was able to re-establish its independent existence.

THE GREAT DEBT THAT had weighed so heavily upon Whittier College following the collapse of the land scheme in the late 'twenties, was at last almost liquidated by the time the United

---

*Chapman alumni from the small classes on the Whittier campus proceeded to various careers: [Drs.] James Deese, Sam Campbell, and Quinton R. DeYoung becoming professors of psychology at Johns Hopkins, Los Angeles State, and Chapman; William R. Eshelman, librarian at Bucknell; Don Poston, Gerald Ford, and Richard Brown, Christian ministers; Gwen Waters, Merton Brown, and Glenn Bickford, serving in other professional vocations.

States became involved in the War. The John Greenleaf Whittier banquet, canceled in the days just after Pearl Harbor, became a Victory Dinner at the Woman's Clubhouse in the fall of 1942 to celebrate the end of the debt.

What had been a Depression indebtedness of over $400,000 had been reduced to $40,000 by the fall of 1941, and to about $4,000 by the summer of 1942. On September 22nd of that year, behind black-curtained windows, but with candlelight cheer, 450 friends of the college watched "the burning of its $410,000 mortgage." It was a moving occasion, a personal triumph for Mr. Hockett and tribute to his prudent management.

With Chapman students to bolster enrollment and with the burden of debt lifted, Whittier was in good shape to weather the uncertainties that lay ahead. Yet, as he was leaving the banquet hall where he had been so honored for what he had done for Whittier College, Howard Hockett was heard to wonder aloud:

"Now, where do we go from here?"

THE ROLE OF WHITTIER during World War II is difficult to appraise. Was Whittier "really" a Friends college? If so, of what kind? and to what extent? And what was this to mean?

Whittier should be viewed, certainly, as being *the kind of Quaker college that it actually was*—growing out of the sort of mid-Western Quakerism from which it emerged, developing in the Quaker-founded town and citrus area in which it grew up, and serving a largely non-Quaker constituency. It was to be judged, then, not by Eastern or Hicksite, but by Western and Orthodox Quaker norms.

The peace testimony of Friends has been part of the Society from its beginning. Condemnation of war has been coupled with efforts toward removal of the causes of war, relief of wartime suffering, and postwar reconstruction. Each war had seen its "fighting Quakers" as well as its conscientious objectors. But with family brothers often following conscientiously quite contrary "leadings," there was a tender measure of tolerance. This was remarkably so at Whittier College during these war years.

Of the 28 Whittier trustees in 1942, 21 were more-or-less Quaker, only one or two were wartime pacifists. But throughout the war, the Institute of International Relations, sponsored by the

American Friends Service Committee and coordinated with the Whittier College summer session, continued to include strong pacifists on its distinguished faculties. For "a spirit of positive tolerance" was one of the Quaker principles accepted by the trustees as among its Aims and Objectives for the college. As for the faculty—of the 40 full-time members in 1942, 20 were more-or-less identified with Friends meetings or the local church. Of these 10 were wartime pacifists, 6 of them men, 3 of draft age and registered as conscientious objectors. The faculty as a whole accepted its stated aim of being "actively sympathetic to the Quaker point of view" and coupled this with "tolerance of spirit." As for the student body—it was less Quaker than either faculty or board. Only 54 young Friends were enrolled in 1942, 13% of the Whittier students. But this essentially non-Quaker student body was infused somehow with attitudes and principles dear to the Society of Friends—respect for the individual, tolerance of differing views, freedom from racial or religious prejudice, friendliness and the ideal of service.

Whittier was a Quaker college, then, of this kind and to this extent.

Most of the college trustees felt duty-bound to support the war. They welcomed approval of the college by the Armed Services for reservist programs, and they sought other means for making Whittier a part of the national effort. They encouraged faculty participation in wartime drives and community service. They were proud of the war activities of the student body, and of those who served. The college board authorized purchase of an appropriate service flag—blue stars on white field surrounded by red border, gold stars to honor the dead.

The Whittier faculty was drawn into the war in one way and another. Benjamin G. Whitten, the librarian, was the only man drafted. At the same time in 1943, Dr. Milic Kybal, Czech refugee and part-time lecturer on Latin American affairs, was called into service. The next year, Elva Brown, dean of women and professor of education, asked for a leave-of-absence to be commissioned Lieutenant (s.g.) in the WAVEs—special waiver as to minimum height. David E. Henley, already on leave, served as regional executive secretary of the American Friends Service Committee. Dorothy Baruch of Broadoaks resigned to develop nursery schools for war-working mothers. Theron Ashby left soon after Pearl Harbor for war work at Douglas Aircraft.

As the faculty shrank in size, there was a bit of doubling up. Several additional classes were needed for men in the Navy V-7 reserves. Under the Defense Training Program, professors took on extra teaching in mathematics and physics. Most of the faculty members participated in some form of wartime work: gave or took First Aid, served as air-raid wardens, donated blood, sold War bonds, helped the U.S.O., wrote to students in military or civilian service—helped Japanese-Americans, European refugees, men in C.P.S. camps.

Additional courses added to the summer sessions in 1942 made possible a Three-Year Plan, allowing students to complete their four-year degrees in three. A regular Summer School had been established in 1939 under the direction of Paul S. Smith. It brought together the work of three separate summer programs—education at Broadoaks, field biology at mountains and beach, and the course related to the Institute of International Relations. Enrollment in the unified and expanded summer sessions was already 285 in 1941.

The Whittier student body became smaller. In the fall of 1942 there were still 185 men on campus including 23 of the Chapman group. By early December, 33 had left college, 86 were enlisted or enlisting in the military reserve programs. By that time some 350 former students and alumni were listed as in war service. During the spring of 1943, more men were called up—in March a busload of 12 were cheered on their way, not without tears—and by commencement time 40 of the 80 men who had started with the Class of '43 were in uniform, with degrees awarded to 14 in absentia.

It was a time of intensified student activity—Bonham's "fiendish" fitness program—and a continuous sequence of student war drives. An original musical, *Cookin' Wiz Gas!* by Bob Dye and Guy Frank, was a U.S.O. benefit. Women collected discarded hose for making parachutes. Sale of Defense Stamps tied in with choosing a Victory Queen. Then—sewing for the Red Cross, First Aid classes, work for the Ration Board, scrapbooks for hospitals, soliciting funds for imprisoned overseas students, donating blood, picking oranges instead of the traditional All-College Picnic, entertaining servicemen home on leave, writing to them and cherishing for them their hopes for peace—and mourning their tragic loss.

For Lt. Bob [Oliver] Mitchell '40, a second gold star was added to the service flag. He went down in the Pacific near Guadalcanal after sinking three out of four Japanese destroyers, and was awarded the Purple Heart and Silver Star posthumously. The *U.S.S. Oliver Mitchell* was given his name.

DR. W. O. MENDENHALL was widely respected as a "peace man" by many who did not share his peace testimony.

Early in 1941, following a Washington conference of college presidents addressed by government and army men, he came back and gave the trustees "a fine explanation of the Quaker attitude toward war and how to cooperate with the [draft] law." After war came, he accepted the fact that the Armed Services approve Whittier for pre-induction training of enlisted men under a quota system that left a certain number of them on campus. He expected the college to do something also for the c.o's.

The c.o's were serving, he felt, in civilian work of national importance. He honored them by placing blue circles along with the blue stars on the service flag displayed from the balcony of the library. These circles were surreptitiously snipped off by some intolerant student, employee, or citizen. New ones were quietly affixed to the flag. An alumnus—naval lieutenant who survived Pearl Harbor—wrote to the Q.C. following his campus visit when on liberty: "I'm awfully glad to see . . . on the service flag , , , the circles for those who have become conscientious objectors." For he honored their fortitude in sticking to their convictions. Again the circles disappeared one by one. A naval reservist decried the vandalism and called for tolerance. "Let's fight to make the world safe for the Conscientious Objector, for freedom of thought." His editorial led to wide comment, many students protesting the circles. To others, also, they did seem out of place.

At this same time, early December 1942, Mendenhall returned from the annual meeting of Quaker college presidents. He was eager to have Whittier join other Friends colleges—Earlham, Guilford, Haverford, Swarthmore—in the Nason Plan there formulated for training a small group of c.o's on the campus. The

Plan was already approved by General Hershey of Selective Service. The announcement that Whittier would offer such training appeared prematurely in the *Pacific Friend*. The Whittier *News* reported that Mendenhall would present the plan to faculty and board. On Monday December 7th, the faculty approved the plan "provided the curriculum could be worked out"—and this the Curriculum Committee was able to do.

Mendenhall then presented the Nason Plan to the college board on December 8th. No motion was made to approve it.

Instead, the trustees discussed "the whole problem" of the relation of the college to the war effort. "In order to clarify our attitude and instruction as to the *procedure toward men in uniform on campus*, it was recommended that a committee be appointed." The emphasis (here added) was not on c.o.'s, whom the college constituency largely disapproved, but on "men in uniform on campus." The committee prepared a resolution. Trustees were called to a special meeting on December 21st. Absent were several of the more militant. President Mendenhall opened the meeting with prayer. The committee reported its "unanimous" recommendation:

> RESOLVED that the Board of Trustees of Whittier College hereby declares its full cooperation in the war effort and offers all facilities of Whittier for training of youth of America to win the war and the peace to follow.

To avoid a showdown vote that would repudiate Mendenhall's leadership irreparably, younger trustees tried to table the motion to adopt. They failed. The Resolution received the necessary votes—it should, one trustee added, be published.

Then President Mendenhall again presented the Nason Plan—perhaps feeling that it might be approved within the meaning of the last phrase of the Resolution. But the motion, made and carried, was that Whittier was not "at the present time in a position to be placed upon the list of colleges" cooperating with the Plan.

The next motion was a directive "that the administration immediately seek" a part for Whittier College in the educational program of the Manpower Commission—that is, a military unit for the Whittier campus.

This Mendenhall could not do.

How much longer could he continue as president of a Friends college whose trustees were "fighting Quakers?"

NEGOTIATIONS WITH THE ARMED Services were carried on by Dean Spencer and Mr. Hockett. As for the Nason Plan, announcement was made "quieting the published rumor"—to some an ugly rumor—that a small group of c.o's would be trained on the Whittier campus.*

In early February 1943, Dean Spencer announced the likelihood that a unit of WAACs would be trained at Whittier. This was not quite "men in uniform" and in football suits. The plan was for teaching them in classes separate from the Whittier-Chapman students.

At their meeting on February 22nd, the trustees were concerned about "the reaction of some faculty members" to teaching such a military unit. The very thought of academic mutiny triggered a militant resolve that the contract of any professor refusing to teach students in uniform would be cancelled forthwith. For this harsh proposal, a substitute motion was offered and carried. A clause would be attached to faculty contracts indicating that the college was negotiating for student military units, and it would be understood that in signing their contracts faculty members agreed to cooperate in this instruction.

Three days later President Mendenhall drafted his letter of resignation.

This was not an angry or even wounded letter. Mendenhall cheerfully overlooked the sharp differences that separated him from his trustees. He simply asked them not to consider him for reappointment at the end of the year. He thought it time to retire. Working with them had been "an enriching experience." He expressed his appreciation of both faculty and administrative staff—their loyalty and sacrifices during the Depression. That was all he said.

The executive committee of the board met March 2, 1943 to consider Mendenhall's resignation.

---

*The other Quaker colleges did not fare well with their programs under this Plan. First the government reduced from 10% to 4% the number of c.o's who might receive such training. Then, within months, the Congress ended the program completely.

None questioned his sincerity in this statement [Harris wrote later], but all who knew the situation understood that a deeper motive was his conscientious objection to participation in support of the war.

Friends urged him to reconsider his decision. Three trustees, named to do so, conferred with him. His opinion was that "the best interests of the college" would be served by acceptance of his resignation. This the board did by unanimous vote, "with regrets and appreciation." Reports in the campus, local, and metropolitan press carried no hint of the inner conflicts that had brought about Mendenhall's resignation. Unaware of them, perhaps, Mrs. Hoover telegraphed her concern and hoped the decision might be changed.

As for the WAACs, no confirmation had yet come of the first published announcement. By May, it was not Girls in Uniform but men who apparently would compose the military assigned to Whittier. Then the Army proposed sending a unit of such size that it would have meant "elimination of all women from the school with complete dislocation of a coordinated college program." This the Board of Trustees could not accept—it was something more than the "full cooperation" intended. In the end, no men or women in uniform trained on the Whittier campus.

To the Test-Act clause for faculty contracts—and to Mendenhall's resignation accepted on March 9th—came unexpected repercussions. Dr. Manford Kuhn, a liberal Quaker and visiting professor of sociology, resigned abruptly to accept a professorship at Mt. Holyoke. Three days later, Dr. Alfred Romer resigned with a sharp letter to the board—and copy to the press. While at Whittier, he had become a convinced pacifist, and he could not sign the arbitrary contract-clause that obliged him to teach a military unit. Romer's resignation was final and left no room for his faculty friends to maneuver. It was a double rebuke to the trustees, and closed the door to compromise.*

A fortnight after publication of Romer's letter, the executive committee of the board accepted his resignation. Discussion followed of "the unfavorable reaction of several faculty members to

*Within a month Romer received a three-year appointment to Vassar, thereafter continued at St. Lawrence University. Friends wanted him back at Whittier, but it was a score of years before this could be proposed to him.

73. Inauguration of Dr. W. O. Mendenhall. 74. W. Orville Mendenhall, sixth president. 75-79. Faculty Members of long service: Dr. O. B. Baldwin, psychology, dean of men; Lucille Verhulst, physical education, dean of women; Dr. Albert W. Upton, English; Alma Anderson, Spanish; Dr. Harry W. Nerhood, history.

80. O. T. MENDENHALL BUILDING, acquired in 1936. 81. LIBRARY reading room. Dr. B. G. Whitten at desk. 82. SENIOR BENCH as rebuilt in the '30s. 83. MASTER PLAN for campus development (1939). 84. FOOTBALL CHAMPIONSHIP team (1934), the second coached by Wallace Newman, the third for Whittier (continued).

85. RUTH HAROLDSON, director, College-Community Orchestra. 86. MARGARETHA LOH-MANN, director, annual Bach Festival. 87-88. POET THEATRE productions: *Journey to Jerusalem* (Wesley Lewis, director); *Emma* (Paul Camp, art director). 84. (cont.) All-Conference: Arrambide (58), Nelson (43), Tebbs (17), Dahlitz (53), Rusk (27).

89. SUCCESSIVE DEANS of the faculty: Dr. J. Herschel Coffin (c), Dr. S. Arthur Watson (l), Dr. Harold F. Spencer (r). 90. JAPANESE Friendship Lamp. 91. WARTIME *Acropolis 1942*, photo by Midori. 92. THE WAR DEAD, later memorialized by plaque. 93. STUDENT WAR WORK, helping to harvest citrus crop.

THERE IS
YET A MAN
WHO CARRIES
A GUN IN
HIS HAND
AND PEACE IN
HIS HEART

RUTH WALKER

★ TO OUR HERO DEAD IN WORLD WAR II ★

1941   1945

ORTHOGONIAN SOCIETY
PAYS HOMAGE TO THE MEMORY
OF THESE VALIANTS WHO GAVE THE LAST
FULL MEASURE OF DEVOTION TO THEIR COUNTRY

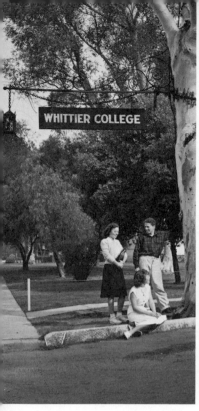

94. Dr. William C. Jones, seventh president of Whittier College. 95. Entrance, welcoming students returning to the campus. 96. G.I.'s, happy to be back in college life. 97. Quonset Huts on Palm Avenue (1946). 98. Provident Hall, war surplus building moved to campus in 1947 to supplement classrooms.

Team, l. to r.
R. Tuttle
C. Sherwood
D. Wardman
G. Martin
W. Moore
R. Hooper
H. Turley
Coach Bonham

99. BASKETBALL CHAMPIONS in 1947, with Aubrey Bonham. 100. TRACK MAN Russell Bonham, who went far and fast also in chemistry. 101. U. S. CONSTITUTION, Dr. Paul Smith lecturing to post-war class. 102. STUDENT COACHES with Dr. Roberta Forsberg. 103. LOU HENRY HOOVER, the Rieber portrait. 104. HOOVER HALL, dedication (1948).

105. ALL-COLLEGE PICNIC, annual event during these years. 106. DANCES by student body and societies. 107. NEW TELESCOPE, Dr. H. Randolph Pyle and students. 108. REYNOLDS BUILDING marked in 1947. 109-110. BROADOAKS: Mabel Rice, professor of education; new Broadoaks School on Whittier campus (1948).

Dr. H. F. Evans, the owner; C. B. Johnson, Dell Coryell

Mattie Wood Gregg, A. M. Otis, R. Ernest Lamb.

111-112. WANBERG HALL—groundbreaking (Dr. Jones, Mrs. Wardman, Mr. Otis); completed building (1949). 113-114. GOLDEN ANNIVERSARY BANQUET: John Foster Dulles upon presentation by Senator Nixon; the program. 115-116. COMMENCEMENT: honorary degree for Clarence E. Pickett; seniors in Amphitheater.

the clause placed on the contracts." The committee voted to eliminate the clause and to rewrite those contracts signed under protest. The provocative measure had not only been arbitrary, it had been unnecessary. And it had utterly violated the "spirit of positive tolerance" that the college board had so recently set as one of its aims.

With President Mendenhall's resignation, the board named Dean Spencer to serve as acting president for the interval between Mendenhall's leaving in the summer and the arrival of his successor. With resolutions of appreciation, the trustees honored Mendenhall at a special breakfast to which community leaders were invited as guests, and he quit the campus for his terminal month of summer vacation.*

Deep hurts and disappointments, of which a good number mark this history, have healed over in large measure by the spirit of good will and enduring loyalty to the ideals of the college.

6

THE CONTINUING COLLEGE PROGRAM
GRIM WAR-YEAR OF TRANSITION

THE PENULTIMATE YEAR of the war—though who could know that?—was a holding operation for Whittier College. Enrollment reached its lowest point and with fewest men since the close of World War I.

In World War II the year 1943-44 was especially grim, and Whittier men were desperately engaged on every front. Though North Africa had been cleared and Mussolini knocked out, there was to be a long year's fight up the Italian boot from Sicily—Salerno, Anzio, Cassino—to Florence. Ruthless bombing of the Nazi heartland and the build-up in Britain prepared for the D-Day assault upon the Normandy beaches in June 1944 and the summer's sweep through France. Action on the other side of the Globe was no less grim. Amphibious operations and mortal conflict cleared the Japanese from islands of the Central Pacific—at Tarawa, at Kwajalein, at Saipan, at Guam—closed slowly toward the Philippines and Tokyo itself.

*During his first dozen years of retirement, W. O. Mendenhall lived for the most part in Whittier, served in wartime and postwar Quaker work, and was welcomed as occasional speaker on the campus.

"How long, how long?!" agonized those, too, at home and on the Whittier campus. "And at what cost in lives!" . . .

Upon accepting President Mendenhall's resignation, the trustees turned at once to Dean Harold F. Spencer. They directed him "to make plans for the coming year as he sees necessary," and expressed confidence in his initiative. Seven weeks later, when it seemed unlikely that they would choose a new president at once, they made Spencer acting president. As such, he provided a transition in administration without disruption.

In his early thirties, Spencer was completing his third year as Dean of the college. He had already won the confidence of both faculty and students. For a year he had doubled as Registrar, and had curricular and academic details well in hand. He was an alumnus of Whittier College (class of '31), with graduate degrees in biology (M.S., U.S.C.; Ph.D., Cornell) and a year's research in Cytogenetics at Michigan State. Married to Pauline Terpstra, earlier of the college faculty, Harold Spencer was a family man and member of First Friends. He had worked harmoniously with President Mendenhall, but was willing to carry out the policy of the board in its full cooperation with the war effort.

From the faculty there were ten resignations or leaves granted in the spring and summer of 1943. These included Mendenhall and Elva Brown as well as Whitten and Kybal, Kuhn and Romer, Henley (who resigned to continue his work with A.F.S.C.) and Baruch. Also resigning were Hadley Marshburn '42, instructor in mathematics, and Dorothy Sheets '39, assistant registrar. These persons had to be partially or fully replaced—for instance, Wilma Bennet received appointment as acting librarian. But there was a good bit of doubling up and teaching in unaccustomed fields to provide the necessary courses. Classes were smaller as enrollment fell, but strain on the regular professors was greater, and surely the quality of instruction suffered. With the reduction in the athletic program, the college adjusted Newman's work and released Bonham part-time to direct city recreation.

THE FURTHER REDUCTION IN ENROLLMENT, and especially the scarcity of men, modified campus life at Whittier.

In the fall of 1943 Whittier enrolled but 294 of its own students, a loss of 30% from the preceding spring, but the number of Chapman students remained about the same. Fall enrollment at Broadoaks fell to 25 regular students, a loss of 50%. In the spring of 1944 there were yet fewer—268 Whittier students, of whom only 39 were men. These were men with physical disabilities—pre-ministerial, pre-medic and others with special deferments—a few men above or youths below draft age. At this lowpoint, Whittier College itself had but *half* the enrollment it had had in the peak fall of 1941.

"It was a woman's year," as the *Acropolis 1944* well said. But not wholly.

The four men's societies, with less than ten members all told, lapsed "for the duration," with the proposal that they merge their social interests into the Associated Men Students. The Senior Class included but seven men. "Chief" Newman directed a program of physical education for the 60-odd men on campus. Sports were essentially recreational, though a basketball team played a nonconference season of 22 games, winning 5.

The A.S.W.C. managed to keep a man as president much of this year. Earle Skinner succeeded Carl Bishop when he was called away. When Skinner left before the end of the term, Jere Rojas [Craggs] took over until the spring election of Bob Cauffman. They tried to maintain some semblance of a complete program of activities, and the Q.C. editor assured her campus and scattered readers,

"Despite necessary changes, we're coming along fine!"

And they were, too. But there was no Football Banquet in 1943 —no football—and Homecoming paled. The women's societies joined to hold their formal—the lack of student escorts made up by inviting servicemen from nearby bases. The fall semester Q.C. rated First Class. The College-Community Orchestra played an All-American concert (including Ernst Bloch's "Concerto Grosso") as part of a war bond drive. Poet Theatre presented an original folk comedy, *Hoosier Parsonage*, as a U.S.O. benefit. Bennie Shaw, a Chapman College Negro student, arranged an evening forum on the Handicap of Color, with particular reference to the crowding of Negro war workers into Little Tokyo, abandoned by the evacuated Japanese-Americans. "Radical" guest speakers condemned this segregation. Resentment (they said) was especially deep in their Negro kinfolk fighting in the armed forces "to preserve democracy in America."

WHITTIER MEN AND WOMEN in wartime service numbered 450 by the spring of 1944. Of these, 23 were women in uniform, and 22 men in C.P.S.

In addition there were uncounted civilians serving in various ways. For instance, Doris Williams '39—daughter of Whittier Williams, first child born in the pioneer town. She had taught physical education in Compton and Ventura junior colleges—and learned to fly. Then she became a civilian instructor, one of the first two women as such, in the Army Air Force. Another was Nate George '31, the track star. He had served 12 years in Y.M.C.A. work in Los Angeles and Monterey. Then he directed a large U.S.O. in Portland for Negro soldiers. There were many others.

Through publication of *The Rock* (edited by Jane Taber Randolph) the college tried to keep in touch with all Whittier alumni and former students in the Armed Services and in Civilian Public Service, carrying news of the campus and of those in camps and combat.

Whittier soldiers, sailors, and marines scattered out round the world. They wrote back their experiences: the draftee training camp for conscriptees—the beauty of Tahiti and willing native girls ("unable to give any firsthand dope myself")—the chance meetings of college mates as airmen in Iceland and in Tunisia. Then came reports of the wounded: Marine Capt. George Krueger, writing of "the reactions of men to the fierce battle" of Tarawa—and Pfc. Pete Lee, wounded in France, hospitalized in England. Airmen were missing: Lt. James K. Daniels, reported down somewhere in China; Sgt. Harvey Patterson, Jr., in Austria; Lt. Jim Gregory, in Germany, and then reported a prisoner. Infantrymen, too: Sgt. Merton Wray '33, captured and imprisoned in Germany (Stalag 3B); and, less fortunate than he, Paul Fouts —first reported missing in the Philippines, then a prisoner, at last presumed dead.

There were those who lived to be decorated, such as Lt. (j.g.) Don Craggs who, together with his skipper (Lt. Franklin D.

Roosevelt, Jr.), was awarded the Silver Star "for conspicuous gallantry" in Sicilian waters. And there were the dead.

Four gold stars more during the college year—and yet three more in the summer months: Lt. Wilson Young and Lt. Wayne Daily, killed in air accidents, the one over Palm Springs, the other over the Aleutians. Ensign Tommy Reed and Lt. Don Winters, presumed dead when their planes crashed in the South Pacific. Landsmen, too, died: Sgt. Roland Crum, killed in action in France, leaving an alumna widowed—and Hobart Cushman.

T/Sgt. Warren McCray—top scoring basketball player in 1943 —was in tanks, landed on the Normandy beach on D-Day. In the break-through that swept toward Paris, he was field-promoted to Second Lieutenant. He was the first American—his captain later wrote for the *Saturday Evening Post*—to see the Eiffel Tower through his binoculars, and he rode into Paris with his unit on August 25, 1944. Thereafter, he received a Bronze Star (his second) for meritorious courage in the capture of enemy troops in Belgium— an Oak Leaf Cluster in Germany—then was killed in action. Of the American youths, the thousands, he was one who saw Paris . . . and died.

Consciousness of these men—their duties and dangers, their service and suffering—was never far from the surface, in faculty and student body alike, during this grim year.

The opening pages of the slim *Acropolis 1944* bore the inscription:

> One struggle is never ending . . . continuing during war and peace . . . kept alive by at least a few . . . this is the search for tolerance, appreciation, and truth . . .

THIS TRANSITION YEAR presented continuous problems to the college trustees. They worked to keep the budget balanced, to maintain their strength in membership, to choose a new president for Whittier College.

With the Great Debt out of the way, interest payments no longer drained resources. But the decreased enrollments meant loss of tuition income. However, compensating for this was the decreased budget for instruction resulting from the shrinkage in faculty. In mid-year Howard L. Hockett gave the faculty "a very favorable report on the financial situation of the College." But he reported to the board that he anticipated an operating deficit for the year of between $10,000 and $15,000. Yet there was always summer session that, under the astute direction of P. S. Smith, could be counted on to turn a profit for the general fund. Its enrollment dropped 25% in 1944, but its gross tuitions still amounted to $13,500 and its net surplus was $6,000. Extension courses added another $3,000 net, and Broadoaks pre-school another $2,000. It was possible to end the year with only $2,500 listed as "decrease of accumulations," that is, operating deficit.

The year was not one, of course, for a financial drive or expectation of major contributions for endowment or development. However, one significant gift came to Whittier College at this time: the home of Mr. and Mrs. Aubrey Wardman.

This beautiful estate, a Mediterranean-style mansion on a three-acre site in Eastridge, overlooked the valley to the sea. The Wardmans had built it in 1925.

> With red-tile roof, the large house faced in on an ample court yard—stone paved, with a central wishing well and corner fireplace, and approached by a winding drive. With its setting of trees and shrubs, this home—as seen against the background of the Puente Hills—was indeed a picturesque villa, one of the most beautiful homes in the area.

Its value was $100,000 when, in the fall of 1943, the Wardmans decided to deed it to the college, retaining a life estate so that they might live out their lives in the home they so loved.* It was their thought that this home, less than a mile from the campus, would serve ideally as a home for future presidents of the college. But they did not "preclude its use for other appropriate purposes connected with the college," or, for that matter, any other disposition of the property according to changed circumstances. This handsome gift brought to $250,000 the total value of their contributions to the college they had already supported for a score of years.

Not realized by many was the sad personal loss preceding the Wardmans' decision to make this gift. In August 1943, Irving Wardman died after brief illness. Aged 44, he was Aubrey Ward-

*They continued to pay all taxes and other charges of maintenance and repairs.

man's only child, and had been associated with his father in management of his telephone properties in Whittier and Downey. It was expected that he would carry on for his father. Though Irving Wardman left a family, none of the grandchildren (it then seemed) would ever make the big house his home.

For Whittier College it was a significant contribution. As acting president, Dean Spencer spoke of the "encouragement and hope" that came with the gift. The president of the A.S.W.C. added his thanks for the students: it was a magnificent Christmas present. Walter F. Dexter affixed the State seal to his personal letter of appreciation sent from his office in Sacramento—this was a heartwarming sequel to that earlier gift of $100,000 made at the beginning of their friendship. College board and faculty joined in honoring Aubrey and Bonnie Wardman at their annual dinner in March. And it seemed fitting that Dexter be named to the executive committee of the Board of Trustees.

Other changes occurred in the list of trustees.

Esek Perry '07, who had served an earlier time as professor and coach, succumbed to a heart attack in the winter of 1943. He had served on the college board for eleven years. A respected Quaker, citizen, insurance man, he had possessed a quiet sense of humor. In the town contest to name the U.S. bomber paid for by Whittier contributions, Esek won the prize with "Earthquaker." He was not a pacifist. The college board established the Esek H. Perry Scholarship Fund, "to perpetuate [his] aims and ideals" of sportsmanship and integrity by providing aid to deserving athletes of good standing. Though Perry's former students, Whittier lettermen, and friends subscribed—and the Sunday School class he had taught so many years contributed $500—the funds in hand by the fall of 1944 were a scant $4,000. Albert J. "Mick" Madden '25 made a further effort, appealing to athletes who had themselves been helped with loans—and it was arranged that payments on outstanding loan accounts would be credited to the Perry Fund. Far from reaching the hoped-for $100,000, it never exceeded $12,500. But "Ek" Perry the man was not forgotten by those whom he had coached and taught.

Another important member was lost to the college board in January 1944—Lou Henry Hoover. In accepting appointment as a trustee in January 1935, she had written,

277

My very early association with the young town, and with my father's friends, the members of the original committee for founding the College, gives me a basis of real sentiment in such a connection, and I can but hope that I may be able to be of some assistance in furthering the welfare of an institution of fine promise.

She and her husband sent a gift of 1,200 volumes (from their White House days) to add to the Whittier College library. She helped in other ways, too, not least by her interest and occasional presence on campus and at board meetings. At the time of her death, the trustees had just decided to select an architect and site for a classroom building, to be constructed as soon as funds and conditions permitted. It seemed natural that, in due time, it should be dedicated to Lou Henry Hoover.

Four places on the board remained unfilled in the summer of 1944, and Lieut. (j.g.) Richard M. Nixon '34 was absent in war service.

AN IMMEDIATE PROBLEM that faced the board in the summer and fall of 1943 was the selection of the next president of Whittier College.

By the end of December, the special committee charged with bringing forward candidates, recommended the appointment of William C. Jones '26 (M.B.A., U.S.C., 1929; Ph.D., Minnesota, 1940). He was then professor of political science and head of the department at University of Oregon, and had earlier served Willamette University. He came with strong recommendations; older trustees remembered him well; the Whittier board was enthusiastic. Invited to accept the presidency of his alma mater, Dr. Jones accepted. On February 7, 1944, the board announced his appointment.

A month later, the president-designate came south to Whittier for a week. Dean Spencer presented him to the faculty—he responded briefly. Gerald C. Kepple '21, vice president of the board, introduced him at the annual Faculty-Board Dinner honoring Mr. and Mrs. Wardman—for the occasion, Dr. Charles B. Spaulding gave a significant address on Postwar Problems of Minority Groups in the Los Angeles area. For a convocation, Dr. Paul S. Smith, who had been Bill Jones' major professor 20 years earlier, introduced him, and Dr. Jones addressed the students on the Idealism of John Greenleaf Whittier:

> The basic tenets by which Whittier ordered his life might well continue to be the guiding principles of the institution to which he gave his name.

As a Rotarian, Jones was then taken to speak before the Whittier club, introduced by his fellow-Rotarian, Harold Spencer. It was a full week, and the president-to-be was indeed heartily welcomed before returning to Eugene to finish his year's work at the University.

As acting president, Spencer continued his responsibilities until Jones' arrival in June to take over his new work. At the end of May, the board minuted its appreciation of Spencer's service as acting president, "so creditably and faithfully carried on" during the year. The letter then sent him spoke highly not only of his "great talent for organization of scholastic matters," but also of his good judgment and his grasp of future plans.

If 1943-44 had been a difficult year in many ways—a grim war year indeed—the transition had been effected with smoothness and large good will.

There remained but one more year of war.

7

WAR'S FINAL FURY—POSTWAR PLANS
THE G.I. CAMPUS INVASION

THE TIDES OF BATTLE had already turned by the time the new president arrived on the Whittier campus in mid-June 1944, but there was still to be a year of bitter warfare. In Europe: the Battle of the Bulge, crossing of the Rhine, nutcracker that broke open Berlin, Hitler dead in his bunker. And in the Pacific: assaults on Leyte and Luzon, on Iwo Jima and Okinawa, then Hiroshima and Nagasaki, and surrender in Tokyo Bay. Death and destruction far beyond man's grasp.

Distant, but aware of the holocaust, Whittier shared the awful costs of war. This final year doubled its known dead. Older alumni—medical Drs. Lowell G. Kramer '23 and James A. Gafford '26, both lost in the last desperate encounters in the Pacific—and younger alumni and former students: Charles Webster, Ivan Wiley, Merlan Emberson, Robert Rotsel, Webber Callicott, and several others but briefly at Whittier. The total number of students and alumni in the armed forces finally reached 550, and 26 more served in the C.P.S.

The spirit on the Whittier campus in this year was one of "carry on." Enrollment fell no further—Chapman students a welcome fifth of the total 335—and in the spring came the first of the veterans. The academic program continued somehow and, despite strains and fatigue, professors wrote, lectured, and led conferences. Faculty joined students in their cultural activities, appeared with them in the Poet Theatre production of *Hamlet* that marked the 50th anniversary of drama in old Founders Hall. And, as prelude to the eighth Bach Festival, the music department presented three days of Brahms, including performance of "The Tragic Overture."

After capitulation of Nazi Germany in May, the end seemed in sight. On June 20th, President Jones spoke for the community at the harbor launching of *S.S. Whittier Victory.** On August 14, 1945, he was meeting with a committee of the board when sirens announced surrender of Imperial Japan. They paused in grateful prayer.

WILLIAM C. JONES '26 was in some ways like Walter Dexter, under whom he graduated from Whittier College. They were of much the same stature; both were undergraduate debaters; both a bit older than their classmates. Both came to the Whittier presidency with plans for its development—though these were quite different. Both were liberals—though not of the same sort. In many ways they were as different from each other as both were from Mendenhall, who served the decade between them.

William Charles Jones was born in Pittsburgh of Welsh parents, and grew up in southern California. His ebullient undergraduate days gave him a rich experience in student life. He majored in history and government, began work in public utilities, then taught high school while taking his master's degree in business administration. He went north to Oregon, spent twelve years in administration and teaching at Willamette Uni-

*Recommissioned in 1966, it was readied for another emergency.

versity. There, in the shadow of the state capitol, he was professor of business and public administration. For a time he studied law, but took his doctorate in political science. The University of Oregon called him in 1941 to become professor and head of the department of political science.

During these years he was an active Congregationalist: a corporate member of the national Board of Home Missions, concerned with higher education for Negroes in the South—a member also of the National Laymen's Committee—and assistant moderator of the Oregon Congregational Conference. Although not himself a Quaker, he was proud that his wife, Helen Fé Haworth '25, was a birthright Friend. Her parents had been missionaries in Cuba, where she was born. They sent her north to Westtown School in Philadelphia. She became a college freshman at Friends University (under Mendenhall), then transferred to Whittier, an eager student and French major. She was related to John Chawner, first principal of the third Whittier Academy. Dr. Jones himself had met or known all six of his predecessors when, aged 43, he succeeded them as president of Whittier College.

No inauguration seemed appropriate in those stark months to induct him into office, beyond an informal reception in the fall and a brief ceremony at commencement. Jones simply entered upon his work, and attended at once the Education session of California Yearly Meeting.

To keep whittier a "truly Christian, a Quaker College"—this was Jones' purpose as he stated it to California Friends on that occasion. And the superintendent, R. Ernest Lamb (beloved Irish Quaker and minister) prayed God's blessing upon him.

Attending his first regular meeting of the college Board of Trustees in August, Jones again stressed that Whittier was "a Christian college and a Quaker college," and he took occasion to sound a strongly liberal Quaker note in condemning the peacetime draft that militants proposed to enact while battles still raged. In his first talk to the assembled faculty in September, Jones added to his definition of Whittier as "Christian and Quaker" his conviction that it should be a liberal arts college. There was nothing incompatible, of course, in Christian, Quaker, liberal, and academic views that one might hold, and Jones invited both board and faculty "to deepen our understanding" of these terms.

Because he was not a Friend, he made a special effort to relate himself and the college to its Quaker roots and heritage. In opening faculty meetings, he often read devotional selections from historic or contemporary Quaker literature. He saw to the appointment of the Yearly Meeting superintendent to the college board. He invited Dr. Mendenhall to address student convocation. He pushed ahead with the Quaker library. He brought distinguished Friends to the campus and bound them affectionately to the college with honorary degrees. He was sensitive to Friends' concerns and testimonies, showed himself understanding of the conscientious objectors. Although he continued active as a Congregationalist, his family also identified itself with First Friends Church in Whittier.

William C. Jones became president of Whittier College expecting it to be a Quaker college, church-related to California Yearly Meeting, which he doubtless assumed to be its principal constituency. And by "constituency" (which he used in its political sense) he meant that body of persons whom the college represented, who presumably supported the college with substantial gifts and students, and to whom therefore the college was in some measure answerable. But within a year—and with more understanding of the Yearly Meeting and the relation of California Friends to the college—President Jones came to think of Whittier, not as a Friends college exactly, but as one "of Quaker ancestry." It had been "established" by devoted members of the Society—its "early support" had come from them— but its appeal had been increasingly to others. Jones had come to realize that the Yearly Meeting was altogether too limited a constituency for the college. He was ready to promote support from other denominational groups, describing Whittier as "unabashedly Christian . . . infused with an overtone of Quaker responsibility in the social order."

The immediate task in August 1945 was to plan for the future. Physical facilities (Jones told the college board) needed expansion "for a student body of 600"—but building would have to wait until after the expected post-war recession. The faculty needed enlargement and strengthening, particularly in business administration and economics. Veterans, soon to come home from the wars, would require no special curriculum and should "find their places in a normal college situation." But Whittier (Jones thought) need not expect a large influx of returning servicemen —they would tend to choose "schools with highly specialized curricula."

But they were already knocking at the door.

THE FULL G.I. INVASION of the Quaker campus did not come at once. However, in the fall of 1945—even without Chapman or a separate Broadoaks—there were 426 students enrolled, including 90 men of whom some were veterans. This 40% increase was matched in the spring by another 40%, "largely due to the influx of veterans." Already the total enrollment of 590 was greatest thus far at Whittier. By the spring of 1947, enrollment reached 928, of whom 556 were men, nearly 500 of them G.I.'s. There was a strong feeling that the college should do its utmost to help in the higher education of these men eager to "beat their swords into plowshares, and their spears into pruninghooks." But quotas had to be established to limit the number of lower classmen to be squeezed into the classrooms.

The number of students still increased, however, until in the fall of 1949 Whittier enrolled 1,374, of whom 815 were men. This was the crest of the G.I. wave. In the spring, enrollment was 1,313; of the 771 men, only half were veterans, of whom 200 received their degrees in June 1950. A year later enrollment dropped back to 1,100 . . . and already some veterans were called back to war.

Whittier College was not prepared to handle these increased numbers—nor were other colleges and universities. At the peak, there were *three times* as many students on the Whittier campus as in any earlier period, and enrollment had *doubled* before even temporary buildings supplemented existing facilities. There was a large measure of goodwill, however, as veterans and C.P.S. men were glad to be back in the mainstream of their lives—and the college was glad to have them.

The G.I. Bill of Rights made possible this higher education of ex-servicemen—and women, for there were 16 ex-WAACs and

WAVEs who enrolled at Whittier. The Veterans Administration paid up to $500 a year for the G.I.'s tuition, fees, books, supplies—and subsistence of $50 a month, more if he had dependents. Larger benefits helped those who had suffered disabilities.

Most of the veterans were new to Whittier—many returning to California after tasting its wonders while in training. They came with a patchwork of college, technical, and military experience. The faculty gave them college credit "for educational achievement" comparable to academic work. The registrar, dean of men, and counsellor to veterans—no less than department advisers—helped fit them back into the scheme of things. But they had to make up what they had missed to meet requirements for their degrees and (in many cases) teaching credentials.

The greater maturity of these men brought a new seriousness to class discussions, a determination to make high grades, an urgency of purpose. In the fall of 1946, six graduate students (all veterans) "made the Dean's list"—40 or more grade points as then calculated. Of the 33 undergraduates on that list, 21 were men. John W. Nicholl had earned 54 grade points—that is, A grades in 18 units. Perhaps competition for high marks was too great. Reported the Q.C.:

> Eager beaver ex-GI's poured into the classrooms to raise the average almost out of sight of fellow students. Forty-two quonset hut units . . . became known for their all-night sessions, as many men did not dare face their wives with low grades.

A good many of the veterans were already married and had children who disquieted their studies. Under the pressure for grades, cheating increased. The Associated Students asked the faculty to assume responsibility for safeguarding their class standing. The faculty then instituted more systematic proctoring and ingenious devices to forestall cheating on examinations. But there was nothing vindictive about these aids to honesty, and examination tensions were seasoned with good humor.

Other adjustments had to be made both by the college and the veterans. Many of these were personal. There were but few indeed of the men at Whittier whose traumatic war experiences left psychic scars that would not heal—aberrations that led in a few cases to tragic violence or to social rejection in the postwar years.

And some war marriages were but short shrift. Ex-majors and Pfc's, leveled out in rank, officer's caste forgotten, heroic acts and citations respectfully ignored. But there was a deep comradeship born of shared fears and dangers and suffering that sent G.I.'s off at times for a quiet beer together, and that made for an even closer fellowship in the men's societies as they revived.

There was reasonable disrespect, too, for regulations as such, after the constraint of military discipline. This was particularly so with some men in regard to "required" physical education courses. They also resisted "compulsory" convocations, and the Associated Students made voluntary three of their four Thursday convocations per month.

The Whittier tradition of "No smoking on campus"—challenged before the war—inevitably modified. To the expected freedom to smoke in dormitory rooms was added general smoking on the parking lot and sidewalk. These men were not boys now. Most of them came back from war drinking. It was at this point that President Jones hoped to hold the line, with strong personal conviction and approval of the trustees. Using legal advice, he rewrote the catalog statement on student conduct:

> Whittier College assumes that it is a community of mature students and faculty working in an atmosphere of Christian democracy. Regulations are kept to a minimum and the maximum of self-discipline and consideration for others is encouraged.

But the college reserved "the right to terminate the enrollment of any student" when it felt that this would be in its best interests. Specifically,

> The use or possession of alcoholic liquor by a student within or without the college is cause for disciplinary action which may result in dismissal.

Beer, wine, and liquor were not served at regular college functions, or at student and society functions regularly scheduled and sponsored, but the policing of students off campus in their informal groups was not, of course, possible. However, general sobriety and decorum seem to have been as high as in the pre-war years (which had not been without their problems), though there was doubtless more post-war drinking at beach parties and during vacations than there had been earlier.

Certain modifications in campus mores came *after* the passing of the G.I. wave—delayed results of the larger social change growing out of World War II.

THE ASSOCIATED STUDENTS had carried on during the last war year with women as successive presidents: Virginia Valentine in the fall of 1944 and then Mary Wiggins. These capable leaders faced doubly difficult tasks, but kept alive Whittier traditions until the return of former students who were part of the influx of veterans.

It seemed somehow "right," in a society ostensibly not matriarchal, to have a man in the driver's seat. So Bob Wright (veteran new to Whittier) was elected A.S.W.C. president in the spring of 1946. Student officers and college administrators formed a Joint Council to consider college problems. To encourage student leadership, the Joint Council nominated, and the faculty named, the annual recipient of the Dexter Award, established in memory of Dr. Walter F. Dexter, who had died suddenly at the end of the war.

Among the A.S.W.C. social activities were, of course, the varied and enjoyable dances. For instance, in 1947 a Boardwalk Promenade took place on the college tennis courts, with a 17-piece orchestra beneath a canopy. A refreshment stand served iced pink lemonade, with raised doughnuts at intermission. It was "stag or drag," attended by 400 students who danced under "twinkling stars and a new moon."

With the returning veterans, the men's societies again came alive. For each of them—Franklins, Orthogonians, Lancers, Penns—a nucleus of six to ten former members met to re-establish their fraternal patterns. But for these older men there was not quite the same involvement in the total student life. Yet the Penns again published the Student Directory; the Lancers pushed ahead with their chapel project; the Franklins presented the Bronze Shoes as a perpetual trophy for the Whittier-Oxy football games; the Orthogonians honored all the Whittier war dead on their memorial plaque in the O. T. Mendenhall Building. To these four long-established was added another men's society in 1948; the Sachsens, Don Donato, the first president.*

*Another women's society began the same year: the Ionians, Janet Leever, the first president.

Some of the pre-war clubs continued—S.C.A., the Peppers, Delta Phi Upsilon—and new departmental clubs started. Cap and Gown, a small group of senior women chosen for scholarship and leadership, served the A.W.S. and the college in a variety of ways. The faculty wrestled long and thoughtfully with the question of religious clubs. Should a Newman Club or a Christian Science club, essentially under off-campus sponsorship, be established on the Whittier campus? The decision was, No, but such groups should certainly be formed by the local churches. This was viewed, not as abridgement of religious freedom, but as safeguarding student liberty that might be endangered by outside pressures. Application for a Quaker club would also have been rejected.

Postwar musical activities continued in directions already established, but with the added vigor of increased numbers of students. Soon, encouraged by President Jones' special interest, a men's glee club again organized. And, for football season, a 30-piece marching band appeared in snappy uniforms—it won first prize in the All Western Band Review in 1948.

Journalistic activities, which had carried on so effectively during the war, experienced new strength with burgeoning enrollment. In 1948, a group of veterans led in publication of *Embryo*, a one-shot literary magazine. Jones, remembering his undergraduate forensics, encouraged renewed emphasis on intercollegiate debating. In 1950-51, Bob Hepinstall and Joe McClure won a radio debate series sponsored by the American Association for the United Nations, considering such topics as the admission of Red China to the U.N. They defeated teams from U.C.L.A. and U.S.C., Occidental and Pomona, and won an all-expense luxury trip to New York.

The Poet Theatre program changed hands in another "reorganization of departments." DeLisle Crawford (M.A., Carnegie Tech) replaced Cooper in dramatics, and directed a varied fare of classic and modern plays, including two more by Maxwell Anderson: *Knickerbocker Holiday*, in which the former Whittier professor twitted the Quakers, and *Joan of Lorraine*. Thesis productions served as training for a few graduate students. The versatile acting of Dave Mintz at this time was a stage in his progress to leading rôles in London and New York under the stage name of David Knight.

Intercollegiate athletics revived and assumed again their accustomed place. "Chief" Newman and Aubrey Bonham, farmed out during the war, evidenced no loss in their old skills.

Basketball got under way at once in 1946. The 1947 team, including such pre-war veterans as Bob Tuttle and Carl Sherwood, won all its conference games, and was judged by a rival coach as "probably the greatest in conference history." These champions were chosen to represent the State in the N.A.I.A. tournament at Kansas City—losing there after the first round. In 1948, the Poets finished as co-champions with the Oxy Tigers. Then in 1949, Bonham's team again won its championship—Bill Moore "the highest all-time Pacific Coast scorer," having made 1,625 points. After a spotty 1950 season, Whittier took the conference trophy again in 1951 with a new combination of men, who won all but one of their conference games. It was Bonham's seventh championship in ten years of conference play—including the co-championship in 1948, but not the nonconference success of 1943.

Baseball also began at once in 1946, the Whittier team winning 18 games in a non-conference season. In 1947 the Purple Sox were undefeated in conference play—in 1949 shared the championship with Redlands—in 1950 again won the trophy undisputed. But, as in prewar days, it was football that roused the greatest student enthusiasm.

The first postwar football team, in the fall of 1946, consisted mostly of veterans, who started off by beating Pomona 18-6, but missed taking the conference title. The 1947 and 1948 teams were memorable for strong players—"Buck" Jarnagan and Jack Brownell, Dick Tucker and Bill Payne—but lost as many games as they won. It was in the fall of 1949 that the Poets took their first postwar championship, with Whittier men chosen for five of the eleven All-Conference places. The Q.C. rhapsodized "the familiar peal of the Victory Bell," and called the year one of the greatest "in Poet grid annals." The 1950 season was almost as successful, and the Poets retained the trophy by tying with Redlands for the championship. Of the 22 chosen that year for all-conference honors, 7 were Whittier men; and the United Press picked Jim Stecklein and Don Axelson for its Little All-Coast team. Then came a post-season game at Christmas time in Mexico City, an All-Star team in the Silver Bowl, Whittier winning to close a brilliant season.

Certainly Whittier was back in business, and football but symbolized the postwar resurgence that came with the invasion of veterans.

8

POSTWAR FACULTY—NEW DEPARTMENTS
PERQUISITES AND PROBLEMS

"To UPHOLD THE HIGHEST academic standards"—this was a primary goal for Whittier College oft repeated by President Jones. He coupled it with his affirmation that Whittier should be a Christian college with Quaker overtones.

When Jones came from University of Oregon to preside over his alma mater one-tenth its size, he spoke kindly of his former professors still on the faculty—Paul Smith, Esther Andrews, Herschel Coffin, Howard Hockett. But he made it quite clear that Whittier, like other colleges, had "suffered a diminution of its academic excellence in the four years of the war." He assured the trustees that "no irreparable damage" had been done, and that he meant to strengthen the faculty at once by new appointments He exerted academic leadership, too, in other directions.

Within the continuing faculty, Jones encouraged professional growth. In 1945 the college board, upon recommendation of the Advisory Committee, approved a systematic plan for sabbatical leaves-of-absence, with approximately half salary.* By the end of the decade a number of professors used such leaves for graduate study or postdoctoral research and writing. In 1946, Jones secured an allocation of funds to pay expenses for professors attending professional meetings on the Coast and in the East. In 1947 he instituted a series of faculty lectures with the purpose of stimulating fresh intellectual pursuits. In 1948 he announced a budget item for the entertainment of professional groups on the Whittier campus. He also made a point of noting with appreciation faculty accomplishments—leadership in professional

*The college had previously granted occasional leaves of absence for advanced study, some of them with partial salary.

organizations, advanced degrees, summer appointments, writing and publishing.

Working with Dean Spencer and the faculty, President Jones sought also to raise the level of academic achievement in the student body. A more formal Honorary Scholarship Group gave recognition to juniors and seniors with high gradepoint averages. The faculty honored them at an annual Scholarship Recognition Convocation, with special lecture for the occasion. On April 6, 1951 (for instance) Dr. Henry J. Cadbury, Harvard professor and Quaker scholar, chairman of the American Friends Service Committee, gave the lecture and was himself honored with a Whittier doctorate.

To keep up the level of faculty grading—and thus the significance of the students' gradepoints—the Dean repeatedly made studies of the actual distribution of grades given by the professors in relation to the "grade curves" established by the faculty itself in 1946. He also reported to the faculty the rating of Whittier College by universities, based upon the performance of Whittier alumni in their graduate schools. Was the grading standard of the college too low? Was the instructional level sufficiently high?

In various ways President Jones fostered cultural values on the Whittier campus.

The college board paid for student admissions to concerts in the Philharmonic Artists series. Dr. John B. Lovell, Jr., of Howard University, spent a busy week on the campus in 1948 as visiting lecturer, speaking in convocation, in English classes, at the faculty-board dinner. Whittier undertook student exchanges with Fisk University at this time. And overseas students—Alfred Rath from Austria, Hanna Petersen from Denmark, Eduardo Keys from Mexico, and others—added to the cosmopolitan character of the college. The summer sessions (directed by Paul S. Smith) continued to enjoy the intellectual stimulation of such Institute speakers as Milton Mayer, Vernon Nash, Ralph Bunche, Aldous Huxley, T. Z. Koo, and Maynard Krueger, University of Chicago economist and prominent Socialist.

If Jones told the assembled students upon first addressing them that, as president, he definitely wanted "a fine football team"— and he got it year after year—his greater wish was for academic excellence. To achieve this, he proposed, not only to expand the faculty, but "to increase the number of departments."

DEVELOPMENT OF THE Whittier faculty in size and specialization went hand in hand with rising enrollment, the G.I. wave that crested in 1949-50.

Immediately upon his arrival in 1944, Jones secured the appointment of Aldus C. Smith (A.B., Willamette; M.A., Oregon; Ph.D., Minnesota) as assistant professor of government. But Aldus Smith, who reflected so closely Jones' own professional life and interests, died lamentably of a ruptured appendix within eight weeks of his arrival.

With the end of the war in 1945, Jones split off economics from sociology to make a new department of economics and business administration. As head he found Spencer D. Pollard (A.B., Harvard; B.Litt., Oxford [Rhodes scholar]; Ph.D., Harvard)— succeeded in a year by Richard C. Bernhard (A.B., Reed; M.Sci., London; Ph.D., Northwestern)—succeeded in a year by Peter F. Palmer (Ph.D., Stanford), who remained for a period of solid work. With him in business administration was a succession of men, Paul K. Schroeder (M.B.A., U.C.L.A.) continuing on the permanent faculty.

President Jones retired older members of the faculty. Maude Evans in home economics, named professor emerita, gave way in 1945 to Gladys Stevenson (Ph.D., Iowa State), who came from teaching at U.C.L.A. In the spring of 1946, the board set 65 as "normal retirement age," with annual appointments beyond that up to age 70. Dr. Herbert Francis Evans and Prof. Harry F. Henderson were forthwith retired and named professors emeriti. Replacing Evans, Jones secured C. Milo Connick (Ph.D., Boston), a liberal Methodist who continued through this and the next period as professor of religion. In Henderson's place, Gerald R. "Jerry" Patton (B.A.S., George Williams) carried on the Y.M.C.A. work in applied sociology.

The second department that Jones split was English. In 1946, he separated Speech and Drama from the work in Language and Literature. As assistant professor of drama, DeLisle Crawford directed Poet Theatre. In mid-year Herold Lillywhite (Ph.D., New York), appointed professor of speech, established profes-

291

sional work in speech correction. Of two other men added in 1950, Lester L. Harris (M.A., Denver, later Ph.D., U.S.C.) continued through the years. For more traditional work in language and literature, Jones added two men to the English department in 1950, Clarence P. Baker (M.A., Harvard) and John A. Stuart (Ph.D., Northwestern).

A third separation, in the fall of 1949, set up a department of Political Science and International Relations. As head Jones secured J. William Robinson (Ph.D., Stanford) who came from teaching at Purdue. P. S. Smith continued as head of History, but gave work in both departments. Soon added was a second man in political science, and Alex DeConde (Ph.D., Stanford) in history.

Additional faculty in the sciences included David F. Bender (Ph.D., Caltech) in physics, who came from teaching at Fisk; John Hamaker (Ph.D., Berkeley) both in chemistry and in general education; Beach Leighton (M.S., later Ph.D., Caltech) the first professional geologist on the faculty; Thomas T. Harriss (Ph.D., Wisconsin) and Paul L. Rice (Ph.D., Ohio) in biology. Of these, all but Hamaker and Rice continued through long years.

In Education there was a succession of chairmen after the war when J. Herschel Coffin was retired to half-time teaching: Wilbur H. Dutton (Ed.D., Stanford), then Edward M. Spencer (Ph.D., Iowa), finally John H. Bright (Ed.D., Cincinnati) who joined the Whittier faculty in 1949 with his friend Homer Hurst (Ph.D., Peabody), later to succeed him. In Physical Education, Elmer L. Johnson (M.Ed., Minnesota, later Ed.D., U.S.C.) began a period of extended teaching. In French, James F. Marshall (Ph.D., Illinois) began a decade's teaching and scholarly research at Whittier. In music theory, William H. Dale (M.M., Northwestern, later Ph.D., U.S.C.) began his continuing years on the faculty. In psychology, Eugene S. Mills (M.A., later Ph.D., Claremont) began a period of fifteen years' teaching, leaving at last to become head of the department and Dean of the Graduate School, University of New Hampshire. He was the only Quaker appointed to the faculty during this postwar period.

There were other appointments, too, of course. Some instructors and professors moved in and out of the academic revolving doors with one short turn. But, with all the changes, it was a remarkably stable faculty. Of the 64 full-time members in 1950-51, *half* had taught at Whittier for five years or more—almost a *third* had been on the campus for at least 15 years—and five persons had served the college for at least 25 years.

But though the faculty had increased 60% in numbers within six years, the student enrollment (as early noted) had already *doubled* by 1947. And if the faculty had increased 77% since 1935, the enrollment had *trebled* in the 15 years from 1935 to 1950.

It was a major administrative problem to find faculty personnel of the kind wanted to meet the goals that Jones had set.

CONDITIONS OF FACULTY employment improved greatly during these competitive years. It was a seller's market for academic wares. Securing a desired professor depended not alone on the salary offered, but on such factors as available housing. Fortunately Whittier had some rental properties at this time. Rewards for services, working conditions, fringe benefits—these assumed greater importance after World War II.

Of prime interest were faculty salaries. Full professors with doctorates, who headed departments, received $3,000 in 1944-45. Increases in the form of bonuses, raises in base salary, and payments to a retirement fund came gradually. By 1950-51 the base for top full professors was $3,875, plus a bonus of 27½% and another 10% pension premium, making the total compensation $5,327 before taxes. This was a 77% raise within the six years. Other faculty salaries increased proportionately, keeping Whittier fairly competitive with nearby colleges.

Soon after his arrival in 1934, President Mendenhall had suggested that some provision be made for faculty retirement, but it was not until the fall of 1946 that, under Jones, the college established a pension plan with Teachers Insurance and Annuity Association. In 1951, upon recommendation of the faculty, Whittier College also became part of the Federal system of Social Security. Younger and middle-aged professors thus began to build up rights and equities in preparation for their retirement.

Group life insurance and group medical and hospital insurance, instituted during these years, further safeguarded professors and their families. The death of Aldus Smith in 1944 and of

William H. Wright the next summer had double underscored the need for such protection. These perquisites made service to Whittier College more attractive.

Another sign of the times was the effort to "organize" the faculty so that its voice might be officially heard in matters pertaining to its welfare. A number of professors formed a chapter of the American Association of University Professors. By this time, too, the faculty members of the Advisory Committee—again, at Jones' suggestion—were elected by the faculty rather than being appointed.

The Policy for Whittier College, drafted by the trustees just before and during the war, finally established both faculty tenure and academic freedom in the summer of 1944. Essentially this was clarification of principles already in practice. It affirmed for the professor

> full freedom in research and in the publication of the results . . . freedom in the classroom in discussing his subject . . . freedom from institutional censorship and discipline ["when he speaks or writes as a citizen"].

But with this freedom was coupled responsible restraint—a warning to the professor "not to introduce into his teaching controversial matter which has no relation to his subject," and a general caution to remember that "his position in the community imposes special obligations." The statement managed to be both liberal and realistic.

In this postwar period—despite the crowding and inflation, the disillusionment and McCarthyism abroad in the land—Whittier was a good place to teach.

DIFFERENCES IN EDUCATIONAL philosophy inevitably led to some strains and tensions within the Whittier faculty.

Although President Jones was in many ways a liberal, he was educationally a conservative. He wanted Whittier to be academically "respectable." He wanted to conform it to traditional norms for the liberal arts college.

The reshaping of Whittier College had never been easy. Long tradition gave the faculty authority in matters of curriculum, degree requirements, and academic objectives. To work around the firmly-berthed faculty, the president could do little more than bide his time and bring in new professors committed to his academic values. But of the faculty of 40 that Jones inherited in 1944, 22 more-or-less supported the liberal philosophy of education that had been Whittier's hallmark for twenty years. These professors still comprised one-third of the expanded faculty in 1950, and of the newer two-thirds, only half were at all permanent.

About three matters President Jones expressed critical concern: the general objectives of the college—the integrated courses —the extent of teacher training.

Within months of his arrival, he asked the faculty to examine critically "the material in the College Catalog dealing with objectives." This the faculty did, and in due time prepared and approved a new statement for the 1946 catalog. Under the heading "Objectives of the College," appeared a general paragraph respecting the founding of the college, the Quaker overtones in its program and its oft-stated purpose, "to educate for Christian Democracy." Within this philosophy "as a matrix," emerged specific objectives:

1. The graduate . . . should take up his life duties . . . with a body of information broad enough . . . to give him a scientific conception of the physical and biological world and the human societies that people it.

2. He should be trained in the skills of criticism . . .

3. He should be able to communicate his thinking . . .

4. He should . . . [be] trained in . . . appreciations and recreational skills.

5. He should have developed a lively concern for the well-being of his neighbors and the world community.

6. Finally, it is planned that in his own way and in accordance with his own pattern he will have found the resources furnished by the Christian Faith.

Following this came "Principles of Organization," affirming that *all* departments of the college should share these goals. For the college

seeks to organize . . . the curriculum around the college objectives instead of around more conventional departmental goals . . . seeks as far as is expedient *to break down the traditional departmental lines* within the fields of knowledge.

Emphasis here added is implicit in the next statement regarding the Integrated Courses in the lower division and the principle of Correlation found in some of the upper-division work.

These statements were not at all what the new president had in mind. They simply reaffirmed the "whole man" philosophy of Coffin as implemented by Upton, said nothing of the new departmental emphasis oriented toward graduate training.

Whether dropped inadvertently or by design, these sections failed to appear in the catalog of 1949. But the faculty raised the question of their reinstatement. After reconsideration, for possible revision or rewording, the statement on Objectives appeared again in the 1950 catalog *unchanged*, but the related statement on Principles of Organization was dropped.

From the beginning President Jones was critical of Whittier's unconventional lower division program. Opening his second year, he "expressed concern" that the faculty reconsider the integrated courses. The next summer he reported to the board that the faculty was spending "most of its energies and resources" on them rather than putting "its main emphasis upon the upper division." The answer of the faculty was to ask Dr. Coffin to give six evening seminars on his philosophy of education. In May 1947 a joint Committee on Planning (trustees, administration, faculty) reaffirmed Whittier's traditional "social service emphasis" and its effort to build a curriculum around "the Whittier Idea," though with equal emphasis upon upper division work. This was certainly what the established faculty members wanted.

Criticism of the integrated courses continued. In 1949 the Randall text, *Making of the Modern Mind*, was dropped under what the students, at any rate, thought was administrative pressure, the book judged "too difficult for the freshmen." But the Q.C. editorialized in its defense and in defense of Dr. Nerhood's so-called Randall Museum of illuminating and enriching excerpts, documents, and pictures displayed weekly to make the text more meaningful. Difficult or not, again the students wanted Randall restored. But attacks upon the program were not without effect, and in 1950, the succeeding Q.C. editor, Bob Plank, pronounced Integration to be effectively dead!—team teaching done for, two of the three great texts deposed, the high purpose "stressing the unity of knowledge" balked by new professors' specialized interests. He was in part mistaken—the program, however battered, survived.

The third concern of President Jones was the "heavy emphasis upon teacher-training." In 1947 Whittier again won approval by the State for its work leading to credentials for teaching all grades from kindergarten through junior college, with special credentials in music, physical education, and home-making. Added in 1948 was speech correction. For Jones this work was incompatible with liberal arts education. The Dean underscored the danger in 1950. In the number of teachers trained, Whittier was 8th among the 31 private colleges, large state colleges and universities giving such training for the State. Half of all Whittier seniors were taking credentials as well as academic degrees. It was true that Whittier had no "education major"—all prospective teachers fulfilled requirements for a departmental or group major—but Jones thought the Whittier program "out of balance." Teacher training spoiled the image he held for his alma mater as a liberal arts college of high academic standing.

Partly because of these views, tensions marred President Jones' relations with a number of his faculty colleagues—notably with Upton, whose work repeatedly confronted Jones' efforts to achieve his goals. But the faculty also frustrated other of his wishes—to classify Newman as coach without faculty status and tenure, to replace Whitten as librarian on his return from military service, to shift the emphasis in music to more popular forms. Some administrative decisions, in a number of cases hasty, were accepted with reservations. It must be said, however, that the Whittier faculty—even as it grew with new appointments—was not an easy one over which to preside.

9

POSTWAR DEVELOPMENT, ENDOWMENT, BUILDINGS
STRAINS AND PROBLEMS

WHITTIER COLLEGE CAME THROUGH the war years in better shape financially than might have been expected.

The accumulated operating deficit was less than $2,000. The old burden of debt was gone, but in getting rid of it the college had depleted its endowment. According to the audit of 1944,

Whittier had total assets of $1,330,000.* Of this, $600,000 was in campus and plant, and $650,000 in endowment assets. Of the latter $150,000 was still tied up unproductively in the campus and Worsham property, about $75,000 was in student loan funds, and some $250,000 still supported annuity contracts. It was a woefully weak endowment fund—less than $200,000 actually produced income to support the educational program of the college. Half the endowment earnings of $20,000 in 1944 was owing to the high price of wartime fruit.

Financial development began auspiciously for President Jones. In August 1944 he called for some Friend to support the Quaker collection in the college library. A month later, Mr. and Mrs. A. C. Johnson made an annuity gift to the college of a store building in the center of Whittier, then valued at $100,000. Their services and gifts to the college had already spanned half a century. Susan Johnson had joined the faculty in 1895, and Clifford Johnson the Board of Trustees in 1902. And she, widowed in 1946, made a final gift of their home near the campus, valued at $25,000 and to be released to the college upon her death, which occurred in 1950. The Clifford and Susan Johnson Library of Quaker Literature honored their names.

No pressing need existed at war's end for seeking special gifts to support the operating budget of the college. As enrollment increased, the trustees raised tuition in four successive stages from $300, as of 1944, to $500 in 1951. Tuition thus kept pace with that of neighboring colleges. For the hundreds of G.I.'s, the Veterans Administration paid tuition and fees amounting to as much as $100,000 a semester. The increasing tuition income more than equalled the budget for the enlarged and better-paid faculty. But this bounty was not looked upon as normal or healthy. An enrollment figure of 750, if no longer just 600, was taken as optimum for the college.

The president and board recognized that Whittier needed the financial stability of substantial endowment.

Sizable gifts for this purpose, however, were not forthcoming. Some contributions came in, such as $10,000 from the Hadley Ranch, still owned by the heirs of pioneer Washington Hadley.

*Hardly more than the total assets of a decade earlier, but in 1934 the indebtedness was $450,000.

The college received welcome bequests, as from the estates of Elizabeth Lum, George W. Marston, Dr. Ralph Herman—further annuities, such as $25,000 from Mr. and Mrs. Jacob D. Williams—property gifts, such as the home of Mr. and Mrs. William Blott adjoining the campus east of Platner Hall. In one way and another the endowment fund increased until in 1951 it reached $1,250,000, which was double what it had been in 1944. But of this total, all but $600,000 was tied up in campus, loan funds, and annuities. A report of 1951 to Western College Association showed $36,000 of endowment income for the preceding year—the equivalent of 6% on endowment investments. If the productive endowment had trebled during these postwar years, it was still thought to be quite inadequate.

The major effort in fund raising, however, had to be directed toward building.

THE NEED FOR NEW COLLEGE buildings, clear enough in 1944, became manifestly greater with the overwhelming tide of postwar enrollment.

Upon President Jones' arrival, the trustees were already looking forward to $500,000 in new building within a five-year period, and "immediate erection of a classroom building." The decision in wartime 1944-45 to bring the Broadoaks school and program to Whittier for more efficient operation, called for a second new building on the Whittier campus. An annuity gift of $60,000 in 1945 from Mrs. Maye Wanberg, a friend of Mrs. Wardman, spurred plans for construction of a men's dormitory.

To match the Wanberg gift, the college launched a financial campaign in the fall of 1945 to culminate in a John Greenleaf Whittier banquet on December 17th at the Biltmore Bowl in Los Angeles. Quotas set for campus and downtown merchants kept committees working. Tickets at $50 per plate—except for faculty and students—brought in most of the $45,000 raised, for 1,000 persons attended the great banquet. Counting the $25,000 annuity-gift from Mr. and Mrs. Williams, the $60,000 goal was more than met. It was the first such banquet held since before the War, and the most successful since Dexter's original banquet in 1923. President Jones thanked Mrs. Wanberg for her generous gift. Ashton M. Otis, as president of the college board, announced "the new dormitory drive" had brought to $250,000 the total of monies "obtained during the past two and a half years" that were then available for building. It was again a memorable occasion.

Toward this larger building fund trustees themselves had contributed sums of from $5,000 to $15,000—Ashton Otis, Cass Rees, Dr. Herbert E. Tebbetts, Dr. Raymond C. Thompson, Mrs. Ella Peasley. Furthermore, the sale of the Broadoaks property for $30,000 added that amount earmarked for a new Broadoaks.* But for no one of the three projected buildings were new funds fully available. Nor could any new building start at that time, because of the scarcity of materials and government restriction on their use. More than a year and a half passed before the first necessary permit could be secured.

To meet the pressing need for housing and classrooms, the college resorted to temporary measures.

For housing married veterans, the City of Whittier, contracting with Federal Housing early in 1946, erected Quonset huts in the park on Palm Avenue between Broadway and Beverly. The college was to have the use of 20 units. In mid-May the college negotiated with the city for its construction of 22 more units (eleven huts) on East Penn Street across from Penn Park and the entrance to Eastridge. This location was strongly opposed by Mr. Wardman as spoiling the view from the [proposed] Wanberg Hall and as "an eyesore for the residents of Eastridge." His alternative suggestion—with the proposal of himself financing neat cottages instead of unsightly quonsets—was to locate this veterans' housing farther up Worsham canyon at the east end of the [proposed] stadium. He spoke up both as a friend and adviser of Mrs. Wanberg, and as a resident of Eastridge. But his offer was brushed aside (as he felt) without due consideration. An acrimonious exchange ensued between him and President Jones that resulted in Wardman's letter of resignation from the college board—though he was prevailed upon to continue, however estranged. The second group of quonsets was then located below Penn Street in what was later to be part of the civic center. Altogether 42 family units were occupied by college veterans.

*The Pasadena property, purchased in 1945 by a group of young Quakers, became the campus of an experimental school that in time became Pacific Oaks College, a degree-granting school of education.

To meet the immediate need for classroom and laboratory space, the college negotiated with agencies of the Federal government. During the year 1946-47, the board applied for five buildings, was approved to receive four, and actually got one. This building at Santa Ana Air Base, was cut in half, trundled 20 miles along the highways, and installed in the college Quad between Naylor Hall and Wardman Gym. Unsightly as the building was, there seemed to be no other place for it. The structure comprised four large classrooms that opened up to make a lecture hall seating 250 (and useful for after-game dances)— four small rooms accommodating the art department—four similar rooms for physics classroom, laboratories, stockroom. The government covered the moving costs up to $6 per square foot. In all the college paid less than $20,000 for this "temporary" building and its equipment that served well for two decades. The name chosen as the result of a campus contest was "Provident Hall." It seemed, in truth, a gift from above.

Permanent buildings came more slowly.

THE BUILDING OF HOOVER HALL was of major importance to Whittier College. It was nearly a decade in realization. The Master Plan of 1939 showed an academic building along Painter Avenue. In late 1943, the board named William H. Harrison as architect and started to raise funds for it. A month later Lou Henry Hoover died. Upon President Jones' arrival, his first undertaking was to press forward with plans for this building. In May 1945 the Herbert Hoover family made a memorial gift of $25,000, and the college named the proposed classroom building Lou Henry Hoover Memorial Hall. The expected cost of the building was $150,000. By the summer of 1945, Jones could report $110,000 in hand or pledges, and he stressed the need for further funds.

In May 1946, the government denied the college application to begin construction—perhaps the plan without the north and south wings might be approved. In any case the south wing posed a problem; to build it would require removal of the Campus Inn. With rising costs, a contractor's bid in August 1946 was $200,000 for no more than the central two-story portion of the structure. The board still hoped to construct the north wing and the cupola, asked for a supplementary bid. Not until May 1947 did the government grant the requisite permission—for the entire building, though the plan for a south wing had been abandoned. At last construction got under way; expected costs had risen to $225,000. The president sought contributions from the faculty no less than the trustees. A $25,000 gift from Mr. and Mrs. M. C. Lautrup named the north wing for them; a gift of $15,000 from Walter Dow named the Maude Hanna Dow Room on the second floor. As the building neared completion in the summer of 1948, $75,000 was still to be raised. Final cost was $250,000.

Dedication of the Lou Henry Hoover Memorial Hall took place in September in the presence of Mr. and Mrs. Herbert Hoover Jr. and Mr. and Mrs. Allan Hoover, who represented their father. Herbert C. Hoover was unable to be present—as elder statesman, he was busily engaged as chairman of President Truman's commission on reorganization of the executive branch of the Government. But Hoover appreciated the interest his wife had had in Whittier, and thought the dedication of the building to her "a fine tribute to her devotion to the college."

Two Hoover mementoes were given to the college—a group of 16th century Chinese porcelains, given to the college in 1945 by the former President, and a fine portrait of Mrs. Hoover, painted by Winifred Rieber (artist wife of Dean Charles H. Rieber of U.C.L.A.). It had been purchased by Mr. and Mrs. Harvey S. Mudd as a present for the national office of the Girl Scouts, of which Mrs. Hoover had been a leader. But women in the New York office "didn't like it," returned it, and Mr. and Mrs. Mudd made a gift of it to Whittier College.

Broadoaks was second of the new buildings. Smaller than Hoover Hall, it presented fewer difficulties. "To keep faith with the Brooks sisters," and to preserve the Broadoaks reputation, the college board wanted to build as soon after the war as possible. In the summer of 1947 the Government declared materials available. In January 1948, the trustees accepted a $66,000 bid for erection of the new school, the site chosen being the Crestwood knoll across Philadelphia Street from the otherwise delimited campus. Financing of this was no serious problem. Not only had the Pasadena property been sold, but the Brooks trust fund had appreciated, and the death of both of the Brooks sisters before 1940 had released the college from their annuity.

William H. Harrison designed an attractive model nursery, beautifully set, approached by the winding road above the arroyo. At the dedicatory dinner in September 1948, Dr. Roy E. Simpson (Dexter's successor as state director of education) gave the address; and Mabel F. Rice, professor of education at Whittier since 1935, began her service as Director of Broadoaks. The college announced scholarships named for the founders of Broadoaks; a portrait of Miss Ada Brooks found appropriate place in the new building; and something of the Broadoaks tradition continued even after the school was uprooted from the shade of the original spreading liveoaks.

The third postwar building to be erected was Wanberg Hall, the first newly-constructed dormitory on the Whittier campus in 25 years. The gift of Mrs. Maye Wanberg in 1945 of $60,000 together with the matching funds raised in the campaign culminating in the John Greenleaf Whittier Banquet that fall totalled about $130,000. Then in 1947 Mrs. Wanberg died, bequeathing to the college properties valued at about $90,000. Mrs. Wanberg had been the widow of Dr. George E. Wanberg, dentist with office a block from the campus. He had interested himself in the work of the Y.M.C.A. Appropriately his life savings were to be used to house young men at the college and to support scholarships for training Y.M.C.A. and other youth leaders.* This bequest consisted of rental properties (soon vacated for faculty housing), but the equivalent value could be invested in the dormitory, income from which would support the George W. Wanberg Scholarships. In the meantime, it became possible to secure a Government loan of up to 50% of the cost of veteran housing, but the trustees were as wary of such loans as they were of other indebtedness. The final cost of $210,000 was somehow met without borrowing.

The site chosen for the George E. Wanberg Memorial building was the beautiful shoulder of the hill occupied by the original homesteading ranch house of the Worshams, just east of the Government Laboratory. By arrangement Dr. and Mrs. Herschel Coffin had remodeled this cottage a decade earlier, expecting to live out their lives in it. Under the shade of pepper trees, it was a

*Mrs. Wanberg had also contributed $60,000 toward the new Whittier Y.M.C.A. building.

cozy and attractive home. But it stood in the way of the new men's dormitory—first college building on the ranch lands, bought for the college the year of the Coffins' arrival in Whittier. The board authorized Harrison to design a three-story reinforced-brick structure to house 92 men. The Coffins moved to a college-owned apartment, a bulldozer cleared away the ranch house, the president and trustees solemnized the groundbreaking—with Mrs. Wardman representing the deceased donor. Wanberg Hall stood complete, furnished, dedicated, and occupied by the fall of 1949, and the Woman's Auxiliary furnished the lounge.

It was President Jones' hope to construct also a new women's dormitory. Contributions for this were insufficient, however, and conservative trustees continued to oppose Federal loans. By 1951 no more than $52,000 had been earmarked for this purpose.

OTHER DEVELOPMENTS WERE not without interest. Another and smaller structure arose above and beyond Fire Hill—and at no cost to the college—a small Astronomical Observatory. Members of the Foundation Society first planned to build it themselves in 1935, materials to cost $200. One of their alumni, William W. Olsen '35, offered to provide a twelve-inch telescope. In due time, the college board approved the site chosen. Olsen, by then teaching at Pasadena Junior College, ground ahead at the lens, but a retired engineer, E. G. Richardson, offered his own eighteen-inch lens and built the mounting and mechanism for it at his San Gabriel home. At long last Dr. Pyle and his students dedicated the completed Observatory at Homecoming in 1947.* Its importance was far greater than its size.

A football field and recreation area were part of the original plan for the college use of Worsham canyon. As a move in that direction, the college removed its lemon grove east of Hadley Field and graded out a women's playing field, thus clearing the Quad for Provident Hall. Next came the leveling and turfing of Freshman Field—at the Penn Street entrance to Worsham canyon, where quonsets were almost placed. The question was how to finance a football stadium up in the canyon itself. It was expected

---

*The City almost blocked this project, for the proposed structure failed to meet Code requirements for school buildings. But the resourceful Foundation mounted the telescope housing on a track and called it a vehicle!

to cost $250,000. Conversations in the winter of 1947 with trustees of the Whittier Union High School District explored the possibility of a joint venture, but it was not deemed feasible.

In the fall of 1949, President Jones directed a campaign for funds for building Memorial Stadium. He appealed to students, alumni, merchants, the College Associates, and parents of Whittier men lost in the war. The A.S.W.C. met its quota of $5,000, but alumni responded without notable enthusiasm. Several pacifists objected to "memorializing war." One alumnus withheld support pending return of the college to the "moral standards" of 1920. The College Hills Property Owners protested that football in the proposed stadium would be noisy and game traffic inconvenient. With insufficient funds in hand, the college broke ground in June 1950—uprooted the orange grove—began grading in September. Memorial Field and track, with 220-yard straightaway, were ready for first use May 4, 1951—an invitational track meet with six lesser college teams, which Whittier won handily. Faculty and students spent a day in mid-May planting "hundreds of thousands of iceplant cuttings" and hundreds of olive trees to protect the cut-and-fill from erosion. Preparation of the field and track (together with grading a baseball field below it) was a good $75,000 start toward the goal of a Memorial Stadium.

Incidental to this development in 1949-51, and to the men's dormitory area on the approach to it, was the acquisition of the Ralph Robbins' home adjoining the campus at the head of Earlham Drive. The elder Robbins had purchased five acres from the Worshams in 1908, planted oranges, sold off lots facing Penn Street, built a handsome home. President Jones felt that this property was necessary for the future development of the college. After his efforts to purchase it failed, he sought legal advice. In the summer of 1950, the college instituted condemnation proceedings under the law of eminent domain. The legality of such action had been tested by U.S.C. and sustained by the Supreme Court. Within a year the court awarded the Robbins property to Whittier College and set the price at $39,000 plus costs—said to be more than the asking price that the college had refused to pay. It was never again necessary for Whittier College to exercise its right of eminent domain; and it may well be that securing the Robbins property in this way forestalled future litigation. The

Robbins' home, scene of student parties in earlier days, became a men's dormitory, College Hall.*

To summarize the development of Whittier College during these postwar years: Three new buildings and other improvements more than doubled the value of the college plant, from $600,000 in 1944 to $1,200,000 in 1951. During the same time the endowment also doubled, from $650,000 in 1944 to $1,250,000 in 1951—though only half of this (as earlier noted) was fully productive of income. Total assets of the college, then, had doubled almost exactly from $1,330,000 in 1944 to $2,660,000 in 1951.

10

THE UNRESOLVED QUESTION—WAR IN KOREA
END OF A PERIOD

"WHERE TO, WHITTIER?" was the question posed by the *Quaker Campus* in the fall of 1949. Bob Plank, editor, invited a series of thoughtful responses from five members of the college board, administration, and faculty. In one way or another they all touched upon the crucial and unresolved question: What, after all, should be the constituency of Whittier College?

"Does the college have a future?" asked Dr. Nerhood in the first article to appear. Giving strong support to the integrated curriculum, he noted realistically that junior-college transfers and departmental specialization had detached the upper division from the Whittier Idea. In what else, he asked, was Whittier unique? No longer Quaker, he said—no longer church-related—was Whittier to be no more than a small residential college "offering training in character and citizenship"?—turning out what he called "happy ditch-diggers"?

Next in the series was President Jones' restatement of "College Goals." He stressed his desire that Whittier be a residence college of medium size, democratic and cosmopolitan, seeking "the highest intellectual achievements" combined with "Christian goodwill, forbearance and responsiveness to human need." Third,

*As part of legal proceedings in this case, the college amended its articles of incorporation to state explicitly that Whittier granted equal privileges to all residents of the State "regardless of nationality, race or religious belief, who possess the required qualifications for entrance." But this had, of course, been the case at Whitter from the beginning.

306

came Dr. Coffin. He stated afresh his thesis that "higher education involves more than higher learning"—it involves "higher maturing." The future of Whittier lay, he felt, in nurturing the "full bio-psycho-socio-spiritual maturity" of its students.

Ashton Otis, president of the college board, hoped that Whittier would "remain a Quaker college," though not narrowly sectarian, and he called upon idealists to dedicate their means to its support and development. Glenn Lewis '15, also of the board, expressed his confidence that "the ship is making headway," and that "the destination is known and approved." He referred to the recently accepted Statement of Policy that had tried to answer the question, "Where to, Whittier?"

It was the sort of question, of course, periodically asked by colleges, especially by the private and church-founded colleges— the kind of question that never stays answered. However, Whittier College was perhaps unique during these years in the persistence of its efforts to phrase and rephrase answers to questions controlling its destiny. Even these five responses to the Q.C. editor's query showed the wide differences of view regarding what kind of college Whittier indeed was—Quaker or not, and of what kind—and what its educational ends should be. Faculty committees repeatedly worked over statements of college objectives— successive presidents and deans sought to reshape the college aims and goals—board committees time and again set themselves to long range planning.

The Western College Association pointed out in 1951 that Whittier was "Quaker in name only." As a statement this was both true and untrue, but certainly no Quaker constituency either could or would sustain and develop Whittier College.* President Jones had pinned his hopes upon proclaiming Whittier a liberal Christian college. He sought support from those denominations that had lost their church-related schools through secularization. For membership on the college board, he therefore secured appointment of Rev. Nelson C. Dreier, superintendent of the Southern California Congregational Conference, Bishop James C. Baker of the Methodist diocese, and Rev. Harold C. Case of First

---

*The trustees modified the By-laws in 1947, at Jones' suggestion, to permit appointment of Quakers other than members of California Yearly Meeting in making up the sixteen Friends who still constituted just over half of the college board.

Methodist Church in Pasadena. Were these not strong Protestant leaders who would tie Whittier to a more-broadly Christian constituency? But how could these churchmen, with other claims upon their interest and influence, do more than simply say a good word for Whittier as the way opened?

The Whittier board also needed a broader regional and professional base. Therefore during these years were added, educators: C. C. Trillingham (Los Angeles County superintendent), John L. Compton '25 (Bakersfield), Einar W. Jacobsen (Santa Barbara)—attorneys and doctor: Emory L. Morris (Santa Ana), Judge Philip H. Richards (Los Angeles), Dr. Homer G. Rosenberger Jr. '34e (Whittier)—businessmen and ranchers: Will B. Wickersham (Los Angeles), James E. Brock (El Centro), John A. Murdy Jr. (Huntington Beach)—and further alumni: Elma [Marshburn] Pearson '14 and Ethel [Koontz] Eckels '25 (both of San Marino).

These, together with Ernest Lamb and Walter Dexter, totalled 16 new appointments within six years to the college board of 30 members, and changed somewhat its character. But Dr. Dreier, Bishop Baker, and Reverend Case all left southern California shortly. Others also withdrew or died after brief tenure. Only five remained for continuing service through the next period of years.

The editor of the Q.C. (John Kelly) put it so simply: "Money is the main problem [of Whittier College] and how to get it is the big question."

> The solution—Answers to this one would win the jackpot ... but ... Whittier will never be able to compete with junior colleges and state colleges until it begins appealing to the moneyed class.

And he thought that certain current college policies (not specified) were not doing that.

He may have sensed the personal gulf that was widening between the liberal college president and the conservative mainstays of his board.

Two HISTORIC FACTORS marked the drift of the United States from V-J Day in 1945 to General MacArthur's peril at the Yalu River in late 1950.

One was the pressure for continuing military preparedness and a standing army with peacetime conscription. The effort during the war to pass a postwar draft bill failed, but Congress did extend the Draft Law through early 1947. Agitation for Universal Military Training began at once. President Jones spoke out against it. Representatives of the American Legion and of the American Friends Service Committee debated the question on the Whittier campus. The Q.C. editorialized in opposition to U.M.T. The controversy was heated the nation over. However, new draft laws passed the Congress in 1948 and in 1951. What might this mean for Whittier College?

A second historic factor was the renewed wave of anti-communism that followed the close of World War II. During the war, of course, the United States had been an ally, albeit an uneasy one, of the Soviet Union. In 1946 Richard M. Nixon '34 ran for Congress as a Republican, defeating Jerry Voorhis, prewar darling of the campus liberals. Nixon had loyal friends in both faculty and student body, but most campus liberals opposed him. Thereafter, they were not inattentive to the notable part he was to play in the inquiries of the House Un-American Activities Committee.

In 1947, as part of the S.C.A. program—renewed with the vigor of the preceding decade—Willa Klug arranged a forum intended to stimulate student discussion of vital issues. In her own view Fascism was a more dangerous threat to American democracy than Communism, and she viewed the current Red-baiting scare as a scapegoat to avert attention from an American-style fascism "promoted by big business." She secured President Jones' permission to bring "a communist, a socialist, and a capitalist" to the campus to lead a student forum—though Jones expected repercussions. Campus interest in the forum grew. The S.C.A. decided to invite the public to the meeting, which changed its character, and Willa Klug herself took material to the local paper. The *News* reported to its astonished readers that James Forrest, educational director of the Communist Party for Los Angeles County, would explain and defend the communist system—that Edmund A. Cooke, a lawyer son of famous labor organizer, would defend the capitalist system—that George K. Roth, secretary of the Whittier Town Meeting, would moderate the proceedings. It was a week already hysterical: Rep. J. Parnell Thomas of the Un-American Activities Committee demanded prosecution of Henry A. Wallace as "favoring the Communists" in Greece, and local supervisors wanted to outlaw the Communist Party in Los Angeles County. Under sudden pressure, Jones cancelled the Forum—he had authorized no such public meeting—and the *News* reported to the citizenry that the conflicting ideologies would be sufficiently explained to students through the college textbooks. The question of Freedom of Discussion was sharply debated, however, in the columns of the Q.C.

Then in June 1950 divided Korea was suddenly at war. Communists from the North invaded the South, determined to reunite and control the nation. Intervention by the United Nations to keep the peace received its principal support from the United States. For this renewal of war, the peace-time military draft and the anti-communist phobia prepared the way.

For Whittier College—as Jones reported to the board in late November 1950—it was again "a day of crisis." He said, "In a situation of complete or partial national mobilization its program can be altered, its financial base weakened, its ideals impaired." He felt that the college "must again examine itself in the pitiless light of a world situation" that would test its stability and strength. "Whittier College is a 'Quaker' institution. It is proud of that appellation." He spoke out for reasonableness and understanding—freedom of discussion—and he lamented the world's drift toward "becoming more authoritarian in its economic, political and social philosophy."

Already the U.N. troops under General MacArthur's command, having reached the Yalu River and threatened the border of Communist China, had triggered an overwhelming counter-offensive of Chinese Reds. Even while students joined in President and Mrs. Jones' annual Christmas party—with singing, story, sweets, sparkling tree, and Santa Nerhood—20,000 U.S. marines and infantry hacked their way back from the Changjin Reservoir toward the Korean coast.

The Whittier football men, playing their post-season game in Mexico City—would they again be drawn off to fight a Third World War on the far side of the Earth?—even before the Second had officially ended?

THE GOLDEN ANNIVERSARY BANQUET of Whittier College on March 31, 1951 was intended as conclusion of the dozen years' off-and-on celebration that had begun, without much success, in 1939,

With a committee (including the able assistance of Duncan G. Wimpress, director of public relations since 1946), President Jones directed the planning. Recalling the importance of Winston Churchill's historic Iron Curtain address at small Westminster College in Missouri in 1946, the committee hoped to signalize the occasion with some speaker of international note. Through Richard Nixon, just then seated in the Senate, the college approached John Foster Dulles, who had been flying about the world patching up agreements toward concluding a peace treaty. From the southern California rim of the Pacific and the rostrum of the Quaker college, might he not wish to say something about it? He accepted the invitation.

This semicentennial year had already been in process of celebration with professional meetings on the Whittier campus— political scientists, mathematicians, chemists, English professors, student teachers, the Youth and Government Conference, the Western College Association. The Golden Anniversary Dinner at the Los Angeles Ambassador was to be the crowning event.

Of the long list of notables invited, however, regrets came from Governor Earl Warren, Lieutenant Governor Goodwin Knight, senior Senator William Knowland, Rep. [Dem.] Chet Holifield, Mayor Fletcher Bowron, Commissioner of Education Earl McGrath. However, 700 persons did attend the beautifully arranged banquet at $100 per couple—$15 to faculty—and ate for their money Jumbo Shrimp Supreme . . . Strained Gumbo en Tasse . . . Boneless Squab Chicken, Narcisse . . . Chocolate Glace, Petits Fours, Demi Tasse.

At the speakers' table, with student and alumni representatives, President William C. Jones '26 made the introductions— Dr. W. O. Mendenhall gave the invocation—the Honorable Richard M. Nixon '34, junior Senator from California, served as master of further ceremonies—Dr. Paul S. Smith of the faculty summarized "A Half-Century of Service"—the A Cappella Choir sang, Eugene Riddle, director—and the Honorable John Foster Dulles, Ambassador-at-large, addressed the audience before him on "Peace in the Pacific." It was a major foreign policy speech, carried by the CBS network of 197 radio stations.

311

In his carefully prepared address, Mr. Dulles outlined the terms for a Treaty of Peace with Japan. It was to be a peace of reconciliation, "not the kind of peace which victors usually grant to a vanquished nation." This peace settlement, while confirming "the cut-back of Japan's territory to her home islands," looked forward to Japan's being "a sovereign and sustaining member of the free world."

> She would contribute in due course to collective security in accordance with her means, but without developing armament which could be an offensive threat . . . Japan would be restored to a position of equality, free of burdensome and discriminatory conditions

The major objective (Mr. Dulles said) was to bring the Japanese people "to live with others as good neighbors."

> The peace would be a peace of trust, not because the past justifies trust, but because the act of extending trust usually evokes an effort to merit trust . . .

This pronouncement of magnanimous peace terms was indeed the effective end of World War II in the Pacific. However, the Ambassador could not but refer in closing to the American contribution to "the United Nations effort in Korea, which fends off danger to Japan, to our Pacific allies, as well as to ourselves" . . .

Attention in Japan focused upon this historic moment. Came a cablegram from a Whittier alumnus and leading journalist in Tokyo:

CONGRATULATIONS FIFTIETH ANNIVERSARY BANQUET STOP ALL JAPAN AWAITING JOHN FOSTER DULLES SPEECH STOP GORO MURATA CLASS OF THIRTY NIPPON TIMES

The Japanese "friendship lamp" had already been restored on the Whittier campus.

But this "United Nations effort in Korea," how great would it have to be? And how far might war in Korea again place the Friends college in jeopardy? And what further anxieties and problems lay beneath the surface upon this gala and momentous occasion?

Little did the gathered friends of Whittier College know that Dr. William C. Jones, with tension grimly visible in his expression that night, had determined to lay aside these anxieties and problems that were only incidental to the world scene.

THE RESIGNATION OF Dr. Jones as president of Whittier College was already drafted that Saturday night of the Golden Anniversary Banquet.

On Monday afternoon, the faculty—meeting at its accustomed hour—was shocked by President Jones' announcement that he was quitting. At the same hour, the college board met on special call to receive and consider his letter of resignation. Earlier that day in Los Angeles, 300 representatives of Congregational churches unanimously elected him the new superintendent of their Southern California Conference, the first layman to serve the denomination in this capacity.

Why did he resign? He assured the faculty in that hour that "no pressure had been applied on him to leave." How important was the reason that he gave, "that Whittier College should move away from the narrow sectarian control still in evidence?" To avoid "acrimony," he decided to withdraw, but then he added that "his relations with the Board were friendly."

Frustrations were evident in Jones' work with both board and faculty—disappointments, too, that support he had sought had not been found. Even the sharp drop in enrollment, the disheartening prospect of large-scale war in the Orient, the tightening of anti-liberalism   these did not force his decision. Beyond his evident desire to give himself more fully to the work of Christian layman, were reasons that perhaps he himself did not fully understand. And he left behind him a college community puzzled why a man of his evident ability could not solve such problems as may have seemed to block the future.

Dr. Paul S. Smith rose in the faculty meeting to speak a word of appreciation for the work of Dr. and Mrs. Jones. It could not then be foreseen that Jones' resignation ended one period—or that Smith would preside over the next period—in the history of Whittier College.

V

NEW DIMENSIONS OF COLLEGE GROWTH

(1951-1967)

GRAVE PROBLEMS CONFRONTED Whittier College at the time of its semicentennial banquet in the spring of 1951. That magnificent occasion, with its historic announcement of peace for Japan, obscured the sobering significance of the 50th anniversary of the college chartering—the 60th, in fact, of its permanent founding in 1891. The glowing tribute to Whittier's "Half-Century of Service" did not fully appraise the long years of struggle and the paucity of enduring achievement. Progress there had been—but grinding poverty was still there.

The unresolved war in Korea, the spiraling inflation in the national economy, the sudden drop in college enrollments everywhere—these were the larger setting for the institutional problems and personal crisis that led to the resignation of President William C. Jones at that time.

For the future of Whittier College, much would depend—perhaps everything would depend—upon the choice of his successor.

1

THE PROFESSOR OF HISTORY BECOMES PRESIDENT
OF THE LIBERAL ARTS COLLEGE

A HOOSIER SCHOOLMASTER, tall and rangy—a shaggy Wendell Willkie of a man, with homespun earnestness, folksy humor, and canny drive—Dr. Paul Smith was ready to begin his thirtieth year as professor of history when, upon the resignation of his former student, he was named President of Whittier College.

Born in 1897 of sturdy Quaker stock, with Pennsylvania and

Virginia roots, Paul Samuel Smith grew up on a farm just north of Richmond, Indiana. He inherited an iron constitution, was early inured to working a long week with chores on Sunday. From boyhood he arose betimes. (Later in life he phoned colleagues at 6 a.m. and wondered why they yawned.) Country school and public high school brought him to nearby Earlham College. There he excelled in public speaking and debate. World War I interrupted his studies—but briefly. Drafted, he was sworn in early on the morning of November 11, 1918, and entrained for camp. The war ended at 11 a.m. The train stopped, Pvt. Smith was mustered out; "a grateful government paid him one dollar for his tour of duty." He returned to his books, and took his A.B. from Earlham in 1919. He went to the University of Wisconsin for graduate work (M.A., 1921) and as a fellow and teaching assistant in the department of History. By 1922 he had taken two years of law and further work toward his doctorate. His Ph.D. thesis (1927) was a study of Copperhead sentiment among Northern Democrats.

Young Paul Smith was a black-haired, bespectacled novice when, aged twenty-five and a bachelor, he came out West in 1922 to head the department of history and social sciences at Whittier College. The salary was $2,000. With the help of a part-time instructor, he taught all courses then given in the vast field assigned him. At first he was ill at ease, frightened some of his students, but soon he became the sort of gifted and popular teacher on whom sophomores played good-natured jokes. Tried by kangaroo court on a Wild West campus day, he was "jailed" only to be "sprung" by his loyal department majors! About him fabulous legends grew. Lecturing intently, his hair unruly, his necktie askew, he would hike up his loosely belted pants to mark a pause or a point. At his classroom jokes he too would laugh—a warmly generous yak (it is said) that could be heard for a quarter mile.

With his tattered oversize copy of "Sir Esmé," his illegibly scriggled reams of class notes, his forensic skill and dramatic anecdotes and moving quotations—he was a first-rate practitioner of "the higher vaudeville." It was memorable to hear him weave a patch in constitutional history, light up a paragraph in Parrington, or sketch in sharp strokes and bright colors that representative American, P. T. Barnum, who pointed the way to the "egress!" As one student remarked, "When you go into P.S.'s class, you never know if you're going to get the Bob Hope show, Dr. I. Q., or Groucho Marx."

Throughout his 29 years of teaching—under six presidents and acting presidents of Whittier College—Paul Smith was a studious and busy member of the faculty. His office was stacked high with books, filing cabinets, piles of papers. There he wrote his *American Political Institutions and Social Idealism* (1928) and *A New Approach to the American Constitution* (1933), published as textbooks. He contributed articles to both the *Encyclopedia Americana* and the *Britannica*. In later research he traced the history of the Electoral College, and the interplay of personal forces in the Constitutional Convention. He reviewed books for historical journals. He lectured widely in southern California on a broad range of subjects and occasions, with a thoughtful mixture of scholarship and current comment. In such addresses he showed a rare sense of timing and rapport with his listeners. He knew just when to throw in a homely phrase from Abraham Lincoln, whose humane idealism and political gifts he knew so well—or an unpublished quote from Woodrow Wilson, historian turned president. Dr. Smith had become the respected spokesman for the faculty when he addressed the semicentennial banquet at the Ambassador in the spring of 1951.

But there were other sides to his complex nature. He was born during the impoverishing depression of the 1890's. A certain string-saving prudence tempered his life. When he came to Whittier to teach, there was no Social Security, there was no pension plan. Professors had to husband their small salaries—save and invest—or retire at last in genteel poverty. They hustled to increase their meager incomes—extra teaching or lectures. It was not yet a time when faculty wives worked. P. S. Smith was one of the leaders of the faculty for twenty years in presenting to the trustees the professors' needs for better and more stable salaries. More than this, he was the chief promoter and director of the summer school. Through a dozen years he so managed it as to pay its instructors well and make a substantial profit for the general fund. This then assured the hoped-for bonus on spring salaries. In all this he was indefatigable. What means the

Smiths themselves acquired was essentially by the exercise of "Hoosier and Republican virtues": careful management, cautious investment, hard extra work. This economic schooling predisposed Paul Smith to the private-enterprise view of life. He admired such self-made men as Walter Dexter, Aubrey Wardman, and Herbert Hoover.

Yet, what was there about Professor Smith that made the trustees think he would really make a good president for Whittier College?

As a matter of fact—some had their doubts. For all of his personal involvement in the affairs of campus, church, and community, a measure of detachment characterized Paul Smith. Was it scholarly detachment, some wondered, or was it "indecisiveness"? Or was he something of a mugwump, in the political sense of being independent?

Smith had been seriously considered for the college presidency in 1943-44. Now, with the resignation of President Jones in 1951, Smith's name was again brought forward—by personal friends among the trustees, by strong voices in the faculty, by alumni and community leaders. The board committee on selection presented his name to the full Board of Trustees at its regular May meeting. No other candidate was urged. Yet there was that lingering question: shouldn't an outside man be brought in? However unanimous, it was a qualified approval that the trustees gave for Smith's appointment.

> This choice [as it was minuted] may lack some of the impetus which new blood might give, but Dr. Smith's general fitness [for] achieving unity out of frictions and factions which have grown up, seems the most important need right now.

For a few quiet and healing years, then, might not Professor Smith be just the man? After all, no president of Whittier College had outlasted a decade. But perhaps the trustees were only hedging their bets.

What was Whittier College in 1951? What were the grave problems confronting it? What "frictions and factions" had grown up in its midst that now called for mending?

FOR PUBLIC CELEBRATION of Whittier's Golden Anniversary, Professor Smith could extol its "Half-Century of Service." But in private reflection, once he had become its president, the fruits of these fifty or sixty years seemed to him woefully meager. Such corporate effort and sacrifice and struggle! So little finally to show for it!

Total assets of the college exceeded $2,500,000, it is true—which was just twice what it had been at the end of the War—but Whittier was still plagued, as it had been from the start, with "an insidious kind of poverty," as Smith soon realized. The Whittier campus, so pitifully small and hilly from the start, was still restricted, its periphery saw-toothed with indentation of private properties. The Worsham ranch, dearly bought in the early 'twenties and dearly paid for in the later 'thirties, was difficult of access and of limited use. The college plant—although three new buildings had been added in the late 'forties to the three permanent buildings of the 'twenties and one permanent acquisition of the 'thirties—was in large part outmoded and outworn: Founders Hall and Naylor, Redwood and Provident, Bolte and old Campus Inn. And another great lack was endowment. Of the $1,250,000 in such funds, only $600,000 was free from annuity obligation to support the educational program.

Gains there certainly had been since the end of the war—beyond the inestimable values in hundreds of young men and women trained and educated. Hoover Hall promised a better "front" for the college, though still lacking its south wing and nuzzling the unsightly hulk of old Campus Inn. Across Philadelphia Street—which bounded the campus as cornered by the O. T. Mendenhall Building and Bolte Hall on Berkeley Way—now stood the new Broadoaks Nursery School on its picturesque knoll above the arroyo. Way around to the southeast stood new Wanberg Hall, just above the United States Government Laboratory —the first college building on Worsham land. And farther up in Worsham Canyon, the long dream of a stadium had gotten as far as Memorial Field completed for practice use and spring track. Solicitation of funds for a new women's dormitory, however, had brought in but $52,000 earmarked for that purpose.

The immediate post-war period of expansion—Smith certainly realized—was suddenly closing. The crest of the G.I. enrollment boom was past. Young men were being called back into military service by the war in Korea. From the peak of 1375 students in the fall of 1949 there had already been a drop of 10% for the fall of 1950—and 10% more for the spring of 1951—at a time when the faculty had been enlarged. There was a squeeze, then, between shrinking tuition income and increased budget. It had been possible, however, for the college to end that year 1950-51 in the black—but with no operating surplus and the threatening of small reserves. Vis-à-vis its sister colleges in southern California, which had forged ahead in the post-war years, Whittier seemed by comparison to be losing ground. Upon reflection, Smith felt that "the college was still abjectly poor in a day when it was difficult for a poor college to be a good one."

Earlier, when asked by a trustee whether, if he were president, he could raise money for Whittier College, Smith had answered with the unbounded confidence of a Walter Dexter:

"I can raise as much money each year as any of the presidents during his entire tenure."

If he couldn't, he added, he should quit or be fired.

It must have seemed highly improbable that he could. But, as for "achieving unity out of frictions and factions," Smith might be able to do that.

Within the Board of Trustees there were certainly differences of view and emphasis. Newly appointed trustees, as already noted, found themselves uncomfortable with the conservative establishment. Personal and acrimonious difference between the resigned-president and the chief benefactor of the college— whatever their basis in misunderstanding—remained an unhealed wound. Wardman was an Achilles, withdrawn in wrath to his tent. Might not Paul Smith be a more-successful Odysseus to win him again to battle?

Within the faculty, too, frictions had developed—few open breaks certainly, but flaws and fracture lines. Was Paul Smith a sufficient Nestor to mend and harmonize these differences?

With the students on campus, with the alumni, with community leaders pretty generally, Smith had wide popular support.

The resolute acceptance by the college board of President Jones' resignation closed a chapter in the history of Whittier College. It was not so clear, however, that the appointment of Paul S. Smith as his successor really opened a new chapter.

It might have ushered in no more than a conciliatory interlude.

Before accepting the presidency of Whittier College, Paul Smith had called on his old friend Aubrey Wardman. As a young professor, he and his wife had played bridge in the home of Aubrey and Bonnie Wardman; thereafter Paul and Lillian Smith counted the Wardmans as friends. But during the years of Wardman's estrangement from the college. Dr. Smith had assiduously avoided seeing him or entering the fray. Now, however, he felt free to call on him.

"Aubrey, they've offered me the presidency of the college."

"Glad to hear it, Paul—and I hope you take it."

"I can't, except on one condition—that you'll come back to active service on the college board."

Wardman thought a moment, his lips pursed. "I've been hurt when the college—and the board—have turned down offers I've made to help. . . . But Whittier College is bigger than any of us, Paul. . . . You can count on me."

What was expected to be a two-year's wooing of Wardman back into the fold, was accomplished in fifteen minutes before Smith undertook his new work.

Otherwise, it was a slow beginning.

No fanfare marked the inauguration of the eighth president of Whittier College. P. S. Smith wanted no elaborate ceremony such as he had helped organize for W. O. Mendenhall in 1934— its ironic recessional, the brisk measures of "Marche Militaire." And once in the President's Office, Smith had his misgivings.

"Things look different from this side of the desk," he said as Jones had said before him.

Smith was now, not asking, but denying. Whereas he had earlier led the faculty pressure for salary raises, he now found himself having to restrain faculty demands. At a faculty meeting during this first year, he paraphrased James Harrington's utopian proposal (made in George Fox' time) that the presidency should be passed around annually from one to another of the professors. But there was no other Samuel to heed and answer "Lord, here am I," and this call was not repeated.

Of the presidents of Whittier College, Smith was the first to be taken directly from the ranks of the faculty. In some ways this made for an easy administrative transition. Everyone in the faculty knew Paul Smith—and his presumed faults. Everybody took for granted his virtues. Few recognized his less-obvious strengths. That he was conservative in temper, friend and mentor of Senator Nixon, was accepted with some show of tolerance by liberal professors. As president (some on the faculty felt) Smith would not rock the boat. And he came into office with no new philosophy of education, no grandiose development program, no announced master plan. There was confidence that all would be well in Zion—but would it?

The downward trend of enrollment continued. Another 16% drop in student body in the fall of 1952, as compared to the preceding fall, further reduced tuition income. Faculty members who resigned were not replaced—the new president notified several recent additions to the faculty to seek other positions. He directed the business manager to reduce expenditures—he asked and reminded the faculty to cut down on telephone calls and to turn off lights after class hours.

Half a dozen trustees resigned from the college board for one reason or another within a year or so. Included were a number of those named to it in support of Dr. Jones' hopes for the college.

It was not an auspicious beginning for the new administration. Faculty colleagues and friends knew of Paul Smith's discouragement. He was uncomfortable in his new office and deeply concerned about the financial position of the college as he studied the ledgers and annual audits. The whole future of the college, he felt, had fallen on his shoulders. One day he asked Ashton M. Otis, president of the college board, whether he should not in fact resign.

"I don't believe, Paul, that the college can stand another resignation."

Queasy for the moment, Smith found the courage to carry on. Perhaps he recalled the dynamic optimism of Walter Dexter under whom he had served in the 'twenties, and the encouraging words of Aubrey Wardman. Perhaps it was a column in the *Times* by Paul H. Davis—college consultant and himself a Quaker—who cited Whittier as an example of *a poor college that needn't be poor!* Perhaps it was the assurance by certain trustees that he would be given large freedom in discharging his awesome responsibility.

At some unmarked point a new Paul S. Smith emerged as college president—one unlike any other, certainly, but genial, self-assured, aggressive, exuding a tremendous air of confidence. The picturesque history professor faded into the years past. Smith put his hand to the plough, and it was soon clear who was driving the team. Not an accident, for sure, was the fact that Whittier College operated in the black that first year 1951-52—and that, despite the drop of $50,000 in tuition income, the year ended with a $40,000 operating surplus! Here stood revealed a man with an uncanny sense of the balance sheet, a Yankee merchant who knew how to meet a payroll and take stock on the back of an old envelope.

But Paul Smith was as much artist as shopkeeper. He was something of a visionary. He played the college presidency by ear, composing strains as he went along. And he soon discovered that he liked being President as he now dressed and comported himself in his new rôle.

Early in the morning one might hear him break into song in his office, a hymn phrase perhaps from his boyhood: "Jesus, wonderful Jesus. . . ."

He adjusted a rose in the bud vase on his desk cluttered with work, ready to begin the day—always for him, a new and wonderful day!

2

NEW APPROACH TO DEVELOPING WHITTIER
AS AN INDEPENDENT COLLEGE

THE NATURE OF ITS CONSTITUENCY was still an unresolved problem for Whittier College. What body of persons or segments of society should it depend on for financial support and students? What public should it serve? Who, finally, should control its destinies?

President Smith's views and purposes gradually clarified.

Certainly it was evident that neither California Yearly Meeting of Friends Church nor the newly organized Pacific Yearly Meeting of liberal Friends either could or would sustain financially a liberal arts college. Although there continued to be about 50 Quaker students of one sort or another in the Whittier student body, few of them were from California Yearly Meeting outside of Whittier itself.* A supporting constituency had to be found elsewhere than in Quakerdom.

From its academy beginnings, Whittier had served some of the functions of a community college. Through the years, the growing college—not alone the football team—was looked upon as a major asset of the City of Whittier. But, though strong support continued to come from business and professional men living in Whittier and nearby, no one wanted the college to be or to remain purely local. Some of the best students from Whittier families naturally wanted to go away to school. Others began their collegiate work in nearby junior colleges, then carried on in state colleges or universities. Long contemplated, the Rio Hondo Junior College became a reality in 1966 to serve the larger Whittier district. And, within driving distance, were Long Beach, Fullerton, and Los Angeles state colleges with their expanding faculties and facilities. These had pre-empted the place of Whittier as a merely local college.

A constituency for Whittier had to be found that would be more-than-Quaker and more-than-local. This President Jones had realized, and Smith was on the joint committee that had engaged with him in long-range planning. Jones promoted Whittier as an avowedly liberal and Christian college. He hoped to woo ducats and daughters from Protestants whose denominations had "lost" their own colleges through secularization. He won but limited support. Liberal dollars were few, and young people from liberal homes often preferred a frankly secular college or university.

President Smith's approach was intuitively different. He too wanted Whittier to be a liberal college with an "open" campus and free classroom. He too wanted Whittier to be an idealistic college in the Christian tradition. He too saw clearly that Whittier must become a largely residential college with dormitories for most of its students.

But Smith sensed the fact that financial support had to come from those who had means. He knew that those who had means were those who had made money. The southern California econ-

*CYM statistics for 1961 reported 143 young Friends from 19 of its churches attending 48 different colleges. Of these 33 were indicated as being in 10 different Christian colleges, including but 14 who were enrolled in Quaker colleges of various sorts.

323

omy was still close to its pioneer roots—there was little inherited wealth such as one might find in Philadelphia or even in Richmond. And these self-made Californians and their wives tended to be conservative in their thinking. Having come up the hard way, they were often persons of keen insight and generous impulse, with an overriding desire to make good use of their means. Few of these capitalists wanted to "turn back the clock," but they cherished their independence. Perhaps with a wisp of nostalgia, they wished for present youth what they had themselves found good in their bustling and thriving lives. They could be brought to see (Smith believed) that, in the swiftly changing economy and technology of the day, youth needed the kind of higher education that Whittier College could give.

Whittier—Smith pointed out to his board, as he did wherever he spoke—was not only an idealistic liberal arts college valuing its Quaker heritage, but it was notably an "independent" college. As such it believed in individualism and free enterprise. Smith preached "the importance of the independent college to the American tradition of the open society." He insisted that if colleges like Whittier are to be the educational spokesmen for such a society, then those who have prospered under it must accept the doctrine of "voluntarism" in supporting their development. But he carefully avoided the "phantom problem" of conflicting interests between public and private education. Especially California, richest of all states in its tax-supported colleges and universities, *needed* the independent colleges and universities— Stanford, Caltech, Loyola, Whittier and the rest. Not only did they educate one-fifth of California's youth (and without cost to the state), but they were a living witness to the pluralism of our society, in which private foundations and government, independent colleges and public institutions joined in good works for the general welfare.

> The private colleges [Smith often said] help keep the public ones free by themselves being fully free, and the state colleges and universities make the independent ones hustle.*

He declared this "competitive partnership" to be the best guarantee of good higher education.

*Of the independent colleges, Smith further said, "their modest size keeps them maneuverable, and their independence makes them imaginative."

Just as Smith was taking up his work as president of Whittier College, the Independent Colleges of Southern California, Inc. was in process of formation. Arch rivals on the gridiron now leagued themselves to present to industrialists and businessmen the proper claim of the private colleges for their financial support. And a state-wide Association of Independent California Colleges and Universities formed to assure protection of their interests vis-à-vis the public institutions and the State Legislature. Smith was involved in the formation of both of these organizations.

Paul S. Smith never had thought of himself as a crusader. Now he became the champion of free-enterprise education. He showed himself unafraid of "ideologies" and of "-isms" so long as discussion was really free and debate was not rigged. He fought to make and keep the Whittier campus open for the exchange of ideas, a marketplace with but minimum policing. Throughout southern California and on occasion far beyond, he was a respected advocate for his liberal-conservative point of view—for American Constitutionalism, for capitalism restrained and responsible to the common good, for Whittier College as the proud inheritor of Quaker tolerance and idealism.

He had found a rationale for Whittier College and the basis for a supporting constituency.

REBUILDING OF THE COLLEGE board was of vital importance. Many were the stalwart trustees who had served the college well and long. Theirs had been a record of loyal devotion to higher education, of sacrificial giving both of time and means.* As they passed from the scene or became inactive, President Smith hoped to see them replaced by men and women who would give a broader dimension to the body that supported the college and

*Six trustees continuing active through 1966—Arthur Corey '24, Glenn Lewis '16, Richard Nixon '34, Cass A. Rees, Dr. Raymond C. Thompson, C. C. Trillingham—had already averaged 32 years of service. Longest (43 years) and oldest in years (aged 91) was Cass Rees, treasurer of the board until 1966.

Four men and women continued in 1966 as honorary trustees—Loretta Cook '05, Edna T. Nanney '11, Ashton M. Otis, and Dr. Herbert E. Tebbetts '10e—having averaged 36 years as members of the board. Otis had served 14 years as its president.

Of the dozen who died during this period, nine averaged more than 30 years as trustees—Bertha V. Coffin, Robert L. Gifford, Milo Hunt, C. Bevan Johnson, J. Chalmers Newsom, Ella W. Peasley, Herman L. Perry, John G. Swain, and Aubrey Wardman—their names elsewhere in these pages.

held it in trust. He asked for and was given freedom in proposing nominations for board membership.

But Paul Smith moved slowly in this and in gathering into his hands the reins of administration. Too slowly, indeed, for some. One was Elden Smith '28, first vice-president of the board. An astute businessman and banker, soon to be chairman of the executive committee of the great Security-First National Bank, he was in despair with his former history professor as college president.

"If you'd just spend a week over at Claremont, you'd see how to run a college!"

Paul Smith was sharp in replying that he had no intention of patterning Whittier after Pomona College—or after Haverford. Whittier had to be its own kind of college, and he had to be his own kind of president. Elden Smith resigned. A period of years healed the breach, and the two Smiths again clasped hands. Elden Smith, invited to give the "charge to seniors" at the commencement of 1960, was honored with a doctorate by his alma mater in 1961. He made a handsome gift of $25,000 for reclassifying the books of the library from Dewey decimal to the Library of Congress system. Only his untimely death in 1964 forestalled his renewed acceptance of board membership.

ELECTION OF RICHARD NIXON '34 as Vice President of the United States in the fall of 1952, was a circumstance of greatest importance in the rebuilding of the Board of Trustees of Whittier College.

Dick Nixon, as he has always been called by his friends, was an outstanding political exemplar of that liberal-conservatism that Paul Smith advocated in the development of Whittier College.

After taking his law degree at Duke University, Nixon returned to California, passed the State Bar examination, and began legal practice in Whittier. His alma mater named him a trustee in 1939. After the War, he entered politics—the story well known—and with a hop skip and jump landed on the Republican national ticket in 1952 as runningmate of General Eisenhower.

Following the Republican National Convention, a Victory

Homecoming on Hadley Field brought out 15,000 or more community well-wishers and dozens of political leaders, including Governor Earl Warren, to cheer the native son and congratulate him upon his nomination as candidate for the Vice Presidency.

The campaign began. Personal attacks, spared the military hero, were heaped upon the young partisan. Democratic charges of corruption aimed at confounding Republican chances by driving Nixon from the ticket. He prepared to vindicate himself to the nation in what was later called his "Checkers speech." A midnight call asked Nixon's old history prof to find and verify a half-remembered quote from Lincoln. Together with Drs. Upton and Cooper, P. S. Smith prowled the college library for the telling item that, in the event, was not needed. Nixon's TV broadcast was a political and dramatic tour de force. An unprecedented flood of letters and telegrams to Republican headquarters overwhelmingly supported him.*

Among Whittier College alumni no less than in the nation, Nixon aroused partisan foe as well as friend. When the Homecoming and pre-election issue of *The Rock* featured Dick Nixon, protests from anti-Nixon alumni beset President Smith. One irate alumna demanded that her name be stricken from the rolls. . . . Had the college erred in honoring its most distinguished alumnus in this way? Smith called another former student for his advice—Dr. George E. Outland '28, professor of political science at San Francisco State College, a staunch Democrat and sometime U.S. Congressman (1943-46). The college was right, Outland said, in exploiting the newsworthiness of Nixon's prominence.

"If any of the Democratic alumni give you trouble, Paul, send them to me!"

The election followed. And in January 1953, Richard M. Nixon was inaugurated Vice President of the United States with Dr. Smith seated with his family.

Evident from the first was Richard Nixon's loyalty to his college, the Quaker college of his kinsmen and cousins. He now could open doors for his friend, the new college president. He

*Given to Whittier College, this collection forms a unique body of research materials for linguistic and psychological study, as the uncounted but estimated 2,500,000 messages represented a wide socio-economic cross-section of the national population.

brought Whittier to the attention of many who had never known it. He supported his alma mater as his means and time permitted.

Unable to give the Commencement address in 1953, he accepted the renewed invitation for June 1954. Some seniors and professors continued a partisan view of their alumnus and trustee, but the greater number were proud and pleased. Attendance was limited to 5,000 on the north bleachers of Hadley Field. The young Vice President, now privy to the highest councils, showed a new grasp of large national and international issues. Honored with an LL.D. on this occasion, he generously devoted the day to the interests of Whittier College: press conference, ground breaking for a new dormitory, twentieth reunion of his class, reception for graduates and their parents and professors, reception for trustees and their guests, dinner at the Wardman home for potential supporters and trustees of Whittier College—a select company of industrialists and substantial businessmen from many parts of California.

The 1960 election year, with Richard M. Nixon the Republican candidate for the Presidency of the United States, was a time of excitement and strong feeling on the Whittier campus. In preparation for the campaign, political biographers scoured the Whittier countryside and campus for intimate or significant details of Nixon's boyhood and college years. Press photographers, feature writers, radio and television teams from NBC, CBS, and BBC interviewed professors who had known him best during his formative student days—Smith in history, Upton in drama, Newman in sports—and they fed quotes and comment, tapes and TV shots to the mass media reaching all parts of the United States and far beyond. Not only was Whittier College receiving unprecedented publicity, but the students on the Whittier campus—and especially those in political science—were getting an inside look at presidential campaigning and a demonstration of the close scrutiny that later life can give to college years. And they viewed the fateful Nixon-Kennedy debates with bipartisan passion edged with an ivied interest.* Small consolation that the

*Published by the U.S. Government Printing Office in 1961 were *The Joint Appearances of Senator John F. Kennedy and Vice President Richard M. Nixon . . .*, and also *The Speeches, Remarks, Press Conferences and Study Papers of Vice President Richard M. Nixon* (August 1 through November 7, 1960). No previous presidential campaign had been so fully covered and recorded.

Whittier man came so very close to defeating the Harvard man in the final tally of votes.

On other occasions, too, Nixon came back to his campus—to address the student body, attend board meetings, dedicate new buildings or break ground for others.

In March 1962, Nixon flew from New York for the Testimonial Dinner honoring Paul S. Smith upon his at-that-time 40 years of service to Whittier College. Some 600 well-wishers overflowed the dining hall of the Campus Inn—leaders of nearby communities and churches, schools and colleges. Stan Sanders '62 spoke briefly for the students, Beryl Notthoff '35 for the alumni. The Board of Trustees upon recommendation of the Faculty, conferred upon Dr. Paul S. Smith its honorary degree Doctor of Laws so that he might continue his presidency of the college as an alumnus.

Jessamyn West McPherson '23—introduced as "one stimulated by Paul Smith's maiden course in American history to become a writer of American fiction"—assured her audience that the course had dealt, rather, with the facts of sociology, and she described Smith as "a superb teacher . . . showing us how knowledge can be made a living part of life." However, it was Smith as "a living link, not with a memory of the past, but with a dream for the future" that concerned her, and his bringing of others into the development of that dream. In doing this, Jessamyn West said,

> He asks us to do what we don't want to do—and we do it. He asks us to give what we don't want to give—and [she concluded with a quip] on occasion, as when last I spoke here, I give more than he asks for.

Then her Milhous cousin, Richard M. Nixon '34—introduced as one "who has served his State well in the Congress, who has served his Country well in its all-but-highest office"—spoke of Smith as a professor who convinced his students "that reading history was much more interesting than reading the best fiction." And he felt that as college president, Smith combined what Woodrow Wilson had called "the man of thought" and "the man of action."

At commencement time in 1965, Nixon again flew to California—dedicated the new college Library and participated in granting honorary degrees to the speaker, Senator Margaret Chase Smith, to Warren Knox '49 (new president of the College of Idaho), and to Bob Hope.*

However, it was Nixon's unstinting help in 1954—and President Smith's wise use of it—that marked a turning point in the rebuilding of the Whittier College Board of Trustees.

ANOTHER FACTOR IN REBUILDING the college board was Smith's realistic approach to the Quaker restriction upon board membership. It did not seem reasonable that Friends should continue to control the college that they could neither develop nor sustain. A change of the By-Laws in 1957 reduced the number of Quakers on the board from 16 to 10 out of a total of 30. And the board now interpreted more liberally what was required of a man to be a Friend. But Smith felt that the number of ten was

> altogether sufficient to guarantee the continuance in the life of the college [of] both the Quaker history and tradition, as well as keeping a strong Quaker stamp on its operations in the present day.

Ashton M. Otis—strong and devoted Friend who had given up his presidency of the board as his deafness worsened—did not oppose the motion that thus changed the By-Laws. But for him and some others it was a sad moment. Officially ended was "control" of Whittier College by members of the Society of Friends— a control that had been but nominal and never sectarian.

"I'm glad I didn't have to preside over this meeting of the board," Otis thought aloud in an audible whisper.

But as a Friend himself, born and bred, P. S. Smith was not unmindful of the Quaker heritage that he cherished for the college. He often quoted the poet Whittier who had declared himself to be "no sectarian in the strict sense. My sympathies are with the Broad Church of Humanity."

Even with this greater freedom from restriction and with the understanding help of the continuing trustees, Smith found that

*A kinescope interview of Nixon, Bob Hope, and Senator Smith was made on the Whittier campus that day by Bob Wright of KNBC. Called "Success: From the Top," it was widely broadcast and shown.

rebuilding the Whittier College board was a slow process. Many qualified men and women were already trustees of similar institutions. Others, Smith discovered, could only be interested in what they felt was "a challenging, not a dubious, situation."

But during the years 1951-1966 fifteen new trustees were named.

AMONG THE NEW MEMBERS of the Whittier College board, beginning in the fall of 1951, was Thomas W. Bewley '26e, law partner of Richard Nixon and City Attorney. He was a Quaker and one-time clerk of Monthly Meeting. Soon he became first vice president, then acting president, and president of the Whittier College board.

In 1953, Walter Knott of nearby Knott's Berry Farm accepted invitation to the board—a conspicuous example and dedicated exponent of free enterprise as he understood it. In 1954—Sada Blake (Mrs. Frank O.) and John D. Gregg '19e. Both began at once to serve the college.*

In 1955—Marius C. Lautrup, Danish-born president of Whittier Sanitary Dairy; Thomas M. Erwin '24e, rancher and state legislator; and LaMotte T. Cohu, birthright Friend, who had been president, general manager, director or board chairman of TWA, Northrop Aircraft, Consolidated-Vultee, and General Dynamics.

In 1957—John Stauffer, who, with Mennonite forebears, had a warm respect for Friends. At that time he was chairman of the executive committee of the world-wide Stauffer Chemical Company, and director of a dozen corporations in the related chemical industry. Both Stauffer and Cohu brought wide executive experience to the Whittier College board.

At the same time Vera Reilly (Mrs. John B.)—her husband a successful local industrialist—became a trustee. In 1960— W. B. Camp, strong Democrat with large agricultural interests in the San Joaquin Valley and in South Carolina. In 1962—Bonnie Bell Wardman, accepting the place on the board of her deceased husband, A. Wardman; and Dolores Lautrup Ball '33 (Mrs. Kenneth L.) filling the place left vacant by the death of her

*Gregg, a business associate of Wardman and president of Rose Hills Memorial Park, was the enterprising son of a Southern family that came into the Whittier area by wagon train from Texas after the Civil War.

father. In the same year—Ezra B. Hinshaw, a leading merchant in expanding Whittier; Clinton O. Harris '34, successful automobile dealer; and Joe D. Robinson, oil industrialist of Fallbrook.* In 1966—Edward J. Guirado '28, scion of one of the early California families and Judge in the Los Angeles County Superior Court.

Such were the new trustees. The older board members "blossomed out in accepting the newcomers with open hearts." They shared a common pride in what they felt they could together accomplish for Whittier as an independent college under President Smith's leadership.

THE FINANCIAL DEVELOPMENT of Whittier College moved slowly at first. Strengthening of the board did not at once result in substantial gifts. It was now possible, however, for President Smith to meet influential people in any part of the country who knew well, or knew about, not only one but several members of the governing board.

Smith began at once his efforts to find money for college development. Times were good. Although truce talks in Korea dragged on for two years, there followed a decade of "peace and prosperity" with unprecedented expansion of the national economy. New as he was in fund raising, Smith was not shy in soliciting contributions—for him, it was not begging but inviting, though he did not hesitate in asking the direct question.

Immediately upon his becoming president of the college, Smith began to raise money to endow the Richard M. Nixon Chair of Public Service. On his way home from the Inauguration in January 1953, he stopped off, by arrangement through an intermediary, to see Jesse H. Jones, the wealthy and generous Texan—Democrat, of course, but Southern.

Smith made his pitch. Jesse Jones replied quietly:

"Dr. Smith, I'm not well impressed with Mr. Nixon."

*Trustees continuing from the preceding years and serving through this fifteen year period—in addition to the six of longest service named on a preceding page—were Dr. Homer G. Rosenberger '34e, grandson of the third president of the college; John L. Compton '25, long-time superintendent of Bakersfield schools; Ethel Koontz Eckels '25 (Mrs. Charles F.) of the pioneer Santa Fé Springs family; John A. Murdy, Jr., Orange County rancher and California state senator (1952-64).

Smith changed his tune—"We at least share in having different opinions"—and asked Jones for scholarship funds for Whittier College. For that, Jones said, he'd give $10,000. Smith thanked him. As he withdrew, his Dallas intermediary whispered, "You got a damn sight more than I thought you would." Next day, Jesse Jones said to his secretary,

"I promised some guy $10,000 yesterday, but don't recall his name!"

She did, however, and the college received a check to establish the Jesse H. Jones and Mary Gibbs Jones scholarship.

Smith continued his efforts on behalf of the Nixon chair, with the help of "Tom" Knudsen, a Nixon supporter. And in time, with $25,000 from Sam Mosher and many smaller contributions, the total approached the hoped-for $100,000, which, when the matter was undertaken, would have modestly supported a professorship.

During his first three years as president, Smith increased the total assets of the college by only $200,000 per year, which was something less than his first brave promise! But by the end of his fifth year net assets had increased by a total of $1,250,000. Of this increase one-half (nearly $625,000) was in additional endowment. Included in this were the substantial grants in 1956 from the Ford Foundation—$300,000 to support improvement in faculty salaries. Not only was Whittier one of the 600 or so independent colleges and universities receiving such grants in varying amounts, but it was among the selected group (one-fifth of the total number) receiving "accomplishment" grants in recognition of their growing financial strength.*

Dr. Smith had the feeling that he could do better in the financial development of the college if its business management was made answerable to him as president rather than directly to the board—an arrangement that had survived, at least nominally, from the crisis of 1930. In 1957 the trustees approved the change in By-Laws that Smith recommended. Although Whittier had had a succession of business managers, there was no question now that President Smith was in fact his own business manager,

*Eight of the 30 California institutions receiving Ford Foundation grants at this time were also given "accomplishment" grants. Other Quaker colleges so recognized were Haverford, Swarthmore, and Bryn Mawr.

with chief accountant, Joseph Rawlinson, efficiently in charge of the business office. In contractual and investment matters, Smith worked closely, of course, with the finance and executive committees of the board; and the college books were, as always, subject to annual audit.

Careful management of the growing yearly budgets permitted at last the accumulation of modest reserves looking toward the replacement of outworn plant and equipment. Within the fifteen years, the regular student body was to double in size. During the same time the tuition rate was gradually raised until it too had doubled. Tuition income therefore rose from $500,000 in the year 1951-52 to $2,000,000 in 1965-66. But individual faculty salaries had also doubled, the size of the faculty had increased by 60%, and other costs rose in continuing inflation. The total annual balance sheet for all college operations had risen to $3,400,000!

During these and the next years, bequests, annuity gifts, and trusts added significantly to the resources of the college. The annuity bequest from the estate of Professor emeritus Herbert F. Evans, valued at $100,000, included the original brick building on East Philadelphia Street (the Reynolds Block) in which the first and third Whittier academies had been held. Emma Hunt, widow of Milo Hunt—Quaker mathematics teacher and college trustee—left their estate of $334,000 to the college as a memorial scholarship fund for their son Wendell, Whittier student killed in a vacation-time automobile accident.

The gift by Bonnie Bell Wardman of $350,000 and the bequest by Aubrey Wardman of $650,000 built the new Library in 1961. Upon her own death in 1966, Mrs. Wardman bequeathed additional stocks and interests valued at over $1,000,000 toward development of the college endowment fund. The Wardmans' many services and gifts to "the campus loved so well" spanned over 40 years and totalled some two and a half million dollars. At Thanksgiving-time in 1966, the City of Whittier renamed the original College Street, which for so long had led through the old town up to the campus, and called it "Wardman Street."

During these years, other bequests were received by the college: $62,000 from the estates of Alice H. Wrede; $50,000 from O. A. Brown; $30,000 from Mrs. John E. Coffin—the Bertha Lindley

334

of pioneer days. The bequest of $170,000 by Ella Peasley in 1958 added to her annuity gifts of $130,000 for a total of $300,000 in construction funds.

Benefactions of various sorts included the living trust for Whittier College set up in 1961 by Arnold and Elsa Blackburn, with an estimated value of $450,000. In 1965 Mrs. Ethel Ball made a gift of $200,000 toward building the new dormitory.

John Stauffer contributed substantial sums throughout the recent decade toward various college projects and buildings, making him the most substantial of the living benefactors of Whittier College, with gifts totalling a half million dollars. To link it more closely with the Los Angeles business community, John Stauffer generously provided a development office for Whittier College on Wilshire Boulevard at New Hampshire.

The total assets of Whittier College had been $2,660,000 in 1951. By the end of 1966, net assets had risen by a whopping $12,000,000 for a total of over $14,500,000. It was a good *fivefold increase!* While much of this was invested in campus expansion and new buildings, well over $4,000,000 was endowment, which had totalled little more than $1,000,000 at the beginning of this period.*

There were still those who shook their heads at Paul S. Smith's management of the college. His desk piled high with correspondence, unopened mail, building plans, scraps of paper with penciled memos—the President himself, like as not, answering his office phone, taking time out for student or parent, putting off faculty members who came for appointments—moseying about the campus, watching construction, giving a groundsman direc-

*Total assets of Whittier College (*Audit* for 8/31/66) were just under $14,000,000. Against this stood current academic liabilities of about $150,000, National Defense Student Loan Funds of over $700,000 and Long-term Indebtedness (Government loans on dormitories and dining facilities) of just over $1,650,000 — totalling $2,500,000. The total net assets, then, were about $11,500,000.

To be added to this, however, were certain bequests and contingencies not shown in the annual audit: The bequest of Bonnie Bell Wardman (not yet distributed from her Estate) was estimated to be in excess of $1,000,000; the bequest-trust of Frank W. Williams, at about $300,000; the bequest of Ted Barber (in probate) at over $450,000 —these together totalling well over $1,750,000.

In addition to these were to be added the $1,000,000 firmly committed by the U.S. Government as a grant toward construction of the new science building, and the contingency gift of $250,000 made by John Stauffer for the same purpose.

These bequests and contingency grants added over $3,000,000 to the net assets of Whittier College, bringing the total to more than $14,500,000.

tions for watering a sick shrub—receiving requests, petitions, reports, plans to mull over and finally accept or reject, or pocket-veto—taking great piles of work home with him at night.

"It's a hell of a way to run a railroad!"

Maybe so, but it was being run—with miles of new trackage, fine new rolling stock, and a new depot!

And the fivefold increase in total college assets (with fourfold increase in endowment) was certainly one measure of outstanding growth during the fifteen years.

3

ENLARGEMENT OF THE CAMPUS

NEW MAJOR BUILDINGS AND CONSTRUCTION

FOR WHITTIER TO SURVIVE and develop as an independent college in competition with the surrounding tax-supported institutions, it had to become largely residential. That is, it had to build dormitories to house the bulk of its increasing student body that was soon to be drawn from a wider geographic area. And it had to redevelop its campus and academic plant to attract and hold good students and faculty.

"You know," Smith would say to colleagues and trustees when he first became president, "Whittier is really a college without a campus."

He was thinking of lawns and vistas.

The original 14-acre campus was awkwardly narrow, hilly, and cut by arroyos. How different from the spacious 220 acres upon which Haverford was established! The gift and purchase of the 5-acre strip along Earlham Drive widened the Whittier campus by 165 feet. But it was obvious in the early 1920's that 19 acres was quite inadequate in size for development of the college. No serious thought was given to pulling up stakes and moving to a more spacious site, as so many colleges had done. There was no money to do this; furthermore, it would have removed the college from the town of Whittier, its principal constituency. The alternative solution of the problem was followed: purchase of the adjacent Worsham Ranch. The assumption was false that this would give the college the acres it needed, for this property was hilly and out of the way. Its broad usable canyon was remote from the old campus—and no plan was proposed for making that area the center for new building.

The "natural" direction for campus expansion was northward from Redwood Cottage, but this land had been subdivided, with homes on most of the lots. Nevertheless, the college built Platner Hall and acquired the Bolte home in this area during the 'twenties. It bought several more properties in addition to the Elks lodge (the O. T. Mendenhall Building) in the 'thirties and 'forties. But it was not until 1948 that the two-block frontage on Painter Avenue was all in college hands; and behind this on Philadelphia and Berkeley Way there were still private holdings.

However, it was the east side of Berkeley Way [later Founders Hill Road] that the college chose as location for the new women's dormitory, and President Smith pushed the purchase of the remaining lots necessary for this project.

Smith was gun shy of Master Plans. He had lived through a succession of abortive building campaigns. Therefore, he did not announce a grand program of fixed goals and rigid priorities. His general plan for campus development was a growing, changing, emerging thing. Although the college retained a firm of landscape architects (Cornell, Bridges, and Troller), ordered a topographic survey (Fairchild Aerial Surveys), and engaged a college architect (William H. Harrison, F.A.I.A.), it was Smith's own views and suggestions that finally prevailed.

Before long Smith eyed the entire block east to Stanford Way [later Haverhill Park Road] for the development of women's dormitories. William and Lorena Blott had already given their home on Stanford Way to the college, retaining a life estate. In time Smith arranged to buy the Howard L. Hockett properties next to it, assuring his widow Alice Hockett of the lifelong use of her home. Smith dickered patiently, waited, traded, never resorted to legal condemnation, which was by then possible for private colleges under California state law. Most of the properties the college purchased at approximately market value. However, at one point near the beginning of this expansion, a prominent trustee grumbled.

"All right, we'll buy it—but no more of Paul's high-priced properties!"

At another point, when two homes stood in the way of completing the second women's dormitory, John Stauffer phoned Smith to say:

"Go ahead and buy—or start proceedings—I'll pay for the lots."

Understandably, an elderly resident (sister of an early trustee) was reluctant to give up her accustomed home. Finally Smith suggested that the college buy a lot across the street on East Philadelphia, clear it of the existing houses, move her home to that site,* establish it upon a new foundation, repaint it and landscape. She was out of her home but a few days (at college expense), her long friendship was retained, and her neighbor accepted a negotiated price.

As the site for a third new women's dormitory, the college bought an acre east of Stanford Way [then renamed Haverhill Park Road] at a cost of $75,000, which was more than the pioneer Quakers had paid for the entire 1250 acres of the original townsite.** Except for one home—about which there was no hurry— the college had at last bought the entire three-block strip of property east on Philadelphia Street from the O. T. Mendenhall Building on the corner of Painter Avenue.

So much for the additional land needed for women's dormitories. But the Whittier campus expanded in a second direction.

North of Philadelphia Street stood the new Broadoaks Nursery School on its three-acre knoll. Except for a narrow entrance beside the arroyo, it was surrounded by homes and multiple dwellings. Smith gradually envisaged this as North Campus, but had some difficulty in carrying his trustees with him in this venture. With endowment funds the college bought Victoria Apartments when it came on the market. John Gregg secured from Rose Hills a substantial office building that was moved to the campus to serve as an Administrative Annex. To provide its site on East Philadelphia, Smith traded a house that the college owned on Park Street. Other properties—the Green Gables on North Painter and smaller houses on Olive Drive—the board purchased one by one. Walter Dexter, Jr. made an outright gift of what had been the home of his grandparents.

*The Whittier City Council passed a special ordinance allowing this to be done.
**This back part of Lot #1 Block H was valued by the P.L.&W. Co. at $150 per acre in the depression times of 1893.

WHITTIER COLLEGE
Independent College founded by Quakers 1887

The campus of Whittier College comprises about 120 acres of land. The first College Grounds of 14 acres was a gift of the Pickering Land and Water Company (1893)—east of Painter Avenue at the head of College Street (renamed Wardman Street in 1966). The south 5-acre strip along Earlham Drive (a gift of Washington Hadley, 1908) included Hadley Field.

The Worsham Ranch of 133 acres—purchased by the Whittier College Syndicate (1923) and paid for finally (1942)—added the broad canyon developed as athletic fields (1951) and stadium (1963).

Gradual acquisition of the 10 acres immediately north of the original 14 acres extended the campus to Philadelphia Street (1926-1967). Development north of Philadelphia Street began with purchase of the William K. Green property (1939). This continued with the acquisition of the surrounding properties (1956-1967) to piece together North Campus bounded by Olive Drive. Purchase of the Murphy Memorial Hospital and what was earlier Alta Park brought the original "College Hill" (1887) within the Whittier College Campus (1966).

CAMPUS MAP OF 1967 ☞

MAP OF THE CAMPUS OF WHITTIER COLLEGE
showing, in addition to the recent permanent
buildings, several older structures.

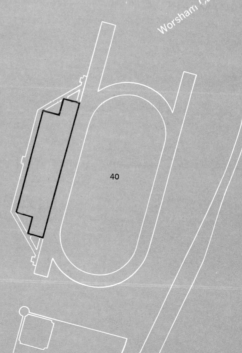

COLLEGE HILLS

Worsham Canyon

WORSHAM

BRYN MAWR WAY

40

39

DRIVE

CANYON

37

38

redrawn by Rolfe Kroll

SYNOPSIS OF EVENTS
Development of the Whittier College campus,
the fourth twenty years
1947-1967

1947.   Provident Hall, war-surplus classrooms moved to college Quad.

1948.   Lou Henry Hoover Memorial Hall, classroom building.

1948.   Broadoaks School of Education, north of Philadelphia St.

1949.   George E. Wanberg Memorial Hall, men's dormitory on Worsham land.

1951.   Memorial Field, practice field and track in Worsham Canyon.

1951.   College Hall (for men) and Robbins property.

1955.   Susan and Clifford Johnson Residence Hall for Women.

1956.   Administration Annex, north of Philadelphia Street.

1958.   Dexter Student Center—Campus Inn and Student Union.

1958.   John Stauffer Lecture-Laboratory, adjoining Hoover Hall.

1959.   Relocation of the Broadoaks School, development of North Campus.

1961.   Peasley Center of Religion, Music, Philosophy—Memorial Chapel (including the Schlicker pipe organ [1963] and Schulmerich carillon), Arnold Hall, and Music Building.

1961.   Roy E. Campbell Men's Residence, remodeling of the Government Laboratory.

1962.   Beverly M. Stauffer Residence Hall for Women.

1963.   Memorial Stadium, permanent seating for Memorial Field.

1963.   Redwood Building removed to Earlham Drive and rebuilt.

1964.   Bonnie Bell Wardman Library, central in campus development.

1965.   Removal of old dwellings to clear the inner campus.

1966.   Murphy Memorial Residence Hall, dormitory with dining facility.

1966.   Dr. Frank Irvin Ball Residence for Women, Haverhill Park Road.

1967.   Acquisition of properties linking Murphy Hall to North Campus.

1967.   Science Building on Hadley Field facing Quad and Earlham Drive.

With audacity, President Smith decided to remove Broadoaks from its knoll. He wanted its "million dollar site" for other buildings. His proposal met opposition in the board—"Move a new building? What an extravagance!" John Stauffer said he'd pay for doing it. The cost was to be $40,000, more than half what the building had cost a decade earlier. The opposition then collapsed, for, "What can you do with Paul when he raises the money!" But from this site Smith could see through the clutter of intervening arroyo and trees, street and poles, old houses and flats turned dormitories and offices. He could "see" down to Redwood Cottage. He could "see" beyond it, down the broad walks and lawns of what he called the Campus Mall, as though they were laid out before him on virgin acres. And Smith's vision shaped and reshaped the architect's successive sketches and plans.

Even before the block of North Campus was fully acquired (several properties not yet purchased in 1966), circumstances permitted a further expansion to the north.

The City of Whittier sold to Whittier College the Murphy Memorial Hospital, separated from the rest of North Campus by no more than a half block of intervening properties (with two of them later acquired to provide a direct pathway). With other hospitals now in the area, the City had found it too costly to operate its municipal hospital. It therefore leased it to the college in 1964 with option to buy. For $70,000 the college converted it into a dormitory for 145 men with dining facility for 200. Early in 1966 the college paid the City $250,000 and received title to the property.*

The 6.88-acre site of this complex of buildings has a history that goes back by stages—it was Alta Park for many years, earlier Reservoir Hill, and at first that original College Hill upon which the Friends' College died a-borning in 1888. Thus, at long last, came home to Whittier College the hilltop of its beginnings. Bounded to north and south by Hadley and Bailey

*The buildings alone had cost more than that. The original hospital unit, of sturdy concrete construction, had cost $100,000 in 1920. It was the gift of Simon J. Murphy, Jr. as a memorial to his pioneer parents, identified with the development of East Whittier. A second gift added a $150,000 wing in 1923, and there were subsequent additions and buildings, including a nurses' home.

Members of the Murphy family expressed themselves as pleased when their memorial building, no longer practicable as a hospital, was taken over by Whittier College.

Streets, it brought to the campus map the names of those two Quaker pioneers and staunch college trustees, Jonathan Bailey and Washington Hadley.

Murphy Memorial Hall constituted one center for men's housing northeast of the heart of the campus. Another center to the southeast, comprised Wanberg, College, and Campbell halls.* Equidistant to the west stood Newlin Hall.

This expansion of the Whittier campus—some 40 parcels of private property costing over $1,000,000—was a notable accomplishment. Without the development of these more spacious grounds and the construction of essential buildings, Whittier College simply could not have moved into the future.

A GOOD PHYSICAL PLANT for the college was what President Smith at times called "educational packaging." He realized how important this was in attracting good students and faculty, and indeed further college benefactors.

Remembering Walter Dexter's apologetic comment of the early 'twenties—"We're proudest of the things we ain't got!"— Smith determined to make of Whittier a college that all might be proud of. All new buildings, he said, should be generously proportioned and of A-1 construction. It took several years to get started. Then one new building followed another, ten of them within a dozen years. Each presented its own problems of financing, of campus site, of planning and construction, of naming. Each had its own story.

The *first* was to be the new dormitory on the corner of Philadelphia and Berkeley Way. This was essential as a first step toward developing Whittier as a more largely residential college. A quiet drive to raise funds in the fall of 1952 added but $60,000 to the $52,000 held over for this purpose.** The death of Susan Johnson, however, had released the Johnson annuity gift valued

*Roy E. Campbell Hall for 32 years served as the U.S. Government Entomological Laboratory. Built upon college property in 1929, it was released to the college in 1961. Converted into a dormitory housing 40 men, it was named for the chief entomologist who had carried on long years of his professional work there, good neighbor and benefactor of the college.

**Ella Peasley, honorary trustee now in her 'nineties, gave President Smith $15,000 in stocks and bonds for this purpose—but would he, kindly, return the paper clips?

Evidently these were the *same* paper clips that the president of Penn College had returned to Mrs. Peasley upon her request when she had made an earlier contribution to that other Quaker college.

in 1952 at about $200,000. This value might be applied if need be to the cost of the new building. Instead, Smith proposed that the college apply for a Federal housing loan of $350,000 to cover all costs of constructing this dormitory. One or two trustees voiced objection: the use of such government money violated their concept of "free enterprise." But the board as a whole approved the low-interest loan (2.75%), keeping in hand the high-yield business block.* The loan was granted and accepted. William H. Harrison planned an impressive two-story building in modern Mediterranean style, with shallow balconies and roof of flat tile, with sheltered patio and spacious lounge. It was to house 90 women. The site acquired and cleared, Smith watched construction at every stage. He himself ordered back the bulldozer to lower the level of the building by a couple of feet—sensing somehow its final relation to future buildings and his dream of a Campus Mall. Upon completion in 1955 this new residence for women students was named Johnson Hall, honoring Susan and Clifford Johnson, beloved classics professor and pioneer banker-trustee, encountered earlier in this history.

The *second* new building to get under way was the Campus Inn and Student Union. The old Campus Inn, makeshift at best, was inadequate to serve an increasingly residential student body. The Student Union had been a dream for 25 years. The student body had put aside small sums looking toward future building, but in 1953 the ASWC voted to assess each regular student $5 per semester for this purpose. It promoted other money-raising schemes, and the Woman's Auxiliary made contributions, until by June 1955 some $32,000 was in hand with assurance of $50,000 and willingness to borrow as much again. Actual construction of the combined Campus Inn and Student Union—to be known as the Walter F. Dexter Student Center—was again to be financed by a low-interest Federal loan of $500,000.

*Most of the industrialists on the board had no fear of Federal aid to education since in their own corporations they had realized the benefits and understood the rationale of subsidies and tax write-offs. Educators among the trustees were well aware of Federal aid to public schools of the state. These men and women, as well as those who had felt or anticipated the weight of inheritance taxes or who were themselves in high Income Tax brackets, looked upon the acceptance of Federal construction loans, student loan funds, or outright grants as simply getting back "some of their own." And even conservative merchants in the community knew that such funds in time filtered through their own cash registers.

A handsome great dining hall, designed by Harrison, with broadly beamed ceiling and massive chandeliers, seated more than 500 students. Adjacent were the efficient modern kitchen and two small dining rooms—the one beautifully furnished by John Stauffer as the President's Dining Room for use on special occasions. Beneath the great hall was basement space, later developed for alumni and student offices. The Student Union consisted of a commodious lounge with picture windows and open fireplace. Below this, on the ground level, were the "Spot" snack bar and booths, and bookstore. The Dexter Student Center was completed in 1958. Then at last the old Campus Inn could be cleared away to make way for the next building.

The *third* construction was the John Stauffer Lecture-Laboratory, first planned as the south wing of Hoover Hall to which it was connected. For this building John Stauffer, not yet on the college board, made an initial gift that approximated the first estimated cost of the building. But development of Harrison's plans to include a full ground floor for seminar and social science (later language) laboratory and office workroom, doubled the original estimates. A proposal by some trustees to cut the cost by cheaper construction—wood frame in place of reinforced concrete—was answered by President Smith.

"I don't think John Stauffer is a stud-and-stucco man."

He expected that some other board members might match the donor's generous gift—but it was Stauffer himself who threw in $70,000 of National Gypsum shares to make his building steel and concrete. Completed finally at a cost of $170,000, and furnished by the donor, it was ready for use in the fall of 1958.

The *fourth* and *fifth* buildings were the Memorial Chapel and the Music Building.

The college chapel was more than 30 years from first plan to actual construction. In 1927 Samuel C. Peasley (Iowa Quaker and kinsman of J. G. Whittier) and his wife Ella Wilcox Peasley made an annuity gift to Whittier of property valued at $100,000 before the Crash, with the understanding that this would in time build an auditorium-chapel. But the Long Beach property, with bus station built upon it by the college, was kept busy paying Mrs. Peasley (soon widowed) her annuity of $5,000 a year through the decades of depression, wars, and recoveries. No money from this gift was available for campus building.*

Without apparent knowledge of this, the Lancer Society was encouraged in 1934 to begin raising funds to build a small chapel. The admirable efforts and determination of these students and their alumni had raised a total of $30,000 by 1954. But plans submitted by the college architect were estimated to cost double this amount. The Lancers asked the college board to make the Memorial Chapel an all-college project. Trustees approved a site near the center of the campus, and ground was broken—but President Smith was dragging his heels!

In the fall of 1958 Smith could but hint that funds might become available for "a more inclusive project." At Christmastime, Mrs. Peasley died, aged 97, leaving a bequest to the college of $170,000 and releasing her annuity gifts that totalled $130,-000. These funds were designated for the building of a chapel and music building. The question of site for the chapel was again opened for reconsideration.

The time had come to jump across Philadelphia Street and create North Campus. Broadoaks gave up its "million dollar site" to the Peasley Center of Religion, Music, and Philosophy, comprising Memorial Chapel connected by breezeway to the double structure of Arnold Hall and the Music Building.

The Memorial Chapel was designed by Harrison in modern ecclesiastical style—with up-thrust laminated ribs, high-ridge roof, pews of blond oak facing pulpit and lectern, the north wall of wood paneling and (in time) resplendent organ pipes. It was to seat 300 or so for devotional chapel services and for student weddings. The building cost some $220,000, of which the Lancers had raised $65,000. Though the Chapel was completed in 1961, it took two more years to make and install the $50,000 Schlicker organ, a special gift of Sada Blake, generous friend and trustee of the college. A Schulmerich carillon—electronic chimes played by keyboard at the organ or automatically on the appointed hour—was the gift of LaMotte T. Cohu of the college board and of his brother Wallace Cohu, in memory of their

*The Long Beach land and building were at last sold in 1961 for $102,000 net to the college.

father, Henry Moore Cohu, a Friend.* Now at high noon and again at vespers, the "Alma Mater" rings out across the campus.

The Arnold Hall wing of the Music Building, Harrison planned to seat 400, with removable chairs and accordion divider. It would thus serve for large classes, for choir rehearsals, and for wedding receptions and public occasions. A bequest from J. Clem Arnold, Berkeley and then Los Angeles newspaper executive—captain of Whittier's first football team in 1893—provided the funds. The name of this hall honors his mother, Nannie Hiatt Arnold, pioneer Friends minister, editor and college trustee.

This and the Music Building to which it was attached were completed in 1961 at a cost of some $380,000. With classrooms, rehearsal and practice rooms, faculty studios, the Department of Music at last moved into its permanent home. This was its fourth move in forty years. Included in the new building was the Peasley Music Library, based upon Mrs. Peasley's original gift of the Carnegie collection of records, worn out and replaced and added to throughout the intervening twenty years.

The *sixth* and *seventh* new buildings were designed to complete the women's quadrangle of which Johnson Hall was the westerly part. The first unit of the Beverly M. Stauffer Residence Hall for Women was already under construction as a separate building by the time the Peasley Center was dedicated. President Smith carried the board with him in his proposal in 1957 to apply for a further Federal housing loan to finance this unit; but it was a year before the government loan of $450,000 could be announced, and another year before all of the property for its building site could be acquired and made available. (The college had dealt patiently and tenderly with old friends in their final years.) The college architect designed a three-story structure to house 92 women, and a large lounge overlooking the central two-level patio. Continuing gifts from the Stauffer Foundation were gratefully acknowledged by naming it for Mrs. Stauffer. This

*A Conn electronic concert organ first served the chapel and then was moved to the adjacent Arnold Hall, valued as a practice instrument and for special occasions. This organ had been given by the manufacturers for use at the Republican National Convention in 1960, and then was a gift to the Republican nominee for the Presidency, Richard M. Nixon. President and Mrs. Smith were still in their box seats at Convention Hall in Chicago when they heard the chairman's final and unexpected announcement: Nixon presented the Conn convention organ to his alma mater, Whittier College.

first unit was completed for use in the fall of 1961. The second was delayed for a year by the difficult acquisition of two key properties. Financed by another Federal housing loan of $600,-000, it was completed in 1962. The three new residences together accommodated 340 women—a significant step toward achieving the general goals of the college.

The *eighth* new construction was not a building in the usual sense. It was the completion of Memorial Stadium, another dream long held but fitfully pursued. Its history went back to 1923 with the acquisition of Worsham canyon, then viewed as a perfect site for athletic and recreational facilities. The post-war drive had completed Memorial Field in the spring of 1951 for track and field use, but without bleachers for football games. With the return of Aubrey Wardman to active service on the college board, it was natural that he would take a hand in furthering this project. For six years he tried first one then another scheme to develop a community stadium on the college field, to be used cooperatively with the high schools, as a means of getting others to share the cost of development—the college itself to invest nothing except the value of the land, and that on a lease. He stood willing himself to contribute $250,000 or more, half of the estimated cost. But at last, in August 1957, when he was turning 80 and had suffered a serious heart attack, he threw in the sponge, though he still felt that the stadium should somehow be achieved. Indeed, he saw clearly that the college would need Hadley Field for essential building. He had always been "athletic minded," as he said, but he had now come to question overemphasis on college athletics. With changing conditions (he wrote to his fellow trustees),

> Whittier College might better use [its] funds and land for engineering and other brain training which will be badly needed by this country in the future.

Then he added his admonition to them: "Think it over!" As for himself, he intended to leave the college money for some other purpose.

President Smith urged the functional completion of the stadium by the college alone; he, too, looked ahead to freeing Hadley Field for other use. Quietly he solicited gifts of $1,000 from alumni and friends and "gifts in kind," and worked his way toward the $300,000 to complete the stadium with permanent concrete bleachers. He avoided draining substantial funds from other ventures. At last in the fall of 1963, the stadium was ready for daytime use, seating 7,000 persons in the lee of Worsham ridge and fringe of trees that afforded welcome shade by 3 o'clock in the afternoon. Wardman himself had not lived to enjoy it or its dedication to the Whittier men, so many of them athletes, who had served and to those who had died in wartime. Memorial Stadium was just 40 years in fulfillment.

The *ninth* new structure on the Whittier campus—the Bonnie Bell Wardman Library—had an even longer history. For it was in 1909 that the college board decided to begin "immediately" to raise "$20,000 [*sic!*] for a permanent library building." The plans came to naught; and the near-miss of a gift for this purpose in the mid-'twenties was sadly noted. Each Master Plan, of course, called for a library building. Acquisition of the O. T. Mendenhall Building in the mid-'thirties gave substantial housing for the library functions and books for 25 years, but this was now outgrown.

After Wardman had given up on the stadium, Paul Smith felt free to chat with him about other needs of the college they had both loved and served so well and long. As an historian, Smith saw the library as central, especially for the social sciences and humanities. Wardman determined what his final gift would be. Aged 83 now and nearly blind, he attended the fall meeting of the college board in 1960. He asked to speak. In a clear analysis of "the changing emphasis in higher education," he stressed the "solid, down-to-earth learning" that was more important than all other campus activities. Respectful attention to an old and infirm friend gave way to a new admiration, as he punctuated his sentences with his cane. It was his intention, he said, to add to his previous gifts "the further sum of one million dollars in moving the college another step forward in its current significant development program." He was quietly cheered, and then he withdrew to be taken home for his late afternoon rest.

Allison and Rible, successors to the architects for Wardman Hall in 1924, were commissioned to design the new library building. Space was cleared for it along Berkeley Way, but Floyd

Rible F.A.I.A. presented sketches for a different positioning of a simple and functional building. He proposed thrusting it athwart the new long axis of the expanding campus, and raising it on structural piers to make it central on the campus without blocking the opening vistas. This daring conception caught Wardman's imagination, though he was never to see its realization. Smith was dubious of others' reaction to the plan. He consulted the international architect-engineer Pier Luigi Nervi in Rome and studied the effect of such a structure at King's College in Cambridge. He came back from Europe convinced. To provide the desired site, old Redwood Cottage—that had earlier housed the library for a decade—had to be destroyed or removed. Smith ordered it sawed in half, moved to the tennis courts, remodeled and stuccoed—at a cost of $50,000—to serve another period for Home Economics and faculty offices. (New tennis courts, beyond Wanberg Hall, were to cost another $38,000.) The library was completed, furnished, and books in place for the fall term 1964.

The building itself, which cost $1,000,000, was financed by Mrs. Wardman's gift of $350,000 and Mr. Wardman's bequest of $650,000. It had been his insistent desire that the Library be named for Bonnie Bell Wardman, his wife of fifty years. It was a tribute to them both that Richard Nixon '34, their friend since his youth, flew to California to dedicate the Library at commencement time in 1965. Herman H. Henkle '28, Executive Director of the John Crerar Library in Chicago, spoke on behalf of the library profession. Jessamyn West McPherson '23 sent her greetings as a writer—and Dr. Smith announced her intention of leaving her valuable collection of books and manuscripts to the Library. Friends, alumni, and Associates contributed special funds for books. Bonnie Bell Wardman herself, with so few months of life left her, was happily honored at the outdoor ceremony beneath the historic liveoak, which lent the tracery of its branchings to the external beauty of the building.

Central indeed as it was on the campus—an illuminated jewel at night—the Bonnie Bell Wardman Library became increasingly central in the academic life of the college. Dr. Benjamin Whitten, librarian, reported that from 1951 to 1966 the collection had grown from 54,000 to 71,000 volumes, which was more

347

than the old library could hold.* The A. A. Clarke gathering of Y.M.C.A. books, the Dr. Herbert Francis Evans bequest of 2,500 books especially valuable in church architecture, the Bayley collection in geology, the designation of Whittier College as a selective depository of Federal documents, purchase of the British Museum Catalog for research purposes—these were among the special enrichments of the library. In separate rooms were the Clifford and Susan Johnson Collection of Quaker Literature and the new John Greenleaf Whittier Collection, including manuscript letters and memorabilia. Other rooms served as college archives, microfilm reading room, library offices and workrooms. The stacks on three levels were designed to hold up to 300,000 volumes. Long reading rooms and open carrels seated as many as 700 students. Use of the college library increased within the first year—book circulation, 50%; student use of the Library for study and research, 60%.

For the central stairwell, rising three floors, the late Albert Stewart of Claremont designed a Memorial Wall, depicting (in sculptured cast-stone against a parquetry of cork) six historic scenes in the life of the Society of Friends: William Penn treating with the Indians and John Woolman uplifting the enslaved Negro, John Greenleaf Whittier as poet and Elizabeth Fry ministering to prisoners, Friends war relief and Quaker missions. In bronze letters at the top: Enlightenment/Peace/Brotherhood. And down through the whole design run broken rays of the Light, upon which are fixed the handclasp of Friendship—the open Book—the dove of Peace.

The *tenth* new building was the Dr. Frank Irvin Ball Residence for Women, for which ground was broken following dedication of the Wardman Library. Occupying the Jessup acre in the block east of Stauffer Residence Hall, this dormitory, designed by William H. Harrison, accommodated 90 women students. It was planned as the first unit for an eventual second quadrangle. Mrs. Ethel Ball, widow of the Portland dentist whose name it bears, was related to the pioneer Hadley and Lindley families of Whittier. She made a gift of $200,000 that enabled

*Actually 31,000 volumes had been acquired, but 14,000 old volumes had been discarded (including normal losses). The collection had therefore been improved in its quality.

the college, with other funds of its own, to complete this $650,000 building in 1966.

THE LARGEST BUILDING on the Whittier campus was already under construction in 1966—the new Science Building. It was for this that, as both Wardman and Smith foresaw, Hadley Field had to be cleared by removing athletics to Memorial Field.

This building, too, has a long history since the first talk of a science building in 1909. Later, when the college built little Naylor Hall for Chemistry in 1918, it contemplated a companion building for Biology; but this appeared only on Master Plans. Whittier College, which had given pre-professional training to so many doctors and scientists, continued through decades to carry on its work with increasingly antiquated laboratories and equipment. Naylor Hall (50 years old) was outmoded and outworn for chemistry; Provident Hall (20 years old) was a war-surplus makeshift for physics; old Founders Hall (60 to 70 years old) housed biology in its basement and in scattered rooms above it, and geology shared the rest of that relic with speech and drama. Yet, during a significant period of years, Whittier had been one of the first among California colleges in number of undergraduates proceeding to university doctorates in the sciences. And a dozen science professors carried on modest yet significant programs of research in pitifully inadequate laboratories.

The need was desperate for new science facilities.

The college board directed Allison and Rible to begin planning in 1964. In 1965 a substantial Federal grant (under the Higher Education Facilities Act of 1963) determined President Smith's decision to proceed even without matching funds fully in hand. The architects designed a five-story structure—as long as a football field. It was to house all of the science departments and mathematics. Included were instructional and research laboratories, lecture halls and classrooms, stockrooms and animal shelters, offices and darkrooms, and a sizable science library. As the plans developed to meet the anticipated needs of the science faculty, the estimated cost increased to $3,400,000. The Federal grant, as supplemented, provided $1,000,000 of this staggering sum. The early contribution of $50,000 from the family foundation of Mrs. Winifred McIntyre of Hillsborough encouraged the

349

participation of others such as Florence A. Hampton in this vast undertaking. A contingency gift of $250,000 from John Stauffer, a challenge to be matched dollar for dollar by other gifts, brightened the prospect of completing the Science Building debt free.

With this great new structure nearing completion, the college made preparations for removing Provident Hall, thus clearing the Quad as a central approach to the second floor of the Science Building. And old Founders Hall*—which had actually been scheduled for removal in the Master Plan in 1917 but served a further half century—again came under consideration, to be removed or possibly remodeled, with due regard for the new buildings and campus vistas.

Such was the prospect in the spring of 1967.

"There will always be need for one more building," President Smith reported to both the faculty and the college board. He was thinking of an auditorium and little theatre, additional classroom building, a student health center, speech and reading clinics with psychology laboratory and testing center. "These," he added, "will come in due time."

But Smith felt that the major building phase in the redevelopment of Whittier College was pretty well fulfilled.

The completion in a dozen years of ten new structures (and the sweeping away of thirty older homes, duplexes, flats, garages) had largely remade the Whittier campus. The costs would have seemed fantastic in 1951 and the securing of such funds wildly impossible. For completed new buildings and their equipment, $5,000,000—for campus expansion, $1,000,000—for moving and remodeling existing buildings and other permanent improvements, $500,000—for a new science building and its equipment, $3,500,000! This Paul S. Smith could add up (on a scrap of paper) for a grand total of some $10,000,000 committed within the period of his presidency for the development of the college campus and plant.

Whittier had in fact become a residential college. Whereas in 1951 it housed 30% of its students, in 1966 it housed 70% of a student body that had doubled in size!

*To which in May 1951 an historic marker had been affixed by the Native Daughters of the Golden West, reading: "Founders Hall/Built by Pioneers/for/Whittier Academy 1894/Home of Whittier College since 1901 . . ." It had been "College Building" from the start, however, and "the home of Whittier College" since 1896.

The college had also become more efficient, with a substantially complete and expanding plant for carrying on its major functions.

But in addition to this was the outstanding improvement in "educational packaging." Beautifully-designed modern buildings, landscaped with old trees and new planting of shrubs and open lawns, made the Whittier campus one of sightly vistas.

President Smith had begun to turn his thoughts to the next great step: the raising of $10,000,000 as further endowment to undergird the academic and instructional program. His conversations about this with Bonnie Bell Wardman resulted in her decision to support this undertaking by a provision in her will. Upon her death in March 1966, the extent of her generous bequest revealed securities and interests valued at more than $1,000,000. It was a great forward step toward the goal Smith had set for Whittier College: total assets of $25,000,000 by 1975.

4

GROWTH OF THE WHITTIER FACULTY,
DEPARTMENTS, AND SCHOLARSHIP

INCREASE OF THE WHITTIER faculty in size and in professional stature had a hard time keeping pace with the spectacular transformation of the academic plant and campus.

With the sudden drop in enrollment in 1951 (of which more presently), the size of the faculty was allowed to shrink proportionately. For six years the number in the student body remained fairly constant. Thereafter it began to rise steadily until by 1966 it had doubled. The faculty was again enlarged. The president and dean—no less than the trustees—having experienced the fluctuations and uncertainties of the 'thirties and 'forties, were wary about committing the college to sudden or permanent increases in staff. But new men and women were added to most of the academic departments. For instance, the departments of History and of Political Science/International Relations, which together had been staffed by 4 men in the mid-'fifties, were staffed by 8 men a decade later. In 1955 Sociology and Economics/Business Administration together comprised 5 men; by 1966, the equivalent of 9. So, too, with English and Speech/Drama—

what had been 6 in all, became the equivalent of 10. In the departments of the natural sciences and Mathematics, there had been a total of 8; this doubled to the equivalent of 16. Altogether the faculty grew during the decade from 59 (of whom 47 were full-time) to a total of 105 (68 full-time). Calculated as "full-time equivalents," the faculty has increased 60% in size.

This was not sufficient growth, some critics asserted. It left Whittier lagging in student-faculty ratio.

While not insensitive to this, President Smith certainly rejected student-faculty ratio as the only yardstick for measuring educational efficiency. Nor could class-size alone be the criterion of good teaching. Smith pointed out that one professor might be more effective lecturing to 400 than some other instructing a class of 40 or leading a seminar group of four! Although there were some large classes, many of the lower division and most of the upper division courses continued through these years to be small enough for optimum small-group teaching.*

The faculty in these more recent years, as in the past, pressed for better salaries.

President Smith had not been insensitive to this, either. However, he did not accept salary-scale as an index of educational effectiveness any more than student-faculty ratio. Increasing the pay of a mediocre teacher, he said, never improved his teaching. But—he did raise salaries.**

When Smith became president in the fall of 1951, the faculty at once sent up a request through him to the Board of Trustees asking for a 10% raise in base pay and in bonus, without evident regard for the second sharp drop in enrollment and tuition income. For the faculty had learned (via unreliable grapevine) that the trustees had $100,000 stashed away that "really belonged" to the faculty. Of the $100,000 in question, half was a building fund of earmarked contributions, and half had been

*A study made for the fall semester 1965 showed that 44% of the classes had fewer than 15 students, that 60% had fewer than 25, and that 87% had fewer than 50. Some of the large classes in the General Studies program, with lectures for 200 to 300 or more students, were provided with laboratory or coaching sections. Taking these sections into account, 65% of the classes had fewer than 15 students, and 75% fewer than 25.

**No general salary increase had been announced for 1951-52. The top base-pay stood at $3,875 plus 10% in retirement funds, but a 27½% bonus was added to this, which brought total remuneration for most full professors to $5,327.

accumulated as an essential reserve fund and was so reported to the Western College Association. There was no obligation to distribute even this modest reserve to the faculty as additional bonus.

By 1951, however, the continuation of the old base-and-bonus system was unbusinesslike and unnecessary. As a first step toward removing it, the trustees at once raised the base salaries 20% adding to that a 10% bonus. But this only figured out as a 3.5% net raise. The faculty minuted its "dissatisfaction."

Through its representation on the Advisory Committee, the faculty tried to formulate a systematic salary schedule that would equalize salaries according to training and experience, rank and length of service, and yet allow some leeway for administrative discretion and judgment. But this effort met two obstacles: First, academic rank had been rather unsystematically disposed through the years by Whittier administrations, sometimes satisfying the instructor's demand for more pay by the solace of higher rank. As a result, several with the rank of "professor" were paid less than others whose rank was "assistant professor." Second, it was important—in the view of president and trustees— that salary should be commensurate with value. By 1958 it was established policy that "larger increases are to be given to faculty members making the most significant contributions," and special funds were used to add to the salaries of three or four professors judged by the administration to be outstanding.

Members of the Faculty Club continued to press for general salary raises. They directed an insistent letter to the trustees by way of the president—then duplicated and circulated copies of it before the board met to consider the matter. This maneuver irritated the trustees; they filed the communication "without prejudice to the case which it pleaded." These businessmen had no intention of dealing with the faculty on a collective-bargaining basis; nor did this tactic of the Faculty Club impress all the professors as properly professional.

However, the trustees did raise salaries, not equally across the board but according to its policy of "merit rating," and they eliminated the outworn base-and-bonus system of payment.

A second policy—continuing from preceding administrations —was the holding of faculty salaries confidential. The college chose not to report its average salaries to the American Association of University Professors, but made them available of course to the Western College Association and to agencies of government upon request. The faculty—and through certain professors, students—kept up the pressure for higher salaries without, therefore, quite knowing what they were talking about.

As a matter of fact, Whittier College salaries increased 100% between 1951 and 1966.* During these years the cost of living also rose, but only by 30%. The faculty was therefore substantially better paid by the end of this period. Salaries had become roughly competitive with those of sister colleges in the area and better than those of many good colleges across the land. Several professors and administrative officers resigned during these years to accept positions at state colleges or universities, but their offers usually included other inducements than mere salary. During the recent decade Whittier lost but one professor to any of the other independent colleges of southern California. A number of those who left returned to Whittier or indicated their desire to do so. Beyond the normal coming and going in the larger academic community, the Whittier faculty remained notably stable.

As in other years, some professors hustled and prospered, taught an extended-day course (late afternoon or evening) or a six-week summer session either on the Whittier campus or at another college or university. Half a dozen added to their income royalties from textbooks or other writing. Several lectured profitably. Others served industry or business in research or as consultants; some added fellowships and research grants to sabbatical salaries. In line with the changing pattern of American life —with the goods of the materialistic and Affluent Society beckoning—a share of the faculty wives brought home a second paycheck by teaching or other employment.

With the wide world to travel, with the good life to enjoy—

*The average for full professors increased from $5,300 in 1950-51 to $10,812 in 1965-66. The average for associate professors, from $4,700 to $8,871; for assistant professors from $4,199 to $7,673; for instructors from $3,952 to $6,532. The average for all ranks increased from $4,560 to $8,731. Further raises for 1966-67 brought top salaries to $15,000.

A fringe benefit added during these years was the payment of full tuition for faculty sons and daughters going *to the college of their choice*, rather than the half-tuition only for those attending Whittier.

executive homes, swimming pools, vacation hideaways—faculty living in the 1960's was far distant from the stringencies and rationing of wartime, from the austerity of the depression, from the pioneering days of sewing bees and box socials, tally-ho or hayride to mountain canyon or riverside.

WITH GROWTH IN SIZE of the Whittier faculty came a strengthening of the departmental structure. Although the president and dean never lost sight of individuals comprising the faculty, there was again an increased emphasis upon the rôle of department chairman.

Rivalry developed for attracting department majors, for these then provided class lists for additional and more specialized courses. To encourage scholarship and the majors' sense of belonging, departments sponsored Greek-letter honorary fraternities. The first of these, Delta Phi Upsilon (the founding chapter at Broadoaks in 1928) came quietly to the Whittier campus in 1945. Beginning in 1959 Pi Sigma Alpha (political science), Alpha Kappa Delta (sociology), Pi Alpha Theta (history), Phi Beta (speech, drama, music) won recognition. For men in science, the Foundation Society continued, and there were various departmental clubs as well.

The interest of new professors after the war had been greater in their own departments than in the curriculum or college as a whole. Yet there were those who pushed "shared administration" so that the faculty voice might be heard formally in deciding matters of general college policy. Traditionally at Whittier College there had been easy communication between administration and faculty. The President's Office continued to be open—and no Whittier president ever lacked for advice! The Advisory Committee that had been set up in the crisis of 1939, and that had been altered by President Jones so that the faculty might elect its representatives, was called upon less frequently during these years, except to consider matters of faculty tenure. If it became gradually clear that President Smith was keeping in his own hands the making of policy decisions (for which, of course, he was answerable to the college board), it was also clear that he informally sought advice widely and reached such decisions deliberately. His administrative committee dealt with extraordinary problems of discipline—there were never many—and the suspension or dismissal of students failing badly in their academic work.

If some professors wanted more power in the hands of the faculty, others were inclined to yawn at faculty meetings, disinterested even in those questions falling within the area of their traditional responsibility. More and more they were willing to leave to committees matters that early faculties had pondered. These committees, named by the president and the dean, carried on much of the academic business. They considered questions of admissions and requirements, courses of study, academic standards and grading, degrees and honors. Most important was the large representative Curriculum Committee, of which the dean was chairman. Other committees—on scholarship awards, scholarship recognition, honorary degrees, social affairs—served special functions. Most of the "academic housekeeping"—catalog and schedule, room assignment and registration, approving petitions covering minor exceptions to rules, and all the rest of the details of smooth running, were carried on efficiently by Dean Harold F. Spencer and then by Dean Roy Newsom with the help of administrative staff. The faculty generally was content to leave details in their hands.

But professors there were, as in any faculty meeting—so merely human were they—who could be persistent or pompous in what seemed to others petty matters. Among the bores no less than the bored were those who watched the minute hand's tedious turn toward five o'clock, at the regular meeting first-Monday of the month, which began with prayer or meditation at 4 p.m.

Some degree of disinterest in the general affairs of the college was certainly a reflection of the greater size of the faculty, the preoccupation of professors with their departments, the marked change in the character of the post-War faculty. Fewer and fewer lived within walking distance of the campus—new housing was on the outskirts of the old townsite. More and more faculty wives chose to work, with resulting decrease in family interest and participation in college life. A dwindling number of professors "supported" student activities, worked closely with societies and clubs, entertained groups in their homes, enriched their lives by attending their colleagues' special lectures and recitals. And there was perhaps some loss in the "vocation" of college teaching, in the sense of commitment and institutional loyalty.

Something of value was seeping away as Whittier College moved forward in becoming more-than-Quaker and more-than-local. But these were manifestations of the changing times, by no means unique to Whittier.

PROFESSIONAL ACTIVITIES of the Whittier faculty broadened markedly during these years.

More and more members of the faculty provided significant leadership in the larger academic community. President Smith served terms as president of Western College Association, the Independent Colleges of Southern California, the Association of Quaker College Presidents. Dean Spencer was on the executive committee of Western College Association and the board of Metropolitan State Hospital at Norwalk. Dr. T. William Robinson throughout these years was a member of the executive committee (and chairman in rotation) of the Institute of International Relations. Dr. John Schutz continued through the years as secretary of the Pacific Coast Branch of the American Historical Association; Prof. Aubrey Bonham was president of the National Association of Basketball Coaches; Prof. Ruth Haroldson continued directing the Women's Symphony Orchestra of Los Angeles. Others, too, served regional and national associations, read papers at professional meetings, received invitations to teach or conduct institutes on other campuses: Dr. Robert W. O'Brien to lecture as exchange professor of sociology, Exeter University, England; Dr. Albert W. Upton to direct an English language institute at George Peabody in Nashville; Dr. James M. Merrill to set up a department of maritime history at the University of Delaware.

Research grants supported Whittier professors in their studies in South America, in Europe, in Washington, D.C., at Harvard—and closer home in nearby research libraries, in problem areas of the County, and on the Whittier campus itself. To keep the trustees abreast of this activity in scholarship, President Smith invited professors to speak briefly at board meetings. For a workshop session in 1959, Dean Spencer summarized the research and current writing of twenty of the faculty. In substance he reported:

Dr. Eugene Mills, on leave at Harvard completing his MS on *Art Creativity*.

Dr. Milo Connick, with a book on the Sermon on the Mount, *Build on the Rock* readied for the press [Revell, 1960].

Dr. James Merrill, returned from a year's study of Civil War Naval history in the National Archives under a Guggenheim grant.

Dr. John Schutz, providing material for the *Encyclopaedia Britannica* on nine southern California cities.

Dr. J. W. Robinson, completing a second volume in collaboration with Dr. [James T.] Watkins of Stanford, a companion to *General International Organization: a sourcebook* [Van Nostrand, 1956].

President Smith, writing the Nixon biographical article for *Encyclopaedia Britannica*.

Dr. Ben Burnett, completing, with co-author Moisés Poblete Troncoso, the MS for *The Rise of the Latin American Labor Movement* [Bookman Associates, 1960 and later in paperback].

Dr. Robert O'Brien, continuing research on the Nixon Papers and on minority groups in southern California.

Dr. H. David Kirk, on the Whittier campus from McGill University, Montreal, directing research on the adoptive family, financed by a U.S. Public Health grant.

Dr. Betty Unterberger, continuing her studies in Soviet-American relations and Soviet foreign policy.

Dr. Edward Stack, with several recent foreign-language textbooks related to his work in the Language Laboratory.

Dr. Gladys Stevenson, retained by Robertshaw Fulton Company to direct research on the physics of the cooking process.

Dr. Inez Hull, associated with Dr. Stevenson in working on the microbiology of the cooking process.

Mrs. Frances C. Hoffman, experimenting on the effect of various sorts of domestic water in the dilution of concentrated drinks and foods.

Dr. Beach Leighton, investigating landslide problems in southern California under a grant from National Science Foundation.

358

Dr. David Bender, retained as consultant by North American Aviation to advise in the field of orbits.

Dr. John Arcadi, researching the histochemistry of the urogenital system in lower animal forms under a U.S. Public Health grant.

Dr. Thomas Harriss, continuing his study of the anatomy of mites.

Dr. Lois James, working on a morphological study of the Macadamia nut.

Dr. W. Roy Newsom and his staff, attempting to devise techniques for the detection of small amounts of beryllium.

During the year appeared in print the Connick and Burnett books above noted, also Gerald R. Patton's *African Detour* (Vantage Press) and Dr. Gladys T. Stevenson and Dr. Cora Miller's *Introduction to Foods and Nutrition* (Wiley Press).

However, no "publish or perish" pressure harried Whittier professors. Some, like Dr. Gilbert McEwen in English, carried on long-range research at nearby Huntington Library. Others simply read widely to enrich their courses, explored related fields, diligently completed doctoral dissertations—or found avenues of community service. Nevertheless, there was increased recognition of scholarship. President Smith said to the trustees in 1961:

> In the Whittier view, there is no necessary conflict between good teaching and purposeful research . . . In a small college it is advantageous for the two to exist together in a proper and complementary balance.

Then he listed some 20 professors who had during the year published professional articles, items in encyclopedias, and book reviews: Dr. William H. Dale, Dr. Raymond L. Erickson, Malcolm L. Farmer, Dr. Eugene E. Gloye, Dr. Lester L. Harris, Dr. Homer Hurst, James B. Moore, Dr. Harry W. Nerhood, Prof. Gerald R. Patton, Dr. H. Randolph Pyle in addition to professors already listed above. And he noted nine books contracted for, published, or reissued during the year:

> Dr. C. Milo Connick, *Jesus: the Man, the Mission, and the Message* (Prentice-Hall, Inc [1963]).

Dr. Charles W. Cooper, *The A. Wardman Story* (Whittier College, 1961).

Dr. Robert W. O'Brien, *Field Manual in Sociology* (reissued by Holt, Winston, 1961).

Prof. Mabel F. Rice, *English is Our Language* (the series reissued, D. C. Heath, 1961).

Dr. Jesse S. Robinson (co-author), *Principles of Marketing* (Pitman, 1961).

Dr. John A. Schutz (co-author) *Peter Oliver's Origin and Progress of the American Revolution* (Huntington Library, 1961).

Dr. John A. Schutz, *William Shirley: King's Governor of Massachusetts* (University of North Carolina Press [in press 1961]).

Dr. Albert W. Upton, *Design for Thinking* (Stanford University Press, 1961).

Dr. Albert W. Upton and Richard Samson, *Creative Analysis* (Whittier College Press, 1961 [E. P. Dutton, 1963]).

In the first half dozen years of this period, Dr. Cooper added four more textbooks—including *The Arts and Humanity* (Philosophical Library, 1952) and *Preface to Drama* (Ronald Press, 1954)—to the four previously published. George Allen published *How to Scout Football* (School-Aid, 1953) and *Encyclopedia of Football Drills* (Prentice-Hall, 1954). Dr. Roberta Forsberg wrote (co-author with Dr. H. C. Nixon) *Madame de Staël and Freedom Today* (Astra Books, 1963) and *Chief Mountain*, biography of Samuel H. Middleton (Historical Society of Alberta, 1964). Beginning in 1957 with *The Rebel Shore* (Little Brown), Dr. James M. Merrill continued writing his highly readable trade books of scholarly research in military and naval history, published by Rand McNally: *Quarter-Deck and Fo'c'sle* (1963), *Uncommon Valor* (1964), *Target Tokyo* (1964, reissued in paperback 1966), and *Spurs to Glory* (1966).

Altogether this represented a very considerable professional and scholarly activity on the part of a teaching faculty in a liberal arts college. Nor has this summary included the creative work of those in the arts: Prof. Elnora Laughlin, traveling, painting, and exhibiting in art shows; Prof. Russell Green, bringing the productions of the college theater to a new level of artistic performance; Profs. Margaretha Lohmann, Ruth Haroldson,

Eugene Riddle, Jerold Shepherd appearing in faculty recitals and directing ensembles.

Perhaps, after all, these fifteen years indeed saw a development in faculty strength and scholarship that had kept pace with the physical transformation of the campus.

But there were also other and new measures of academic growth during these same years.

5

THE CURRICULUM—CONTINUING PROGRAMS
AND ACADEMIC DEPARTURES

THE FUNCTION OF THE FACULTY—in the Whittier view—was essentially to teach, and the college curriculum was the framework within which the professors carried on their instruction. The curriculum, however, was not considered the mere aggregate of courses described in the college catalog. It was also the pattern and sequence of the courses required by the faculty and by the departments as the basis for an earned degree.

The curricula of American colleges had become pretty well standardized. Credits circulated as academic currency—perhaps often a specious specie—characteristic of the high degree of academic mobility enjoyed in American society. But despite accrediting associations and nationally administered tests, no criteria really existed for evaluating very satisfactorily what went on in college classrooms—or in student heads—and certainly much collegiate education was spurious. But President Smith could be irked, as when a colleague suggested that Whittier might well become "the Swarthmore of the West," and he retorted, "Why not Swarthmore, the Whittier of the East!" Not that Whittier was self-satisfied, but that Smith felt it had to become better in its own way.

Periodically the faculty restudied and restated its larger human objectives for the college. It then proceeded to reshape the Whittier curriculum toward realizing these objectives in the lives of the students. But no revolutionary rethinking characterized this period—no ferment comparable to that of the mid-'twenties under the inspiration of Dr. J. Herschel Coffin or to that of the mid-'thirties under the leadership of Dr. Albert W. Upton. In its curricular pattern, the college continued in the general direction that President Smith had himself helped to set. It is notable that, with the coming and going of collegiate experiments across the land, the Whittier Idea and its modification persisted for 40 years.

Smith quoted Woodrow Wilson's unpublished complaint that "Nobody specializes in the relation of things." He thought that the General Studies (or Integrated Courses as they were earlier called) should do just that.

GENERAL STUDIES AT WHITTIER came under increasing criticism as the period wore on. Smith named Upton the co-ordinator (1958) and then director (1963) of General Studies, believing that he would be an articulate counsel for the defense, as he had been the articulate architect in redesigning the curriculum in 1936. If Smith felt that Upton had some of the failings of genius ("he could make unworkable ideas plausible, [and he] overestimated the speed at which education could take place"), he also felt that Upton's more official leadership would bring improvement in the lower-division program, to which they had both given so much thought.

For surely the parts of this original and enduring program "did not make a consonant whole," and its "public relations were poor" both with students and faculty generally. No satisfactory means had been devised for bringing newcomers into the scheme or even orienting them to it. New professors felt themselves to be department "specialists" and came from training in graduate-school scholarship. They had not had seminars in "the relation of things." Young instructors when brought into the program, saw no academic future in becoming "generalists." Nor did they have or take the time to work closely in team teaching. The use of student coaches as discussion mediators in quiz sections was only fully developed and successful in one or two courses. Some lecturers to large required classes never mastered the art and craft of "the higher vaudeville." Others were timorous in venturing outside their "fields" in noting significant relationships.

Those closest to these courses were more aware of the real

problems than were the carping critics on the sidelines. For Upton, General Studies were meant to help the students in

> getting a clear idea of the rules that work best wherever you go in life. They are harder to learn [he felt] than the little rules and require a better kind of education.

And he hammered away to keep in repair as well as to improve the curricular structure he had earlier built.

Upton's own course—at first called Significs and then Basic Communications—continued under the innocuous title: English 1 and 2, First Year Reading and Composition. This new minting of the old coin made it easier for registrars in the transfer of credits. But the course developed along its original lines. The linguistic theory and critical exercises—published as *Design for Thinking* and *Creative Analysis*—received national attention following an extended article in the New York *Times* in 1960.* How did the discipline of this course succeed in raising significantly the I.Q. of its students? The students themselves and their coaches knew. Interpretation, definition, classification, problem-solving—even with *Hamlet* and *Moby Dick*—were a difficult "brain training" for many freshmen. However much generations of students groused, they increasingly appreciated the results of the course in their later studies and lives.

The broadly historical courses in "general education" were rechristened Social Studies—someone had objected that "social science" was a misnomer. Dr. Harry Nerhood continued for years to introduce freshmen to Dr. Coffin's Whittier Idea and boomed basic concepts of Western Civilization with Randall's *Making of the Modern Mind* in hand. Under student pressure for change, Northrup's *The Meeting of East and West* was added for the second semester, although its inclusion hardly supported the basic theory of the course. Not without a certain affection was the invitation to John Herman Randall to address a Whittier convocation in the spring of 1966. No college, perhaps, had been more faithful in presentation of his broad view of the great historical ideas that have shaped our minds.

---

*Richard W. Samson, former student and assistant, collaborated with Upton in writing *Creative Analysis*. Samson gave a further and more popular exposition of this critical theory in *The Mind Builder* (Dutton, 1965).

Two of the original textbooks also survived in Social Studies III and IV for sophomores: Esmé Wingfield-Stratford's *History of British Civilization* and Vernon Parrington's *Main Currents in American Thought*. During the first years of this period "Sir Esmé" was a sort of household god for Whittier students. "It would be a happy stroke of fortune," Charles A. Beard had said, "if it could supplant some of our dry manuals in colleges." Whittier students were a little proud that *they* used it. An alumnus, recuperating in Korea from battle shock, pondered its wisdom: "Mankind has its own gait and will not tolerate hustling."

Dr. Forsberg returned from England, having lunched with Wingfield-Stratford at his country home. She had found him, in his early 'seventies, "gallantly mannered, easy to talk to, and very humorous." Students enjoyed her report of his library, his original Gainsborough, "golf balls stacked on top of books and tennis shoes stuffed in a bookcase." The gentleman scholar, cultured sportsman, patriot and soldier-pacifist—he typified the personality integrated and fulfilled. The Sachsens honored "Sir Esmé" as the serious theme of their Homecoming float in 1955 and carried off the prize.* When this philosophical history at last went out of print, Whittier arranged to reprint important sections of it. There was no implication that its interpretation of British Civilization was sacrosanct, or that it made unnecessary the reading of other historians. But it did clarify the British roots of historic American attitudes and institutions, the rich texture of our common heritage. Long on allusion and scant on dates, its paragraphs were spun to ponder, demanding close reading and illuminated teaching. When students, and some of their professors who really did not know the work, condemned it, both Smith and Upton would rise up in defense: "Forsooth!—if you'd just read the blamed thing before damning it!" And when in 1964 dissident students mounted a concerted attack upon the course and its text, the faculty committee in charge reduced the class hours and credits from five to three—but *added more extended sections of Sir Esmé!*

In the field of the natural sciences, it had been hoped that General Studies would "introduce the student to the scientific

*Esmé Wingfield-Stratford's title was a Whittier honorific; but "Sir Esmé" he remained until unknighted by the disenchanted.

method" and that a meaningful relationship would develop between this and the analytical discipline of Whittier's unique freshmen "English" course. But these science courses faced rather special problems: the great inequality of student preparation and interest, the inflexibility of science prerequisites for advanced and professional training, the emphasis upon scientific technology in the training of the professors themselves, with the scanting of philosophical and historical perspective. Various and valiant efforts were made to develop courses in this area—but by the mid-'fifties science majors were excused from them to plunge at once into their chosen specialty.

Other parts of the General Studies program also withered. The work in Fine Arts for sophomores, which had early fragmented, lost its integrative course in Aesthetics, eliminating two units of the requirement. What had been a 40-unit block of work in the first year (1937-38), and remained 36 units for most of twenty-five years, was reduced to 32 required units by 1966—except for the science majors and optionally for those who elected departmental science courses. For them the integrated course requirement had been reduced to 20 units.

Notwithstanding the special problems, General Studies continued and sought to implement the continuing broad objectives of the college.

DEPARTMENTAL MAJORS and specialized training were strengthened at Whittier while General Studies underwent modification. This reflected the development of the faculty.

Degree requirements remained what they had been, specifying a departmental major with the option of a "group major" in two or more related departments. No new departmental majors were added to the curriculum. In all, some eighteen departments offered majors, several indeed presented two or three different major programs. In Art, only a group major was possible. No major at all was given in Education, nor were Education courses accepted as part of group majors. But the Department of Education—and the wider Division of Teacher Education—continued to prepare significant numbers of teachers, all of whom (as in the past) fulfilled requirements for departmental or group majors in subject fields.

Course offerings in many of the departments increased greatly. In History, the number of undergraduate courses rose from 31 to 51, with such new titles as The Anatomy of Revolution, Russian-American Attitudes, the World Beyond Europe [Africa, India, Asia]. In Political Science/International Relations courses increased from 25 to 35, with such titles as Dynamics of Public Policy, Asiatic Governments, Model United Nations. In Sociology/Anthropology the number jumped from 29 to 49 with new interest in Racial and Minority Groups, Population and Migration, Sociological Aspects of Religion. In Psychology the count went up from 18 to 35, with Theories of Motivation, Psychological Aesthetics, Psychobiology. All courses cataloged were not given each year and such departments as Biology and Chemistry added few courses to those already given. But the expanding curriculum reflected both the broad changes in the nation's culture and the "knowledge explosion" in its intellectual life.

Though Whittier became more and more regional and national, it continued to enrich life for the city's expanding citizenry. The Summer School, which Smith had himself developed and directed, served many teachers and others in the Whittier area. The Institute of International Relations sponsored by the American Friends Service Committee was still integrated with a summer session credit course until the Institute itself changed pattern. The Institute had continued 25 years on the Whittier campus—not without community criticism. It moved its annual programs to a mountain retreat; but occasional Institutes, with a balancing of viewpoints upon such controversial issues as Disarmament and Red China, continued to be presented by A.F.S.C. on the Whittier campus, as in 1961 and 1965. President Smith and President Bewley of the college board were able to carry more conservative trustees with them in the policy of keeping the Whittier campus notably open as a forum for divergent views—and they had small patience with demands for "equal time" or arbitrary "balancing" of speakers.

Extended-day classes, earlier established for adults in the community, increased in number and size. Such courses served a variety of educational needs, kept Hoover Hall busy in late afternoons and evenings, provided extra teaching for professors who wanted it. Not directly a part of this, but of special significance, was the program established under a grant from the Fund for Adult Education (established by the Ford Foundation).

Developed by Dr. Betty Unterberger, this experimental program in Adult Education grew rapidly, drew wide and favorable attention to Whittier College, and continued for a period of five years. Community citizens of widely different vocations and backgrounds were drawn into groups for the discussion of a broad range of vital topics—from "Parenthood" to "Aging in a Modern World," from "The Ways of Mankind" to "Russian Foreign Policy," from "Economic Reasoning" to "Tension in Southeast Asia." Group leaders were not lecturers but stimulators and referees of discussion that was based upon selected reading. In the final year of the program, Dr. Unterberger had 56 groups (some thousand persons) organized in Whittier and in the metropolitan area from Laguna Beach to Baldwin Park and from La Puente to Downey. The goal of "a citizenry free through knowledge" was close to the larger purposes of Whittier as an independent college. But when the Fund discontinued its support in 1959, after about $60,000 in grants, the Liberal Arts Center closed and its program lapsed. This happened not only in Whittier but in other parts of the country where similar centers had been established. The Whittier project had not become fully self-sustaining, as hoped, and upon this its continuance had been conditioned. Otherwise, the venture in Adult Education was highly successful, served the larger community well "in a time when the public intelligence was being subverted by the propaganda of extremist groups in the name of 'freedom.' "

But the main business of Whittier College, President Smith realized, was the liberal arts education of its on-campus students.

Pre-professional and professional curricula continued at Whittier in the patterns earlier established, with the addition of three-two programs in Engineering carried on cooperatively with other institutions. Three years of general education at Whittier College, with prescribed courses in the sciences and mathematics, prepared a student to go on for two more years at Colorado State, Southern California, or Stanford University to earn an engineering degree plus the A.B. Pre-professional A.B. courses of study sent Whittier students on to professional schools, as in the past, to become medical doctors, dentists, attorneys, ministers, social workers. Other students proceeded to university graduate schools for academic doctorates to enter fields of research or college/university teaching. Preparation of public school and high school teachers continued to be an important but decreasing function of the college. During these years the Whittier student body doubled in size, but the number of graduates receiving teaching credentials dropped to one-half what it had been.

In 1966 the college was sending about one-third of its seniors on to graduate and professional schools—one-third directly into teaching—one-third into business and allied vocations.

PROGRAMS OF GRADUATE STUDY developed along with departmental growth. A few graduate students in the early 'thirties earned the master's degree in child development on the Broadoaks campus of Whittier College. Then the college established a fifth-year program for preparing high school teachers. This called for some supporting graduate courses in several major departments. But limitation in faculty, library, laboratory resources—and in educational budget—restricted the number of master's candidates. Yet, through the next score of years, a trickle of graduate students completed M.A. and M.S. degrees in biology, chemistry, English, history, home economics, speech and drama. Master's theses in the college Library attest creditable accomplishment, as did the subsequent professional success of those who wrote them. Less exacting master's degrees in education met the professional needs of Whittier alumni and others teaching in the area.

In the mid-'sixties, however, with increased research on the part of the enlarged faculty, more formal programming of graduate work was approved by the Graduate Committee for master's degrees in sociology, psychology, and political science. In sociology, Dr. Robert W. O'Brien undertook a cooperative master's program with Pacific Oaks College (on the former Broadoaks campus in Pasadena). This was a further move in the direction of academic ties with nearby independent colleges.

Establishment of the Intercollegiate Program of Graduate Studies in 1953 constituted the outstanding cooperation of this kind in the state.

As early as 1899 there had been some talk of a Confederation of Southern California Colleges. All were weak—Pomona and Occidental, no less than Whittier, sustained by their prep students. In 1907 representatives of denominational colleges met. They found no agreeable "basis of union" except that all should be Christian and look toward some dim future in which they foresaw themselves as the bases of a great Christian University. Academic cooperation, when it came, was to have a different emphasis.

In 1951 began conversations and discussions stimulated by Dr. Ernest C. Colwell of the Fund for the Advancement of Education (also set up by the Ford Foundation). He envisaged a new sort of graduate school education, hardly possible within the great university establishments, but attainable perhaps by "pooling the interests" of adjacent liberal arts colleges already giving some graduate work. Claremont Graduate School did this for its associated colleges—Pomona, Scripps, Claremont Men's College. Might not Occidental, Redlands, and Whittier cooperate with the Claremont colleges to develop a distinctive graduate program in the humanities and social sciences? With an exploratory grant of $10,000 from the Fund, the seven colleges set administrative and faculty committees to work. They developed a first plan (rejected), then a second, and finally a third, which secured an initial grant of $120,000 to launch the Intercollegiate Program of Graduate Studies in the fall of 1953.

This was to be no ordinary graduate school. The I.P.G.S. was not to supplant graduate work in the several colleges but to supplement and enrich it. The seminars were to be broadly interdepartmental. Several professors from related fields and different colleges formed with young instructors and graduate students a community of scholars, centering their study and discussions about a large theme—such as (for the initial year) Society and Ideas in Flux, with focus on the Renaissance; and Public Interest and Property, with focus on Institutions and Loyalties. Hopefully there would in time be young men and women with M.A. and Ph.D. degrees coming from these colleges with not only a sufficient mastery of one field of learning, but also a marked understanding of "the relation of things," which Whittier itself had been seeking so earnestly at the undergraduate level.

Participation of Whittier College in the I.P.G.S. was both ac-

369

tive and minimal during this period. Professors Cooper, O'Brien, and Schrickel served in succession as "fellows" and members of the Council—Burnett and Merrill, as instructors, were among the early "interns." A few Whittier students took the interdisciplinary seminars as part of their master's work. But Whittier continued to have only a small graduate department, and saw itself essentially as an undergraduate college.

But this did not minimize the value to Whittier College as a whole of its various programs of graduate work.

THE COPENHAGEN PROGRAM of overseas study for undergraduates came into being in 1959 after two years of planning. It greatly enriched the experience of those students and professors who participated in it—and in some measure of those who remained on-campus in Whittier. It was certainly one factor in making Whittier College increasingly cosmopolitan.

In the earlier periods of the college, returning missionaries and Student Volunteers, gave something of a world perspective to Whittier students, as did the few professors who traveled or studied abroad. Then there were those who served A.F.S.C. overseas and the international Y.M.C.A., and refugee scholars who became members of the faculty. Such inveterate world-travellers as Dr. Jesse S. Robinson (who flew off in alternate semesters), as Prof. Jerry Patton (who safaried the Sahara in his camper), as Dr. Harry Nerhood (who circumnavigated and then visited the Soviet Union) stimulated student interest in the wide but shrinking world. Professors Connick, Patton, O'Brien and Riddle conducted summer study tours (for college credit) to Europe and the Near East and behind the Iron Curtain. In the late 'fifties the time was ripe for developing some sort of overseas study program for Whittier College.

The choice of Denmark was more than a happy accident—though O'Brien and Patton already used the efficient services of the Danish International Student Committee of the University of Copenhagen. This small North European country was in many ways an ideal setting for the Whittier venture. A modern and progressive state with an ancient culture, Denmark was a microcosm for studying social and economic problems, a point of vantage for viewing European history, politics, and arts. More than this, most Danes in the intellectual community spoke good English. Courses and seminars for Whittier students could be conducted in English, thus opening the program to students whose major interest was not foreign languages.

Negotiations, urged on by Patton and O'Brien, resulted in agreement between the college and D.I.S. for a one-semester program at a basic cost of about $1,500. This covered transportation (by plane from New York and return), college tuition, board and room in a Danish home, a ten-day pre-study tour with brief stays in London, Paris, Amsterdam, rural Denmark, a mid-term trip to Berlin, field trips in Denmark, evenings in theatre and concert-hall. President Smith flew to Copenhagen and (in the words of the Danish press) "inspected his troops," confirmed his enthusiasm for the undertaking. Successive faculty directors, the first being "Jerry" Patton, brought various emphases to the studies and modifications in the arrangements. The student group grew from 25 to 75, including a number from other colleges and universities as further enriching the program. Students returned from their term abroad with an enlarged view of European affairs and of their own cultural roots. The Danish lecturers —John Danstrup, Knud Jørensen, Knud Voss, Knud Helm-Ericksen—and D.I.S. director Ole Scherfig and his associate Hanna Mørch became well-known names on the Whittier campus. "Copenhagen" floats were popular entries in the Homecoming parade; the Q.C. carried columns of political and social comment by its overseas reporters; the *Acropolis* featured as many as six pages of pictures with extended legends.

COPENHAGEN, I.P.G.S., ADULT EDUCATION, and enlarged departmental majors were all part of the curriculum as a growing dimension of Whittier College.

Other developments lay in the future. President Smith looked toward a broadening of opportunity for the student's independent study. Again, he quoted an unpublished note of Woodrow Wilson:

"Self-direction breeds self-control, and self-control is the assurance of free institutions."

THE ENLARGING STUDENT BODY OF
GRADUALLY CHANGING CHARACTER

DURING THIS PERIOD Whittier College reflected the changing constituency from which it drew both its development funds and its students. Clearly Whittier was becoming more-than-Quaker and more-than-local as it sought to meet the challenge of its time and place. However rich its heritage and unique its character, it had to accommodate itself to the rising standards of the day.

Growth in enrollment posed problems for a college that prided itself upon being small. It threatened the very things, the very intangibles, that had distinguished the liberal arts colleges of the past—the *je ne sais quoi* that brought a disproportionate number of their alumni into Who's Who. But if the time had passed when a poor college could be a pretty good one, it had also become increasingly true that a small college as such could hardly meet the educational demands placed upon it in the 1960's.

During most of its history, Whittier had no choice as to its size. Except for a brief moment during the G.I. boom, when there were more qualified applicants than could be admitted, the college always wanted and indeed needed to be a bit larger than it was. In 1913 it desperately hoped for 100 collegiate students; in the 'twenties for 400; in the 'thirties for 500. Only after World War II did enrollment surge ahead until it reached a peak in the fall of 1949. Of the 1374 at that time 1220 were regular undergraduates.* Then came a drop of 10% in 1950—and a further drop of 16% in 1951, at which time the regular student body stood at 895.

President Smith at once appointed one of his former students as full-time director of admissions. George Tenopir '48 (M.A. 1949) left a successful career in teaching to organize the work of his new office. His assignment was to secure both more and better students for Whittier College, students drawn from a widen-

*Only the regular undergraduates (full-time freshmen, sophomores, juniors, seniors) are used as an index, as they comprise what constitutes the basic student body. Not included are graduate, special, and unclassified students—nor those in the extended-day courses. Spring semester enrollments were characteristically smaller than fall enrollments, by as few as 20 students or as many as 100. Unless otherwise indicated, fall enrollments are those compared.

ing constituency. The number of applicants for admission increased, and the standards for admission were raised. The size of the Whittier student body remained quite stable for six years, while the college developed dormitory and dining facilities for accommodating more residence students.

The number of local students increased among the applicants for admission, but "local" was an expanding word. The City of Whittier doubled during these years, largely by annexation, as the old town was already built up. In addition to the City of 60,000, there was the neighboring area with 250,000 more. And a vast population reservoir—the 8,000,000 of four contiguous counties—was brought within an hour's drive of the Whittier campus by the growing complex of interconnecting freeways. Everywhere were large school systems. Even the "local" district developed seven high schools where there had been but one at the close of the World War II.

Such was the burgeoning population of southern California, the fruits of persistent migration to the Land of Promise, and of the postwar "baby boom." With this came pressure on the part of parents to get sons and daughters into a college of their choice. College prep students became over-anxious as to grades and test scores, and made simultaneous application to three or four colleges. During the years when Whittier enrollment doubled, the applicants for admission increased fivefold. Roughly two-thirds of these were considered qualified to do creditable college work—one-third finally formed the next freshman class.

Dean Tenopir and his staff reached out to a widening circle in their interviewing of applicants. In addition to high school transcripts and College Board test scores, other objective indices were also used. Not inflexibly bound to any of these, however, the college was alert for evidences of unusual aptitude, leadership, creative gifts. Some "late bloomers" might still be admitted provisionally, with a chance to prove their worth in college. By 1966, 50% of those admitted came from the top 10% of their high school classes.

After six years of more selective admissions from among the increasing number of applicants—and with the first of the new dormitories constructed—the size of the Whittier student body was allowed to increase. The enrollment in 1957 jumped by a hundred. In the fall of 1960, with a freshman class of 460, the regular enrollment of 1285 surpassed the crest of the G.I. wave. In the fall of 1966, the number reached 1799. By this time, then, Whittier was half-again as large as at the postwar peak—double the 1951-1957 plateau—thrice the highest point of the 'thirties— quadruple the best years of the 'twenties—ten times the enrollment of 1916!

During this time, the student body became proportionally less local than it had been. By 1964, hardly 20% of the students came from the Whittier area—about 20% from outside the State— (including 5% from abroad)—another 20% from central and northern California—and some 40% from widely scattered communities in southern California. The college had housed but 30% of its student body in 1951; in 1966 it housed 70%. And for this now-largely residential and enlarged student body, Whittier provided a notably expanded campus, enlarged plant, strengthened faculty, and broadened curriculum.

Whittier had become one of the largest of the so-called "small colleges." It had kept pace in size with its near sisters, Occidental and Redlands, but remained smaller of course than the cluster of Claremont colleges. If Whittier became largest of the Quaker colleges, the others too had grown—and even Haverford, richest and all but smallest, decided to enlarge. This was all part of a widespread change in the academic economy of the independent colleges.

But President Smith foresaw a leveling off in numbers for Whittier, and a yet more selective policy of admissions.

OTHER CHANGES ALTERED the character of the Whittier student body.

The proportion of men to women had always been a concern for colleges that recognized one of their objectives to be social. After World War II, with the incoming veterans, men outnumbered women 3 to 2. As enrollment fell, this disproportion righted itself, but in the fall of 1951 there were still a few more men than women. By the next fall, the situation reversed: women outnumbered men. In 1962 the balance of the sexes was 7 women to 6 men, roughly the proportion of girls to boys graduating from the high schools.

117. PAUL S. SMITH, eighth president of Whittier College. 118. RICHARD M. NIXON, commencement speaker (1954). 119 THOMAS W. BEWLEY, president of the board. 120. BOARD OF TRUSTEES (1965).

Lewis, Knott, Rosenberger, Erwin, Rees, Trillingham, Robinson, Smith, Cohu, Murdy, Compton, Hinshaw, Harris.
Seated: Eckels, Blake, Nixon, Wardman, Stauffer, Thompson, Ball.

121. SENIOR PROFESSORS—Dr. Albert W. Upton, English, director of General Studies; Dr. W. Roy Newsom, chemistry and Dean; Dr. Robert W. O'Brien, sociology and I.P.G.S.   122. FROM FIVE CONTINENTS—Ron Snowden and students from nine foreign countries.   123. "SIR ESME" FLOAT in the Homecoming Parade (1955).

124.   JOHNSON HALL, Residence for Women (1955): lounge, main entrance, patio.

125. PROFESSORS LONG HERE—and there: Prof. Elnora Laughlin, painting; Dr. William
H. Dale, musicology, with John Danstrup (political science) and Knud Voss (art history) in Copenhagen; Dr. David F. Bender, physics.   126. INTERIM THEATER, scenes
from *Macbeth* (1963).   127. COPENHAGEN, Whittier students (1959).

128. WALTER F. DEXTER STUDENT CENTER (1958): Campus Inn, Student Union.

129. PROFESSOR-SCHOLARS with their recent books—Dr. Ben G. Burnett, political science; Dr. C. Milo Connick, religion; Dr. James M. Merrill, history.   130. FORENSICS STUDENTS, with sweepstakes trophies (1963), Mr. Gerald G. Paul, director.   131. A CAPPELLA CHOIR (1960), Prof. Eugene M. Riddle, director.

132. PEASLEY CENTER OF MUSIC, RELIGION, PHILOSOPHY (1961): Memorial Chapel, Schlicker organ, Arnold Hall and Music Building.

133. PROFESSIONAL PROGRAMS for teachers, dieticians, clinicians—Dr. Homer Hurst, secondary education; Dr. Cora Miller, home economics; Dr. Lester L. Harris, speech correction; Lola B. Hoffman, reading clinic.   134. SPRING SING, the Athenian entry (1952).   135. MODERN DANCE, physical education activity.

136. JOHN STAUFFER LECTURE-LABORATORY (1958)—John Stauffer, college trustee.
137. BEVERLY M. STAUFFER RESIDENCE HALL FOR WOMEN (1961-62).

138. PHYSICAL EDUCATION — professors, directors, coaches: Wallace J. Newman, Aubrey R. Bonham, Alyss G. Sutton, John H. Godfrey.   139. INTERCOLLEGIATE ATHLETICS—basketball and football.

140. MEMORIAL FIELD/STADIUM in Worsham Canyon (1951, 1963)—crowds, cheer and song leaders.

. ADMINISTRATORS—H. F. Spencer, Dean (to 1963), W. R. Newsom,
[ma]n (from 1963), George Tenopir, admissions; B. G. Whitten, librarian.
. RHODES SCHOLAR, Stan Sanders, with J. W. Robinson, political sci-
[enc]e. 143. LANGUAGE/LITERATURE—G. D. McEwen, English; G. M.
[Ri]sty, German.

[1]4. BONNIE BELL WARDMAN LIBRARY (1964). 145. MR. AND MRS.
[W]ARDMAN—Bonnie Bell Wardman and Aubrey Wardman.

146. SCIENTISTS long on the faculty—geologist Dr. Beach Leighton; biologists Dr. Lois E. James, Dr. John Arcadi, Dr. Thomas T. Harriss. 147. COLLEGE BOWL, winning contestants, with Dr. Harry G. Schrickel, psychology. 148. PRESIDENT AND MRS. SMITH (and friend) greeting Dr. and Mrs. Raymond C. Thompson.

149. SCIENCE BUILDING, architects' perspective. 150. CONSTRUCTION viewed by John Stauffer and Paul S. Smith.

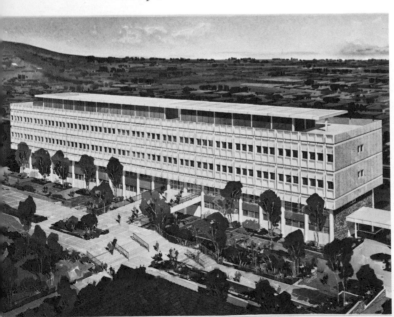

From the viewpoint of religious affiliation, the pattern did not change greatly during the period. But there seemed to be a loosening of established religious ties.

Methodist young people continued the largest group, as they had been for half a century. In 1955 they comprised 25% of the student body, Presbyterians 15%, Congregationalists 8%, Baptists 7%, Episcopalians 6%, Quakers 5%, Christian Scientists 3%, Mormons 2%. Catholics had become twice as numerous as Friends. During the next decade, Protestants continued to make up two-thirds of the total, but with some decrease in the proportion of Methodists. (However, 22% of the students declined to state their religious preference.) Friends remained at 50 or so in number, but had decreased to 3% of the total. In 1966 Moslems had a slight numerical edge on the Quakers, and Catholics were as numerous as Methodists. There was no telling, of course, how meaningful or how perfunctory was a student's declaration that he was Jewish or Christadelphian, Unitarian or agnostic.

One notable religious phenomenon on campus during the mid 'fifties was a group of strongly evangelistic students. They petitioned the faculty for recognition as the Varsity Christian Fellowship, to be affiliated with chapters on other campuses. But the faculty denied the petition, partly because outside organizers invaded the campus, partly because aggressive evangelism disquieted the dormitories, as sinners were called upon "to look to the salvation of their souls." What seemed to some the denial of religious liberty, was by others interpreted as safeguarding the rights of privacy and the campus tradition of Friendly tolerance. The policy was sustained: no religious clubs on campus under direct sponsorship of outside groups. However, a local Christian Fellowship continued for the next years.

The appointment to the Whittier faculty in 1956 of a college chaplain was intended to give general direction to religious interests on the campus. Rev. Robert T. Bobilin (M.Th., U.S.C.) and his successor Rev. Wendell A. Hook (B.D., Union; Ph.D., Edinburgh) worked with a student and faculty committee in arranging and conducting voluntary chapel services. These were nonsectarian, within the Protestant tradition of the majority of the student body. But, with the changing temper of the times, comparatively fewer students attended them. Sunday morning services in the Memorial Chapel undertook to give resident students a "church on campus," but they also were poorly attended, and were temporarily discontinued in 1966. The Friends unprogrammed meeting, held for a score of years at 8:30 a.m. in the O. T. Mendenhall Building, had very few students among its regular Sunday worshippers.

A good number of the college students participated in the activities sponsored for them by the Whittier churches—Wesley and Pilgrim fellowships, young Presbyterians and Friends, Canterbury club and Christian Science Society, Aquinas and then Newman club, the latter with chapel-hour meetings on campus. These, too, were part of the religious life of Whittier College students.

As for political views, students (for all their making up of their own minds) tended to reflect the politics of their families.

A sampling in 1956 showed 58% to be Republican, 27% Democrat, 12% Independent, 3% Don't-Knows. Part of the "apathy" that student leaders and Q.C. editors decried through successive generations—on the Whittier campus as on others—evidenced no more than the frustration of activists at the unruffled poise of their peers. Young Republicans gained approval as a campus club at this time.* Young Democrats also organized. National elections, of course, increased campus interest in partisan politics.

Regarding celebrated alumnus Richard M. Nixon, it was hard for students to be nonpartisan. Some were proud of his political achievements and of the nationwide identification of Whittier College with him—"Oh, yes, I know; that's where Dick Nixon went." Others were just as proud of being anti-Nixon. President Smith was able to balance his personal friendship and support of his distinguished former student with his championship of campus freedom in politics and opinion, something that Nixon himself valued. But Smith could be irritated by occasional lapses in courtesy and good taste on the part of overzealous students and faculty: the professor who placarded his car with anti-Nixon posters at the Library entrance, or the Q.C. editor who reprinted a smear-Nixon diatribe on the eve of election!

By and large it was nonpartisan political activity that drew

*After the 1964 elections, the group reorganized as a chapter of the (moderate) California College Republicans.

the greater student interest: preparation for annual sessions of the Model United Nations, or the annual excursion of Pi Sigma Alpha to Sacramento for informal discussions with the Governor, state officials, legislative leaders. Of course there were a few student extremists on the Whittier campus, Right and Left, but the bulk of the student body seemed to be in the bipartisan middle, as might be expected, with the liberal tendencies of youth predominating.

The cosmopolitan character of the Whittier student body continued, but with a proportional increase in the number of students from abroad. By 1965 more than a hundred foreign students were enrolled, comprising 6% of the total, and a widening range of racial backgrounds was evidenced on the Whittier campus. In addition to a few from European countries, from Africa, from Latin America, from Japan and Korea, from Taiwan and Vietnam, came a contingent of students from Iran, Kuwait, and Saudi Arabia. For some of these, special instruction was provided. They lent cultural enrichment to campus and dormitory life. For the President's Christmas Party in 1963, a large group from far lands appeared in their homeland costumes to share in the spirit of the occasion.

The various racial strands in the complex of American society became increasingly evident. The state sending the most students to Whittier, second to California itself, was Hawaii. Warm ties had existed between Whittier and the Islands for three decades, bringing a succession of attractive and popular students. By 1960 the college had an Hawaiian Club of some 50 students. The Polynesian, Chinese, Japanese, and assorted Caucasian components of Hawaiian culture were woven into the pattern of campus life, with Bill Kinaka as A.S.W.C. vice-president in 1963 and others also in student leadership.

The Whittier student body had always been open to those of the so-called minority races. American Indian, Mexican-American, Californiano, Japanese-American, and Jewish students enriched campus life through the years with their talents. The faculty also had long been interracial, with regular or visiting professors identifiable as Amerindian or Arab, as Oriental or Negro, as European-Caucasian (Nordic or Mediterranean) or Semitic. They were all living specimens for freshmen who practiced "classification" by sorting photos of the sculptured "Races of Mankind" by Malvina Hoffman.

Of interest is the place that Negro students have occupied on the Whittier campus. From the time when George Anthony graduated with the academy class of 1899 and proceeded to become a medical doctor, there have been occasional though never many Negro students at Whittier.* In one way or another, they made their mark as athletes, scholars, student leaders. No campus position or honor has been closed to them: team captain, society president, member of the student executive committee, student body treasurer. Both Bill Kelly (in 1959) and Stan Sanders (in 1963) served as president of the Associated Students. Kelly, trained in applied sociology, entered international Y.M.C.A. to work in Sweden. Sanders, outstanding all-round athlete and major in political science, received a Rhodes scholarship in 1963. He was the first Whittier graduate so honored, for Judge Frank G. Swain '11e (Rhodes scholar half a century earlier) had not proceeded to a Whittier degree. Sanders was one of the two American Negroes thus sent to Oxford, the first in this century.**

A campus open to students of all races was part of Whittier's Quaker heritage. When other colleges suddenly "pioneered" in exchange programs with southern Negro colleges, Whittier quietly continued its interchange with Fisk University and at times with Howard that had been going on for a score of years. When some national fraternities were at last breaking their stubborn racial barriers, Whittier societies simply continued their practice of decades, choosing men and women for membership without racial discrimination, on the basis of friendliness, leadership, and personal interests.

Not all individuals on the Whittier campus were free from delimiting prejudices, certainly, but in general the spirit was one

*There had never been a separate listing or tabulation of Whittier students according to race or national origin. Foreign students were kept track of because of the legal requirements regarding entry visas. Religious preference was noted so that community churches might welcome and invite new students to their services.

**Returning from Oxford to study law at Yale on a fellowship, Stan Sanders visited his home in Watts during the summer of 1965. He identified himself with the protest (though not with the violence) of family neighbors and newcomers to the area. The next Sunday morning, with presence and poise, he spoke of the experience from the pulpit of First Friends Church in Whittier.

of openness to all as the college became gradually more cosmo-politan.

Another change in the character of the Whittier student body resulted from the drastically increased costs of independent higher education.

The cost of attending Whittier College doubled during the period. Tuition climbed from $500 per year in 1951 to $1,260 in 1966—board and room from a minimum of $500 to a minimum of $700—student body fees from $24 to $50 a year. These increased costs, like those at comparable colleges, were greater than the 30% rise in general cost of living. They reflected the changing demands made upon higher education—demands for larger and better faculties, for larger and better teaching facilities, for larger and better libraries.

As a direct result of this, more and more Whittier students came from families in the higher income brackets. Young people from homes with but average means were increasingly likely to go to junior college, state college or university. Thus Whittier, which earlier drew a large share of its capable and ambitious students from town and country homes of limited means, had gradually become a college drawing from urban and suburban homes of more wealth. This socio-economic shift was evidenced by increasing sophistication in dress, in cars, in attitudes, in social mores. Students had more spending money. In larger numbers their fathers were professional men and business executives. For their sons and daughters, they coveted success in the Affluent Society, professional and business careers rather than service vocations such as teaching, religious education, youth work.

Could a poor boy or girl still go to Whittier College? The answer was certainly, Yes. And many did.

For the student with a good record and marked ability, the college itself offered greatly increased numbers of larger scholarships, grants and loans. California state scholarships and National Defense Loan Funds added materially to these. Altogether 50% of the regular students received some form of assistance, other than that from their parents, or "worked their way" in part by table-waiting or other employment on campus or in the community. Despite the increased costs and the larger number of students whose parents could and did pay for them, the student

379

body continued a fair balance of those who, highly motivated, scrounged and worked and borrowed their way through college to gain the kind of education they wanted.

7
WIDENING RANGE OF STUDENT ACTIVITIES
AND INTELLECTUAL INTERESTS

"WHAT KIND OF PERSONS make up the Whittier student body?" A student journalist asked two professors as the basis for a Q.C. article in 1957.

Dr. Paul A. Albrecht, newcomer in psychology, found Whittier students "congenial, well-mannered and considerate."

> Intellectually [he said], they were conforming and dependent ... [they] accept the world as it is ... the necessity of adjusting to life's problems.

He judged them "serious-minded" but uninterested in "purely intellectual pursuits." He observed among them "no violent reaction to authority."

Dr. Albert W. Upton, that campus veteran, also thought Whittier students well adjusted. "Today's undergraduate is not confused himself; he just baffles his confused elders." Upton found no maladjusted "crusaders" on campus, but rather those who worked for improvement, not reform. "Whittier is not bothered by intellectuals" he said, and added tongue-in-cheek, "—probably has only one and a half." Rather, Upton saw Whittier students as "healthy, gregarious animals" whom the college should help to become "self-supporting individual human beings with ideals."

The student journalist, Charles Adrain, brought together his own comment:

> No rebels without a cause raise their bloody banners on the Whittier College campus. There are not even any rebels WITH causes ... The middle way now seems the most sensible way.

He added ruefully that the student had reached "an intellectual stalemate." Seeing good and bad in all proposals for reform, he hesitated to give himself wholeheartedly to any of them.

This student analysis of the mid-'fifties was made at the beginning of a decade's growth in enrollment, scholarship, and sophistication. Ironically it was prelude to a time of student ferment, rebels without cause, revolutionaries without anatomy, intellectuals without perspectacles.

And these were to be heard from at Whittier as part of the widespread student unrest in colleges and universities across the land.

But first, something about the interests and activities of the "healthy, gregarious animals" with ideals, the well-adjusted and unconfused, the serious-minded and nonintellectual—all those with the great middle-class utopian dream of successful job, happy marriage, home with kids, place in the sun, stake in the economy, share in the responsibilities and security of the Great Society.

ATHLETICS AND SPORTS underwent no overt de-emphasis during this period. But "a saner community attitude" developed and even inter-campus student raids pretty well ceased. Other phases of student life brought about a better "balance of interests." In the total program of Health, Physical Education and Recreation a broadened base came with the work of Dr. Elmer Johnson and later Dr. Hilmi Ibrahim, but without diminution of intercollegiate athletics. And why not doctors, lawyers, ministers, professors, engineers, businessmen, educators who as undergraduates trained and disciplined themselves by such activity?

Whittier continued its magnificent record of achievement in the field of sports without apology and within the Southern California Intercollegiate Athletic Conference. With various changes and occasional strains and squabbles, it served well through the years.* Moreover it led the way toward other forms of co-operation among the neighboring independent colleges—in fund rais-

*Something of a controversy resulted from the CBS televising of Whittier College home games on Memorial Field during the 1964 football season. Between the halves of each game the presidents (or representatives) of the two contesting colleges were introduced to speak and to show film views of their campuses, in this way reaching a large general audience throughout the entire region with valuable academic promotion. A subsequent SCIAC ruling, however, required its consent for any further TV broadcasting of Conference games—an action that President Smith protested as infringing college sovereignty in the matter of its public relations. The point became academic indeed, as no sponsor was found for the next season's telecasts.

ing, in graduate studies, and (to a limited extent) in student promotion.

Football teams, coached by George Allen (later with the Los Angeles Rams), won the conference championship in 1952, and second place or tie-for-second three of the other years, from 1951-1956. Don Coryell and then John Godfrey coached Whittier teams, which won an amazing string of eight consecutive championships or co-championships, 1957-1964. Gary Campbell was an outstanding quarterback of the late 'fifties, a Little All-American.

The 1961 team of SCIAC champions was star-studded: Captain John Sherman, an All-Coast half—Dennis McMaster, Dick Peter, Dave Okura, Stan Sanders, Little All-American tackles, guard, and end. Their teammates were hardly less distinguished. "Undefeated, untied, and untouched [*sic!*] in regular season play" with conference teams (Occidental, Pomona, Claremont Men's, Redlands), this 1961 team also beat San Diego, Santa Barbara, Davis, Pepperdine, and Cal-Western by solid scores, with never less than a three-touchdown differential! It was a season, too, of thrills: Cliff Dudley intercepted a pass in his end zone, returned it 101 yards for a TD in the Claremont game. Stan Sanders, receiving, scored on a 78-yard pass play the third play of the Redlands game! Only in a post-season NAIA game did the team suffer defeat. The eight-years triumph was broken in 1965 —"the worst season in 14 years"—which allowed the Oxy Tigers to win back the bronze shoes that had remained for an unbroken decade at Whittier.

In basketball, Whittier teams were less frequently champions than in the previous period. But they won three conference titles, three ties, and three second-places in fifteen years. The 1959 champions enjoyed a 17-game winning streak, placed three men on the All-Conference team: Bill Johnson, Carroll Hooks, and Herm Mason, the last also a NAIA All-American. Nationally recognized as an outstanding teacher of this team sport, Aubrey Bonham—who completed three decades of coaching at Whittier —was elected president of the Basketball Coaches of America in 1962.

As in 1932-33 and again in 1941-42, Whittier honored three

championship teams in 1958-59: football, basketball, and baseball.

In 1957, Wallace "Chief" Newman returned to part-time coaching. For his outstanding achievement he was elected in 1958 to the National Football Hall of Fame and was signally-honored by the California State Legislature in 1964. Upon George Allen's resignation, Newman again coached baseball. In eight years he developed two championship teams and one second-place. His final retirement in 1964 rounded out 35 years of coaching at Whittier, but he continued teaching a course in Insurance.*

In the minor sports, too, these years had their high moments.

Track continued to be dominated by Occidental. But Whittier in 1952 made a good second-place showing, with Gordon Jones (captain) and Russell Bonham, both faculty sons and later university professors. There was a Cross-Country championship that fall, Jim Lawrence the team captain. Russ Bonham was the Whittier "athlete of the year" in 1954, the third-ranking collegiate miler in the nation. In the succeeding years Coach Aubrey Bonham developed many track and field men who made fine individual records: Billy Colbert, Stan Sanders, Ned Lazaro among others.

In the middle of the 'fifties—and even though Whittier had no pool of its own—swimming came into its own as a competitive sport under the coaching of Dr. Elmer Johnson. Jerry LaBonte, champion breast-stroke swimmer, paved the way in 1956 for Whittier's first SCIAC championship in this sport.

Then, in a still lesser sport, Whittier won distinction in 1962. Paison Loaharanu—pre-medical student from Bangkok, Thailand—became the U.S. national champion (singles and doubles) in badminton—the Woman's Auxiliary contributing funds to send him East to the tournament.

In women's sports and athletics emphasis was still on healthful development and recreational skills. The applied courses of Alyss Sutton in the Dance—with coeducational groups in Folk

*With his interest in Indian affairs and the history of the southern California tribes, he advised State and Federal officials on matters of Indian land claims and education. He was especially concerned about a fair presentation of Indian culture in the textbooks used in California schools.

and Square Dance, Social Dance, Modern Dance—enjoyed wide interest, active participation and occasional exhibitions.

There was plenty for the "healthy, gregarious animals" to do to keep fit.

THE SOCIETIES AND SOCIAL LIFE continued in much the pattern already set. But the men's and women's societies comprised a smaller proportion of the total student body as its numbers gradually doubled and dormitory life and associations served a larger number.

To the established five men's societies—Franklins, Orthogonians, Lancers, Penns, and Sachsens (in order of seniority)—was added Los Quijotes in 1951-52 with Pete Reyes as president. Jimenez, Rozales, Gonzales formed the roster along with others such as Green, Gross, and Sturdevant—all pictured in Basque berets. But this society failed to win pledges in 1954 and faded from the scene. To the women's societies—Palmers, Metaphonians, Athenians, Thalians, Ionians—was added the Vestician Society in 1960, Carol Shonborn the first president. And there were additional clubs of a social nature: The Docians for "more mature women," Hui O'Hawaii for those coming from the Islands, and the Arabs Club. The Green Peppers survived from earlier years as a loose gathering of the off-campus women students.

As a popular dance for the student body, the Lancers sponsored the annual Mona Kai, for which students wore Hawaiian shirts, muu-muus, leis, straw hats, and bare feet! The Orthogonians' Side Saddle Hop brought out Western dress and accessories including raised beards. Sachsens offered the Snowball Christmas dance. Franklins found their theme in the Roaring 'Twenties. And there continued the society formals and informals, the Intersociety, and the Poetess Prom as in previous years.

The changing social life and styles were reflected in the successive volumes of the *Acropolis*. Campus dress followed the tides of fashion for both men and women, and the terrible terrible strain of final examinations brought women out in sloppy attire that would have done credit to Vassar. For much of the year many men roamed in T-shirts, Bermuda shorts, hairy legs and sandals—or in haberdashery running from Ivy League to Western campus.

384

For all the new conventions, there was less uniformity than there had once been.

AESTHETIC AND LITERATE activities drew a smaller proportion of student participation as the student body itself grew and departmental specialization sharpened.

A notable exception to this was the vitality of Spring Sing, certainly the most popular musical activity. The societies and other groups supported this annual event, with everything from barbershop quartets to impressive 50-voice ensembles vying in competition for the prizes. And, under the musical direction of Dr. Lester E. Remsen and others, a uniformed student band marched and toodle-dooed in the pageantry of football seasons.

Other musical activities were essentially functions of the Music Department: student, senior, and faculty recitals—and informal musicales as in the past. What had so long been the Whittier College-Community Orchestra under the direction of Ruth Haroldson, withdrew to independent and county sponsorship as the Rio Hondo Symphony, with but personal and historic ties to the college. The A Cappella Choir under Eugene Riddle carried on with annual tour and home concert. The Bach Festival maintained its long tradition under the direction of Margaretha Lohmann, with a national broadcasting of its 25th observance in 1962. Dedicating the new Schlicker pipe organ in Memorial Chapel, a series of concerts exhibited the full range of this crowning instrument, with performances by Robert Prichard of the faculty and by guest artists including Herbert B. Nanney '40 of the Stanford faculty, whose benefit recitals a quarter-century before had raised initial funds for the chapel itself.

The work in drama continued to be handicapped for want of adequate facilities. Dr. E. Ray Nichols, as director of Poet Theatre, produced a varied program of classics such as *Macbeth* and *The Imaginary Invalid*, contemporary dramas such as *Inherit the Wind* and *Diary of Anne Frank*, and Broadway comedies such as *Harvey* (Nichols himself playing Elwood) and *No Time for Sergeants* (with a capable Charles Tillitson in the lead and popular professors filling small rôles and costumes). The abandonment of Founders Hall for public performances moved Interim Theatre (as it was called) to the nearby Woman's Club in 1958.

As a summer venture Nichols presented melodrama for several seasons in the new Bird Cage Theater at Knott's Berry Farm. In 1961 Prof. Russell Green (M.F.A., Yale) came to Whittier from the University of Tennessee. A gifted and demanding director, he produced a succession of largely contemporary dramas—*The Crucible* and *Dark of the Moon*, *The Little Foxes* and *Our Town* —as well as popular musicals, *The Fantasticks* and *Bye Bye Birdie*. His was a high level of artistic achievement, with such gifted students as Joe Curtis and Lynn Hutchinson. An excellent little theater in the Whittier Civic Center near the campus had become available and continued to be used for college productions by Green's successor, Dr. Robert M. Treser.

Forensics as a student activity has been woven in and out of the history of the college. Under Dr. Nichols' coaching—and with a new forensics organization in 1960—Whittier won a series of intercollegiate debates and individual contests. This program continued with Gerald G. Paul as director. Forensic teams represented Whittier creditably in the invitational debate tournaments at Harvard University. A large number of Whittier men and women engaged in ever more tournaments and contests —winning a "first place sweepstakes" at the Pacific Southwest Forensics Fall Tournament in 1963. Participation in these activities proved valuable training for pre-legal students and campus leaders.

As for the art of writing, Whittier never fostered an enduring literary cult. Student writers of verse and story there have been, a lonely few. Occasionally literary magazines were born to die without further issue. In 1965, the A.S.W.C. sponsored *Figs and Thistles*, and a number of students did worthwhile writing in the journalism courses of James B. Moore.

The chief outlets for student writers continued to be the *Acropolis* and the *Quaker Campus*.

The traditional form and purpose of the college yearbook imposed limitations upon the creative talents of the *Acropolis* editors and staff writers. So did the steady rise in production costs and the increasing number of activities to be subsumed. But the photography, much of it by Robert Dill, was often first class. And the written text—captions, legends, summary paragraphs, theme statements—were functional if only occasionally sprightly. *Acropolis 1961* (Bob Davis, editor) was judged Excellent in national competition: *Acropolis 1963* (Pat Licata and Tony Realyvasquez, editors) was rated one of the top twenty among a thousand. Working on the Whittier annual was certainly worthwhile experience for the hundreds who comprised its staffs.

The *Quaker Campus*, though briefly bi-weekly, continued as the weekly publication of the Associated Students, the elected editor a member of the executive committee. The Q.C. was a competent but rather colorless college paper. Typically it reported a fair share of the news, devoted too much space to sports, relied largely on syndicated cartoons, covered society and chit-chat, editorialized and columnized against student apathy, bad manners, and cheating. It won no great prizes, stirred no great controversy, caused no great problems. Then, in the spring of 1955, an anonymous mimeographed sheet IMPACT! hit the campus—it would print, it said, *what the Q.C. dared not print!* Its revelations were not shattering. But as a result, the Q.C. assumed a more aggressive stance—perhaps encouraged by President Smith's comment that, as far as he was concerned, "There is no issue too hot for the *Quaker Campus*, regardless of the consequences."

A succession of editorial Davids proceeded to sling brickbats at assorted giants from behind the protective wall of campus Freedom. But the Q.C. staff shrank and, with it, coverage of campus news. However, serious features increased. The Q.C. became, not the Voice of Whittier College (as it proclaimed) or even of the Associated Students (to which it belonged), but of a small and self-perpetuating clique. Though these students brought occasional distinction to their paper—special contributions by Eric Bentley (on Campus Sex Habits) and by Bertrand Russell (against U.S. policy in Vietnam)—they filled its pages with their own forensic protests, at times with their own three-column photos! Rated First Class in 1958, the Q.C. won no further national honors during this time.*

The Q.C. reported the suspension and later censoring of the Redlands student paper—and the firing by Occidental students

*In 1964 to celebrate its semicentennial, the Q.C. ironically brought to the campus William Knowland, editor and spokesman of conservatism. Two years earlier Harold H. Story '16, founding editor and liberal, came to the campus to address a reunion of the former Q.C. editors.

of their editor. But the Whittier editors hardly appreciated that
—though repeatedly censured by the Whittier College Board of
Trustees and by the A.S.W.C. executive committee, and earnestly counseled by the college administration—their student
paper had not been *censored!* In attempted belittlement a Q.C.
editor characterized President Smith thus: "From his office we
will never have snap decisions, no flash of sword and mad dash
forward, no daring crusade or do-or-die cause . . ." But he added:
"we do have freedom of the press." That, of course, was good.
But he said nothing about the responsibility of student journal-
ists. Nothing about Smith's calculated decisions, steady pressure
forward, dedicated crusade leading Whittier into a larger and
freer life.

"NEW CAMPUS RENAISSANCE"—this was the self-confident phrase
used by editors of *Acropolis 1962* for what they felt was a notable
advance in the intellectual maturity and scholarship of Whittier
students.

One aspect of this was the awakening of a good number of
students to the challenge of self-direction. The columns of the
Quaker Campus were not the only expression of student ferment.
In some ways the earlier image of the Whittier College Family
had turned sour, and for some students the head of the family
was no longer the vocative "Papa Paul" but the accusative "Pa-
ternalist!" Smith became the symbol of Authority against which
(not whom) adolescence was in revolt. Some students wanted to
call the president to account weekly in open meeting—President
Smith countered by holding Monday mornings open for individual students or small groups who wished to drop in for a
chat. As many as four hundred in a year—thoughtful students—
did visit him thus to talk about college and life, personal problems and anxieties.

The Free Speech and Free Sex movements that made head-
lines on other campuses echoed faintly at Whittier. There were
a few beards and other hallmarks of the truly "ethnic"—long
stringy hair and unscrubbed faces, war-surplus jackets and
huaraches. Following an evening's protest meeting, a hundred
or so marched [drove in sports cars?] to the president's home
[press photographer alerted?] to call Smith out in bathrobe and

blanket [ill with the flu!] to answer their charges that Whittier truckled to "wealthy donors" and refused the campus to an eminent "Marxist economist." As a matter of fact, the college board had just confirmed a very liberal Policy Statement that, while keeping student organizations and their sponsors answerable to the college administration in matter of controversial speakers, left the faculty free to invite such speakers to address their classes. Thus, with good effect, an avowed Communist spoke to political science students, discussing Marxist revolutions in the critical climate of the classroom with its perspective of history.

But this was not freedom enough, some felt, The college library should circulate copies of *The Tropic of Cancer!*—the librarian insisted that he was running the library. Nor would the college bookstore stock Henry Miller!—paperbacks available on the lower shelf downtown. Women students were regulated by antiquated dorm rules imposed by a Victorian administration that thinks "sex doesn't exist"!—on the contrary, the rules were those developed by the dormitory councils, and the administration knew only too well that sex did. Perhaps, in truth, the image of the Whittier Family was still as valid as ever, with the same squabbles about late dates and liquor, impertinence to Father and deceiving of Mother that otherwise marred domestic tranquility in these and other times.

There were amusing moments. Students staged a daytime protest march in 1965 with placards—the press to provide coverage, the college president for sure in his office. Twice the two hundred circled Mendenhall Building. Smith invited them into the great hall, greeted by name a number, hinted that they lay aside their signs, encouraged them to sit down on the floor, disarmed them with answers to their questions, invited them to drop in any Monday morning. Of course some students, who had marched for the fun of it, felt a bit foolish. Within months no one remembered what the protest had been about.*

Students had characteristically resisted attending required convocations—typically thought them a waste of time, as apparently did many of the faculty, judging by their non-attendance.

In the 'sixties the A.S.W.C., with increased funds, set up a

*It was a student demand for further raising of faculty salaries.

389

substantial budget to pay lecture fees, often of $500 and even of $1500. Smith invited an elected student representative to be co-chairman with him of the joint Convocation Committee, and students played a prominent part in programming and introducing speakers. Presented now were more controversial figures with widely divergent views. But Smith held no brief for the tit-for-tat balancing of opposite numbers.

> The college graduate will have to handle himself in a world in which he will be assailed by ideas in every conceivable combination of imbalance . . . He needs to get out of college the ability to make up his own mind instead of having it made up for him.

On Tuesday mornings at convo hour, usually at the First Friends Church, the committee presented "a parade of peddlers of special causes": such old-time socialists as Norman Thomas and Upton Sinclair, and such assorted contemporaries as Paul Sweezy and Sam Rosenwein (not at the church), Felix Green and Linus Pauling, Drew Pearson and Carey McWilliams—Robert Welch and Max Rafferty, William Knowland and Ronald Reagan. There were others, too, such as James Farmer, Margaret Mead, S. I. Hayakawa, Edward Teller—and neighboring humorist Richard Armour.

President Smith came under strong pressure from conservative citizens and Friends and from some members of the college board, but won general acceptance (and most welcome community support from the Whittier *Daily News*) for the educational value of this program. After all, the older speakers were but "living pages from our national history," and those still in the thick of it were "laboratory specimens of contemporary thought." In the fall of 1964, the college board minuted its approval "with specific commendation for the work of Mr. [Chester] LaRue," then the student co-chairman of the joint committee.

This procession of convocation speakers stimulated the intellectual life of the Whittier student body. But for Smith convocations were just a side show; the classrooms were the main event.

A further index of the "new Campus Renaissance" revealed itself within the general context of protests, at Whittier as on campuses across the land. It was a significant student concern for academic standards.* Was Whittier sufficiently restrictive in the matter of admissions? (Students should be added to the Admissions Committee!) Was the faculty adequate in size, in quality, in salary-schedule? (Students should publish their evaluation of professors!) Was the curriculum keeping pace with the times? Criticism centered on General Studies—texts, methods, examination procedures. Spurred by the A.S.W.C. "exec," the Q.C. led the pack with its hue and cry—assailing "Esmé" and Parrington. The large co-curriculum committee of leading students and faculty met throughout 1964-65, making a creative analysis of the program and formulating suggestions for improvement.

Dr. Upton, a key member of the committee, could view the ruckus with some perspective. A decade before he had observed that Whittier was free of crusaders and intellectuals, its students adjusted and unconfused. Others had then described them as congenial, considerate, conforming—no rebels, no causes!

But this ferment was good—this interest of so many students in the real business of the college. Good, too, were the stimulating convos, the growing sale of good paperbacks at the student store, the increased use of the college library, the better balancing of campus interests.

A spectacular symbol of this gradual change came in the success of the Whittier College team entered in the General Electric College Bowl competition in the spring of 1964. Coached by Prof. Harry Schrickel, the students—John Guidas, Chester La-Rue, Joellen Mann, Jan Takahashi—flew weekly to New York City to match wits with teams from other colleges. They won five successive TV victories (the limit) to make Whittier one of nineteen championship colleges, the only other from California being Pomona College.**

In a real sense, the superb performance of these fine academic students was more than an exhibition of their personal gifts and

*Within a single week, student dissidents at Wellesley and Rutgers no less than Whittier characterized their academic programs as "mediocre."

**The Whittier team defeated in succession teams from Illinois Institute of Technology, Drew University, Indiana State College, Lewis and Clark College, and Marshall University.

Other Quaker colleges chosen in one year or another to enter teams were Haverford, Swarthmore (thrice a winner), and Earlham, which in 1965 lost only its fifth contest.

display of their remarkably specialized learning. Theirs was a team performance (well coached) for a college that had always made much of team sports. The alacrity with which they fielded hard questions, sized up the bases, threw for the out at home plate attested the values of their unique training in General Studies—disciplined interpretation and analysis, classification and manipulation of data, with emphasis upon "the relation of things." The Whittier professors—well pleased not to be themselves thus tested—were proud of their students, and of the broad range of knowledge that they so surely possessed and controlled.

It was part of the whole picture—as was the championship football team televised that fall—the opening of the new Bonnie Bell Wardman Library—the Q.C. editor thumbing the college catalog to find something new to criticize in his next issue!

For persons with the long view of its history—and with a closer look at this period under the amazing leadership of Paul S. Smith—Whittier College had indeed achieved new dimensions of outstanding growth.

Epilogue

FOURSCORE YEARS IS YOUNG *in the life of collegiate institutions, though Whittier is as old as the oldest in its region, save only two. Yet at the time of the fumbled founding of Friends' College in 1887, John Greenleaf Whittier himself had just turned 80, having been farm-born near Haverhill in Jeffersonian days of the young Republic. And eighty years before his birth takes one back to mid-Colonial times and the death of His Majesty George I, too-Hanovarian to speak English. And yet another fourscore years brings one to young George Fox at the start of his Friends ministry in Cromwell's England, Charles I not yet beheaded! Foreshortening history in four such leaps does lend a certain perspective view to the Quaker College in California, and lengthens the time-value of its years.*

Yet eighty years is but a short span. Still living at this present writing are those—they are but few—who recall the first struggling decade of the Whittier colony and academies. But there are a dozen presently professors and trustees who at this time have served Whittier College through the half-life of its collegiate history. If the pioneering and founding were before their time, the middle and later periods are yet green in memory—high moments and forlorn hopes, minor triumphs and poverty, choices made and indecisions survived as the college under successive leaders sought to find its place and its purposes.

Whittier College has repeatedly tried to redefine its relation to the Society of Friends (itself anomalous and enigmatic) and to its Quaker roots—to redefine its educational philosophy and to implement this in the curriculum—to redefine its co-curriculum and to revaluate its student activities—to redefinite its rôle in the immediate community and to move with the changing times.

These pages have traced such themes while detailing the Human Comedy with its ever-recurring campus scenes and ever-new dramatis personae. If professors have grown old with varying grace and wisdom, freshman boys and girls have always been of an age "to go to college" and to begin the crucial stage in their maturation, looking toward the enrichment of their lives

393

and the fulfillment of their talents. Their scenario has been the eternal spiraling and cyclic design of life itself . . .

The history of a living institution ends with its story still in progress. But as never before, the present Whittier College promises a bright future up the avenue of years—a future dedicated to the ever-greater service of youth and of Society. And Our State (in the poet's words) need not fear "the skeptic's puny hand" nor "the blinded bigot's rule" so long as its colleges stand firm by the ethical bases of their heritage and what John Greenleaf Whittier called THE BROAD CHURCH OF HUMANITY.

C. W. C.

ACKNOWLEDGEMENTS AND SOURCES

IN LIEU OF FOOTNOTES, an encumbrance for a book of this kind, a running account of sources will hopefully serve the reader. However, a full set of marginal notes has been prepared, to be found in the Whittier College archives.

The number of persons to whom the author is under obligation, and the size and range of his debt, make acknowledgement difficult. Mere mention of names in these pages will signal personal gratitude—and omission must often be construed as untold appreciation.

Book sources for the history of Whittier and of Whittier College included: Benjamin F. Arnold and Artilissa Dorland Clark [eds.], *History of Whittier* (Whittier, 1933), consisting of contributions by old-timers and pioneers; Herbert E. Harris, *The Quaker and the West, the First Sixty Years of Whittier College* (Whittier, 1948), enriched by its author's experience of decades of service to the college; Loverne L. Morris, local historian for, *The Historical Volume and Reference Works*, vol. II (Whittier, 1963).

Standard California and regional histories were drawn upon: those of John Caughey, Robert Cleland, Glenn Dumke, Carey McWilliams, and the earlier Maurice H. Newmark. The [Drs.] Walter Lindley and J. P. Widney, *California of the South* (New York, Appleton, 1888) was of curious interest. The histories of neighboring colleges (Occidental, Pomona, Redlands) provided perspective, also the histories of such Friends colleges as Haverford, Earlham, Guilford. Among the relevant Quaker histories were: Rufus M. Jones (*Later Periods*), Louis T. Jones (*Quakers in Iowa*), T. Eugene Coffin (*Living Waters Flow West*). Edwin Scott Gaustad, *Historical Atlas of Religion in America* (Harper, 1962) and Frederick Rudolph, *The American College and University, a History* (Knopf, 1962), were useful, as were occasional works in social and economic history.

Books relating to persons included Elbridge Amos Stuart, *Stuart and Allied Families* [Hadley, Lindley, etc.] (New York, 1938); privately published pamphlets by Charles E. Tebbetts (on members of his family), by H. E. Harris (on Noble B. Renneker), by J. J. Jessup *et al.* (*Campus Echoes* [honoring Absalom Rosenberger], 1930), by Levinus Painter and Laura Meigler (on their sister *Anna Moroy Painter*); J. Herschel Coffin, *The Story of an Educational Adventure* (Whittier, 1928) and *The Soul Comes Back* (Macmillan, 1929); Charles W. Cooper, *The A. Wardman Story* (Whittier, 1961); Elbert Russell, *Autobiography* (Friendly Press, 1956).

Serial volumes used as sources included the more-or-less annual *Catalogue* of Whittier Academy (1891-1894) and of Whittier College (1895-1905); thereafter the quarterly Whittier College *Bulletin* (1906-1967), which included an annual *Catalogue* number, various brochures, and occasional pamphlets, such as the publication of John Foster Dulles, *Peace in the Pacific*, together with Paul S. Smith's "A Half-Century of Service" (Whittier, 1951). The students' *Acropolis* appeared serially, first as an annual and then as a somewhat-quarterly; it became a regular yearbook in 1915, and continued thereafter with but one interruption. The Minutes of *California Yearly Meeting of Friends Church* were published annually (1895-1966) [W. C. Quaker collection]; for half a century it printed full reports of the president of Whittier College as well as other reports on the college. Articles on Whittier Academy and then College appeared in Quaker journals: the mid-Western *Christian Worker* [Earlham College library], the *Christian Workman* [Whittier, First Friends Church vault] and its successors the *Pacific Friend* [W. C. Quaker collection] and *California Friend*. In the mid-'twenties a number of national journals included articles by J. Herschel Coffin and others on "The Whittier Idea"; and in the next decades, articles on the linguistic work of Albert W. Upton. Occasional articles—such as Harry W. Nerhood, "Whittier, California: the Life of a Boom Town in the 'Eighties" (1945)—appeared in professional journals. Feature stories about the college and news items about former students have been the chief substance of *The Rock*, publication of the Whittier College Alumni Association.

Newspapers have been an important source for this history from the beginning: the *Graphic* [unique file, Whittier *Daily News*], the *Pointer* [few issues surviving], the *Register* [microfilm, Whittier Public Library], the Whittier *News* and more recently *Daily News*. To celebrate the city's Golden Jubilee in 1937, the Writer's Section of the Whittier A.A.U.W. prepared a series of historical articles for the *News*. Harry W. Nerhood wrote three articles for the *News*, "Early History of Whittier College" (2/3/44 ff.); during the next two decades Loverne L. Morris wrote feature articles on pioneer families of the area for the *News* and *Daily News*; James B. Moore, an historical sketch of Whittier College for the *Daily News* (75th anniversary issue, 10/10/62). This issue, rich in local and college history, reprinted the long puff for "the magic little city" of Whittier from the Pasadena *Star* (1887). Other newspapers in the Whittier area, the *Reporter* and the *Pictorial*, have included items of interest. The Los Angeles papers, the *Times* and *Herald-Examiner*, have printed news and sports stories about Whittier College [clipping file, W. C. archives] and reports of special occasions.

The *College Quill*, short-lived in the spring of 1907, was the first student paper [W. C. archives]. The *Quaker Campus* has been continuous since September 1914 as a source of useful data regarding both students and faculty. A series of ten historical articles, "Through the Years, the Intimate Story of Whittier College" by Bessie Manning (Q.C. 11/6/31 ff.) was based upon fresh interviews with the founders. Fugitive student publications have had their interest.

Such—with the addition of programs and the like—were the printed sources for this work.

Unpublished sources also provided important substance. For later years, the president's annual reports to the Board of Trustees were mimeographed and bound; for the years 1938-1943 there were reports of the Dean and the Comptroller [W. C. files]. Reports and applications to foundations, to the California Coordinating Council for Higher Education and the U.S. Office of Education, to the Western College Association and the California State Board of Education included useful material. From 1918, reports of the annual Audit furnished financial data.

Official minutes constituted a valuable source: minute book and stock register of the Pickering Land and Water Company [W. C. vault] and the original town plat [Whittier Public Library]; minute book of the board of trustees of Friends' College [W. C. vault]; minute book and stock register of the board of directors of Whittier Educational Association [W. C. vault]; minute books of the board of trustees of Whittier College from 1918, and of its executive, finance, and building committees [W. C. vault]; minute books of the Whittier College faculty from 1903 [W. C. vault] and of its curriculum committee [Dean's office]; minutes of Whittier Monthly Meeting (First Friends Church) and of its Ministry and Oversight, of Pasadena Quarterly Meeting, of Whittier Quarterly Meeting, of Huntington Park Monthly Meeting, of Whittier W.C.T.U. [Friends Church vault, with appropriate permissions]; minutes and other records of Whittier College Auxiliary [W. C. cabinet]; minutes, ledger, and subdivision map of the Whittier College Syndicate [W. C. vault]; minutes and records of Pacific Southwest School of the Y.M.C.A. [W. C. vault]; minutes and ledgers of Whittier Home Oil Company [W. C. vault]. Various files and records in the college vault, in the President's Office and in the offices of the Comptroller, of the Registrar, of the Dean of the College (Copenhagen program, I.P.G.S., etc.), of the Deans of students and of admissions, of the Department of Education yielded important data.

A number of MS theses, dissertations, critical and research papers were of historic interest: the early senior theses of Coila Carter, Gertrude Mills, and Caroline R. Sharpless, and a course paper by Ruth Ann Mohler (1927) [W. C. archives]; William Feeler, "History of Whittier College" (M.A. thesis [U.S.C.], 1919); Albert W. Upton, untitled paper on the Whittier College curriculum read to the faculty in 1937 [W. C. archives]—also Alfred Romer's syllabus for a new Physical Science course, mimeographed and printed forms of textbooks for the Life Science, Significs, and Fine Arts courses, and graduate student reports on the coaching system [W. C. archives]; Edward R. Miller, "The Educational Program of a Church-related College, A Study of Whittier College of the Society of Friends" (Ph.D. dissertation [Yale], 1942); Kenneth G. Beyer, "An Historical Development of Three Problem Areas within the Whittier College Curriculum" (M.A. thesis [Whittier], 1951); Herbert R. Larsen, "An Analysis of Whittier, California, as a Regional Center" (1964).

Manuscript reminiscences and biographical materials included: William V. Coffin, "Autobiography" [courtesy of Mary C. Kimber]; the Washington Hadley papers [W. C. historic Hadley desk]; Burritt M. Hiatt, "Reminiscences of Whittier College 1903-04" [W. C. archives]; Frank W. Crites, "The Rock" and Gertrude M. Cox "A History [in verse] of the Class of 1912"; Absalom Rosenberger, "Memoirs of My Life" [courtesy of Dr. H. G. Rosenberger Jr.]; Absalom and Florabel Rosenberger, "Sketch of First Friends Church, Whittier . . . Its Pastors. . . ." [W. C. Quaker Collection]; Louise Whipple and Lucia W. Smith, "A Sketch of Broadoaks School" [W. C. archives]; Paul S. Smith, MS notes covering the years of his presidency; and various biographical sketches and material found in the Genealogical Cabinet, Friends Historical Association [W. C. Whittier room].

Manuscript letters of John Greenleaf Whittier, relative to the Quaker colony bearing his name and to the Whittier College in Iowa, are in the John G. Whittier collection [W. C. Library].

Sources of a different kind were tape recordings, moving picture film, photographs, and scrapbooks. Available were an interview with John J.

Jessup taped by Harry W. Nerhood; interviews with Whittier pioneers taped by Loverne L. Morris and J. Edward Perry (Whittier Area Historical Society); talks by Richard M. Nixon and Jessamyn West McPherson at the Testimonial Dinner honoring Paul S. Smith, taped by Gerald G. Paul (1962) [Whittier Public Library]. The promotional film, "Horace Goes to College" (1917) was rediscovered and reprinted; later films in color and sound included "Continental Campus—Whittier in Copenhagen" (1963), "The Whittier Story" (1964), "East Wall West—Berlin Seminar of Whittier in Copenhagen (1966) [W. C. Public Relations]. Photographs relevant to Whittier Academy and Whittier College were found in the college archives and various offices; in the Whittier Public Library, including the collection made by the Whittier Area Historical Society; and in private collections. Scrapbooks and albums from Horace S. Haworth, Lois Johnson Ogilby, Anna Tomlinson, Gertrude Cox, W. V. Coffin, the "W" Club, and the Public Relations Office included assorted photos, snapshots, legends, programs, and memorabilia.

Additional acknowledgement for photographs used as illustrations: Margaret Fulmer (Whittier Public Library), Barbara Little Smith, Dr. Herbert E. Tebbetts, William H. Harrison, Miriam Ostrom, Paul Todd and Barbara Todd Kennedy, Jeannette S. Cox, Dr. Homer G. Rosenberger [Jr.], Anna Bell Taber, Dr. Harry N. Wright, Walter Dexter [Jr.], Berenice B. Steele, Clyde Clevenger, Richard C. Harris, Whittier First Friends Church—various departments of the college and members of the faculty—Ralph Barton, Robert Dill, Eugene E. Gloye, Ed Prentiss and Cummings-Prentiss Studio.

Interviews with a number of present and former trustees and professors, students and alumni provided valuable data and insights. Informal contacts and conversations with a larger number during recent and earlier years supplied relevant details, illuminating at times the hard facts of reports and records, minutes and audits.

INDEX

principally of the recurring names and selected topics of special interest in the life and development of Whittier College

Evans, Maude D., 237
Evolution course, 107, 119, 138, 195-97

faculty, 90-91, 162-63, 204, 215, 228, 147-48, 291-94, 351-61
faculty salaries, 60, 68, 136-37, 156, 209, 212-13, 234, 241, 293, 316, 332, 352-54, 389
faculty tenure, 136, (204), 249, 294
Farmer, Malcolm, 359
Fascism, 255-56
financial crises, 57-60, 114-15, 134, 148, 153, 205-07
financial development, 38, 122-23, 148-50, 205, 238-39, 332-36
Finch, Olin, 113, 124-25
football, 48-49, 53-54, 95, 112-13, 124-25, 145-46, 176-77, 220-21, 253, 288, 382
Ford Foundation grant, 333; Fund for Adult Education, 367; Fund for the Advancement of Education, 368-70
forensics/oratory and debate, xii, 54, 70, 84-85, 126, 143, 287, 386
Forsberg, Roberta, 360, 364
Foster, Gordon, 258-59
Foundation Society, 174, 355
Founders Hall, 38-43, 76-78, 121, 184-85, 350
Franklin Society, 143-44, 173-74, 218, 220, 286, 384
freedom of speech, 310, 325, 388
Friends' College (Whittier), 15, 16-24, 25-26
Friends colleges, 9-11, 391
Friends Reconstruction unit, 129, 140
Friends, Society of/Quakers, 9, 58-59, 61, 97-98, 122, 162

General Education Board, 149-50, 189
General Studies, 362-65, 301
George, Nathaniel, 178, 274
G.I. enrollment, 283-86, 318
Gifford, Robert L., 325
Girls' Cottage, see Redwood
Glee Clubs, 111, 144, 173, 220, 254, 287
Gloye, Eugene E., 359, 398
Godfrey, John, 382
Golden Anniversary Banquet, 310-12, 314, 317
graduate programs, 192-94, 228, 368-70
Great Debt, the, 183-84, 205, 211, 213-14, 233, 240, 263
"Greater Whittier College" plan, 121
Greene, L. M., 69, 118, 122, 147, 198
Green, Russell, 360, 386
Greenleaf Hotel, 14, 20, 21, 26, 39, 51

Green Peppers, 211, 384
Gregg, John, 331, 338
Guilford College, 10, 115
Guirado, Edward, 171, 332

Hadley, Emilie V., 37, 43, 92, 147
Hadley Field, 57, 93, 345
Hadley, Hiram, 41, 50
Hadley, Mary T., 63, 65
Hadley, Washington, 7, 23, 34-36, 39-40, 42-43, 55-56, 63, 75-82, 91-93, 114, 239, 298
Hampton, Florence A., 350
Hanna, Vernon, 141, 174
Haroldson, Ruth, 254, 357, 360, 385
Harris Amphitheater, 142-43, 150
Harris, Clinton O., 332
Harris, Herbert E., xii, 67-68, 72-73, 78-80, 85-6, 90, 95-96, 106, 136, 142, 151, 162, 173, 179-80, 182-83, 196, 207-9, 212, 219, 222-23, 245, 248, 250, 255
Harris, Lester L., 292, 359
Harris, Richard C., 183, 185, 208, 218
Harrison, William H., 301-03, 341-45, 348
Harriss, Thomas T., 292, 359
Hartley, Reuben H., 17, 22-24
Harvey, C. W., 14, 18, 21, 30, 38-40, 51, 56
Hazzard, George L., 30, 75, 81
Healton, Burtis, 70-71, 97
Henderson, Harry F., 110, 291
Henkle, Herman H., 347
Henley, David E., 165, 246, 265
Hiatt, William M., 54, 63, 75-76, 92
Hildreth, Marjorie, 217, 219
Hinshaw, Ezra B., 332
Hockett, Howard L., 84, 90, 106, 111, 141, 162, 205, 207, 209, 211-13, 220, 232-33, 264, 275, 289, 337
Hoff, Esther, 230
Hoffman, Frances C., 358
Homan, Walter J., 190, 230
Honor Code, 125, 170
Hook, Wendell A., 375
Hoover Hall, 301-02, 318
Hoover, Herbert C./family, 29, 140, 169, 222, 278, 301-02
Hoover, Lou Henry (Mrs. Herbert C.), 16-17, 28, 222, 225, 234, 254, 277-78, 301-02
Hope, Bob, 330
Howard, Bailey, 148
Howling Hundred, 113, 146, 253
Hull, Inez, 358
Hunnicutt, George B., 48, 54

Hunnicutt, William P., 100, 102
Hunt, Milo, 325, 334
Hurst, Homer, 292, 359

Ibrahim, Hilmi, 381
incorporation of Whittier College, 74
Independent Colleges of Southern California, 325
Ionians, 286, 384
Institute of International Relations (A.F.S.C.), 264, 366
Integrated Courses, 243-44, 295-96, 362
Intercollegiate Program of Graduate Studies (I.P.G.S.), 368-70
Ishikawa, Sam, 261

Jackson, Lydia, 33, 35, 45, 53, 67, 91, 101-102, 122, 147
James, Lois, 359
Jessup, Elias, 16, 17, 32, 34, 40, 44, 50
Jessup, John J., 50, 52-53, 55, 60, 92
John G. Whittier Banquet (1923)/later Banquets, 153-54, 156, 158-159, 179, 189-90, 193, 233, 299
Johns, Ray, 178
Johnson, A. Clifford, 47, 57, 66, 81, 91, 122, 147, 157, 179-80, 298, 341
Johnson, C. Bevan, 33-34, 147, 179, 225, 325
Johnson, Elmer, 292, 381, 383
Johnson Hall, 340-41, 344
Johnson, Susan H., 47, 50, 53, 60, 65, 92, 103, 340-41
John Stauffer Lecture-Laboratory, 342
Joint Council, 169-70, 172, 175, 199, 217
Jones, Helen Fé Haworth, 173, 281
Jones, Jesse H., 332-33
Jones, Louis T., 165, 170, 175, 200, 204
Jones, William C., 141-42, 173, 278-82, 289-91, 294-97, 301, 305-08, 309-11, 313, 314

Kelly, Robert L., 225-26, 227
Kelsey, Rayner, 80-81, 83-84
Kepple, Gerald C., 143, 149, 278
Kerr Laboratory of Home Economics, 236
Kimber, John Shober (Sr.), 118, 122, 132
Kimber, Morris, 118-19, 128, 135-36
kindergarten, see Broadoaks
Knott, Walter, 331
Knox, Eugene, 126, 143, 173
Koontz, Ethel, 173, see Eckels
Kuhn, Manford, 270

Lamb, Ernest, 281, 308
Lancer Society, 218, 231, 286, 343, 384
Landreth, Verne, 178, 221, 253
La Rue, Chester, 390, 391
Laughlin, Elnora, 360
Lautrup, Mr. and Mrs., M. C., 302, 331
Leighton, Beach, 292, 358
Lewis, Charles E., 90, 106, 114
Lewis, Glenn, 307, 325
Library, 36, 53, 114, 121, 186, 235, 346-48
Life Recruits, 140
Lillywhite, Herold, 291
Lindley, Hervey, 5-8, 14-15, 17, 19, 21-23, 30, 43, 56, 127
Lindley, Ida, 33
Lindley, Ida B., 127, 136
Logan, Edith, 144-45
Lohmann, Margaretha, 163, 254, 360, 385
Los Quijotes, 384

McClean, Clarence G., 191, 204
McCorkindale, Leonard, 175-76
McCray, Warren, 275
McEwen, Gilbert, 359
McIntyre, Winifred, 349
McKee, Jane W., 191-94
McPherson, Jessamyn West, vii-xv, 142, 144, 329, 347
Madden, Albert, 146, 277
Maple, Amos C., 123, 179
Marshburn, Dr. W. V., 100
master plans for Whittier College, 93, 121, 148, 184-85, 239, 337
Matlock, William H., 83, 90, 106
May Day Festival, xi, 96
Memorial Chapel, 342-43
Memorial Field/Stadium, 304-05, 345-46
Mendenhall, Mary, 204
Mendenhall, Mrs. O. T., 235-36
Mendenhall, W. Orville, 223-27, 229-30, 234, 238, 240-41, 245, 247, 255, 257, 267-69, 270-71, 293, 311
Merrill, James M., 357, 358, 360, 370
Metaphonian Society, 173, 174, 384
Milhous, Frank, 122
Milhous, William and Frances, 188
Miller, Cora, 359
Mills, Adrian, 86, 112
Mills, Eugene S., 292, 358
Mills, Levi, 74, 76, 91
Minchin, Elwood, 84-85
Mitchell, Bob, 267
Monument to John G. Whittier, 105
Moore, Anna, 47, 53, 60

Moore, James B., 359, 386, 396
Muchmore, Lyman J., 90, 107, 119
Murdy, John A., Jr., 308, 332
Murphy, Col. Simon J., 30, 40, 123, 339
Murphy Memorial Residence Hall, 339-40
Murray, Augustus, 72-73
Murray, Verl and Earl, 111, 122, 123, 144
Music Building, 342-44
Music Department activities, 49, 52, 110, 220, 254, 287, 385

Nanney, Edna Thornburg, 96, 200, 325
Nanney, Herbert B., 254, 385
Nanney, Leslie C., 106, 108
Nason Plan, 267-69
National Youth Authority (N.Y.A.), 214, 216, 232
Naylor, Addison and Rebecca, 32-33, 81, 114, 122, 147, 150
Naylor Hall, 123, 318
Nerhood, Harry W., 247, 306, 349, 364, 370, 396
Newlin Hall, 237
Newlin, Thomas, 88-90, 91-92, 94, 101-103, 105, 114, 115-116, 120, 133, 136, 148, 201, 225, 236
Newlin, T. Elwood, 5, 7, 17, 23, 34-36, 39, 43-44, 52, 55, 56, 91-92, 129
Newman, Wallace, 177, 221-22, 252-53, 273, 288, 383
Newsom, J. Chalmers, 325
Newsom, W. Roy, 247, 250, 356, 359
Nichols, E. Ray, 385-86
Nixon, Richard M., 218, 309, 311, 325-30, 332, 344, 347, 376
Nordyke, Clayton B., 28-29

O'Brien, Robert W., 357-58, 360, 368, 370-71
Occidental College, 24, 48, 50, 51, 54
Orchestra, Whittier College-Community, 173, 273, 385
Orthogonian Society, 218, 286, 384
Ostrom, Gustaf E., 106-107, 120, 136, 162, 167, 174, 250
O. T. Mendenhall Building, 235-36
Otis, Ashton M., 299-300, 307, 321, 325, 330
Outland, George E., 171, 327

Pacific Oaks College, 300, 368
Painter, Anna, 136
Painter, John, 5, 7, 17, 25, 30, 64

Palmer, Irene, 178, 204
Palmer, Peter F., 291
Palmer Society, 173, 174, 384
Panunzio, Constantine, 165
Parrington, Vernon (textbook), 244, 296, 364
Patton, Gerald R., 291, 359, 370-71
Paul, Gerald G., 386, 398
Peace Corps, 140
peace testimony, Friends, 129, 264
Peace Movement, 257-58
Peasley Center of Religion, Music, and Philosophy, 342-44
Peasley, Ella (Mrs. Samuel C.), 188, 300, 325, 335, 340, 342-44
Penn College, 10, 45, 51, 123, 133, 155
Perry, Esek, 85, 106, 136, 145, 148, 162, 176, 177, 198, 235, 277
Perry, Herman L., 147, 157, 205, 235, 325
Pfuetze, Louise, 230, 246-48
Phelps, Guy Fitch, 196-99
Pickering, Aquilla H., 3, 5-8, 13-14, 25, 26, 32, 43
Pickering Land and Water Co. (P.L.&W. Co.), 5-8, 18, 26, 27, 30, 31, 34, 36, 38-41, 43, 55-56
Platner, David and Jennie, 187
Platner Hall, 184, 187
Poet Theatre, see drama
Pomona College, 25, 39, 50
pre-ministerial training, 89, 104, 118-19, 190-91
pre-professional curricula, 367-68
Preparatory Department, Friends' College, 26-29
Preparatory Department, Whittier College, 57, 67, 84, 99, 107-08
presidents of Whittier College, 64, 88, 116, 133-34, 155-56, 224-27, 278, 314-19
Prohibition, 62, 84-85, 137
Project Method, 163, 167
Provident Hall, 301, 350
Pyle, H. Randolph, 170, 250, 304, 359

Quaker Campus (Q.C.), 109-10, 138, 142, 174-75, 193, 217, 255, 258-59, 387-88
Quaker colony and town, 8-11, 13-15, 27, 54-57, see Whittier, city
Quaker education, 59, 69, 104-120
Quaker students in Whittier College, 101, 168, 191, 265, 375
Quakers, see Friends
Quonset huts, 300

403